apu 905

A HISTORY OF
BEAMINSTER

Frontispiece: Shadrack Street *from a drawing by H. W. Colby*

A History of
BEAMINSTER

Marie de G. Eedle

Phillimore

1984

Published by
PHILLIMORE & CO. LTD.
Shopwyke Hall, Chichester, Sussex

ISBN 0 85033 575 2

Typeset in the United Kingdom by:
Fidelity Processes - Selsey - Sussex

Printed and bound in Great Britain by
OXFORD UNIVERSITY PRESS

This book is dedicated in affection and gratitude to
Kathleen Pim of Beaminster
whose Daniel ancestors lived here for so many generations

CONTENTS

      — water supply — refuse collection — housing   166
15   PEOPLE AND SOCIETY: Churches — National and elementary schools
      — grammar school — community life — leisure activities   180

      Postscript 198
      Appendix I: Population of parish of Beaminster 1801–1981   .   . . 199
      Appendix II: Chairmen of Beaminster Parish/Town Council 1894– .   . 199
      Appendix III: Chairmen of Beaminster Rural District Council 1895–1974   199
      Notes and references 201
      Bibliography   213
      Index 218

LIST OF PLATES

(between pages 110 and 111)

Plates 2, 8, 18, 24, 25, 26, 28 and 38 are reproduced by kind permission of the Dorset Natural History and Archaeological Society. Other plates appear by courtesy of the following: Mrs. Mary Walbridge (1 and 40); Mr. S. H. Godsell (11 and 17); Mr. E. J. V. Williams (23 and 32); Dr. R. Conway (21); Mr. and Mrs. W. J. Brooks (22, 29 and 31); Mr. R. C. Bugler (27); Miss K. Pim (20); Southlands College, Wimbledon (30); Mr. R. C. Travers, 33, 35, 36, 37 and 39); Mr. A. G. Walbridge (34).

Photographs were taken as follows: for plates 3, 4, 5, 6 and 19 by Leslie Brooke; for plates 7, 10, 15, 16, and 27 by Bob Keller; for plates 9, 12, 13 and 14 by John Eedle.

LIST OF TEXT FIGURES

Figs. 4 to 8 incl. are reproduced by kind permission of the Wiltshire Record Office; fig. 10 by kind permission of the Congregational Church, Beaminster; fig. 11 by courtesy of Mr. and Mrs. W. A. Stiby; figs. 12 and 13 by courtesy of Mr. and Mrs. W. J. Brooks.

ACKNOWLEDGEMENTS

I am greatly indebted to Miss Margaret Holmes (former Dorset County Archivist) and staff for their kind assistance over the many years I have been carrying out research at the County Record Office. I should also like to thank Mr. K. H. Rogers, Wiltshire County Archivist, and his staff for their help in connection with wills and inventories. Mr. Roger Peers, Curator of Dorset County Museum, and Mr. John Sales, Curator of Bridport Museum, helped me locate useful Beaminster material.

I am immensely grateful to Mr. Simon Alford, Historic Buildings Inspector, and Mr. Bob Machin, Bristol University Resident Tutor (Dorset), for valuable information and advice about Beaminster buildings. I should like to express my gratitude to Mr. Warren Riglar for giving me access to the most interesting records of the Congregational Church at Beaminster and allowing me to quote from them.

I have to thank Canon Timothy Biles and contributors to the parish magazine for permission to quote extracts. Mr. J. Stevens Cox, publisher, has kindly allowed me to quote from *Life in Beaminster 1864-1910* by A. P. Codd.

My most sincere thanks are due to the many people, from Beaminster and elsewhere, who so willingly provided information, showed me over their houses and lent documents and photographs. I can only hope I have not forgotten anyone:

Mrs. Joyce Banks, Mr. and Mrs. D. J. Barrett, Dr. J. H. Bettey, Mr. and Mrs. I. Boyer, Mr. R. J. Branchflower, Mrs. Sylvia Bridle, Mr. and Mrs. W. J. Brooks, Mr. R. C. Bugler, Mr. A. Cleal, Dr. R. G. Conway, Mr. T. G. Crew, Mr. H. Dawe, Mr. and Mrs. W. Day, Mr. and Mrs. G. A. Dearlove, Mr. and Mrs. J. W. S. Dunell, Mrs. Daphne Dupont, Mrs. Irene Elix, Mr. G. Frampton sen., Mr. S. H. Godsell, Mrs. Joan Graveson, Dr. and Mrs. T. Green, Mr. A. V. C. Greenham, Mr. A. K. Hardy, Mrs. Norah Harrison, Mr. and Mrs. N. H. Head, Mr. J. Hine, Mrs. Ann Hudson, Kitson & Trotman, Mr. M. J. Lester, Miss S. Lunn, Mr. and Mrs. K. J. Macksey, Rev. P. D. May, Mr. and Mrs. F. O. Meddows-Taylor, Mr. B. J. Murless, Mr. B. Newbery, Mr. S. A. Oliver, Mr. E. J. Parker, Mrs. Heather Penman, Mr. P. G. Perry, Miss K. Pim, Mr. W. C. Poole, Mr. & Mrs. A. J. Pratt, Miss F. Reynolds, Mr. K. H. Rogers, Mr. G. J. Runyard, Mr. and Mrs. H. G. Russell, Mr. and Mrs. R. F. Scott, Mr. and Mrs. R. N. Sjogren, Rev. N. R. Skinner, Mr. F. J. Sprackling, Mrs. Ivy Sprackling, Miss S. Stenhouse, Mr. and Mrs. W. A. Stiby, Mr. and Mrs. K. M. Stobart, Mr. and Mrs. A. G. Tomkins, Mrs. Mina Towers, Mr. R. C. Travers, Miss E. S. Trotman, Mr. B. Tucker, Mr. and Mrs. Tye, Mr. and Mrs. R. Vickery, Mr. A. G. Walbridge, Mrs. Mary Walbridge, Mr. A. J. Wallis, Mr. and Mrs. H. B. N. Walters, Mr. and Mrs. A. M. Webster, Mrs. Audrey Welsford, Mr. N. C. Welsford, Mr. J. M. Whitaker, Mr. G. J. Whitehouse, Miss M. Woodward.

Messrs. Leslie Brooke, Bob Keller and Warren Riglar gave me great help by photography. The maps and the line drawings at chapter ends were drawn by my husband, John Eedle, for whose patient help and support in all aspects of the work words are inadequate.

MARIE DE G. EEDLE

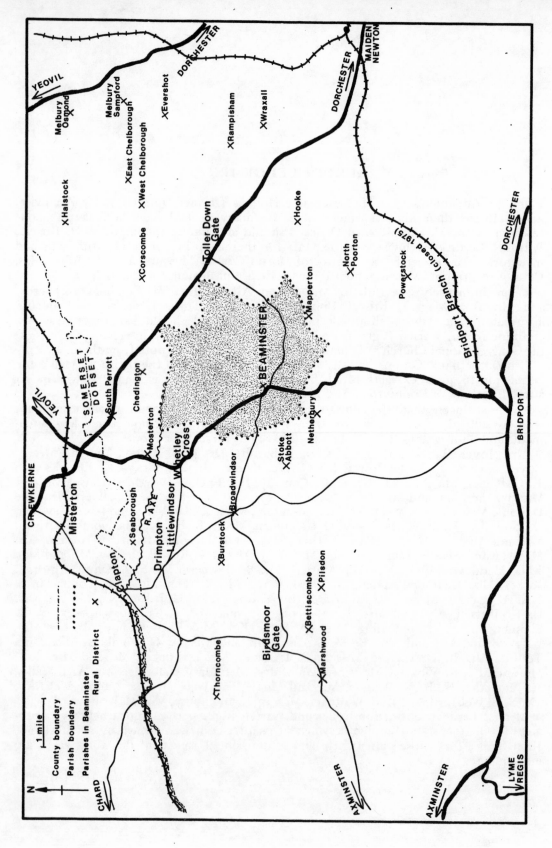

Fig. 1. Sketch map of Beaminster and surrounding area about 1950.

INTRODUCTION

'Behind the features of landscape, behind tools or machinery, behind what appear to be the most formalized written documents, and behind institutions . . . there are men, and it is men that history seeks to grasp . . . The good historian is like the giant of the fairy tale. He knows that wherever he catches the scent of human flesh, there his quarry lies.'

Marc Bloch in *The Historian's Craft*

IN 1796 William Marshall wrote: 'On Beaminster Down, one of the broadest and richest circles of scenery this Island affords is seen with every advantage. In variety, extent and richness, considered jointly, I know nothing that equals it.' The view that Marshall so much admired has changed less than many other views in southern England in the past two hundred years. West Dorset is still a green land of curiously shaped hills, secret valleys, small villages and hamlets, with a very few — and fairly compact — towns. Beaminster, one of these few, is almost entirely encircled by hills: I feel that its inhabitants must always, and more especially after an absence, have found pleasure in the familiar sight of their home 'from above'.

So much of the past is here with us in Beaminster, and recognisable. Walking through the bluebells in Edmund Coombe Coppice — the valley may have got its name from a 15th-century member of the Strode family of Parnham — I remember that it was already called the 'old warren' in the early 17th century: this was to distinguish it from the 'new warren' enclosed not long before by Sir Robert Strode, the area of which is today still marked in places by ruined stone walls. Climbing to the top of the down past Langdon fields, a delightful picture is conjured up by the thought of Richard Bridge's 18 donkeys going round the paths here about 1800. Driving through Horn Hill Tunnel brings to mind that great character Henry Crocker, who in 1904 expressed the view that it was 'a dangerous and troublesome building, and that it would be cheaper in the long run to take off the roof'!

While working on this book, I was all the same aware of the amount of change going on the whole time. This is true even in a few years of living in Beaminster: there have been many changes in the shops, and farms and fields have found new owners. It must always be remembered that much of what we tell of people in the past amounts only to a camera shot held frozen at one particular moment — immediately afterwards the subject walked away and did something quite different.

Beaminster's first historian, so far as we know, was the solicitor John Banger Russell (1760–1827), who described himself, rather delightfully, as a 'Curious Person'. From 1779 to the 1790s he recorded items about the history of the parish and that of neighbouring parishes, and his writings are the only source we have for many important facts. Inquiries have failed to trace the manuscript, but Richard Hine quotes extensively from it in his *History of Beaminster* (1914); two notebooks which belonged to Hine and apparently contain extracts copied from the manuscript still exist. John

Banger Russell was, it seems, writing mainly with a view to supplementing Hutchins' *History of Dorset*, the first edition of which had been published in 1774. While full of praise for this valuable work in general, Russell comments on the inevitable errors and inadequacies due to Hutchins having to rely on information from other people: 'he is most deficient in the Western Part of this County which he does not seem to have visited & unfortunately there were but few Curious Persons resident there . . .'. Russell hoped that his work would encourage someone else to revise and enlarge Hutchins' *History* as a whole. This project was in fact begun in earnest about 1792, with Richard Gough as editor; one of his assistants was John Banger Russell, and volume 1 of the 2nd edition, which covers Beaminster, appeared in 1796.

It was left to Richard Hine to produce a separate printed book on the history of Beaminster about a hundred years later. Hine's book is a veritable storehouse of information, and the later researcher, retreading the same paths, cannot fail to be impressed with the high degree of accuracy and the painstaking transcription of such a vast amount of detail.

Since Richard Hine's time, however, the study of local history has been transformed by a new approach, and new techniques for tackling the sources, many of which are only recently available, and would not have been known to him. This book is largely based on my own study of the primary sources; my aim has been, in adopting a chronological rather than a thematic approach, to show the development of Beaminster, stage by stage, from earliest times. I have dealt in some detail with the farms: the area in which the town is set and its staple occupation — agriculture — receive next to no attention in Hine. I have given more thought to the later 19th century, which was too close to Richard Hine, and I have obviously been able to carry the story further, to the middle of the present century. It has been said that Beaminster, because of its surroundings and history, has always been a place of 'characters' — I feel I have got to know some of those from the past quite well! It is however impossible to deal adequately with individuals in a book of this size and scope, and in the more recent periods justice simply cannot be done to the superabundance of interesting material about people of all sorts and conditions.

The story is told in four parts — the dates are of course only approximate. Part One (before 1500) outlines the scanty archaeological information for the area in prehistoric and Roman times, and pieces together what is known of the development of the agricultural settlements within the parish from the first recorded mention of the place-name to the end of the medieval period, by which time Beaminster had acquired certain urban and industrial features.

In Part Two (1500-1700) we have a small but growing market town, of some relative importance in the area, whose inhabitants are often engaged in farming, industry (particularly wool-cloth making), and shopkeeping at one and the same time.

Part Three (1700-1850) describes a developed community, still growing, but only moderately. In the earlier part of the period, hemp and flax manufacture is becoming more important than wool-cloth, but there are many other small industries. Towards the end of the period, industries begin to fail, and the community is struggling, while places elsewhere advance.

Part Four (1850-1950) brings the story up to the end of the Second World War. With the disappearance of the small industries, the fact that the railway did not come near the town, and the flight from the land, the population fell. Beaminster became something of a backwater; in the early 1900s it was described as 'this bright and busy, though sequestered, West Dorset town', and it was only the advent of motor transport which put an end to this isolation. The further development of the town in response to the needs of retirement and tourism is outlined in a postscript.

'Julia' — memorial to his sister erected in
the Square by Vincent Robinson of Parnham

PART ONE — BEFORE 1500

CHAPTER ONE

THE FRAMEWORK

The Natural Setting

BEAMINSTER LIES near the head of the valley of the river Brit, which rises to the north of the town. It is cut off to the north and east by the chalk downs which reach a height of between 700 and 800 feet on a ridge some two miles away. Beyond the downs, the land slopes away again to the river Axe, the northern boundary of the parish. On the slopes of the downs, the Chalk gives way to the Upper Greensand; the base of the Greensand is very wet where it rests on the Fuller's Earth Clay round about the 500 to 600 foot contours, and this has caused numerous landslips in the distant past, for instance on Dimstone Hill, on White Sheet Hill, and near Langdon.

The headwaters of the Brit are on the impervious Fuller's Earth Clay, resulting in innumerable little streams over a wide basin. At the southern edge of the town the river, on its way to Bridport, passes through a narrow gap left by flat-topped hills between 300 and 400 feet high, composed of the Bridport and Yeovil Sands, capped with a few feet of Inferior Oolite Limestone. The river must have had an earlier name 'Wooth', probably derived from Old English *wop*, sound or clamour: the name 'aqua de Wooth' (Wooth Water) occurs in 1288, and Watford was the home of Philip de Wothford. The name survives today in Wooth Grange. The later name 'Brit' is a back formation from a form of the name of Bridport, and not the other way round, as might be supposed.[1]

The town of Beaminster itself stands in a level area on the Fuller's Earth, at the junction of a number of tributary streams of the Brit, the streets fanning outwards along the courses of these streams, so that the pattern of the settlement is star-shaped.

Prehistoric Period

By 3000 B.C., the clearance of primaeval forest in England generally had already been under way for several thousand years, and settlements were a well established feature of the landscape, though people were still semi-nomadic. Few of the Neolithic settlement sites of the first Dorset farmers are known as yet, and it is by no means certain whether these are to be sought mainly on the high hills and downland, or in the low-lying valleys, with the cultivation of the high lands being the result of an expansion on to marginal lands under pressure of population. West Dorset, where archaeological sites of all periods are comparatively rare — this may just mean that they have yet to be discovered, or are inadequately recorded — is almost a complete blank. Two finds of Neolithic flint axe-heads have been made in Beaminster and the vicinity. In 1962, the fore-end, about three inches long, of a finely polished axe-head of light coloured flint, was found on the site of the new school at Newtown (ST 479019);[2] a partly polished flint axe-head was found in the valley of the river Brit south-west of Netherbury (Patley Wood Farm).[3]

A ridgeway route, probably of prehistoric date, runs across Beaminster Down, entering the parish by the Hore Stones, at a junction with the road from Dorchester to Crewkerne, and leaving it again at Horn Hill (see Fig. 2). This road, designated the 'Northern Trackway' by Professor R. Good, seems to be a continuation of the Berkshire Ridgeway which enters Dorset in the north-eastern corner, and continues along the chalk escarpment in a south-westerly direction across the county.[4] The route, being mainly on high ground, would have been preserved from later ploughing, unlike the many other prehistoric tracks which must once have existed, affording access to fields from farmsteads and villages farther down in the valleys.

By the beginning of the Bronze Age (about 2000 B.C.), most of the countryside was being heavily exploited, but the settlements of the earlier Bronze Age have not so far been found in Dorset. The later Bronze Age settlement at Shearplace Hill, on high chalk downland near Sydling St Nicholas, about a dozen miles east of Beaminster, may have its origins in the earlier Bronze Age. It consisted of a single farm on which had stood a small circular wooden hut and a circular barn on one side of a small yard, which was approached by a track through its own small rectangular fields bounded by banks. This site may represent an extension of settlement from the better lowland areas to the less favourable uplands.

Many hundreds of Bronze Age burial mounds survive on the high land, often on spurs overlooking the valleys, where probably their builders actually lived. Four bowl barrows were recorded on Beaminster Down in 1952. Two of them had been ploughed. The third, 65 yards north of the ridgeway road, measured 53 ft. by 70 ft. in diameter, and was 6 ft. high; the fourth, 480 yards north of the third, measured 66 ft. by 96 ft. in diameter, and was 10 ft. high. The third and fourth barrows had been opened by Samuel Symes Cox in 1874, but the two vessels found were much damaged in removal; one of them contained a number of bones, with charred wood lying near.[5]

In 1912 another barrow was opened on Beaminster Down south of Wellwood Farm, near the western hedge of a field (ST 47770352). It was 34 ft. in diameter, with a ring of large flints about a yard wide not far under the surface, the remains of a retaining wall. In the barrow was found a vessel with the burnt bones of a child inside. From its position, in a small hole dug to contain it in the clay below the wall, it was presumably not the principal interment, but either a subsidiary or a secondary one; if the latter, the ringwall must itself have been an addition as it sealed the urn-hole. The vessel was described as 'rather like a barrel in shape, 7½ in. diameter at the bottom and 9 in. at the swell, originally 12 in. tall'; in 1955 this was said to be a late Bronze Age cremation in a Deverel Rimbury barrel urn, but the vessel has since been listed among collared urns of the early/middle Bronze Age. In 1955 the investigator could not find any trace of this mound, but at ST 47780348 was a probable bowl barrow, much spread, with a diameter of 82 ft. and a height of about 1 ft.[6]

The existence of other barrows in the Beaminster area is attested by the name Barrowfield west of the town, and Long Barrow Lane just over the boundary in the parish of Stoke Abbott.

The most characteristic sites of the Iron Age (from 600 B.C.) are the hill-forts, of which there are 30 or more in Dorset. There are forts on the top of Pilsdon Pen, Lewesdon, Lamberts Castle, and Coneys Castle, all a few miles west of Beaminster overlooking the Marshwood Vale. The archaeological evidence points to increasingly large numbers of weapons, and the hill-forts may indicate the development of organised warfare. These massive constructions prove that there was plenty of labour available, and considerable social cohesion, and they must also have functioned as focal points for their area, that is as religious, cultural, or trading centres. Large numbers of Iron Age rural settlements have been identified, both on the chalk downlands and limestone hills of the county, and in the river valleys. Finds in the upper reaches of the river Brit, quite near the town of Beaminster, suggest Iron Age settlement there. A bead rim of Durotrigian (late Iron Age) ware was noted on the west side of the river (ST 477008) with some Romano-British pottery.[7] In 1963 Captain J. Cobham found a cast bronze coin of the Durotriges in his garden at 'The Walnuts' near Prout Bridge: it was identified as Mack's type 340, and dated to A.D. 50-70 or rather later.[8]

Romano-British Period

After the Roman conquest Dorset seems to have been garrisoned with newly built forts, of which two fairly small ones have been identified, one at Hod Hill, north-west of Blandford Forum, and the other at Waddon Hill, about two miles west of Beaminster. Waddon was a suitably shaped hill to take a fort which would control one of the routes to the south-west, through the Pilsdon and Lamberts Castle range. This route is the continuation of the 'Northern Trackway'; the old way passes near Waddon Hill Fort, and was doubtless used by the Romans, though there is no known evidence of any agger (bank) or flint metalling of this date. The eastern side of Waddon Hill, where the approach is fairly easy, was more heavily fortified than the other three, where the fort was built above steep slopes. The fort was excavated between 1959 and 1969. Five main buildings were found in the interior: one possibly the *principia* or headquarters, another the *prætorium* or commandant's house, a further building which was either barrack blocks, stables, or a hospital, and two buildings which may have been barrack blocks for cavalry. The fort was occupied A.D. 50-60, with maybe one or two further years either way, and it was probably established about the same time as Hod Hill was abandoned, as part of a general forward movement to secure the province against Caractacus in South Wales. Its abandonment was due, it is thought, to the need for men elsewhere, either in East Anglia after Boudicca's revolt, or in the south-west, where there may have been trouble at South Cadbury.[9]

The main Roman roads constructed in this area of Dorset were the road from Weymouth via Dorchester to Ilchester, and the road from Dorchester to Axminster; other minor roads have yet to be identified. In addition there was of course a multitude of trackways and lanes; many of these had been in use since time immemorial, and many more appeared as farmsteads and villas multiplied. Four Roman villas have already been discovered within about a dozen miles of Beaminster: at Maiden Newton, Wynford Eagle, Thornford, and Halstock. It would not be surprising if more were found in West Dorset, because the preferred sites are on the clay lands and in the richer alluvial valleys. The villa at Halstock, seven miles north of Beaminster, which was first discovered in 1817, is currently being excavated. The villa complex, with winged corridor buildings, extends north and south of Common Lane, the medieval and probably earlier road between Halstock and Corscombe, which goes on south to join the 'Northern Trackway' on Beaminster Down. There is evidence of occupation from 2nd to 4th centuries A.D., and it is possible that the site had been continuously occupied since the later Iron Age.[10]

There have been a number of Romano–British finds on the west side of the river Brit south of Beaminster. Near Parnham ice-house (ST 473006), there were surface finds of late Romano–British colour-coated ware, flints, clinker and coal, which may indicate some industrial activity.[2] Captain Cobham found a small piece of samian ware near the 200 ft. contour south of Edmund Coombe Coppice (ST 473008),[11] and a further chip of samian (form 27) at 'The Walnuts' (ST 480012), together with Romano–British black coarse ware. Coarse ware, including flat rimmed 'pie-dishes' and 3rd- or 4th-century A.D. flanged dishes, was found at ST 477008, and sherds of coarse ware in a field west of Hams Mill (ST 478010).[7] Two Roman coins were dug up near the premises now Aplin & Barrett in the centre of the town during sewerage operations in 1967: these were identified by the British Museum as (1) Maximian, A.D. 286–305, and (2) Constantine I, A.D. 306–337 (mint of Treveri).[12]

Romano–British pottery has also been found at two sites on the downs north of Beaminster. On Buckham Down, roof tiles were found as well as pottery, on a southerly slope about 550 ft. above sea level, on the west side of a field south of Buckham Down Farm (ST 476031). The other site was on Mintern's Hill, in the south-west corner of a field (ST 487035), where the pottery was found in rabbit scrapes.[11] This is near the line of an old drove way known as Axnoller Lane, and field names 'Small Walls' and 'Bench Walls' farther south-east along the lane could suggest buried buildings. (There are, however, lynchets in 'Small Walls'.)

Place-name, Minster, and Settlement

In the earliest known reference to Beaminster by name, the form used is BEBING-MYNSTER, minster or church of (or associated with) BEBBE, a female personal name.[13] This record, which may go back to the 7th century, is found in a Saxon charter connected with St Peter's Abbey at Gloucester. The actual manuscript which survives occupies the first three pages of a register compiled by the monks of St Peter's in 1393–7 under Abbot Walter Frocester,[14] but there are a number of features which suggest that the basic document was composed in the 9th century, by putting together material, based on oral tradition and possibly on earlier authentic documents, regarding the foundation and endowments of the Abbey. The surviving manuscript falls into three parts, the first purporting to be a foundation charter of Ethelred of Mercia granted to Osric, founder of the Abbey, in 679. This is followed by a list of benefactions, starting with the words 'aduinxit Etbebing mynster illic & on port lande ad illam ecclesiam cxx cassatorum in occidentalibus saxonibus', which record a gift to St Peter's Abbey of 120 cassati or hides of land in Wessex at Beaminster and on Portland. It is not clear from the text whether this benefaction dates to the time of the foundation

(679) or to that of the last abbess Eafe, who died in 757.[15] In explanation of the gift of land so far away, it has been suggested that it may have been made by a princess of Wessex, Cyneburgh, possibly on entering a nunnery at Gloucester.[16] The rest of the document is a charter of confirmation issued by Burgred, King of Mercia, in 862.[17]

The next reference to Beaminster is in the form BEGA MONASTERIUM: we are told that Wulfsige III, Bishop of Sherborne, died here in 1001 or 1002.[18] The form BEGMINISTER was used in 1091 when St Osmund, Bishop of Salisbury — the see was transferred from Sherborne to Salisbury in 1075 — gave Beaminster to Salisbury Cathedral.[19] This form is thought to come from the name of St Bega: according to tradition, she was the founder of a monastery, known as St Bees, in Cumberland in 650.[20] Perhaps Bebbe and Bega are one and the same person. The Swedish place-name scholar Anton Fagersten, however, proposes an entirely different derivation of Beg-minister from Old English *Beag*, a ring, which he suggests is used in a topographical sense in connection with a well marked bend of the river Brit.[21]

Christianity was well established in central Dorset in Roman times: the 4th-century Christian cemetery just outside Roman Dorchester is evidence of a sizeable community there. The British Church of the post-Roman period was probably less organised than was the later Saxon Church, and its mission was based mainly on travelling saints. There are few records, and the existence of a saint, and the sphere of his efforts, are usually only attested by the naming of a church in his honour. There is evidence to suggest some sort of ecclesiastical foundation at Sherborne, Wareham, Iwerne Minster, Milton Abbas and Cerne Abbas in pre-Saxon times,[22] so there could well have been a minster (an endowed religious community) at Beaminster.

The existence of a minster would not of itself necessarily imply a substantial nucleated settlement, though it has been pointed out that Beaminster seems to occupy the remains of a large sub-oval enclosure, which may be traced partly in field boundaries, and partly in street lines; it is suggested that such an enclosure could denote a pre-Saxon planned ecclesiastical settlement,[23] but there is no evidence on which to date it.

Little is at present known about early Saxon settlement in Dorset, but the Saxons are not thought to have been in control of the county until comparatively late; they were in Dorchester by 675. The place-name *ham* (farm or settlement), which is believed to indicate an early phase of settlement, is found in West Dorset: there are, for example, the villages of Portesham and Rampisham. It is likely, however, that many of the farm names, such as Buckham in Beaminster and Greenham in Broad-windsor, are derived from *hamm*, water meadow. Anglo–Saxon finds from Hardown Hill, near Morecombelake, apparently secondary barrow inhumations, suggest pagan burials there between the mid 5th century and the mid 6th century, but the signifi-cance of these is not clear.[24]

There is a possibility that in the earlier stages at least Saxon settlement may have occupied the lighter upland soils, moving short distances down to the heavier valley soils later on. The settlements may have been of a dispersed type: there is now some evidence to suggest that the familiar nucleated village may only have become the norm after the end of the Saxon period. We have no Anglo–Saxon material from Beaminster, and so we cannot be sure that there was a settlement precisely on the site of the present town. The development of a nucleated centre would, however, be likely to have occurred earliest at places in a single lordship, and more especially those belonging to the king or to an important ecclesiastical or lay personage: we have already noted that Beaminster was a manor of the Bishop of Sherborne before 1002. As the central place of a hundred, it was also a place to which people would have to come to transact legal business, and a certain amount of trading activity might be expected to spring up there.

The early Saxon Church was organised on the basis of mother-churches, with semi-collegiate groups of secular clergy serving a widely spread area. St Aldhelm, first Bishop of Sherborne, reorganised the Church in Wessex in the early 8th century, and it is likely that many of the Dorset 'minsters' were churches of his foundation; as we have seen, there may have already been a church at Beaminster. Minster churches share certain characteristics, which often enable them to be recognised at a much later date. The first of these is the use of the word 'minster' in the place-name. The second indication is a church with a substantial Domesday estate, often at the centre of a hundred. The third feature is a group of dependent churches. Beaminster qualifies on all counts, except that of the Domesday estate — the church is not mentioned in the Domesday survey. Beaminster was the centre of a hundred, and links certainly existed between the churches of Beaminster, Netherbury, and Mapperton. (The nature of the link raises a question, in that Beaminster and Mapperton were later chapelries of Netherbury: Mapperton was so described in 1291, while Beaminster remained a chapelry of Netherbury until 1849.)

Where was the Saxon minster? It is usually assumed that it was on the site of the present church, and there are strong reasons for accepting this view. The church is built on a mound, with a steep drop to the south; this seems too high to be natural or just a build-up of graves, and it could even be a pre-Christian sacred site. With the tradition attaching to it, and the sacredness of the ground, it is unusual for a religious site to move. But then why did Beaminster become a chapelry of Netherbury, and not the other way round? This suggests a certain lack of continuity inconsistent with the same site having been occupied by the 'minster' and the parish church without a break. The church, too, appears to be wrongly placed for the town, in that normally a church is entered by its south door. Here the main entrance has to be on the north, and a possible explanation is that the church is an early medieval addition to an already existing settlement. The minster having ceased to function for one reason or another (see below), perhaps the prebendaries of Salisbury Cathedral (lords of the manors) and the townsfolk decided, may be in the 12th century, to build a church on a new site, and one more convenient for their growing town. Only excavation of land in the immediate vicinity of the church would perhaps tell us whether the minster did stand there.

If the minster was not on the same site as the present church, where could it have been? In early manor court records, the common at the end of East Street, which borders Langdon farm on the south, is sometimes called 'HOLY moore' and not 'HOLLY moore' as in later records: the earliest instance found is a Beaminster Prima presentment going back to at least 1565. Two possible sites for the minster are tentatively put forward: one near the town end of the common, and one near the Langdon end. There is a tradition that the area by Prout Bridge now occupied by Bridge House,

Brook House, and Satyrs was once associated with a religious house of some kind. No record has been traced of any such community, but the garden walls here have unusual footings composed of large blocks of dressed stone.

Alternatively the minster could have been on the Langdon estate. The Bishop of Salisbury kept Langdon when he gave 'Beaminster' to the Cathedral in 1091 (see Manors): it must have been his Domesday demesne farm, and so possibly the site earlier of a residence of Bishop Wulfsige of Sherborne. (Langdon is an attractive site on a shelf at the base of the Greensand, with good water supply; it has a south-westerly aspect, was earlier well wooded, with access both to arable and downland above, and to meadow on the clay of the valley below.) The old way to Langdon from Two Rivers leads past 'Higher Hilly' field, a 300 ft.-high knoll, which is almost encircled by the river Brit and its tributary, the circle being completed by an artificial cut-off from the river. Could the 'ring minster' have stood here?

What happened to the minster at Beaminster? The history of Saxon minsters at the critical period in early Norman times is very obscure, but where something of it can be glimpsed, for example in Domesday (1086), the minsters appear either to be in a state of decay, or undergoing some process of transformation. By no means all churches whose existence is otherwise vouched for are mentioned in the Domesday survey, and perhaps the most usual reason for not finding an entry is that the church belonged to a religious body or to an ecclesiastic. When a clerical estate owner got possession of a church he could redistribute its revenues as he thought fit, and a bishop might well divert the endowments of a smaller minster to his own episcopal church or 'head minster'. There is no reference to a church or clergy in the Domesday entries for any of the smaller Dorset 'minster' places: Charminster, Iwerne Minster, Lychett Minster, Sturminster and Yetminster are all lacking in this respect, as well as Beaminster. It is perhaps significant that so many of them belonged in 1086 to bishops or monasteries. Beaminster, Charminster, and Yetminster all belonged to the Bishop of Salisbury, and one possible conclusion is that, their endowments having been appropriated by the Bishop, the churches had decayed or declined to parochial ones, served by an appointed priest.[25]

Another fate which had overtaken some minster churches with their secular colleges of priests in the later 10th century was conversion to a strict monastic order on the Benedictine model. The name of Wulfsige III of Sherborne was closely associated with this monastic revival, and in 998 he obtained permission to eject the secular canons from Sherborne Abbey and introduce Benedictine monks.[26] Is it possible that this is what happened in the church at Bega Monasterium?

Whatever its exact status at the time, the religious establishment at Beaminster could well have fallen victim (like Wimborne) to one of the Danish raids by which Dorset was ravaged between 998 and 1016, when Wessex passed into Danish rule under Cnut.

Parish Boundary

Minsters served a wide area, and it has been suggested that there was one in each hundred; the hundred, which emerged in the 10th century, was an administrative unit, forming a region within the shire. Beaminster was centrally placed in the hundred of

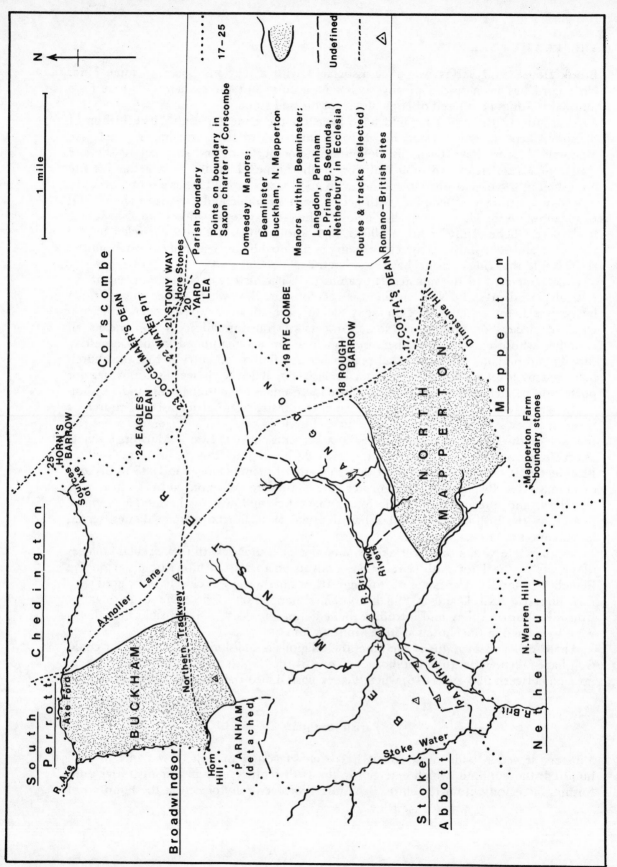

Fig. 2. Sketch map showing boundaries of parish and approximate extent of manors.

Beaminster, which was held by the Bishop of Salisbury. A reconstruction of this hundred, and its offshoot, Redhone hundred (part of which lay to the south-east and part to the north-west of Beaminster hundred), suggests that together they probably included the following places: Beaminster itself, Buckham, Wellwood, Netherbury, Bowood, North and South Mapperton, North Poorton, Stoke Abbott, Little Windsor, South Perrott, Mosterton, Chardstock (a detached area), Corscombe, Toller Whelme, and Catsley.[27]

If the boundaries of a Beaminster minster parish did once include all or many of these places, in later Saxon times it was certainly less extensive. For example, by the beginning of the 11th century at the latest, the boundary between Beaminster and Corscombe parishes had been defined. There are two Saxon estate charters of Corscombe,[28] the first of which dates to 1014 and consists of a confirmation by Ethelred of the gift of land to Sherborne Abbey; Professor G. B. Grundy has concluded that the bounds of this charter are those of Corscombe ecclesiastical parish excluding Toller Whelme to the south and Benville to the east. The second charter, of Cnut in 1035, covers a somewhat larger area, and Grundy considered that here the bounds excluded only Benville.[29] Nine points (Nos. 17–25) of the second charter — the last two of which occur also in the first charter — cover the whole of the Beaminster boundary with Corscombe; tentative identifications are shown on Fig. 2. No barrows have survived in the positions indicated for 'Rough Barrow' and 'Horns Barrow'. The Hore Stones, two large sarsens, which today are just inside Corscombe parish, are not mentioned in the charters.

We have already mentioned that there was a definite link between Beaminster, Netherbury, and Mapperton. At some stage, perhaps in the 12th century, as further churches were built, each of these places must have acquired a smaller 'parish' area of its own. In answer to a visitation enquiry of the Dean of Sarum (1613), the churchwardens of all three, in separate presentments, say that neither the minister nor the parishioners go on perambulations of the parish, and no record of beating the bounds has so far been found. Churchwardens' accounts, with details of rates made for the repair of the church, survive for Beaminster from the mid 17th century, and during the Civil War period it was for some years an entirely separate parish, with its own incumbent, to whom Beaminster tithes were then allocated.[30] In 1849 the Order separating Beaminster and Netherbury stated that Beaminster had been treated as a separate and distinct parish for *civil* purposes from time immemorial,[31] and this must certainly have applied since rating for poor law purposes was introduced in the 16th century.

The boundaries of Beaminster ecclesiastical parish, still a large one, with an area of just over 5,000 acres, were first shown on the Tithe map of 1843. The Ordnance Survey Act of 1841 provided for the ascertainment and marking out of parish boundaries, which were to be for the first time an integral part of the O.S. map, and the agreed boundaries appeared on the first edition of the large-scale maps; for the Beaminster area these were published in 1890. The surveyor used the Tithe maps of Beaminster and neighbouring parishes, and information provided by 'meresmen' from both sides of the boundary; the meresman for Beaminster was Charles Lawrence, then in his late sixties, a great walker, who 'knew the parish thoroughly'.[32] Three Boundary Remark Books covering the perambulations of January to June 1885 show a number of points (for example, Horn Hill Tunnel, Axe Ford, Ramsmoor Coppice, Parnham) where differences of opinion and doubts arose.[33] The queries were later officially settled in 'Boundary Reports', but these were destroyed in an air raid in the Second World War.

The very same points — emerging quite independently — were the ones which caused problems when a survey of Beaminster parish boundary was carried out for the Dorset Archaeological Society in 1980. The purpose of the survey was to record how the boundary was marked at the time, and if possible to suggest reasons why it followed a particular course. The ecclesiastical boundary coincides with that of the modern civil boundary (1894), its length being approximately 14.3 miles; over one third is water, following the rivers Axe and Brit and their tributaries. About another third seems to accompany roads or the course of old roads no longer in existence: for a mile the boundary follows the Northern Trackway over Beaminster Down, and some stretches follow the hedge of the old drove road from South Perrott to Dorchester, which is known variously as Axnoller, Crabb Barn, Raspberry, and Hooke Lane. The only actual boundary stone found was one remaining out of four which used to be at Mapperton Farm (O.S. 6-inch 1st edition) along the farm track between the tree known as the 'Posy Tree' and the farm buildings. No record or explanation has been traced of these stones, the remaining one of which seems to be a sarsen; the boundary goes right through some of the buildings.[34]

The Manors

Within the parish there were several manors or land units; some of these land allotments could well date back to Roman times, and have been incorporated by the Saxons in their own territorial arrangements after their late entry into Dorset. For the sake of clarity, the history of the manors is here continued beyond 1500. Their approximate extent is shown in Fig. 2.

The first unit we know of is the 120 hides at Beaminster and on Portland which were given to Gloucester Abbey; the list of benefactions to the Abbey, which is carried down to the reign of Burgred (852-74), ends with a statement that all these lands belong 'now' to the church of Gloucester.[35] When next we hear of Beaminster, it belonged — no charter survives, so we do not know when it was acquired — to the Bishop of Sherborne, a new Saxon diocese established in 705: we are told that Wulfsige III died at his episcopal manor of Bega Monasterium in 1001 or 1002.[18] The see having removed to Salisbury in 1075, it was St Osmund, Bishop of Salisbury, who held Beaminster in 1086 (Domesday).[36] (It was not, as Hutchins says, the first of nine manors for the provision of the monks of Sherborne Abbey[37] — the nine are those preceding, not following, the words 'These nine manors described'.) Beaminster, together with Netherbury, was given by St Osmund to Salisbury Cathedral in 1091;[19] the first cathedral at Old Sarum was consecrated the following year. A new cathedral at Salisbury itself was begun in 1220. It may have been about this time that Beaminster and Netherbury became five manors, each attached to a prebend of the cathedral: Beaminster Prima, Beaminster Secunda, Netherbury in Ecclesia (also called Beaminster Parsonatus), Netherbury in Terra or Yondover, and Slape.

Prima, Secunda and Parsonatus. Beaminster parish included Prima, Secunda and part of Parsonatus. A sub-division of 'Beaminster' had taken place by 1226 (at the latest), when Valentine is known to have been prebendary of Secunda.[38] The grant of a market in 1284 (see Chapter 2) was made to two prebendaries, those of Prima and Secunda. There is no simple relationship between the lands allocated to the prebends and the two-fold Domesday division between the Bishop of Salisbury and his sub-tenants. No maps exist for the three manors, and the only rent rolls or surveys are a rent roll of Secunda dating to 1472-3,[39] surveys of all three manors made in 1649,[40] and a survey of Parsonatus in 1819.[41] In 1472-3 land was held of Secunda at Axnoller, Shatcombe and Coombe, and at Beaminster 'in vico orientali' (East Street); the last part of the roll has perished, but there were at least 70 holdings in East Street, and it has been suggested that the street may be a medieval suburb of the town.[42] In later records however, both the other manors have holdings in East Street.[41, 43] In 1649, when the lands of the Dean and Chapter were surveyed, the Commissioners concluded that the manors of Prima and Secunda were 'soe intermixed as that the lands belonging to each . . . apart wee cannot perfectly distinguish or discover'.[40] From 17th and 18th-century court books and the Inclosure Award of 1809, it can be seen that the manorial lands were indeed scattered and intermixed. Buildings, the *White Hart* for example, and fields, for instance 'Earth Pit Meadow' in Whitcombe Road, were actually part in Prima and part in Secunda.

It is probable that the prebendaries (lords of the manors) of both Prima and Secunda originally had some land in a demesne or manor farm worked by the villagers. In the Secunda rent roll (1472-3), the tenants paid rent, but some also paid sums of money for 'works' (presumably commuted into this money payment earlier on), while others paid for 'all rents and works'; there is even one mention, obviously an error, as it comes right at the beginning of the survey, of 'works . . . hoeing'. There are three references to pieces of demesne land then held by tenants:[39] probably the prebendary had let the demesne out piecemeal to the villagers, perhaps earlier in the 14th century when direct management of demesnes declined owing to economic conditions. Where the cloth industry developed, as it did at Beaminster (see Chapter 2), the lord of the manor must have benefited from an increase in the rent-paying industrial population. The tenants of Prima and Secunda seem to have gained from the fact that the lords were absentees and had other concerns, for this probably accounts for the unusually favourable customs of the manors. (John Curteys, for instance, who was Prebendary of Beaminster Prima from 1466 to 1471, was not only a canon of Salisbury Cathedral, but the incumbent of Stanton Harcourt, Oxon. and High Ongar, Essex.[44]) There is a record of the customs presented at a court for Secunda in 1599,[45] but they were the same for both manors, and must have been established much earlier; the tenants enjoyed considerable security of tenure, with low entry fines and annual rents. Apart from obtaining a market grant in the 13th century, the greatest gift of the prebendaries may well have lain in simply allowing the place to run itself, although no actual form of self-government developed.

In 1598 the manor of Beaminster Prima was leased by Robert Pinckney, canon of Salisbury Cathedral, to Peter Hoskins of Langdon and his assigns for three lives, and Beaminster Secunda was similarly leased to Hoskins by Canon Thomas Coldwell in the following year.[40] After the Hoskins family, the manors of Prima and Secunda were leased to many different tenants for lives or years until the mid 19th century, when they were vested in the Ecclesiastical Commissioners, and were sold by them to Samuel Symes Cox.[46]

Langdon. When the Bishop of Salisbury gave 'Beaminster' to the cathedral at Salisbury in 1091, he retained Langdon, which must have been his Domesday demesne or home farm, although it is not mentioned by name; in 1293 the value of the Bishop's estates at Langdon was assessed at 115s. 10d.[47] In 1294 the Bishop was granted free warren in various demesne lands in Dorset, including Langdon.[48] We know of one occasion when a Bishop of Salisbury was at Langdon, for on 28 September 1316 Roger Martival transacted some business there.[49] The manor was leased out subsequently, the first lessees we hear of being the Hoskins family. Writing *c.* 1625, Thomas Gerard says that this family 'that dwelt not far from the town had enjoyed the fee farm of it for some descents'.[47] They seem to have obtained the lease in the later 16th century: no member of the family is listed under Langdon tithing in taxation records of the earlier part of the century. In the probate inventory of the goods of John Hoskins (1613), the most valuable item was the lease for years of the farm of Langdon, assessed at £1,000.[50] In 1630, in a court case between the Bishop of Salisbury and Peter Hoskins (son of John) and Peter's son John, the Bishop claimed that the lease, which was worth £250 a year to the lessees, had been acquired by the defendants' father and grandfather 'at a verry meane and invaluable consideration'.[51]

In 1645 John Hoskins' estate at Langdon was sequestered,[47] but after the Restoration it was returned to the Bishop and his lessees. A lease of 1661 states that the lessees must allow customary tenants as much of the timber growing on their tenements as they need for repairs, and must deliver to the Bishop every year a roll of surrenders and admittances to copyhold lands.[52] No court rolls of Langdon seem to have survived, and there may not actually have been any copyholders at this time. A survey made *c.* 1663 detailed 503 acres,[53] much the same as in the Tithe Award of 1843. The manor of Langdon had many subsequent lessees — it was sometimes leased for years, sometimes for lives — but in 1869 it became vested in the Ecclesiastical Commissioners (subject to a lease of 1826), and fell in hand to them in 1884.[54] The farm was sold after the First World War.

Parnham. This was described as a separate manor, held by socage of the Bishop of Salisbury, as of his hundred of Beaminster;[55] Parnham appears nevertheless as a sub-manor of Beaminster Secunda in 1472-3, William Strode being a free tenant holding a capital messuage or house for which he paid 20s. a year.[39] In the 17th century the demesne land of Parnham adjoining the house (in the parish of Beaminster) was about 72 acres, and there were also 100 acres of freehold land at East Hewstock.[55] Some land held copyhold of the other manors was rented out, according to rent rolls of Richard Strode 1438-46[56] and later accounts of Parnham manor.

We know from Domesday of two other manors or land units which were in, or mainly in, the parish of Beaminster. *Buckham* (Bochenham), in the north-west corner of the parish, to which also belonged Wellwood (Welle), was held by the Bishop of Salisbury at the time of Domesday.[36] It included what became South Buckham, North Buckham, and Buckham Mill, though some of the land attached to the mill was in the parish of South Perrott; the land of the manor in Beaminster was about 500 acres.

North Mapperton (Maperetone), in the south-east corner of the parish adjacent to the parish of Mapperton, included what became the two Marsh farms, and Storridge, which like the Marsh farms belonged in Tudor times to the lords of Wraxall and Rampisham, must have also been included; the land of the manor was about 600 acres. 'Maperetone' was held at the time of Domesday by Arnulf de Hesdin,[57] a distinguished man who was a tenant-in-chief in 10 counties. William of Malmesbury gives us a cameo picture of this man, saying he was remarkable for his skill in agriculture, and for his bounty in relieving the needs of the poor. A business-like personal interest in the management of his estates is suggested by the striking increase in value Domesday reveals on many of his manors.[58] North Mapperton, where the value increased from 40s. before 1066 to 60s. at Domesday, is a good example.[57]

The Hore Stones at 'Corscombe Corner'

CHAPTER TWO

THE MEDIEVAL SETTLEMENTS

Domesday Survey 1086

THE DOMESDAY SETTLEMENTS recorded are purely agricultural; no urban or industrial features are mentioned. As we have just noted, at the time of Domesday there were settlements at Beaminster, Buckham and North Mapperton.[1]

Beaminster was held by the Bishop of Salisbury. Before 1066 it had paid tax for 16¼ hides; in 1086 four sub-tenants held 10¼ hides, and so the Bishop must have had 6 hides of the taxed land in his own lordship. (A hide was a unit both of tax assessment and land measurement, notionally reckoned at 120 acres, but probably varying in practice.) There was arable land available for 20 ploughs, but we hear of only 11 plough teams at work altogether, 9 of which belonged to the sub-tenants and their men; a possible explanation is that on most of the Bishop's land sheep were more profitable than growing crops.

The Bishop's lordship was worth £16. He had 19 villagers ('villeins'), 20 smallholders ('bordars') and five slaves under him. The normal holding of a villager was perhaps 30 acres, though it might be only half this; smallholders were of inferior status, having maybe five acres of land. All would have to perform some labour on their lord's demesne or 'home farm'. Besides the land for which tax was paid, the Bishop had in lordship two carucates (enough land for two ploughs) which had never paid tax — this may have been either land recently brought into cultivation, or land on his home farm (or both). There he had two ploughs and a mill rendering 20d. In a survey of Langdon farm c. 1663[2] we find 'Milford Lands': on the Tithe map of 1843 this is 'Metforlands', and runs down towards the Brit near where an artificial watercourse, taking water off from the river, has been constructed at some date. This seems a likely site for the Domesday mill. The survey also mentions fields called 'Great Sart' and 'Little Sart': on the Tithe map 'Great Scite' lies near 'Metforlands' between the house and the river. *Sartum* is a medieval Latin word for assarting, the clearing of woodland for cultivation, and here we may have a reference to an assart on the Bishop's home farm.

In the Domesday record the woodland, and some of the pasture, is described in terms of linear dimensions, using the league (probably 1½ miles) and the furlong or quarenten (probably one eighth of a mile). The areas concerned cannot have been strictly rectangular, so a simple multiplication of the two measurements quoted must result in exaggeration. An area of more reasonable size (say about half), which fits better with the total acreage estimated for the various manors, can be produced by taking these measurements as the maximum length and breadth only. In the Bishop's lordship, there were in addition to the arable, 33 acres of meadow and very considerable

20

areas of pastures and wood; the pasture was 1 league long and ½ league wide (say 360 acres), and the woodland 1½ leagues long and ½ league wide (say 540 acres).

The lordship of the sub-tenants was worth £7. One of the men was French: Humphrey de Carteret held 1¾ hides. The other three were English: Sinoth (5 hides), Algar (2 hides) and Brictwin (1½ hides). On their land they had two villagers, 19 smallholders, two cottagers ('coscets', with very little land, perhaps only a garden) and 11 slaves; between them they had nine ploughs and two mills rendering 28d. There were 40 acres of meadow, pasture of 32 acres, and other pasture 4 furlongs long and 2 furlongs wide (say 40 acres). The woodland was described as 13 furlongs long and 9 furlongs wide (say 585 acres).

Before 1066 Buckham had paid tax for 3 hides. In 1086 it was held by Walter of the Bishop of Salisbury, and the value was 30s. There was land for three ploughs, of which 2¼ hides were in lordship, with one plough and two slaves. There were three three villagers and four smallholders and they possessed two ploughs. There were 4 acres of meadow and 30 acres of pasture; the woodland was 4 furlongs long and 2 furlongs wide (say 40 acres). One hide in Wellwood, held by Osmer, also belonged to the manor of Buckham; there was land for one plough here, and one smallholder, and it was worth 40d.

Before 1066 North Mapperton had paid tax for 3¾ hides. In 1086 it was held by Arnulf of Hesdin, and there was land for three and a half ploughs. There were two ploughs in lordship, and three villagers and 10 smallholders with one and a half ploughs. Meadow was only of 8 acres, but there was pasture 1 league long and 4 furlongs wide (say 240 acres), and woodland 5 furlongs long and 4 furlongs wide (say 100 acres). The value was 60s.

As to the size of the Domesday population, there were 82 recorded adults at Beaminster, 12 at Buckham and 13 at North Mapperton, and it is possible to make a very rough estimate of the total population, based on these figures. If we assume that the slaves were counted individually, but that all others (sub-tenants, villagers, smallholders and cottagers) refer to heads of households, and multiply the latter by 4 or 5, we arrive at the following: Beaminster, between 280 and 346 people, Buckham, between 42 and 52 people, and North Mapperton, between 52 and 65 people. This adds up to quite a large population, but the counties of Dorset, Somerset and Wiltshire were among the more highly populated areas of England at the time of Domesday, having a population of between 8 and 11 recorded adults per square mile.[3] Domesday was not necessarily, as is often assumed, the beginning of a period of assarting fresh lands: this process had probably been going on for at least the previous two centuries, just as we have evidence that it continued in many places for the two centuries following Domesday.

Agriculture

Hardly any medieval deeds or manor court records seem to have survived for Beaminster, and this means that for information on farming, the main occupation, we have to rely on an interpretation of later records — the earliest are 17th-century court books of Beaminster Prima. The parish comprises a variety of farming land. The

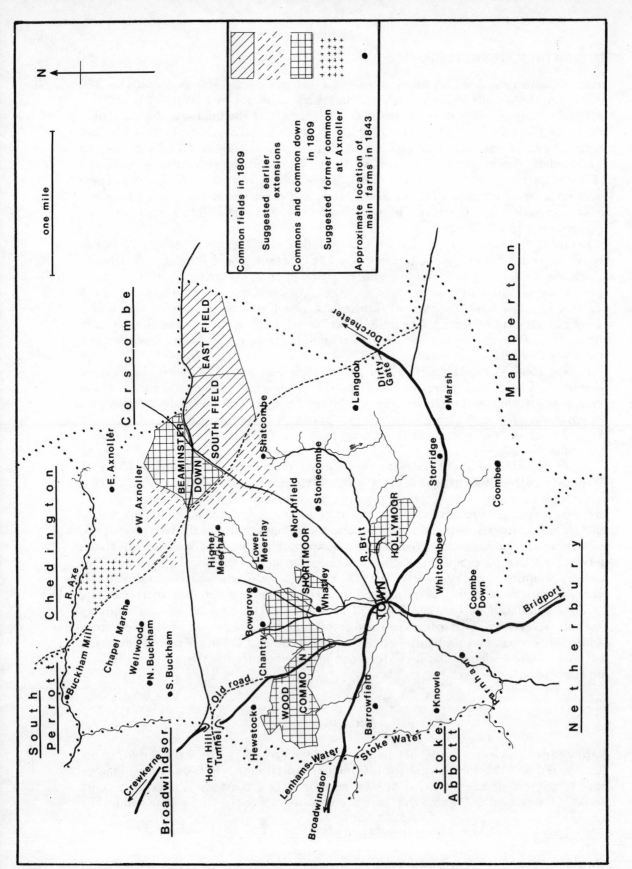

Fig. 3. Sketch map of parish showing commons and common fields and location of farms, earlier 19th century.

Legend:
- Common fields in 1809
- Suggested earlier extensions
- Commons and common down in 1809
- Suggested former common at Axnoller
- Approximate location of main farms in 1843

one mile

N

South Perrott

Chedington

Corscombe

Mapperton

Broadwindsor

Stoke Abbott

Netherbury

R. Axe
Buckham Mill
Chapel Marsh
Wellwood
N. Buckham
S. Buckham

E. Axnoller
W. Axnoller
E. Axnollér

BEAMINSTER DOWN
EAST FIELD
SOUTH FIELD
Shatcombe

Higher Meerhay
Lower Meerhay
Northfield
Stonecombe

Bowgrove
Chantry
WOOD COMMON
SHORTMOOR
Whatley

Hewstock
Horn Hill Tunnel
Old road
Crewkerne

Lenhams Water
Stoke Water
Broadwindsor

Barrowfield
Knowle

TOWN
R. Brit
HOLLYMOOR
Whitcombe
Coombe Down
Bridport

Langdon
Dirty Gate
Dorchester
Storridge
Marsh
Coombe

Parnham

higher areas of the chalk down, with their superficial deposits of clays and loams, are suitable for grazing, and to a certain extent for cultivation. Most of the arable is on the fertile soils (Foxmould) of the Greensand, and the well drained soils of the limestones and sandstones on lower slopes. The Fuller's Earth Clay in the valleys, sometimes poorly drained, is basically grassland for permanent pasture.

At the time of the Inclosure in 1809,[4] there were two large common fields adjoining Beaminster West Down, comprising 290 acres between them. The fields were named South Field and East Field, South Field being on the west of East Field (see Fig. 3). The names suggest that logically there must at one time have been a third field with the name North or West Field, but there are confusing statements in manor court records: in one instance, two half acres are said to be in the Southfield *or* Westfield, and 1½ acres in Westfield.[5] Elsewhere, a half acre of arable is said to be in the bottom furlong of the North Field, with North then crossed out and East substituted.[6] There is a reference to two closes of meadow called 'Northfields' in the early 17th century;[7] much later we find the farm named Northfield farm on White Sheet Hill, well to the south of South Field! A third field of common arable (West or North) could have lain in earlier medieval times on what was later called Beaminster West Down (131 acres); this could have been turned over to sheep grazing in the 15th century, when there must have been a large increase in the sheep population owing to the development of the wool and cloth trades.

In the earlier Middle Ages, owing to pressures of population and subsistence farming, there was probably more land under the plough in West Dorset than there has been since. The common fields of Beaminster were certainly much larger at one time. There are several areas of lynchets on the slopes of White Sheet Hill, pointing to an extension of cultivation down the hillsides in a time of land shortage — today most of them are overgrown and much too difficult to use. It is impossible to date the lynchets, and indeed, in view of the large Domesday population, which seems to have been fairly static subsequently, they could be as early as 11th century. Shatcombe Field nearby was a common field,[8] and there was a field at Shatcombe named Bean Lawns: lawns is a local name given to strips of arable land, suggesting a common field connection. We find references to arable land in Meerhay Field and Little Meerhay Field.[7] The common fields must also have stretched down north of the ridgeway road to West Axnoller, where in the 18th century there was quite a little hamlet, with six houses and 34 inhabitants. Field boundaries here have the characteristic reversed S shape, which is thought to have been produced by the method adopted in ploughing a strip, and there are field names like Hookey Lawns and Butts. The latter name often refers to the short or butt ends of common arable strips. (The medieval archery butts, which were still standing in the late 18th century, were close to the road on the south side of the down.[9])

South Field and East Field were the common fields of the manors of Beaminster Prima and Beaminster Secunda, and the areas of the parish which lay outside these manors had no share in them. They are, it must be noted, a long way (two miles or more) and a steep climb (500 feet) from the town of Beaminster. It has been suggested, in connection with the location of settlement, both in the past and in areas where men still walk to work today, that round about 4 km. (2½ miles) is the critical distance beyond which the decline in return for effort becomes significant enough to necessitate a modification of the system, for example by the establishment of a secondary settlement. The limits of most medieval parishes would probably all be within this compass of their village or villages. Normally, however, the grazing, where less attention was required, would be at the farthest distance, and the arable nearer; in the case of Beaminster, this is reversed, as the commons (apart from Beaminster West Down) were nearer to the town than the common arable.

Is it possible that the original agricultural settlement was nearer to the arable on the down, for example half way up on the Greensand? Could there have been at one time other common fields nearer the town? There are intriguing references in manor court records to 'common Barrow Field',[10] by that time obviously no longer 'common'; Barrowfield farm lies on the west of the town, near the road to Broadwindsor. Common fields could have stretched on both sides of the road here, and also farther east to Fleet Street and North Street, between the town and the common pastures at Beaminster Wood and Shortmoor. (This would put a different complexion on the Northfield references already mentioned.) Most of this land offers suitable arable soils. Unless further early records come to light, it is unlikely that we shall ever know the answers.

At the beginning of the 19th century, there were common lands belonging to the manors of Prima and Secunda at Beaminster Wood, Shortmoor, and Hollymoor (235 acres altogether), and also on Beaminster West Down (131 acres), on which the tenants had rights of pasturage. Beaminster Wood Common, which extended from Hewstock to Whatley, was rather more than a mile in length, and averaged a quarter of a mile in breadth; Shortmoor lay to the east of Beaminster Wood, and Hollymoor was on the way to Langdon[4] (see Fig. 3). In medieval times all the tenants of Prima and Secunda — tenants of Parsonatus were excluded — would have had rights on all the common lands in the parish, including Axnoller Moor for which special arrangements were later made (see Chapter 4).

We hear of three corn mills in later medieval times, the same number as in Domesday, There was a mill on the land of Beaminster Prima, probably near the site of Hams Mill: in 1525 Philip Spelt held for life a water mill called Beaminster Mill, to which all the customary tenants had to bring their corn to be ground. He had to keep in repair the buildings and ditches, and all the mill machinery: the document specifies ironwork, brazen bearings, cogs, rungs, 'betyngs' and 'leyengs'.[11] Beaminster Secunda had its own mill, which was held by the Fairewells in 1472-3,[12] and this was probably along the river off East Street. A taxation list of 1332 mentions John Langgeddonesmull,[13] on the Langdon estate.

Place-names provide evidence of medieval settlement, some of it in enclosed farms.[14] Buckham (Old English *bucca*, he-goat) and Wellwood (O.E. *wielle*, spring) featured in Domesday. Langdon (O.E. *lang dun*, long hill) is mentioned by name for the first time in the 13th century: in an account of cattle customarily left by one bishop to another in manors of the Salisbury diocese, eight oxen (a plough team) were left at Langedone.[15] Axnoller (a compound of the river name Axe and O.E. *ator*, alder-tree) occurs in the 13th century, as does Chapel Marsh in the Latin and French forms of *Capella* and *La Chapele*.[14] Twelfth-century pottery was found in a field at Meerhay Manor, mainly towards the north end (ST 487028), when an orchard was ploughed in the late 1950s;[16] in a taxation record of 1327 we find an entry '. . . atte Merheye' — 'hay' means an enclosure, while 'mere' is probably O.E. *mere*, lake, rather than *(ge)maere*, on a boundary.[17] Shatcombe is recorded in the 14th century, 'combe' being the valley, while the first element may be O.E. *sceat*, corner or angle of land.[14] Robert of Combe[18] was probably farming at Coombe Down Hill to the south-east of the town.

There must have been a house at Parnham (O.E. *per*, pear, and *hamm*, water meadow by the river): the name 'de Perham' occurs in a deed, and the Poulets or Paulets granted land in Parnham in the later 14th century.[19] The Jerards inherited Parnham through a marriage with the Paulet family, and a branch of the Strode family moved to Parnham in the reign of Henry VI (1422-61) when Richard Strode married Elizabeth, daughter of John Jerard.[20] The name of East Hewstock, where the Strodes lived previously, occurs in the 13th century, and seems to derive from O.E. *heafod-stocc*, head-post, one on which a criminal's head was fixed after beheading. According to Sir John Strode's survey *c.* 1628, in earlier times signs of the walls and moats of the medieval house were to be seen — some traces of moats are visible today. When Horn Park House was built in 1911, the foundations of the medieval house were found, together with stone and earthenware roof tiles and medieval pottery.[21]

Communications

The town of Bridport, six miles south of Beaminster, was prominent in medieval commerce; we already hear of the rope and net trade there at the very beginning of the 13th century. Medieval routes from Bridport to Beaminster probably followed both sides of the river Brit, where they can be traced by lane and footpath today. The western route came by Waytown, Netherbury church, and fields west of the river, to enter Beaminster by way of St Mary Well Street. The eastern route came by Oxbridge to the lower part of Netherbury; at the sharp bend in Crooked Lane, it probably ran straight on near Parnham House and across Parnham Park along the avenue of trees, on the line of an old public footpath (closed in 1809), to emerge at Hams. (The 'crook' in the northern end of the lane looks like the result of a diversion at a later date to take the route farther away from Parnham House and along the Bridport road.) A meadow 'next Portwaie Lane', somewhere near Parnham, is mentioned in the 1620s,[7] and this eastern route may have been called the 'Port Way'. (Port was a term used of a market town in the Middle Ages; on the whole it seems more likely here to refer to Bridport than Beaminster.)

Beaminster was an inland distribution head for Bridport, and a natural centre for the surrounding area; it seems to have been very well served by inland routes fanning out in all directions, though of course they may not have all been in use at the same time. Tracks which can still be traced today by road, bridleway or footpath — if sometimes broken in places — led to Crewkerne (over the top of Horn Hill), South Perrott, Chedington, Corscombe, and Halstock. From the end of East Street a track led across Hollymoor to Langdon and Higher Langdon, possibly emerging at the great junction near the Hore Stones. Whitcombe Road was not developed as a through route till the later 18th century; a branch from the Langdon route would have gone directly on to Hackthorn Hill to join the old drove way — here known as Crabb Barn Lane — which ran from South Perrott to Dorchester.

There were plenty of travellers on the roads in earlier medieval times, many of them ecclesiastics visiting their estates to receive rents and their bailiff's report, or on visitation to parishes within their administrative care. The Bishops of Salisbury had a residence at Chardstock, which was convenient for West Dorset. Simon de Gandavo (1297–1315) was in Beaminster on three occasions. Roger Martival (1315–30) was at Chardstock, which was one of his favourite residences, on 26 September 1316, and at Langdon on 28 September. The Bishop's records travelled with him on his journeys, by pack horse or cart, and we may imagine a long retinue trailing over the rough tracks, by Birdsmoor Gate and through Broadwindsor, to take the old route over Horn Hill and Beaminster Down. The next morning they were off again by the Dorchester road to Puddletown.[22]

Urban Features and Growth of Industry

As we have noted, nothing of an urban or industrial nature is recorded at Beaminster at the time of Domesday. Some time in the next 200 years, the settlement began to develop in that direction. This was probably connected with the cloth industry, the Fuller's Earth Clay on which much of Beaminster is situated being no doubt exploited. With the invention of the fulling mill, from 1200 onwards the industry moved out to the countryside from its centres in populated towns, which did not encourage these mills in their vicinity. The availability of water power naturally affected the siting of fulling mills, and former corn mills in rural river valleys could readily be adapted for the process, which consisted of thickening or felting the cloth. At a fulling mill, two wooden hammers, each of which weighed several hundredweight, fell alternately on the cloth as it lay in the trough; the hammers were controlled by a revolving drum, attached to the spindle of a water-wheel. The buildings of these early fulling mills were often converted later on to other uses.

There was a marked increase in wool-cloth making in England in the 13th century, and this was the reason behind the numerous market grants made to village overlords, whereby it was hoped that the villages would develop local trade and cloth-making, and bring profit to them. The grant of a market and fair to William de Ewell and Thomas de Rupton, prebendaries of Prima and Secunda, is recorded in 1284:[23] a market could be held every week all day Thursday, and a fair every year in September, lasting three days. The trade surnames recorded in the Lay Subsidy of 1332, for example Brasgheter (worker in brass), Deygher (dyer), Chaluner (blanket-maker), Glover, Tanner, Couller (maker of tubs for liquids), and Taillur (tailor) suggest that a little industrial and trading centre had grown up in the town of Beaminster. The subsidy, which was levied on movable goods or personal property, not on real estate, lists 49 taxpayers in Beaminster tithing, paying 60s. 10d. between them. Twelve people paid 1s. 6d. or 2s. 0d., 29 paid 1s. 0d., seven 10d. or 8d. (the minimum), while there was one individual who paid 4s. 0d.[18] It was a thriving, but not a wealthy, place.

In 18th-century land tax returns, the area covered by the tithing of Beaminster comprised the town and lands pertaining to it, together with the farms of the out-parish nearby on the south, that is at Knowle, Parnham, Coombe Down, and Coombe. There were separate subsidies in the 14th century for the tithings of Langdon and

Mapperton. Langdon tithing (not the same as the manor) included in the 18th century Langdon itself and all the hill farms from Langdon round to the north and west, that is at Shatcombe, Stonecombe, Meerhay, Axnoller, Chapel Marsh, Wellwood, Buckham and Hewstock. In 1332 this agricultural area seems to have been better off than the town: 23 taxpayers paid 47s. John le Blount (Blond) paid 6s. 8d., while John de Legh and James Husee paid 4s. each, and John Wetherhog 3s. There were 11 people who paid 2s. each, and eight others paid 1s. 6d., 1s., or 8d.[13] Mapperton tithing included the settlement at North Mapperton, which later became the farms at Marsh and Storridge, but the taxpayers there cannot be distinguished from the rest of the tithing in Mapperton parish.

It is possible to make a very rough guess as to the size of the medieval population of Beaminster parish (excluding North Mapperton), based on the number of taxpayers recorded in the subsidies. Using the 1332 Lay Subsidy, which contains a larger number of taxpayers than the 1327 Subsidy, and taking Beaminster and Langdon tithings together, the total number is 72 names. We do not know how many people would have been exempt from the tax because their possessions did not exceed a certain minimum, or the extent of evasion; if we allow a third to cover these, double the number for women, and assume that children formed 40 per cent. of the population (estimates for the proportion of children at various times range from 33.3 to 50 per cent.), we arrive at a figure of 360. This would not suggest any increase since Domesday, when in an already well populated district an estimate of between 322 and 398 people was made for Beaminster (including Langdon) and Buckham. We cannot of course be sure that the areas covered are identical on the two occasions. The population of England as a whole is thought to have more than doubled over this period; the rate of growth would have been slower in the already thickly populated areas. If the urban community in Beaminster was growing, perhaps it was by attracting people off the land.

The Lay Subsidies come at what may have been the peak of the medieval population in England. In the late summer of 1348 the Black Death reached the country; successive outbreaks of the plague led to a considerable fall in the population, and it is possible that there was little net increase in populations generally between the mid 14th century and the early 16th century. Such evidence as is available suggests that this is true of Beaminster (see Chapter 3). We have no information about the effects of the plague at Beaminster, though we do know that half the parishes in the county of Dorset lost their incumbents in 1349.[24] It must, however, be remembered that land vacated as a result of the plague meant more land and better prospects for those who survived, and in a cloth area there would have been plenty of demand for wool and food in the later 14th and the 15th centuries, to keep the farmers busy. Among the few surnames from the Lay Subsidy of 1332 which are again found in the Beaminster Secunda rent roll of 1472-3 are Dyer, Glover, and Wether (hog).[25] Unlike so many of the markets founded in small places over the 200 years before the Black Death, which failed to survive, the market in Beaminster is very much a going concern when we hear of it again in the early 17th century.

The townspeople were able to rebuild the church in the later 15th century, and to add the splendid west tower. Most of the great rebuilding of parish churches which took place in the century or so before the Reformation was done at the expense of the parishioners, and was financed by parish functions and by gifts and legacies. Two figures on the west front are thought to be those of donors and various suggestions have been made as to the people represented. The figure on the right has been described as a fuller, but it is difficult to identify the implements he carries as any connected with this trade. The figure on the left is usually called a pilgrim, with wallet, staff and scallop-shell badge on his hat.[26] Parish gilds or fraternities, which were common in medieval times, also contributed to the building and maintenance of their churches; one of their functions was to provide candles for lighting, each gild looking after its own particular altar. The will of William Mason (1504) leaves 8d. each to five fraternities in the church of Beaminster.[27]

St Mary's Church

The parish of Netherbury, together with Beaminster, was a 'peculiar' of the Prebendary of Netherbury in Ecclesia, a canon of Salisbury Cathedral. (A peculiar was a parish in a special jurisdiction of its own, not in the normal jurisdiction of archdeacon and bishop.) Presentations to the benefice by the prebendary or his lessee are recorded from the 16th century. The vicarage house and glebe were at Netherbury. The same vicar served both churches: some corrections to the list of vicars in Hutchins[28] have been published by G. D. Squibb,[29] who also provided the names of six more early vicars.[30] (The dates are those when the names occur.)

William de Vicumbe	1295
Geoffrey Huse	1297
David de Stapelbrigge	1338, 1342
Bryan Sloman	1385
Roger	1429
Stephen Stanlake	1479

Two further vicars were Robert de Grondwell 1374 and John Algar 1534.[31]

St Osmund's gift of Beaminster and Netherbury to the church of Salisbury in 1091 does not mention a church at either place,[32] and we do not know exactly when their churches were built. The bowl of the font at Beaminster is 12th century, and there is a small section of re-used moulding with dogtooth ornament incorporated into the rood loft staircase. Both Beaminster and Netherbury are dedicated to the Virgin Mary, suggesting that churches were either built or remodelled in the 12th century, when a preoccupation with the cult of the Virgin coincided with the multiplication of parishes. We know that there was a church with this dedication at Beaminster by the 13th century, because the market grant fixed the eve, day and morrow of the Nativity of the Virgin Mary (that is 7, 8 and 9 September in the old calendar) as the days for the annual fair.

Many parish churches were reconstructed very extensively in the decades around 1300. The earliest work *in situ* in the present church at Beaminster is in the east end of the north aisle wall, which seems to have been the end of the north transept of a 13th-century cruciform church without aisles and with a central tower. The 13th-century piscina with trefoiled head at the east end of the south aisle wall suggests that this may also include some original masonry forming the end of the south transept. On

16 December 1298 Simon de Gandavo, Bishop of Salisbury, wrote to the Dean of Salisbury's representative asking for an inquiry to be made as to the appropriated churches in the Archdeaconry of Dorset which remained unconsecrated, and reminding him of the diocesan rule that any parish church still unconsecrated two years after its walls were standing was inhibited from the celebration of divine service. In a further letter of 23 August 1303 the bishop expressed surprise that in spite of his earlier instructions, several churches, including those at Beaminster and Netherbury, were still unconsecrated. He further notified his intention of coming to consecrate the church of Beaminster himself the following month; from the bishop's itinerary we see that he was in Beaminster on 1 October.[33]

The church was again rebuilt in the later 15th century and early 16th century, and this is the 'fair Chappelle of Ease' mentioned by Leland.[34] The walls are local rubble-stone and ashlar, with ashlar dressings. The chancel and tower arches are panelled, a sign of late medieval date and characteristic of this area. The nave arcades are of five bays: the three western bays are late 15th-century work, the capitals of the piers having carved vine-foliage, while the other two bays are plainer early 16th-century work, probably inserted after the removal of the central tower. The medieval roofs of the nave and chancel may have been of the wagon-shaped form which is found so often in the south west; the present roofs are 19th century. The aisles were added in the late 15th century, but their pentice roofs are of 17th-century date. Very late in the medieval period, there was a great passion for demolishing central towers and building western ones. The tower at Beaminster was built about 1500: the will of William Mason (1504)[27] gives instructions for his body to be buried 'under the new tower' of the church. The tower is the most elaborate in Dorset; a striking feature is the wealth of figure sculpture on the west front, which includes the two figures already discussed. The south-west annex abutting on the tower was built in the 16th century, possibly as an ossuarium, where the odd bones dug up in the churchyard would be kept; it was later called the 'mort-house', and was at one time shut off from the rest of the church.[35] The only early monument now remaining in the church is a blue marble slab (with brass inscription) inserted in the floor of the south aisle, which was once part of the altar tomb there of Sir John Gone (*not* Tone), chaplain, whose will is dated 11 December 1497.[36]

Chantry of Robert Grey. In 1406 a licence was granted to Robert Grey of Beaminster to give two messuages, 40 acres of arable land, 12 acres of meadow and 10 acres of wood (62 acres in all), for the maintenance of a chaplain to celebrate divine service daily at the altar of St Mary and St Juthware in the church of St Mary of Beaminster for ever, for Robert and his wife Christina and for their souls after death.[37] The chantry chapel may have been at the east end of the present south aisle: a parclose screen separating an area here from the rest of the church was removed in 1658.[38] Tradition connects St Juthware, who was martyred, with Halstock, a village seven miles north of Beaminster. Her body was taken to Sherborne and buried in the church of Wulfsige III on the same day as his Translation;[39] the dedication of the altar at Beaminster may hark back to the connection between Wulfsige and Bega Monasterium.

William Vale was the officiating priest of the chantry in 1408, and two other chaplains are recorded in the registers of the Bishop of Sarum. In 1421 Walter Salke, chaplain, exchanged with John Aleyn, vicar of Powerstock, pr. to the chantry of St Mary and Juthware in the prebendal church of Beaminster; in 1429 John Napper, chaplain, exchanged with John Comeland, vicar of Whitchurch.[40] The will of Robert Grey, eldest son of Robert and Christina, who married Joan, heiress of Kingston Maurward,[41] leaves to William 'chaplain of my chantry' and his successors the testator's new psalter, together with goods belonging to the chantry, such as missal, chalice, vestments and other ornaments. Robert Grey also directs (1419) that his body should be buried in the church of the Blessed Mary of Beaminster in front of the altar of St Juthware, and leaves 13s. 4d. to the maintenance of the chapel.[42]

In 1526 Walter Grey, patron of the chantry, granted to John Ernley and William Page the next presentation to the chantry for one turn only.[43] Roger Eyars was chaplain in 1534.[44] At the time of the dissolution, the value of the chantry was £6 3s. 4d., of which 2d. was deducted for rent paid and 12s. for the tenth. The remainder of the money was received by the incumbent John Myntern annually to his own use; there was no other preacher, school, poor, or beadman to be paid for or relieved out of it. The chantry had one chalice weighing 7 ounces, and certain ornaments worth 8s. 4d. The chaplain must have had a cow, as there was for sale one cow worth 10s., in the custody of the churchwardens.[45]

The property previously owned by the chantry was leased out by the Crown to various people from time to time.[46] In 1549 a grant describes the chantry house with garden and orchard as worth 3s. 4d. a year; the house stood to the west of the churchyard, and in 1630 Sir John Strode built his almshouse on land formerly belonging to it (see Chapter 5). Lands leased out to E. Mitchell in 1564 included closes called Estewood House and Kyte Crofte. Kite Croft is not far away on the Tithe map of 1843 from some of the land then called Chantry, of which some 70 acres can be identified, lying on both sides of Chantry Lane: 25 acres called Chantry were in 1843 part of Whatley farm, while 19 acres were part of Chantry farm, six acres of Bowgrove farm and 20 acres of North Buckham farm. A transfer of North Buckham by George Keate to Anthony Larder in 1690 mentions four closes (22 acres) which were parcel of the dissolved chantry called Beaminster chantry,[47] and a lease of North Buckham to Thomas Hitt in 1715 includes five closes known as Chantry.[48]

Hillary Aisle. The north chapel or eastern extension of the north aisle of the church is said to have been built by a John Hillary of Meerhay in 1505; there is an earlier medieval piscina in the south wall and the chapel may incorporate re-used features. It is possible that it was built as a chantry chapel, but there does not seem to be any record of a *second* chantry, unless the details have become confused with those of the chantry of Robert Grey: a grant of 'le Chauntrie ground' in 1586 could just possibly refer to a different chantry.[46] Two hundred years ago John Banger Russell was unable to find out the origin of this chapel while local descendants of the Hillary family were still alive: 'I have applied to the Family of Mills of Meerehay, but can get no Information from thence'.[49]

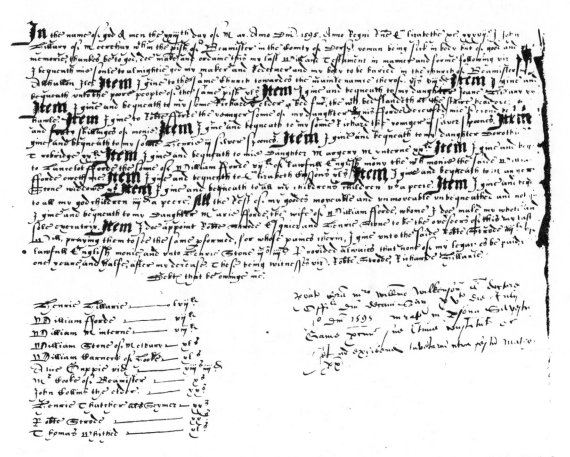

Fig. 4. Will of John Hillary of Meerhay, yeoman (1595). It directs that his body should be buried in the church of Beaminster in 'Allhallow Ile' and gives 40s. to the poor of the parish (lines 4, 5 and 6).

The will of another John Hillary (1595) directs that his body be buried in 'Allhallow Ile',[50] and many members of the Hillary and allied families are buried beneath the paving stones of the chapel. Most of the brass inscriptions have been lost, but three which turned up elsewhere were restored to the church and are now on the west wall of the chapel. There used to be a wooden board, painted white and lettered in black, over the north window, with details of the later history of the chapel; this has been replaced by a brass tablet on the wall left of this window. The tablet records that the chapel built by John Hillary was 'beautified' by Mrs. Mary Mills of Meerhay in 1767, repaired by William Clark in 1794, and restored and entirely re-roofed by Mrs. Mary Cox of Beaminster Manor House in 1898. Because they, and not the parish, kept the chapel in repair, the owners of Lower Meerhay were not liable for church rates.[51] In 1685 Mr. John Hillary and Mr. William Mills were presented by the churchwardens for 'not repairing of the Ile which do beelonge to Mr. Hillery'.[52]

Chapel at Chapel Marsh. There was at one time a chapel on Chapel Marsh farm near Axnoller; J. B. Russell, writing in the later 18th century, says 'the site . . . could not long ago be easily discerned, but the Ruins of the Walls are now gone'. The chapel, which may have been destroyed at the time of the Reformation, was presumably a chapel of ease to St Mary's church in Beaminster, and could have been for the use of the inhabitants of Langdon tithing, who lived a long way from the parish church.[53]

12th-century font in St Mary's Church

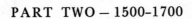

PART TWO — 1500-1700

CHAPTER THREE

TOWN AND PARISH 1500-1700

Population

IN THE TWO HUNDRED YEARS from 1500 to 1700, evidence for Beaminster's population is patchy: sources of information on total population consist almost entirely of taxation assessments based on tithings, and ecclesiastical censuses based on the parish, and the two are not easily reconcilable. There is in addition the unique record, the Protestation Oath of 1642, which was in effect a census of all males of 18 years and over. Estimates of population can be only approximations, but they are enough to indicate a substantial increase, from rather below 500 in 1500 to something like 1,500 in 1700.

The first source after 1500 is the Tudor Lay Subsidy assessments. In 1525 a tax was levied on the value of either land or goods, whichever was the greater, or on wages; it is believed that this assessment affected all but the poorest people, the lower assessment limit being £1. The return lists 63 in Beaminster tithing, and 12 in Langdon tithing, a total of 75 names.[1] (North Mapperton taxpayers cannot be distinguished from the rest in Mapperton tithing, so will have to be excluded.) If we assume that two-thirds of the men paid tax (the other third being too poor to be assessed), the number in Beaminster and Langdon would be 112 males. Doubling this for females, and assuming that children formed 40 per cent. of the population, would give a total of 373.[2]

Another extensive subsidy paid in 1545, with the same lower limit of £1 (assessed on land or goods only), gives 95 names in Beaminster, together with 51 names in 'Langdon & Chedington' tithing.[1] Chedington alone had 10 taxpayers in 1525 when Langdon had 12; splitting the total of 51 proportionately would give 28 in Langdon in 1545, making a total of 123 for both Beaminster and Langdon. A similar calculation to that used for the 1525 figure (again ignoring North Mapperton) produces a total population of 613.

The Muster lists made in Tudor times of men and their armour are supposed to include all men between the ages of 16 and 60.[3] In the 1542 list there are 111 names for Beaminster, and 20 for Langdon; if we add the names from the shorter 1539 list which are not common to both, the maximum number of names becomes Beaminster 134 and Langdon 22, a total of 156, which confirms that the figure of 123 derived from the subsidy of 1545 is not excessive. Without pretending an accuracy for the calculated figures which they do not possess, we may reasonably suggest that a population which in the first quarter of the 16th century was below 500, had risen by the middle of the century, and was now comfortably above that figure.

The returns of a census of families taken in every diocese in 1563 do not seem to have survived for Dorset. A further ecclesiastical census was called for in 1603, this time enumerating communicants and recusants (Roman Catholics). There are several papers in a made-up file of churchwardens' presentments which give such figures for a number of peculiars of the Dean and Canons of Salisbury Cathedral; all are undated except for one Wiltshire parish, but this bears the date 1603, and it is likely that the others are of the same date. Netherbury and Beaminster are dealt with in the same report but separate figures are given.[4] At Beaminster there were 600 communicants 'or thereabouts', no recusants, but three people who 'refuse to communicate'. The number of communicants is obviously in round figures, but assuming communicants (over 14) at 60 per cent. of the population, the total population of Beaminster would be about 1,000. This would mean that since the earlier part of the 16th century the population of the parish had more or less doubled. The country as a whole was experiencing a population boom over this period, but the big increase at Beaminster suggests that there was some migration into the parish. Another ecclesiastical census known as the Compton census took place in 1676, but there are no statistics for individual Dorset parishes.

The list of all male inhabitants of 18 years and over who subscribed to the Protestation Oath of 1642, pledging themselves to defend the Protestant religion, the King and Parliament, included 420 names in Beaminster;[5] there is no record of anyone having refused to take the oath, although the names of absentees and refusers were to be recorded. It has been estimated in the work of the Cambridge Population Group that men above the age of 18 made up 31 per cent. of the population, and that a multiplier of 3.2 can be used to convert the number of subscribers into a rough estimate of the size of the community. This gives a population of 1,344 in the case of Beaminster, suggesting another substantial increase in the earlier 17th century.

Finally we come to the returns made in connection with a tax levied during the period 1662-74 on the number of hearths in a house. Persons having an income of less than 20s. a year or property worth less than £10 were exempt, as were those too poor to pay church or poor rates. The assessments covering 1662-64, which have been printed, are well preserved for Dorset, but the number of chargeable entries or households for Beaminster Town is only 68, and there is no information regarding exemptions.[6] The most likely explanation for such a low figure is that many inhabitants of the town had been unable to repair their houses after the great fire of 1644; we know that the compensation money was very slow in coming.

The Hearth Tax assessments for 1673 provide details of chargeable entries, and of those who were certified exempt, which make more sense. On this occasion there were for Beaminster Town 168 chargeable households with 54 exemptions for which certificates were issued, that is 222 in all. Langdon tithing had 26 chargeable households, and no exemptions,[7] and we may at this date allow three households at North Mapperton in Mapperton tithing. Paupers, that is those who did not pay rates, did not need certificates, and so it is necessary to add something to the above, at least for Beaminster. If we assume that certified and non-certified exemptions together should amount to at least one-third of the total (a proportion which has been found to be about the average in Surrey), the total for Beaminster Town is increased from 222 to 252. The number of households in Beaminster, Langdon, and Mapperton would then be 281, which multiplied by a factor of 4½ to 5 — the average number of people to a house in Beaminster in 1775 was in fact 4½ — produces a total population of between 1,264 and 1,405. It seems probable, in the light of the various commercial and industrial activities which will be described later, that most of the growth was taking place in the town, rather than in the farming community.

The 17th-century growth in the population is supported by the fact that galleries were built in the church in order to increase the accommodation. The nave, chancel, aisles, north chapel and Parnham pew could accommodate (according to mid-19th-century figures) 569 people, so that at the beginning of the 17th century, there may have been only just enough room for the communicants, estimated at about 600. As early as 1638, churchwardens' presentments refer to a loft which had begun to be built, but had not been finished.[8] In 1657 approval was given to build a 'new gallery in the north part of the church', and seats there were sold in 1658.[9] A south gallery was also built at some time for, as we learn from J. B. Russell, 'The two old Galleries were against the North and South walls'.[10] The 'new singing larte', for which there is a list of subscribers' names in 1697,[9] must have been at the western end, although Russell does go on to say that a west gallery was built in place of the old galleries when these were removed 'somewhat more than 40 years ago' (about 1750); this gallery went all across the church from north to south, and extended in breadth from the west wall to the first pillar.[10]

Urban Status

In the last chapter we noted the development of an urban community in Beaminster in the medieval period, with the grant of a market in the 13th century. The large level area at the head of the valley of the Brit, with communication routes fanning out along its tributaries, was a good natural site for a town. Beaminster was the site of an early religious foundation, and in the Anglo–Saxon era the centre of an ecclesiastical estate and the administrative centre of a hundred, although, as we have seen, there is no actual evidence of any substantial settlement at that period. Perhaps at this point we should look at the nature of Beaminster's urban status, and compare it with other towns of the pre-industrial era.

It is difficult to define a town, though many attempts have been made. Some of the criteria which have been put forward — defences, a mint, planned streets, a special type of house and shape of plot — [11] were not features of Beaminster. It never obtained borough status, a step with which the accident of overlordship must always have had much to do. A market town was in an entirely separate category from a borough in medieval eyes, and Beaminster has similarities with a number of other small towns or large villages in West Dorset and South East Somerset, such as Abbotsbury, Cerne Abbas, Martock, and South Petherton, all of which had markets, but did not develop any form of self-government.

By the period 1500-1700 Beaminster possessed certain other features by which it can fairly be recognised as a town. It was no doubt in the bottom tier of towns, the category into which fell the majority of places — several hundred — considered to be towns in pre-industrial times.[12] (The first tier consisted, besides London, of seven or eight major cities, while the middle tier included perhaps a hundred or so places.) Beaminster was distinguished from a purely agricultural village by its market, one of those which *had* survived out of a much larger number of medieval grants, and its specialisation in the cloth and allied trades, in which a flourishing middle class was engaged. It was also characterised by a population of greater size than all the surrounding parishes except Netherbury. The populations of Netherbury parish and Beaminster parish were much the same, but Beaminster had a higher density in the town area. Netherbury's population was scattered over a wider area, and it had two separate roadside settlements — Melplash on the Bridport to Beaminster road, and Ashe (Salway Ash) on the Bridport to Broadwindsor road. In the 1520s the minimum population for a 'town' tended to be 500, or slightly less, so at this point Beaminster probably just about qualifies; in the 1670s, when the minimum would be nearer 1,000, Beaminster has clearly qualified.[13]

Beaminster had a community function beyond its own immediate limits. Quarter Sessions were held here during part of the reign of Elizabeth, and on a number of occasions in the 17th century: Michaelmas 1625, 1627, 1628 and 1629, and again in 1664 and 1665.[14] The market house is referred to as the 'sessions house' in Q.S. Order Book of 1630, and there must have been a court room above where sessions were held. It was at one time envisaged that a 'House of Correction' might be set up in Beaminster. There was apparently only one such house, at Sherborne, and in 1638 the Judges of Assize gave directions that more should be erected. The Quarter Sessions Court, finding 'this County not able to performe soe chardgeable a worke', did not make a general order: 'And yet uppon the motion of severall gentlemen of the Westerne Division . . . (whose care this Court doth much commend) doth give directions and order that they may at the charge of that division erect an house of correction at Bemister for the setting on work of masterles and idle persons and for the punishment of vagabonds and other malefactors within those partes, desiring them to goe on with a worke of soe great use and benifit. . . .'.[15] No subsequent references have been traced to the setting up of a house of correction and with the advent of the Civil War soon afterwards it is likely that the project was never put into effect.

The community function, both as a market or shopping centre and as a focal point of local government administration, was one which Beaminster was to retain in succeeding centuries. It is difficult to say what the real area of influence of the town was at the period under discussion. It has been suggested that six miles or so is the distance a man could walk to attend a market and return home the same day. The villages or hamlets in the following parishes, which were later to be included in the Beaminster Poor Law Union, are all within six to eight miles: Bettiscombe, Broadwindsor, Burstock, Chedington, Corscombe, East Chelborough, Evershot, Halstock, Hooke, Mapperton, Marshwood, Melbury Osmond, Melbury Sampford, Misterton, Mosterton, Netherbury, North Poorton, Pilsdon, Powerstock, Rampisham, Seaborough, South Perrott, Stoke Abbott, West Chelborough, Wraxall. (See Fig. 1).

Lay-out of the Town

At the beginning of the 16th century many English towns were in a decayed state. Beaminster may have been one of the exceptions, as a result of its involvement in the wool and cloth trade — we have noted that the church was rebuilt in the late 15th century and early 16th century. Apart from the church, the most noticeable features of the town would have been the market place and the streams which ran along most of the streets. (See Fig. 9).

Leland, who visited Beaminster in the course of his travels in the earlier 16th century, described it as follows: 'a praty market town . . . and usith much housbandry, and lyith in one streat from north to south: and in a nother from west to est'.[16] The street to the north was probably the one we know as Fleet Street; this ended at 'the Townesend' (Abbot Browns), where the Willmott family had a mill in the 17th century. When the roadway in Fleet Street was opened up in 1907 to lay water mains, the old stream bed was exposed with the remains of an oak conduit in it; several 17th-century ox and horse shoes were found in the gravel. In medieval times and perhaps as late as the 16th century, this stream must have run above ground across the market place (Fore Place), continuing down Church Street and St Mary Well Street, which possibly together constituted the street to the south mentioned by Leland. In the earlier 17th century the whole of this street was known as Church Street; later the name was changed to Mary Well Street, which was applied to the whole street in the 18th century. In 1692 the cost of the 'Stone Bridg that was new built in Mary Well Street' came to £1 18s. 7d.; Hams Bridge, over the river Brit on the narrow way between St Mary Well Street and the Bridport road, was rebuilt in 1691 for £1 8s. 4d.[9] At this time the parish pound for stray animals adjoined the church on the south-east; the old pound was filled in and the area incorporated in the churchyard in 1840.[17] The other main streets — Hogshill, North and East (which began at the Fore Place) — are also named in 17th-century records. Shadrack Street occurs in the forms Shittrick and Sheetrick,[18] and is probably derived from O.E. *scite*, dung, and *ric*, stream or ditch.

Leland further tells us that the river Brit, rising to the north of Beaminster, 'descendith as yet a smaul water down by the est end of Bemistre under a litle stone bridge of 2 praty arches'. The bridge was probably already called Prout Bridge, as the name John Proutes occurs as early as 1332;[19] before turnpike days of the 18th century, it was only wide enough for foot passengers. Gilbert Adams, mercer, by his will of 1627 gave £5 for repairs to Prout Bridge and Lane's Bridge (in Church Street).[20]

In the market place stood the town hall or market house, a building with handsome arched pillars.[21] Gilbert Adams gave £5 to the market house in 1627, 'to be imployed in the Building of the same when it shall be ended and finished'.[20] Near the market house were set up shambles, 'standinges with penthowses [awnings] for butchers to sell their meat in on Markett dayes and other tymes'.[22] There would also have been a number of more permanent shops and craftsmen's workshops. Near the shambles, we are told in J. B. Russell's MS. of the later 18th century, there was a fine market cross 'adorned with Carved work with a high ascent of Steps'. The cross, which was probably late medieval and of similar type to those at Maiden Newton and Stalbridge, became ruined; the remains, Russell says, had been removed 'some time ago'.[23]

In and near the Fore Place, there were a number of inns: inns were an important feature of any market town in this period, much business being transacted in them on market days, as well as drinking! The chief inn was the *King's Arms*, on the south corner of Hogshill Street; it is mentioned in a book of alehouse licences in 1619.[24] Now a restaurant, it retains some mullion windows on both east and north fronts; on the east front, where there are two 19th-century windows with canted bays, the southern one is built into the former carriage way.

The *White Hart*, on the north side of Hogshill Street, is mentioned in a document of 1636; the old building had mullion windows and a massive portico entrance.[25] The inventory of the possessions of John Hoskins of the *White Hart*, dated 1680, gives us a good idea of the premises.[26] The value of his goods was nearly £65. There were four rooms on the ground floor: hall, parlour, kitchen and milk-house. The hall and parlour had very little furniture in them, only table boards (usually for long narrow tables), forms, and a settle. The milk-house was used for cooking: it had five spits, a jack to rotate them, two dripping pans to catch the juice, and two basting ladles. There were several hooks (two pot hooks, five crooks) from which pots were suspended in which to boil food, and a number of such pots, metal vessels with handles (four crocks, three kettles, three skillets). In the way of tableware, the innkeeper had two dozen pewter dishes, 15 flagons for beer and cider, three quart pots and four pint pots, a dozen old silver spoons, and a little silver bowl. The kitchen was used for brewing — it contained one brewing tub and 'other tubs used about the brewing', and there were eight hogs-heads, seven half hogsheads, and five little barrels. Two hogsheads of beer, one of cider, and a firkin of sack stood ready for customers.

On the floor above, there were four chamber rooms, named as hall chamber, kitchen chamber, broad chamber, and cellar chamber; there was also a cock-loft, probably a half storey over. All the chambers had standing bedsteads with feather mattresses, curtains and valances; the broad chamber and the cellar chamber had in addition trestle bedsteads and dust beds (mattresses stuffed with chaff). All except the cellar chamber were furnished with table boards, and two had a little board or side board as well. The table board in the broad chamber, which was obviously the best bedroom, was round, and had its own 'carpet' or table covering. The hall chamber had four joined stools and three chairs, the broad chamber a dozen chairs, and the kitchen chamber three chairs and two forms. A dozen pairs of sheets, six board (table) cloths, and six dozen table napkins were kept in the kitchen chamber.

The *Red Lion*, at the corner of North Street, is named in 1618.[24] Henry Hoskins was paying church rates on 'the Lion' in 1664, and we have the inventory of Henry Hoskins senior, innholder, who died in 1680.[26] The rooms of his inn are listed as kitchen, hall, middle room, buttery and white hall, with hall chamber, middle chamber, buttery chamber, and garret above. The kitchen was used for brewing probably, and the hall for some of the cooking as well as for eating, while the middle room was also used for meals. The white hall was in use as a bedroom. The total value of Henry Hoskins' possessions was £57.

The two great fires

Fire must have been a constant hazard in the town when most roofs were thatched. With the increase in population from the later 16th century, and the building of houses with two or two-and-a-half storeys, and even a few three-storey ones, a great deal of property was at risk in a small area. We know of two major fires in Beaminster in the 17th century. The first occurred during the Civil War, when on Palm Sunday 1644 soldiers of the Royalist army of Prince Maurice, which had occupied the town, are believed to have fired their muskets into the thatched roofs. (The town as a whole was Parliamentarian.) Fire started in the gable of a house in North Street, and in two hours virtually the whole town was destroyed: only East Street and part of Church Street escaped. Besides barns and stables, 144 houses were burnt — there were probably only about 200 houses in the town at this time. In 1645 the Parliamentary army was at Beaminster, and Joshua Sprigge, the historian, records:

> The train and most of the foot quartered on the top of an hill: some laid in Beaminster Town, a place of the pityfulest spectacle that man can behold, hardly an house left not consumed with fire.[27]

The total loss was estimated at £21,080. The inhabitants applied to Parliament for help, and obtained an order for raising £2,000 out of the sequestered estates of George Penny of Toller Whelme, the money to be employed in repair and new building of the houses of the poor. The commissioners who distributed the money stated in January 1647 that they had assisted about 160 persons — those in greatest need rather than those who had sustained the most loss — and had allocated £1,540.[27] The actual money was however slow in coming. On 5 April 1648 an agreement was made between George Penny and certain leading inhabitants for the money paid so far to be made up to £300, and for 'timber trees now standing' on lands at Chedington and Hooke to the value of £500 to be designated for use. All inhabitants of Beaminster to whom these trees belonged were to be allowed at all reasonable times in the year within the next three years to fell the timber, and to 'make one or more convenient sawepitts' for sawing it up. In consideration of £300 in money, and £500 in timber, Beaminster people were to wait another three years before any more of the money owing was paid. Then Nicholas Poyntz, heir to a lease granted earlier by Penny, would begin to pay off the remaining £1,200 at the rate of £100 a year. The first quarter's payment was to be made on 24 June 1651, and similar payments during the 12 years 'in the common hall or markett howse' of Beaminster.[28] Without funds to rebuild, it must have been a long time before the town returned to normal.

The greater part of Beaminster was burnt down again on 28 June 1684, this time by an accidental fire. The normal practice was followed of applying for an official brief, so that collections could be made in every part of England.[29] Seventy-seven people claimed to have lost property and goods, and 51 people goods only; the property was worth £9,161 16s. 6d., and the goods £4,522 8s. 4d., making a total of £13,684 4s. 10d. The sum distributed, which was said to be 'the whole money' collected, 'necessary charges . . . only excepted', was £1,035. The distribution took place during two different periods between October 1686 and October 1689.[30] This fire, coming only 40 years after the earlier one, must have affected the fortunes of the town for quite some time — the further down the urban hierarchy, the more lasting the effects of such disasters.

The market house and the shambles were extensively damaged in the 1684 fire: the damage was assessed at £500 (the market house) and £30 (the flesh shambles). A letter dated 17 April 1690 from Carleton Whitelocke (of Hersham, Surrey, son of Bulstrode Whitelocke, a leading Parliamentarian) to Mr. Hitt of Beaminster, authorises him to receive brief money on his behalf and 'lay it out in building or repairing the market house or such part of it as you and Mr. Strode shall think most convenient and proper'. Carleton Whitelocke was at the time lessee of the Manor of Langdon, to which the profits of the market and the ownership of the buildings had become attached. There were nine flesh shambles, three belonging to Thomas Hitt, two to Isaac Gerrard, two to Edmund Stodgill, and one each to William Hallett and James Daniel (the butcher); all received some compensation for their losses.[31]

The new house of Frances Tucker, which was destroyed in the fire, had stood for a short time not far from the market hall. In 1670, on reaching the age of 21, Frances (daughter and heiress of William Tucker) entered into a contract with Thomas Reeves, carpenter, to build a house of good stone, three storeys high, with three rooms on each floor.[32] The house was finished by 1673, but she had only lived in it for a brief period. Her claim for loss in buildings amounted to £500, the highest amount claimed for a private house.[33]

On the north side of the Fore Place at the corner of Fleet Street and North Street, was a house which still bears today a unique record of the 1684 fire. No. 12 The Square (a newsagent's) has on the Fleet Street gable a panel which reads:

> This Towne
> Burnt in 1684
> Howse rebuilt
> in 1687. W.L.

The initials probably stand for William Lacke, clothier, who sustained a loss of just over £235 in buildings.[33] The 17th century house seems to have consisted of the present shop divided into two rooms (shop and living room), with two rooms on the first floor, and two attic rooms above. The original entry was possibly to the left of the Fleet Street shop window, where there is a straight joint in the outside wall.[34]

There are a few other 17th-century buildings near the centre of the town: these include No. 5 Church Street (*Eight Bells*), and No. 56 Hogshill Street, which has a large Tudor-arch fireplace on the ground floor. Nos. 19 and 21 North Street are mid-17th century; No. 21 has a canted bay of two storeys. On the outskirts, and so surviving the fires, are several large 17th-century houses; they are exceptionally fine, with a high quality finish, and show progress towards a more symmetrical plan. These houses are described in Chapter 6, when the Tithe Map of 1843, in conjunction with the commercial directory, makes it possible to identify all the more important houses in the town.

CHAPTER FOUR

AGRICULTURE AND INDUSTRIES 1500-1700

Farming and Land Use

IN THE EARLIER 16th CENTURY, Leland described the way between Bridport and Beaminster as 'in an exceding good and almost the best vain of ground for corne, and pasture and wood, that is in al Dorsetshire'.[1] As we have seen, the parish of Beaminster comprises a variety of farming land. In the 15th century there was a contraction in the arable in favour of enclosures for sheep; the vast flocks in Dorset were commented on by travellers during the 16th and 17th centuries. The other main farming occupations were the rearing of cattle, and dairy-farming, the production of milk to be turned into butter and cheese.

The main source for some aspects of farming in Dorset in the 17th century are the inventories attached to wills, which have survived for a number of the parishes which were 'peculiars' of the Dean and Chapter of Salisbury Cathedral. The inventories cover the middle sections of the community, the richer landowners' wills being proved in higher courts, while the poor were not required to make a will. Inventories had to be compiled for all goods of a total value of more than £5. An analysis for 1573-1670, made by computer, reveals the rising wealth of many of the substantial yeomen farmers over this period. It shows that in the mixed farming region of the West Dorset claylands, livestock represented 38 per cent. of the total wealth of the average farmer, the dairy cows making up much of the value of this holding. Fifty per cent. of clayland farmers had sheep, the average size of the flock being 40; this is a smaller proportion of farmers and a lower size of flock than on the chalk farther east, but the sheep from these rich lands were of higher value. Some of the clayland farmers had little or no arable at all; most had a lower proportion of their wealth in crops than those of the chalk or heathlands.[2]

Details of arable crops, stock, and farming implements are given in a number of Beaminster probate inventories. Away in a class by himself, with assets amounting to £480 (apart from his lease for years of the farm of Langdon, appraised at £1,000), was John Hoskins of Langdon, gentleman; he owned horses, cattle, sheep and swine to the value of £200. Corn was grown on the farm in some quantities, and 'his Corne in the Barnes & bartons and his greene Corne in the feildes' was valued at £80 in 1613; his 'waynes, sulles [ploughs], iron chaynes and all other plough stuffe' were worth £10.[3] A court case between the Bishop of Salisbury and Peter and John Hoskins (1630) dealt with a complaint that the Hoskins family had turned up the pasture grounds at Langdon and converted them to arable 'for their owne great benefitt' at the time, but the lessening of profits in time to come.[4] A survey of Langdon made about 1663 stated that John Hoskins (grandson of the

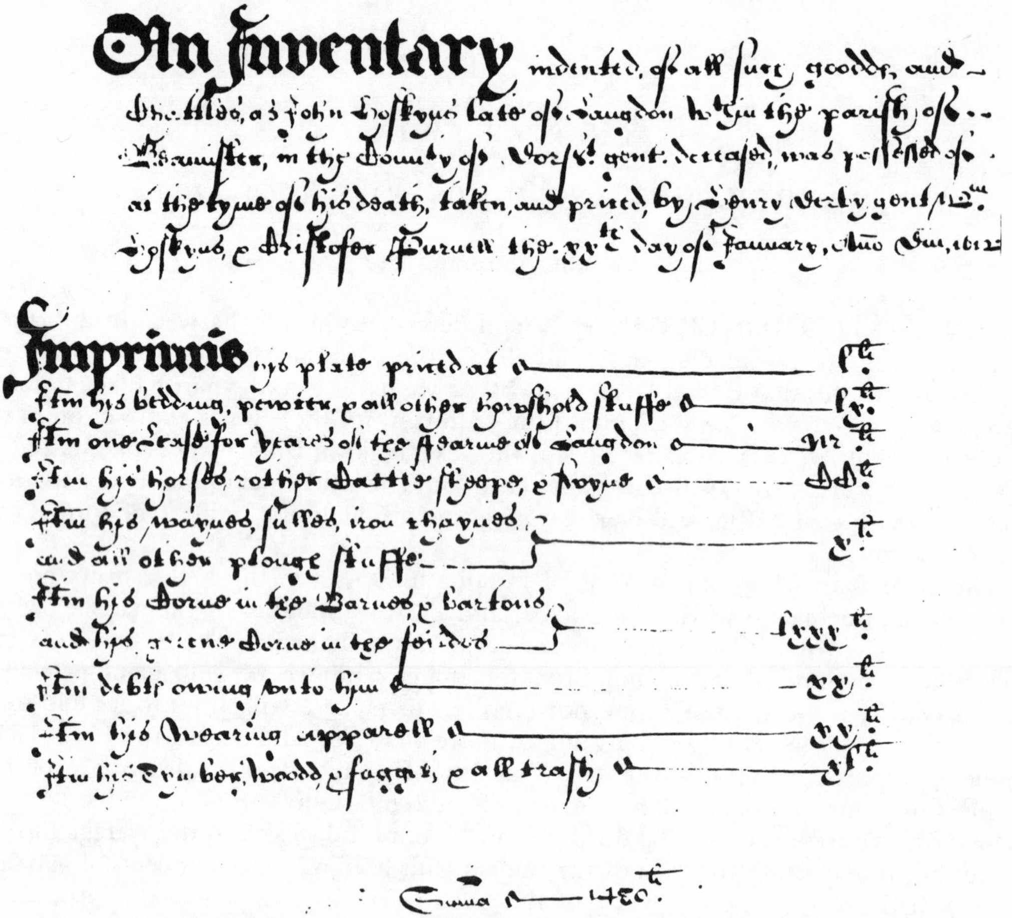

Fig. 5. Probate inventory of the goods of John Hoskins of Langdon, gentleman, taken 20 January 1612/13. His household goods were highly valued: (silver) plate at £50, and bedding, pewter and other items at £60.

earlier John) had impoverished the grounds by overploughing them.[5] Leases of Langdon granted by the Bishop after the Restoration refer to 'Two Quarters of good cleane sweet and well winnowed wheate being the Rent newly increased'.[6]

Some other inventories of Beaminster farmers of the earlier 17th century, all of whom were content to call themselves husbandmen, range in value from nearly £90 to under £10. The total assets of John Daniel, who was probably farming at Knowle, were £89 13s. 4d. in 1628,[3] well above average for this decade in the computer analysis.[2] He had corn, wheat and barley worth £12; his main farm assets were however divided almost equally between his flock of 54 sheep worth £20, and his other animals — seven cows and calves valued at £10 10s. 0d., five young beasts at £7 10s. 0d., and a horse and two pigs at £4. His hay was worth £4.

Henry Thatcher, probably in the Meerhay area, had a few acres where he was growing wheat, oats and barley to the value of £6 in 1600, but again his stock was his greatest asset. Twenty wethers, 31 small sheep and 10 lambs were worth £14 15s. 0d., and three kine, one steer, one heifer, two geldings and a pig were worth £13 10s. 0d. He had two pails, a trendle (a large wooden tub with handles used for working the butter grain), and three cheese vats. He also had hemp seed, a 'weight' of hemp (32 lbs. in Dorset), and 30 'runnes' of yarn (a run was a measure); the value of all his goods amounted to £55 1s. 2d.,[3] about average for this date in the analysis.[2]

The possessions of William Trivett (1616) and George Damett of Axnoller (1610) came to less than £10. They worked as labourers, Trivett having a hatchet and an axe, and Damett a spade, pickaxe, and 'other necessary tools'. William Trivett had one heifer and three sheep, while George Damett grew a little hemp. Both men owned a spinning wheel and hand cards for opening and straightening wool.[3]

In the later 17th century William Milles the elder, gentleman, of Meerhay, left assets amounting to £701 9s. 0d. Of this sum, £563 10s. 6d. was in money and in bills, bonds and surrenders, but he had seven bullocks, 66 sheep and lambs and one horse worth £45, and in the field 1½ acres of wheat and the same area of barley were valued at £5.[7]

Examples of inventories of men calling themselves yeomen disclose assets ranging from £185 to just over £50. John Munden (total assets in 1700 £184 14s. 7d.) possessed 10 horses and 19 cows worth £74, and 60 sheep worth £26. In the buttery were 16 bushels of barley and one bushel of wheat, in the barn barley and wheat valued at £3, while four small mows of wheat and some barley and beans in the barton were worth £12. He had three sulls, two pairs of harrows, two drags (a heavy harrow), together with harnesses and halters. In the chamber over the hall were 100 cheeses.[7]

Lancelot Mills of Chapel Marsh (total assets in 1684 £141 7s. 3d.) owned animals worth £132, including 21 cows and one bull valued at £60, and 80 sheep and lambs at £22. He had a 'zule' (sull), and a pair of harrows, but his corn in mow and in barn was worth only £1 6s. 8d.[3] John Ireland of Axnoller (total assets in 1684 £88 15s. 8d.) was clearly engaged in dairy work. There were seven pails in the entry, a churn in the chamber over the hall, two butter barrels in the passage, and a cheesesteane or cheese press in the kitchen. There were moreover 30 small cheeses in the chamber over the kitchen and more in the chamber over the parlour. He had nine milch cows, six small heifers, two bullocks and a colt worth £28 10s. 0d. His sheep, 36 couples (that is a ewe and one lamb) and 24 hogs or hoggets (yearlings), were valued at £15. He also had a yoke of steers, a mare, and another colt worth £10.[7]

Richard Batten (total assets in 1694 £61 18s. 7d.) was also engaged in dairy work: in the milk-house were nine milk pans, one churn and one cheese tub, and in the chamber over it one cheeserack, one cheesestane, four cheese vats and 42 small cheeses. He had two 'torns' (spinning wheels). John Oliver of Whately (total assets in 1684 £52 5s. 6d.) was the owner of four cows, two yearling bullocks and a calf valued at £12; there were three pails and a butter barrel in the hall, and cheese vats in the buttery.[7]

The tenants of the manors of Beaminster Prima and Beaminster Secunda made rules for the pasturing of sheep and cattle and the management of the commons.[8] A presentment made in the reign of Elizabeth was re-presented and confirmed in 1651, and

Fig. 6. Probate inventory of the goods of John Munden, yeoman, taken 3 January 1699/1700. Five rooms are mentioned: hall, buttery, hall chamber, buttery chamber and chamber over the outhouse.

similar ones were made in 1658 and 1673: sheep only were to be kept on Beaminster Down (20 for a tenement and 10 for a cottage), and cattle and horses were to be kept only in Hollymoor and Beaminster Wood Common (three for a tenement and two for a cottage). Sheep and cattle belonging to strangers, and tenants' animals kept on the wrong commons, were to be impounded. No tenant was to keep any sheep or cattle on either of the cornfields at Beaminster Down (South Field and East Field) after corn or grain had been sown until it had been cut and carried away. Two tenants were to be elected every year at Michaelmas to act as wardens. Any tenant offending against any of these orders was to pay 3s. 4d.; half of this was for use of the wardens, a further quarter for use of the hayward of Beaminster Down (his job was to protect the commons from stray cattle), and the final quarter was to go to the poor of Beaminster. No tenant was to carry away the earth out of the commons, highways, or lanes, though he might make a marle pit in the commons for 'the better improvement of his Customary Lands so as it bee in a convenient place and without prejudice to any of the tenants of this Mannor'.

A presentment of 1605 (re-presented in 1651) shows that 40 years earlier (1565) a parcel of common called Axnoller Moore, on which all the tenants had previously intercommoned, had been allotted to the tenants of Axnoller in lieu of their common in Beaminster Wood and Hollymoor which was obviously a long way from them; as the tenants were few, each enclosed his separate share with his own fields.[8] A somewhat similar arrangement seems to have been made for mutual convenience in connection with land out to the east of Langdon on the parish boundary. Here seven closes, one of which was called Corscombe Corner, had (it was stated c. 1663) been 'antiently' taken into Langdon farm, by a composition made between the lessee and the tenants of Prima and Secunda which permitted them to intercommon on a sleight or sheep pasture on Beaminster Down belonging to Langdon.[5]

It seems that in 1605 an order was made that the commons 'as yet undivided' should be allotted in individual portions to tenants 'that every one may have & take to his owne use the furses and other fewell growing uppon the porcon to him allotted . . .'; in 1658 it was resolved that the commons of Beaminster Wood and Hollymoor should be divided into six parts, each part to belong to an agreed number of tenements and cottages, which would be solely entitled to the pasturage and fuel of their respective section, but these arrangements were apparently not carried out.[8]

About six-sevenths of the land in the two large common fields was in the hands of the neighbouring farms at Meerhay, Stonecombe, Shatcombe, Northfield, Langdon and West Axnoller, when these fields were inclosed and allotted in 1809. We do not know how much earlier this process of consolidation of holdings had started; the 1649 survey of Prima and Secunda gives no information about the location of individual holdings.

Farm Holdings and Estates

The only information we have for this period comes from deeds and court books, and some of the larger farms were not within the manors of Prima, Secunda, and Parsonatus. The impression gained is of a complex pattern of land holding, changing perhaps more frequently than one might expect. The land in the immediate vicinity of the town was in innumerable small holdings of a few acres here and there. some of these may have together constituted a small farm, but many belonged to townsfolk plying other occupations. Some of the later large farms, for example Barrowfield and West Axnoller, were still in a number of units. It is noticeable that all the farmhouses of the 'out-parish' are sited on the spring line between the 500 and 600 foot contours. Many of the existing houses are 17th century: of these all but one were built in the latter part of that century, a period which seems to have been a very prosperous one for West Dorset pastoral farmers.[9] A detailed picture of the majority of the farms cannot be obtained before the Tithe map and Award of the mid 19th century, but in two exceptional cases – Langdon and Parnham – there are 17th-century surveys and other sources giving a great deal of information.

Langdon. The lawsuit between the Bishop of Salisbury and the Hoskins family (1630)[4] and the survey made *c.* 1663[5] combine to give a good picture of the manor farm. Before it was taken over by the Hoskins family, probably in the later 16th century, a considerable amount of the woodland noted at Domesday must still have remained. The Bishop stated that at the time the lands had been leased to the Hoskins they had been 'plentifully stored and set with great quantety of Tymber Trees'. He complained that Peter and John Hoskins had 'in the space of Seaven or Eight yeares now past cut downe or caused to be cutt downe . . . and rooted up to the number of One Thousand Trees of Oake Aysh Elme and such like timber trees . . . to the value of fifteene hundred pounds . . . and the same they have disposed of to their great enrichment . . .'.[4] Lessees of estates were not infrequently guilty of such misdeeds, but it was not unknown for bishops themselves to supplement their income by cutting down all the timber on their properties! We have already mentioned the large scale conversion of meadow and pasture grounds to tillage which was carried out by the Hoskins family. They were also accused by the Bishop of 'wasting' the houses on the manor; perhaps they turned off the copyholders and pulled down the cottages.

The survey describes the 500-acre farm as bounded on the east and south with the lands of George Penny (Toller Whelme), Mrs. Frances Tucker and Mrs. Ursula Hoskins (Storridge and Mapperton Marsh), on the north with Corscombe farm belonging to Sir Andrew Henly, and on the west with Beaminster Downs, belonging to the prebends. The fields and their acreages are given as follows:

	acres
Hill Close	37
Brockehay	20
Thorney Craft and Orchen Wood	25
Great Sart	30
Little Sart	10
Milford Lands	14
Great Meadowe	14
Nete Meade	8
Two place Grounds and Black Orchard	20
Turly Moore and Shoareing Greene	20
Plaine Close	10
	208

continued opposite

(continued)

	acres
East Downe	25
West Downe	25
Two Lower West Woods	20
Higher Westwoods and the moore	20
Blacke Spine	8
Rowe Downes	12
Oakey Close	8
Rusly Downe	20
Three Shatcombe Closes	9
Two Little Closes	6
Plotts and orchard	2
	363

Three Closes near Beaminster Down	15	
Corscombs Corner	10	
Marlpitt	50	
Bottom Close	20	
Hoskins Corner	20	
by a new survey they contain in all		140
		503

Parnham. The Strode family had become well established here since the arrival of Richard Strode in the earlier 15th century. William Strode had done a certain amount of building by 1500, but it was Robert Strode who about the middle of the 16th century largely rebuilt the house. To this period date the hall with its two porches, and the wing, originally the kitchen wing, immediately adjoining the hall on the north; the present service wing to the north-west was built as a separate structure in the 17th century.[10] The house had 18 hearths at the time of the 1664 Hearth Tax.

Details of Parnham and its estates are given in a survey made by Sir John Strode about 1628.[11] He tells us that his father John (Robert's son, whose arms with the date 1559 are in the glass of one of the east windows in the hall) built a gatehouse and a schoolhouse and made walls round the 'Inner Court' and the garden. Sir Robert Strode, Sir John Strode's elder brother, built a wall round the 'Base Court' and enclosed a 'new warren' with a dry stone wall. There was an ancient grist mill below the house on the river Brit (near the present Mill Ground Cottages), but it was now 'suffered to lie ruinous and decayed for the advancement of Bemister Customarie Mills', the mill belonging to Beaminster Prima farther up the river.

The demesne freehold lands, totalling 87 acres, part of which were in Netherbury parish, were as follows:

- Croft Meads as far as the mill stream on the west – 10 acres
- Hams and grounds lying under the new warren and the bowling green, also hopyard grounds, all lying west from the mill stream as far as 'fair Oak' – 6 acres
- Little close called 'dry close' lying under the lane from Bowling Green to Beaminster Mills – 4 acres
- Warren anciently called 'Longlands', beside the ground called 'Daniel's Knowle' taken into the warren by Sir Robert Strode in exchange for some part of Edmond Coombe – 10 acres
- Pasture called 'West Leaze' next to the warren on the south – 20 acres

— School House Mead (3 acres) and West Mead (12 acres) on the east of West Leaze
— Mead behind the barn — 8 acres
— Part of Bowling Green and Quarr Close — 8 acres
— Part of meadow between 'the Row of Ashes' and the lane from Beaminster to Bridport —
   6 acres

There were also copyhold lands used as demesnes to Parnham, consisting of Edmond Coombe and Edmond Coombe Hill called the 'old warren', together with meads and arable lying under the hill, and the remainder of Bowling Green. Many of these enclosures still had the same names two hundred years later when they can be identified on the Tithe map.

On the other side of the lane from Beaminster to Bridport were 'grounds lying under Coome downe hill being sometimes several closes but now lying open & in common to the hill for sheepe', Coombe Down Hill itself, and a number of arable closes on the south-east side of the hill; details of Coombe Down farm were left unfinished in Sir John Strode's notebook.

To Parnham also belonged 'divers closes, land, meadow & pasture, known by the names of East Hewstock, Mill Close, Hullet Downe [elsewhere the last two are called Milch Close and Hewlets], containing about 100 acres', which were then on lease to the Pitt family; Lancelot Mills also held three closes called Hewstock.[11] This was the farm known in the 18th century as 'Horne'. The park of deer called Horn Park, 'paled in with cleft pales of oak, and containing about 70 acres', was apparently in the parish of Broadwindsor adjacent to East Hewstock;[12] in the 18th century it was part of the farm known as 'Park'.

When Sir John Strode died in 1642, he left instructions in his will that he was to be buried in Beaminster church beside his father and mother, and many members of the family are understood to have been buried there.[13] In 1956, when the flooring of the south aisle had to be renewed, the Strode family vault was re-discovered near the Strode memorials. The original entrance, now covered with quarry tiles, is a stone slab, with a flight of stone steps going down to the tomb. The vault contained 14 lead coffins, some of the lead of which had perished. Of the seven inscriptions which could be read, one was the coffin of Catherine Strode, wife of George Strode, who died in 1746 and is commemorated with her husband on the fine marble monument in the aisle; the other six were of members of the Oglander family who followed the Strodes of Parnham. It was not possible to read the names on the seven coffins which were underneath.[14]

Woollen-Cloth Industry

Thomas Fuller (Rector of Broadwindsor 1634–41) said of the county of Dorset that it could 'Cloathe it self with its own Wooll and Broad-cloath made thereof . . . And as they are provided for warmth in their Woollen, so for cleanliness with their Linnen-cloath . . .'.[15] After agriculture, the main occupations of Beaminster during this period were cloth-making, and hemp and flax manufactures. For many people these were secondary occupations; for a few it was industry which provided their chief livelihood. The short wool of Dorset sheep was not of the best quality and much of it

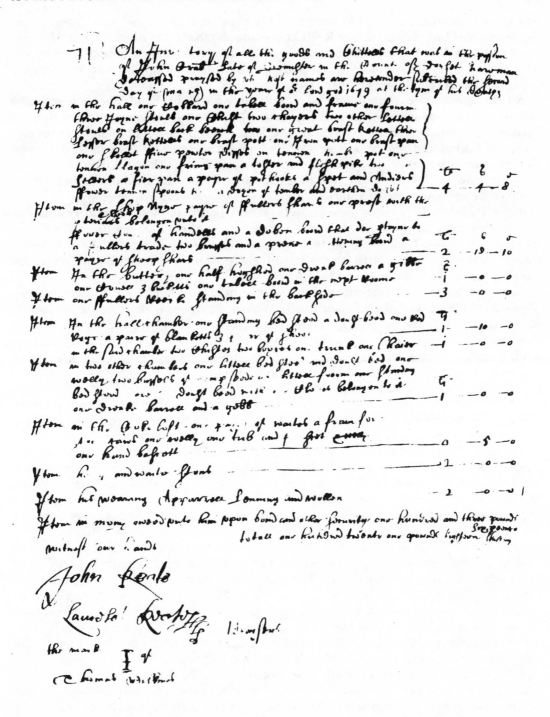

Fig. 7. Probate inventory of the goods of John Crab, shearman, taken 2 March 1679/80. Among the items in the hall were a skillet, five pewter dishes and a tin (tennen) chamber pot.

was made into coarser fabrics known as 'kersies' or 'dozens', which were lighter than
the traditional broadcloth; Lyme Regis had a considerable trade in the export of these,
particularly to Brittany and Normandy.[16] In the Somerset–Devon border country the
new serges, made from coarse wool, and with a worsted warp, became increasingly
important during the 17th century.

All the processes except fulling were still carried out by hand: the first spinning
machines were not introduced until the late 18th century, and power-looms did not
become common before the 1830s. In the West Country capitalist clothiers usually
bought the wool and sent it out for spinning, which was mostly done in the cottages.
The spun wool was then woven out by the weavers, who worked on their own looms
at home, and finally the cloth was finished and sold by the clothier. Daniel Defoe
includes Beaminster (about 1700) in the Dorset towns 'principally employed in the
clothing trade'.[17] In a court case in 1627, it was said that there were in Beaminster
'divers cloathiers who doe keepe many people on worke which sell their cloaths to
merchants that doe trade them beyonde the seas'.[18] In 1656 James and John Willmott
owned mills and a watercourse at the top of Fleet Street[19] — the Willmott family are
later described as wool-staplers and clothiers.

Our main source of information about people in the clothing trade is the inventory
of goods made at the time of their death. William Burges was described as a clothier
in an inventory made in 1679, but the total value of his goods only amounted to
£16 7s. 2d.; he had a pair of looms and a spinning-wheel in his workshop.[7] William
Lacke, also a clothier, had in 1692 several remnants of new wool cloth worth £10, but
was owed the sum of £40 in 'desperate debts', the particulars of which were said to be
recorded in a book of samples of cloth.[3] Lancelot Keate, clothier, by his will of 1683
left to his son 'six pair of cloth sheers . . . and all materials that belong to the Cloth-
working Trade', together with a pair of looms;[7] in 1668 he had issued a Trade Token,
featuring what has been described as 'two hands holding some instrument'.[20]

The most interesting inventories are those of John Crab ('sheerman'), and the two
John Hearnes, both serge-makers. In 1680 the goods of John Crab were worth
£121 18s. 6d., of which £103 was money owed to him upon bond and other security.
In his workshop were 'nyne payre of fullers shares . . . fower courst of handells and a
doben board that doe pertayne to a fullers trade'. (Raising the nap was done by
drawing a 'handle' set with teasles over the cloth; often the cloth was laid over a
board and the handles drawn over this in a horizontal position, and this was called
'dubbing', the number of courses given with the handles varying with the quality of
the cloth. The raised surface was then cut down again, using the huge ponderous
shears traditional to the industry: a very good 16th-century carving of a pair of
fuller's shears can be seen in the church at Cullompton (Devon), on one of the spring-
ers of the fan vaulting on the south side of John Lane's aisle.) In the cock-loft there
was a frame for stock cards for opening and straightening wool, and in the back yard
a fuller's rack on which cloth would be hung to dry.[7] (See Fig. 7.)

John Hearne, who died in 1695, was worth £253 10s. 0d., £100 of which was in
'Money Due on Booke'. He had wool valued at £60 in the wool loft, and serges, both
dressed and undressed, and worsted yarn worth £50; there was a dye-house on the
premises. The John Hearne whose will was proved in 1716 was apparently his son;
there were more rooms on his premises, but one of them was still a dye-house. This

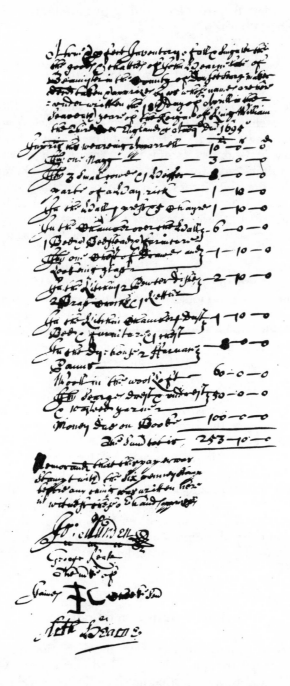

Fig. 8. Probate inventory of the goods of John Hearne, serge-maker, taken 18 April 1695. He owned three small cows and one heifer worth £8, and part of a hayrick.

John Hearne had 23 dressed and undressed serges valued at £28, together with 29 spinning pounds of worsted yarn (£5), and a pair of looms. His total assets were £183 4s. 3d., of which £100 was in one bond.[3]

Hemp and Flax Manufactures

Flax and hemp were grown all over Dorset in medieval times: flax must always have been sown in small patches to weave into linen cloth for clothing, and hemp would be needed for halters, nets, cords and traces. There was a flourishing commercial rope and net industry in Bridport.[21] Acts to promote the growth of the two crops were passed in Tudor times, and the development of flax and hemp manufactures was further encouraged by the vicissitudes that the woollen cloth industry went through during the Thirty Years War (1618–48), which led to unemployment. Huguenots coming into England after 1685 introduced different forms of manufacture, for example into sail-cloth,[22] the demand for which was increasing as ships began to carry more sail.

The growing and working of hemp and flax, labour intensive occupations, fitted in well with dairy farming, and the possibility of these multiple sources of income must have attracted people to West Dorset, and accounted for some of the population growth. The soil was very suitable for the cultivation of hemp, as Thomas Fuller testified: 'England hath no better than what groweth here betwixt Bemister and Brydport, . . . our land affording so much strong and deep ground proper for the same . . .'.[23] In 1610 George Damett had an acre of green hemp at Axnoller.[3] John Munden, yeoman, had 10 bushels of hemp seed in the chamber over the hall in 1700,[7] and there are numerous other references in inventories of farmers and others to hemp and hemp seed in store. The townsfolk asked for the balance of the funds which were allocated to Beaminster after the fire of 1644 to be laid out in a stock of hemp and wool for employing the poor.[24]

William Keate (will 1676[3]), Henry Newman of Meerhay (will 1683[7]), Richard Way (will 1690[7]), and John Horsford of Langdon (marriage 1702) were all engaged in the weaving of sackcloth. In 1695 Lancelot Hoskins was making sail-cloth.[25] The Jessop family were weavers: the inventory of John Jessop (1690) mentions four pairs of looms in the workshop,[7] and the will of Robert Jessop (1707) describes him as a linen-weaver. Robert had two pairs of looms, a pair of warping bars, and two spinning wheels in his workshop; his assets (totalling just under £18) included flax and thread worth £4 and linen worth £1.[3]

Other Industries and Crafts

Tanning had been carried on in Beaminster from medieval times, the numerous streams providing the water needed for this industry; allied occupations were those of glover and saddler. Gloving had also been carried on since the medieval period, though we do not know the extent of the industry; the gloves were of leather, and used in jobs like hedging. The inventory of George Baker, glover (1622), details assets worth £55 3s. 10d., but most of this was in money out on loan, and his leather and skins were valued at only 10s. 0d.[3] The inventory of Peter Filldew, saddler (1705), gives a detailed description of his stock-in-trade. In the shop, valued (with a few other items) at £11 7s. 6d., were the following:

> one dozen of spurrs, one dozen of hackney whipps, four dozen of bridles, five & twenty pair of stirrup leathers, twelve cruppers, six new saddles, twelve saddletrees, one pillion, one dozen & halfe of webb garths, about three halfe pieces of webb, three curry combes, six brushes, eighteen pair of stirrup irons, one dozen & halfe of snoffles, halfe a dozen of bitts, one dozen of mane combes, eight sheep skins, thirteen calve skins, eight hogs skins, three pieces of hide leather, two dozen of saddle strapps, one dozen of leather girdles, three foot stools, four pair of side leathers.

Peter Filldew also kept an alehouse. The contents of his cellar and cider house (mainly hogsheads full of beer and numerous pewter drinking vessels of various sizes) were valued at £22 13s. 0d., and his total assets came to £90 10s. 6d.[7]

In the inventories of other common craftsmen and tradesmen we often find their stock-in-trade and working tools listed. For instance, John Bower, glazier (1622), had glass and lead to the value of 16s. 0d. and glazing tools worth £1, his total assets amounting to £16 2s. 2d. The goods of John Ford, shoemaker, were valued in 1635 at £26 11s. 0d.; leather and shoes accounted for £4, but he also possessed two kine, two heifers and one bullock worth £9 6s. 8d. In 1710 another shoemaker, William Clift, with total assets of £53 13s. 8d., possessed shoes, leather and working tools worth £7 10s. 0d.; he had £40 in money in the house and out on security.[3] We know from deeds that William Clift was at No. 18 Hogshill Street where he had a shop, hall, kitchen and buttery on the ground floor and a bedroom over the hall.[26] A tailor named William Dent (1688) had in his workshop five remnants of serge and 12 remnants of cloth valued at £10 5s. 0d.; six remnants of shag (long-napped rough cloth), a remnant of kersey, some buttons and silk and a small quantity of ribbon, galloone (narrow braid) and tape were valued at £3. His goods and chattels were worth £97 5s. 0d. altogether; of this £60 was in money.[3] Brewing and malting were common occupations: the inventory of Robert Mason, maltster, which was taken in 1674, valued 'the barley and malt that was in the house' at £4, out of a total of £24 5s. 0d.[7]

Markets and Communications

Whereas hundreds of markets which existed in the early 14th century failed to survive the subsequent decline, the market at Beaminster was not only still functioning in the early 17th century, but presumably trade was growing, since a new market house was built. The inhabitants claimed during the Civil War that it was a 'great market town'.[27] By 1663 the value of the tolls, profits, etc. of the market, which had somehow become attached to the Bishop's manor of Langdon (although originally granted to two prebendaries of Salisbury Cathedral), had 'advanced' to £20 'at least', though the fair was 'of little value'.[5] After the fire of 1684, which may have hastened a decline due to other causes, the market may not have regained its former importance. It was no doubt mainly non-specialist, dealing generally in commodities such as cattle, meat, and dairy produce, but it would also have sold hemp, flax and linen goods produced locally. Its influence would be restricted to a purely local area of half-a-dozen miles or so.

By the 17th century the larger markets tended to specialise, and there were a number of these in the vicinity. To the north Chard (12 miles) specialised in cattle, and Crewkerne (7 miles) in cattle and sheep. Bridport (6 miles south) specialised in linen, hemp, rope and twine, and there were also markets at Lyme Regis and Axminster to the south-west. The really large important markets were at Dorchester (17 miles), Sherborne (20 miles), and Yeovil (15 miles); these sold not only cattle and sheep, but provided the more pastoral areas with corn. At Yeovil market, which was important for north-west Dorset, leather, hemp, and linen figured largely, as well as butter and cheese.[28]

A major trading event for West Dorset was the fair which was held for four days during Whit-week each year on Whitedown Hill, between Crewkerne and Chard, at the junction of three major routes. There were very important sales of cattle and leather, attended regularly not only by people from places nearby, but also from a distance of up to 16 miles. Beaminster, about a dozen miles away, was among the parishes of origin of both buyers and sellers of leather, in trade records of the earlier 17th century; John Locke of Beaminster, who sold regularly at the fair, must have been a well established tanner.[29]

From the late 16th century, traffic on the roads multiplied, owing in the main to the increase in foreign and internal trade. Much travelling was also done by well-to-do people, some of whom have left accounts of the bad state of the roads: Celia Fiennes, for instance, about 1700, recorded that westwards from Dorchester 'the wayes are stony and very narrow'.[30] Poor people too were often on the roads, many of them moved on by the overseers of the poor to the next parish, lest they became a burden on the poor rate. Some who had been issued passes by the J.P.s at Quarter Sessions were given charity money by Beaminster churchwardens. One entry in the accounts (1666) reads 'gave 3 semen that had thare Ship taken away by the Hollener with a passe that lodg in town all night, 8d.' Another entry, in 1667, records 'To A man & 3 children with a pass from London from the hospitall his Leggs burnt of, 1s. 0d.'[31]

By the Highways Act of 1555 the primary responsibility for roads, including the main highways, had been laid on the parishes through which they ran. On four (later six) days in the year every person holding land to a certain value, or keeping horses or plough, had to send a cart and two men to work on the roads; other inhabitants had to labour themselves. Unpaid surveyors of the highways (waywardens) were appointed among the parish officials; their job was to view the roads three times a year, and to organise the repairs. Highway surveyors' accounts survive less often than those of other officials and none exist for Beaminster. Churchwardens' books record, however, that in 1670 George Beere and John Gudge of Axnoller were appointed surveyors for the parish, and in 1691 John Herne, waywarden, was paid for the rebuilding of Hams Bridge.[31]

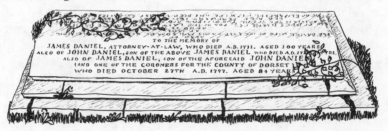

Gravestone of James Daniel in Knowle burial ground

CHAPTER FIVE

PEOPLE AND SOCIETY 1500–1700

Local Administration

A NUMBER OF AUTHORITIES were concerned with the different aspects of local administration during this period. The manorial courts exercised their traditional jurisdiction, regulating the entry into and surrender of copyhold or customary lands, and such items as the cutting down of trees and underwood for repairs and for fuel. The management of commons and common fields was dealt with through these courts: the appointment of wardens for the commons and a hayward for Beaminster Down has already been noted. A constable or tithingman for Beaminster town was appointed by the manor court of Beaminster Prima; the office of constable originated in that of tithingman, and the two terms became more or less synonymous — sometimes a tithingman was a sort of deputy constable.

The Justices of the Peace, who held a central position in local government as the county authorities, were generally responsible for law and order; they were concerned with an increasing variety of matters, and we come across illustrations of this in connection with Beaminster. In 1629, information having been received that there were neither stocks, ducking stool, nor pillory in Beaminster, an order was made at Michaelmas Quarter Sessions that Peter Hoskins, lord of the manors of Prima and Secunda, should have a pair of stocks made and set up within 10 days, and a ducking stool and pillory before Christmas.[1] The constable of Beaminster informed the Quarter Sessions Court in 1630 that a company giving puppet shows had been causing a lot of trouble in the town, because they 'doe exercise their feats not only in the day tyme but alsoe late in the night, to the great disturbance of the Townsmen there, and the grievance of divers of the Inhabitants who cannot keepe theire Children and Servants in their houses by reason that they frequent the said shewes and sights late in the night in a disorderly manner'. The company were ordered to leave the county.[2] A complaint was made in 1636 that the constables and other inhabitants were 'fearful to goe abroad in the night tyme to execute theire office and negotiate theire businesse', because of the fierce dogs kept by alehouse keepers and other 'meane inhabitants'.[3]

The J.P.s were concerned in 1626 with a serious outbreak of the plague at Bridport, and it is probable that Beaminster was also affected, because that year Michaelmas Quarter Sessions were held at Dorchester instead of Bridport or Beaminster as was usual. Burials recorded at Beaminster for 1626 were however only 18.[4]

Vestries, originally concerned only with church affairs, became more important during this period, as the operation of the poor law through the parish officials began to transform the ecclesiastical unit of the parish into a civil one, eventually ousting the tithing as a unit of administration; this process was not completed in Dorset until about 1800. No vestry minutes have survived for Beaminster prior to the 18th century.

The Poor and Charities

In medieval times the poor and sick had been dependent on alms given by the monasteries and on the charity of the better-off. After the dissolution of the monasteries, many parishes had some sort of alms collector, and the office of overseer of the poor may have originated in this way. Under a series of Acts in 1572, 1597, 1601 and 1640, the responsibility for relief of the poor was laid on the parish. Unpaid overseers were appointed annually by the J.P.s from lists drawn up by parish vestries, and their job was to maintain the poor, the majority of whom were of course the aged and disabled, widows and orphans. Funds were provided by local taxation in the form of a poor rate.

The earliest record of the overseers of the poor for Beaminster is an account book covering the period 1630-74.[5] This shows that regular monthly payments – the sums ranging in the 1630s from 1s. to 6s. – were made to certain people, several widows and a child being specified. There were also a large number of casual payments each month, for example for rent or the cost of repairs to a house, and for items of clothing such as a pair of shoes. Where possible, work was supposed to be provided for the poor to off-set the expense: when the compensation money was being allocated after the fire of 1644, the inhabitants wanted the £400 which remained to be 'conferred as a stock to their common workhouse to procure materials of hemp and wool for employing their poor, who were both numerous and idle'.[6] It seems unlikely that there was actually a workhouse at this date, but the poor may have been employed in their own homes. In 1635 there was a complaint at Quarter Sessions that 'many poore of the towne of Bemister doe usually goe abroad into the feilds adjoyninge and teare hedges and fences of many inhabitants ... notwithstandinge the parishoners have provided sufficient fuell for the poore there'. The constables or other officers were authorised to 'apprehend all such hedge tearers as they shall finde there ...'.[7]

Disputes frequently took place between parishes as to their liability for poor people, and these had to be settled at Quarter Sessions. In 1626 Beaminster and Broadwindsor had a difference of opinion concerning providing for 'one Gartrude Elbie an aged & impotent woman'. It was reported that she had lived at Beaminster with her kinsman for the past two years without any interruption, but 'about a short time sithence she went by the instigation of her kinsman to Broadewynsor where she could not be received but only one night for pittie'. The court ordered her return to Beaminster, adding that 'for such goods as is alleged by inhabitants of Beaminster that she carried thence to Broadewynsor & there now remaine', these should be delivered to Beaminster on demand.[8]

It was quite common in the earlier part of this period for parishioners to leave money in their wills to be distributed amongst the poor of the parish. For instance, in 1573 William Spelt left 4d. 'to the poore mens boxe', while John Hillary left 40s. to the poor in 1595.[9] Gilbert Adams in his will (1627) named nine poor tradesmen, to each of whom he left 40s., and also 23 other poor folk of the town, who were to receive 20s. each. He further gave £200 to the poor of the parish to be bestowed at the discretion of his executors, and £5 to be distributed after his funeral.[10]

Several well-off members of the community gave sums of money to be kept as 'a stock' for the poor by the overseers, whose receipt is entered in the account book. Richard Hillary of Buckham, by his will dated 1629, left £10 'to be kept in the poore man's boxe', and lent out on security.[11] Forty pounds, which Henry Hillary had given by his will (1639), was lent to Anselme Wall in 1642. Sir John Strode, who died in 1642, left £5 'to be imployed and lent to poore tradesmen upon sufficient security' (June 1647). In 1652 this money was lent out in three parts: £2 to Robert Meech upon the bond of Mr. Henry Hillary his surety, £2 to James Willmot upon the bond of Joseph Symes, and £1 to Widow Leakey upon surrender of part of her house.[5]

Gilbert Adams' almshouse. Gilbert Adams left £40 in 1627 for the building of a house for the poor of Beaminster, together with a further £20 for its maintenance. A house, later known as the Gilbert Adams Almshouse, was built in Beaminster, and a number of poor people lived rent-free in it.[12] About a hundred years later, the house, which was in East Street, was taken over as the parish workhouse (see Chapter 9).

Sir John Strode's almshouse. Another almshouse, a small one storey building with ham stone mullion windows and Tudor-arch doorway, which still stands adjoining the churchyard on the west, was erected by Sir John Strode of Parnham. In the front wall is a stone inscribed 'God's House. Sit Honos Trino Deo. Anno Dom. 1630'. During a recent restoration, two fireplaces were found; the one at the west end is thought to be original. The almshouse was built on land belonging to a chantry, presumably that of Robert Grey. George Strode, Sir John's grandson, in his account of the original endowments settled on the almshouse, detailed rents from four houses apparently still standing on the chantry lands in 1630, one of which was described as 'a house which was antiently the Chantry House'. The other endowments consisted of two-thirds of Bilshay farm in Loders and certain quit rents. Six poor people of good behaviour were to be chosen from Beaminster or elsewhere at the discretion of the heirs of Sir John Strode.[13] 'Steps of Stayres' were laid next to the almshouse in 1647.[14]

Tucker's Charity. A major charity was that of Frances Tucker, who by her will made in 1682 and proved in 1689, gave from the income of the part of her farm called South Mapperton £20 a year for the maintenance of a schoolmaster to teach 20 of the poorest boys of the parish of Beaminster. He was 'to take care of their manners', catechise them, teach them to read and write, and 'in some competent measure to cast an account'. A further £30 a year was to be employed for binding out as apprentices three or more of these boys, one or two of them to be sent to sea. The trustees and executors appointed by Frances Tucker refused to act, and fresh trustees were appointed more than once by the Court of Chancery, the whole thing culminating in a lawsuit on behalf of the boys; it was not until 1703 that the trustees appointed William Combe as schoolmaster. The school used an upper room in the 'annex' attached to the south-west corner of the church, which then had a separate entrance from the churchyard up a flight of steps.[15] It was quite common for part of a church to be used for a school at this period: at North Cadbury in Somerset, two alphabets are written in black letters on the wall of the vestry.

It may well be that Frances Tucker endowed a school which already existed in Beaminster. We hear in 1634 of a schoolmaster whose name was Launcelott Crabb,[16] and there are entries in churchwardens' accounts for 1651 and 1663 of items for a schoolhouse. It seems quite likely that Thomas Spratt (1635-1713), who became Bishop of Rochester, once attended this school. He was born at Beaminster, being the son of a Thomas Spratt who was curate there in the early 1630s, and he later stated that he had received the rudiments of education 'at a little school by the churchyard side'.[17] He was evidently well known to Frances Tucker, who left him a fourth part of her farm called North Mapperton.[15]

Puritanism and Early Nonconformity

During the reign of Edward VI (1547-53) the effect of the Reformation began to be felt in parish churches. As we have already seen, the chantry of Robert Grey in the church of Beaminster was dissolved, and its property confiscated and granted out to lay persons. Roods and images were taken down; the beginning of the stairs which led up to the rood-loft can still be seen to the south of the chancel arch at Beaminster. Orders were made to pull down stone altars and replace them by wooden communion tables, often in the body of the church. In 1606 the churchwardens of Beaminster stated: 'our communion table standeth not in our chauncell but standeth in the middle allie of our churche to the good likeing of all the parishioners'.[18] (Under the regime of William Laud, Archbishop of Canterbury in the 1630s, the High Church movement endeavoured to have communion tables returned to the east end of the chancel.)

In 1549 the vicar and churchwardens of each parish were required to make an inventory of all the vestments, plate, jewels and bells in their church; two years later the Privy Council ordered that such church plate as remained should be taken into the King's hands for his use, the churches being allowed to keep only the least valuable chalice and paten for Holy Communion. An inventory of church goods for the parish of Beaminster is dated 1552: the parish was permitted to keep the worst chalice (of two), and one cope of white satin, together with all the table cloths and surplices.[19]

Attendance at church was compulsory, and churchwardens had to report regular absentees: there are frequent examples of this in the presentments of Beaminster churchwardens. In 1631 it was presented that John Hillary of Buckham and William Hoskins the younger 'doe often depart out of the Church at the beginning of the Sermon, and not returne againe during all Sermon tyme...'.[20] It may be that as more conservative churchgoers they disliked the increasing tendencies of some of the clergy towards Puritanism, and the preaching of long sermons; certainly John Hillary of Buckham was no friend to Puritanism. His name was crossed out on the joint present-ment made by the other church officers at the time of Archbishop's Laud's visitation in 1634; they had nothing to present on controversial points. John Hillary put in his own long series of presentments. He reported the curate Thomas Spratt because he did not read Evening Prayer according to the form prescribed in the Book of Common Prayer:

... first hee doth reade parte of Evening prayer (as much as pleas him) and then doth call forth such as are to be Catechized and soe doth aske them a question or two out of that Catechisme ... but upon those questions doth preach and make a sermon (at the least) the space of an hower & a quarter, if not more ... the people often tymes are kept in church till it be almost v of the clock.

He also objected to the fact that, in his own absence, his fellow churchwarden John Crabb and Mr. Spratt had allowed an unlicensed minister to preach, 'who preached very much against the Kings booke of lawfull recreacons'.[16] (The Puritans wished to prohibit Sunday games after divine service, but Charles I had recently re-issued a declaration put out by James I, in favour of certain traditional sports.)

In essence it was Puritanism, becoming divorced from the Church, which turned into Nonconformity; in the later 16th century and earlier 17th century, when Puritans were still members, if wayward ones, of the Church of England, the documentary evidence is to be found only in records of the Church. From churchwardens' presentments about 1600, we learn that while there were no recusants (Roman Catholics) in Beaminster, there were three people 'which refuse to communicate'.[21] In 1634 John Hillary's presentments included one to the effect that 'one Thomas Conway of Beaminster doth keepe & to his house doth frequent private congregacons tending to Conventicles'.[16]

Most of the Anglican clergy supported the king, and during the Interregnum many were ejected from their benefices in favour of Puritan candidates. The livings of Netherbury and Beaminster were separated during this period, and Beaminster had its own incumbent, the nonconforming minister Joseph Crabb; he however succeeded to Netherbury also in 1657, and was incumbent of both parishes until 1661.[22] It was during his incumbency that there was a solemn ordination of nine ministers in Beaminster church, at a service lasting several hours, in the presence of a great assembly of both clergy and laity.[5]

After the Restoration, nonconforming ministers — including Joseph Crabb — were ejected in their turn. Episcopal returns made in 1669 reported the congregations or conventicles still in existence despite the Conventicle Act of 1664, which was intended to suppress them: the return of Bishop Seth Ward of Salisbury for the south-west of Dorset shows that there was considerable nonconformist activity in certain areas here. In Beaminster a group of 100 met at the house of Lancelot Cox in East Street, though the worshippers were described as 'people unknown, from London and places distant'.[23] In the late 17th century and early 18th century some rural chapels acted as regional as well as local centres.

In 1672 the Declaration of Indulgence permitted public worship by nonconformists; the place had to be 'allowed' and the teacher 'approved'. Three forms of printed licence were issued. Two were for teachers: one licensed a teacher to teach one specified permitted congregation, with further licence to teach in any other allowed place, while the other was a general licence to teach in any allowed place. The persons to whom licences were issued include Ambrose Clare (a minister) and William Craine, both of Beaminster, who had a General Preaching Licence; John Willis was also given a licence to teach in Beaminster. The third form of licence was for a place: two houses were licensed in Beaminster, those of Lancelot Cox and John Locke (a tanner who lived in North Street), and also the 'room under the Market House'. Preachers and places were all described as Presbyterian.[24]

Services probably continued to be held in the house in East Street which had belonged to Lancelot Cox. Records of Beaminster Secunda (1695) refer to 'all that house or structure now commonly called the meeting house situate in Eastreet . . . between the dwelling houses there of Joshua Cox on the one side and of Thomas Boel on the other side . . .'; the house was for the use of Thomas Hoare and his wife Mary. The Rev. Thomas Hoare, for many years before he took sole charge of the chapel in 1714, assisted the Rev. Thomas Crane, former vicar of Rampisham, who seems to have been the first minister.[25]

People and Families

What do we know about individual people or families during this period? It was not until about 1400 that surnames became settled and hereditary. Only one of the names in the 14th-century Lay Subsidies can be identified in the subsidy of 1525: there was a Robert of Combe in 1327 and 1332, and in 1525 a John Combe. In the Muster lists of 1539 and 1542 and the Lay Subsidy of 1545, about one hundred different surnames can be counted in Beaminster and Langdon tithings.[26] Only just over half these names are still to be found in the list of those who subscribed to the Protestation Oath in 1642;[27] it is not surprising that all except one of the Langdon surnames (that is, those of people engaged in farming) are among the survivals. In 1642 there are about two hundred different surnames, so nearly a hundred and fifty new names have appeared, and must relate to the period of exceptional growth in the town in the later 16th century and early 17th century. We have already discussed the Strode family in connection with Parnham. Some other important families — Hoskins, Hillary, Daniel — can be traced right through from the 15th century, and in 1525 they are all found in the top bracket of taxpayers, assessed at £20 and over. The Hoskins (principal family) and the Hillarys had died out in Beaminster before 1700.

Hoskins. The name occurs in the rent roll of 1472, and there are a number of men with this surname in 1525. The Beaminster Hoskins derive from Roger of Hereford,[28] and the head of the leading family (Henry or Harry, Roger's grandson) was the highest taxed person in 1525: he paid on an assessment of £60 (in goods), more than John Strode. Sidelights thrown on the Hoskins of Langdon in the earlier 17th century suggest that they were colourful characters. We hear of Peter (Henry's grandson) and his eldest son John in more than one episode. In 1630 Peter, evidently annoyed at the court order to set up the stocks, told John to pull down the shambles erected by Peregrine Percoty and put the stocks and pillory in their place. The stocks had before 'beene placed in another more fitt and convenyent roome in the Markett place', and John gave out that he had put them in place of the shambles just because Percoty was employed by Sir John Strode, one of the J.P.s responsible for the order.[29] During the lawsuit with the Bishop of Salisbury already mentioned, Peter and John threatened to cut down all the rest of the trees on the Langdon estate, and waste the lands 'bare & barren', if they were not granted a further lease.[30] Peter was also involved in a legal battle with William Tucker regarding trees which Tucker had cut down on land that he leased to Hoskins at North Mapperton. In his letter of 18 April 1636 to

Sir John Strangways, who had been appointed to investigate on the spot, Peter asks for matters to be deferred until he has consulted his solicitor in London, describing himself as 'an old & blind man whoe have long since left off to deale in mine owne affaires'. This special pleading did not work: Strangways pointed out that Peter's son John was equally involved, saying, 'I am sure hee is noe stranger unto it nor can it possibly soe bee but that from tyme to tyme hee hath given you a full information of the proceedinges therein'.[31] John Hoskins, who later purchased the manor of Purse Caundle, wrote his own whimsical Latin epitaph, to be found on a grave slab in Purse Caundle church;[32] he died in 1651.

In 1664 Mr. Henry Hoskins (probably Peter's second son) occupied a house in North Street with five hearths[33] (perhaps nine or ten rooms), no doubt an earlier building on the site of the Manor House. We are told that the Hoskins family had in the town 'a considerable estate, with a neat house belonging to it', and that part of this house was rebuilt by Mary, only daughter and heiress of another John Hoskins (son of Henry), who married William Gifford in 1685.[34] There is a memorial tablet to this John Hoskins and his daughter in the north aisle of the church.

Hillary. This surname also occurs in the 1472 rent roll. In 1505 a John Hillary of Meerhay built the Hillary Aisle in the church, and in the 1525 Lay Subsidy John Hillary was assessed at £40. The Hillarys had two farms, at Lower and Higher Meerhay, in the 17th century. They also owned land at Buckham from the later 16th century, and the John Hillary who styled himself 'of Buckham' in 1634 also comes through to us as something of a character. We have already mentioned the separate presentments he made in 1634: his first long list of parishioners 'who did not bow at the name of Jesus' was followed by two further lists containing names he had omitted, including those of most of his own relatives, ending with 'and soe now you have all, nisi me fallit memoria'.[16] This family too died out with female heirs, all named Elizabeth: in 1634 Elizabeth, daughter of John of Buckham, married Robert Mohun, while Elizabeth, daughter of John of Lower Meerhay, married William Mills some time after 1645, and Elizabeth (presumably daughter of Henry of Higher Meerhay) married William Stephens in 1665.[35]

Daniel. The Daniels feature in deeds of land near Parnham, no doubt at Knowle farm, as early as 1385, when Nicholas Poulet or Paulet confirmed to John Daniel and his wife Cristina four acres of the land of his demesne, and granted them the reversion of a garden called 'Langheye'.[36] In 1525 a John Daniel paid tax on £20. The Daniels were nonconformists: in 1684 James Daniel, attorney, and his two sons John and James, were reported by the churchwardens for 'not frequenting their parish church at divine service'.[37]

Among other surnames persisting from the earlier 16th century to the mid-17th century, and in many cases into later centuries, are Ireland, Mintern, Newman, Wilkins, Gudge; all of these belonged in 1525 to a substantial middle class of yeoman, taxed on between £10 and £20. The better-off representatives of the families of Keate, Ford, Painter and Stone were slightly lower in the scale, being assessed at between £4 and £10, while the holders of the names Nile, Chick, Baker, Guppy and Wilmott were labourers, taxed on wages of £1. Other names found in the 1545 Lay Subsidy, though not in 1525, include Derby, Damytte (Dematt), Hallett, Horsford and Jessop.

Among the 'new' surnames of important families coming in from the later 16th century onwards are Cox, Russell, Hitt, Symes, Conway, Lacke, Tucker and Mills. Robert Cox, son of Robert, was baptised in 1585. Ralph Cox occupied a house with seven hearths (a large property) in East Street on 1664.[33] In 1667 Lancelot Cox issued a Trade Token, with his initials on one side and a skull pierced by an arrow on the other.[38] A John Russell was overseer of the poor in 1656;[5] no connection has been traced between the 17th-century Russells and the John Russell who set up as solicitor in the mid-18th century (see Chapter 10).

In 1664 Mr. Thomas Hitt owned a house with five hearths in East Street,[33] doubtless the house known as 'Hitts'. J. B. Russell, writing in the late 18th century, says that the property of the Hitts family 'was great, being upwards of £600 a year', and that one of their descendants still owned the mansion 'which belonged to them before the time of the Great Rebellion . . .'. The Hitts were also owners of a farm at Whitcombe.[39] Mr. Joshua Symms or Symes lived at a house in East Street with four hearths in 1664;[33] this must have been 'Farrs', which was later connected with the family.

A Trade Token with a wool-comb on one side was issued by William Conway in 1667;[40] his branch of the family came from Stoke Abbott and he was buried in the churchyard there in 1720.[41] The Lackes were also in the cloth-working trade; the marriage of a Peter Lacke is recorded in 1588, and William Lacke was living in a house with five hearths in the Fore Place in 1664.[33] William Tucker, father of Frances Tucker, was a prosperous mercer, and also owner of land at North Mapperton which his daughter inherited on his death in 1654.[42] The Mills family were prominent yeomen: a William Mills, as we have noted, married the Hillary heiress of Lower Meerhay, while Lancelot Mills was farming at Chapel Marsh at the time of his death in 1684.

Although the town as a whole was strongly Parliamentarian, families must have been involved on both sides during the Civil War. John Hoskins took an active part on behalf of the king; his estate at Langdon, which he held on lease from the Bishop of Salisbury, was sequestered. So were the estates of John Hillary at Lower Meerhay, Robert Mohun at Buckham, and Sir John Strode at Parnham.[43] It is possible that Charles II stopped briefly at Parnham on his way from Bridport to Broadwindsor, where he spent a night in September 1651. He decided not to halt at Beaminster as he had intended, being struck 'by the melancholy aspect of the place', still suffering from the effects of the great fire seven years earlier; so he went on, perhaps by Long Barrow Lane, 'over a high conical hill called Chartknolle [Gerrards Hill]'.[44]

After the Restoration, small regular payments were for a time made to indigent soldiers who had been faithful to Charles I, and the names of a number of Beaminster men eligible to receive these are recorded in 1664 and 1665: John Hawkins, John Dabbin, John Mills, Lancelot Forde, Stephen and Robert Gerrard, Ellis Coles, John Tinker, Nicholas Hardy, Clement James, John Reade, William Hoskins, William Lea, William and Henry Keech, Thomas Notthey, Henry Peach and William Furser senior, all of Beaminster, and William Beard, Lancelot and George Hallett of Axnoller.[45]

The Monmouth Rebellion of 1685 again found Beaminster families in opposite camps. Nineteen Beaminster men 'wanting from their Homes in the tyme of the Rebellion' were tried at Dorchester. Four were convicted of high treason and sentenced to transportation; others may have been executed. The 19 names (amended slightly from other sources) were as follows: Joseph Strong, Charles Strong, Charles Strong junior, Thomas Sargeant, Richard Meech, William Bugler, Thomas Bugler, Samuel Bailey, Edward Doun, Samuel Hoskins, Richard Hoare, John Canterbury, Philip Dunning, John Dunning, Lancelot Cox, John Hearn junior, John Gerard, Ralph Cloud junior, and John Hoskins. We also hear of one Simon Poole, who was put on board a frigate bound for Barbados, but died at sea.[46] Many of those ranged on the side of Monmouth came from nonconformist families: of the men listed above, Joseph Strong, Charles Strong, William Bugler and Philip Dunning had been reported in 1684 for not attending the parish church.[37]

James Daniel, attorney, had a surprising escape at the time of the rebellion. The story goes that having fled from the battlefield of Sedgemoor, he managed to get to his house in Hogshill Street, but as there was a price on his head it was unsafe to remain there. He went out at the back and across the fields, and hid under the straw in a barn on his farm at Knowle, where (so we are told) against all odds, the pursuing soldiers failed to find him. He decided to be buried on this spot, where he had been preserved by divine providence, and his wish was carried out when he died at the age of 100 in 1711. The small burial ground still exists, and inscriptions on the 10 tombstones record his burial and the subsequent burial there of a number of his descendants.[47] In 1835 a white marble tablet to his memory, recording his 'wonderful concealment', was placed on the north wall of the Congregational chapel in Whitcombe Road.

Doorway of East Axnoller farmhouse

PART THREE — 1700- 1850

CHAPTER SIX

TOWN AND PARISH 1700-1850

Population

WE HAVE SUGGESTED that at the end of the 17th century the population of the parish was somewhere in the region of 1,500. In 1801, at the first census, it was 2,140, an increase of some 40 per cent.; this is a very much slower rate of growth than in the preceding period. It compares, however, with an increase in England and Wales over the same time of about 53 per cent.; in the country as a whole, from about the mid-17th century there seem to have been periods of slight decline interspersed with periods of slight recovery, before renewed substantial growth set in from the mid-18th century.

What do we know about the actual size of the community at Beaminster between the late 17th century and the beginning of the 19th century? At this time Dorset formed part of the Diocese of Bristol; in 1735 Bishop Secker visited the county and made notes on the parishes, and these were continued by Bishop Newton in 1766, when details of the number of families in each parish were entered. Unfortunately, there are no figures for the 'peculiars', of which Netherbury (with Beaminster) was one.[1] In 1775, however, 26 years before the first census, a survey of Beaminster was made by Samuel Cox, in which he found a population of 1,955.[2] He divided the population between the town, to which he attributed 1,708 inhabitants, and the out-parish, where the inhabitants numbered 247. The people are listed, street by street and house by house, in columns under the headings of husbands, wives, widowers, widows, single men, single women, male children, female children, male servants, female servants; children constituted about 45 per cent. of the total. The summary shows 390 houses in the town and 41 in the out-parish, which included the individual farms and farm cottages, and the hamlets of Axnoller (6 houses, 34 people), Meerhay (10 houses, 51 people), and Stenfy or Stintford Lane (6 houses, 33 people). Some of the entries in the survey are a bit ambiguous, the totals transferred to the summary do not entirely agree with the sheets, and there are errors in the arithmetic of the final totals. However, the net differences are not large, and the picture given of the community is likely to be pretty accurate.

Parish registers, which are our only source before 1775, give some idea of what was happening to the population. Registers are defective before March 1736; after this they are complete and the entries clear and well kept. In the 39 years from 1737 to 1775 inclusive, there were 30 more christenings than burials. Over the period christenings tended to rise, but in the 1740s they were exceeded by burials (502 burials, 408 christenings) — there were several very bad harvests in England during this decade. From the 1750s burials tended to decline, except for a few unusually heavy years: in 1758 there were 117 burials, in 1759, 60 and in 1767, 86, and there must have been epidemics.[3] There would have been some under-registration of births in the parish registers because of the Congregational community. (The only non-conformist burial ground was the small private one of the Daniel family, and the few burials here can be ignored.) Most of the early records of the Congregational chapel, which is unlikely to have had more than about a hundred adherents, were lost in the fire of 1781. However, the addition of three or four baptisms a year over the 39 years 1737-75 — later in the century the average was over four — would bring the total excess of baptisms over burials to between 150 and 200. We have no information about migration into or out of the parish.

From 1776 to 1800 inclusive, the 'natural' growth as shown in the parish registers was 457 (1,505 christenings, 1,048 burials). From Congregational records we may now add a further 112 christenings. This estimate has been made by adding together the christenings of children of Beaminster residents for 1777-89 (57) and 1797-1800 (19), and proportionately for the years 1776 and 1790-96 (36), which are missing.[4] This results in an amended figure for natural increase of 569, whereas the net increase between the Cox survey (1,955) and the first census (2,140) was only 185. If we now look at the years 1801 to 1810 inclusive, the parish registers show an increase of 342 (677 christenings, 335 burials),[5] to which may be added further christenings at the Congregational chapel (50),[4] making a total of 392. The census increase over this period was in fact only 150 (1811 census, 2,290).

Between 1775 and 1801, and at all the decennial censuses between 1801 and 1841 except one, the actual population increase in Beaminster was very small, and well below the national average. (The exception is 1811-21: the large national increase counted at the end of this particular decade is partly attributed to the return of the armed forces after the Napoleonic wars.) It is generally accepted that from the 1780s the absolute growth of rural populations in England and Wales was much slower than that of the new urban and industrial areas, as the pace of migration from the country-side quickened. The individual sets of figures may not be wholly reliable, but perhaps what we are seeing in the case of Beaminster is a migration out of the town already starting by the last quarter of the 18th century, which may denote the beginning of the decline in local industries. We know from other sources that emigration was taking place in the 1830s and 1840s.

Between 1801 and 1841 the population of the parish rose to 3,270, its highest ever; this is an increase of 53 per cent. overall, as compared with the increase of 79 per cent. for England and Wales. In 1841 the census report records 2,938 people in Beaminster 'town and parish', and 332 in 'Langdon tithing'; in the former there were 581 inhabited houses, in the latter 61. This indicates a considerable increase in the population of the out-parish: Langdon tithing (the main part) had contained only about 34 houses in 1775. A circular distributed in the town in 1848 pointed out that the parish church lay in the south-west extremity of the area, and proposed the erection of a new district church:

> Towards the North and North-East lie the suburbs of New Town, Short Moor and the Green; the Hamlets of Higher and Lower Meerhay, and outlying Farms on the Hills to the distance of three miles. These Suburbs and Hamlets are mostly of recent date; are inhabited mostly by poor people, are populous and are increasing . . .

The area to be allocated to the new church would contain about 1,000 inhabitants, it was suggested.[6] So Holy Trinity Church came to be built, at the very time when the population of the parish actually began to fall.

Most of the larger parishes in the Beaminster Poor Law Union (established in 1836) also reached their population peaks in 1841 — some of the smallest ones had already begun to decline. The only places which were to show further slight gains were Misterton and Evershot, where the railway passed within a mile or so of the village centres.

Town Development

In 1775 the houses in the town were distributed as follows: Fore Place 17, Hogshill Street 55, Fleet Street 66, North Street 39, The Green 35, East Street 96, St Mary Well Street 80,[2] a total of 388. (Cox's own summary shows 390). The name Clay Lane occurs in early 18th-century records, but in this survey houses along the lane must have been included in Hogshill Street. When Hogshill Street was newly made up as a turnpike road in 1777, the usual course of the stream there was obstructed, and a covered channel had to be made for conveying the water. At the same time it was ordered that 'a Dipping place shall be made where thought most convenient for the use of the inhabitants';[7] this was opposite No. 26. The stream which crossed to the south side of the street near No. 53 — which was only put under the pavement in 1910[8] — ran down through the tan-yard to the bottom of Shadrack Street. Both Shadrack Street and Church Street were included in St Mary Well Street in 1775; in 1791, when the town was responsible for the bridge there,[9] Shadrack Street was known as Little Street. Up to 1832 St Mary Well Street proper consisted of an open stream with a cobbled pathway on both sides in front of the houses; it was known locally as 'Duck Street'.[10] East Street in 1775 covered Prout Bridge, East Street itself, Whitcombe Road and the Bridport road — the last-named appears as South Street in the 1830 directory.

A number of improvements were made in various parts of the town by the Bridport 2nd District Turnpike Trust (see Chapter 8) during the later 18th century. Even at that date there were often no bridges suitable for the traffic on turnpike roads, and in 1775 the trustees met to consider plans for building a new bridge over the river at Prout or Bride Bridge. Several masons agreed that it could not be done 'without taking away Farmer Clift's Wall & a part of his Court before his House and if that is done the way into Mr. Dunnings Barton will be blocked up and the Water will be thrown into his House [Bridge House]'. It was decided that the steps of the existing bridge should be taken down and that the road over the bridge 'should be made convenient for people on horseback as well as on foot' and that 'a gutter be made under the Road leading from Bishop Dunnings to the river in order to carry off the water from his house'. Not long afterwards it was agreed to widen the bridge at the north side 'so that carriages may occasionally pass over', and in 1778 William Miller (alias Brinson) and William Mills were paid £15 15s. 0d. for the job.[7] (The high-pitched arch built over the river proved dangerous to traffic, and about 1839 the bridge was lowered.[10]) The main road between the *Red Lion* and the corner of Whitcombe Road was widened and straightened in two places about 1800.[7]

In 1784 a bridge was built by William Brinson near the turnpike gate at South Gate: this may be the bridge at 'Sansford Lake', which was one of those for which the turnpike trustees were responsible in 1791.[11] In 1810 it was ordered that 'a causeway be made for the convenience of foot passengers by the side of the road from the south end of the Turnpike House ... to the Gate entering into Mr. Gundry's Field called Hams'.[7] This must be the paved strip shown in the water-colour by H. Codd,[12] and it looks as if part of it still remains in front of No. 2 South Gate, where there are three rows of blue lias setts, with space between them for more. The whole is about 2 ft. wide and identical with a strip of paving six setts wide in front of Bridge House, which may also have been laid down by the turnpike trust. Such causeways would at that time have been above the level of the muddy road. It is interesting that the Act of 1819, which prohibited the trustees from repairing the foot pavement in any town, specifically exempted 'footways or causeways by the sides of that part of the said roads which passes through the town of Beaminster which have been from time to time kept in repair by the trustees of the 2nd District'. The Act of 1830 expressly forbade the trustees to spend any money on repairing, lighting, or improving any street in Beaminster.[13]

Fires and fire-engines

There had been yet another serious fire in Beaminster in 1781. J. B. Russell records that on 31 March 'Between the Hours of 4 and 5 in the morning, a Fire broke out in a Back Building belonging to the King's Arms Inn ... In the course of Three or Four Hours all the Houses on the West Side of the Street leading from the Market Place to the Church (two only excepted) were destroyed. At the same Time, two Houses near the Pound, with the School House, and several Houses near the Alms House, together with all the Houses in Church Street and Schederick Street ... and Eight Houses on the South Side of Hogshill Street, besides Stables, and other Buildings, were entirely consumed. The whole number of Houses destroyed amounted to upwards of fifty'. The total loss was more than £8,000, about £6,000 being insured;[14] soon after the Great Fire of London, several fire insurance companies had been formed in the capital, and the Sun Office, established in 1710, was not long afterwards effecting insurances all over the country. The sum of £805 was raised by subscription in Beaminster and in towns and villages all over Dorset, contributions also being made by Crewkerne, Chard and Yeovil; this money was distributed to those who were not insured.[15]

In 1786 there was another smaller fire. 'Early this morning', wrote J. B. Russell on 27 May, 'a Fire broke out in the East Street in Beaminster, which consumed 4 Dwelling Houses, & damaged 3 or 4 more — some of these were the Oldest Houses in the Town'.[16] In 1842, we are told, upwards of 40 houses and outbuildings were destroyed in a fire.[17] Two houses in the Fore Place adjacent to the eastern end of the market house, which were occupied by Thomas Pine (grocer) and John Marden (linen draper), were never rebuilt after being burnt down in 1844.[18]

At the time of the terrible fire of 1684, fire-fighting equipment in Beaminster probably consisted only of buckets of water filled by hand from the river or drawn from private wells, and ladders brought to the scene by neighbouring householders. Some time in the later 17th century, the first fire-engines, which were of course entirely manual, began to be manufactured: the town of Dorchester had bought a fire-engine by 1676.[19] The first fire-engine of which we have any record in Beaminster was bought by public subscription in 1712; the engine itself cost £35 5s. 0d., and the total expense including bringing it from London came to £40 14s. 10d. The number of people subscribing to buy the engine was 135, and the largest subscription (£1 1s. 6d.) was paid by 12 leading townsfolk.[20]

In 1753 the Vestry resolved to buy a new fire-engine, to be paid for out of the poor rate; the engine chosen was one of Newsham & Ragg's 'Fourth Size' engines. In a broadsheet issued in 1728, Richard Newsham of Smithfield, London, who had patented his first fire-engine in 1721, claimed that his 4th size engine (there were six sizes) would hold 90 gallons in the cistern, and discharge the same quantity per minute. Thomas Strode of Parnham was asked to obtain the engine and ship it to Bridport; the engine cost £44 2s. 6d., 40 yards of leather pipes cost £11 12s. 0d., and freight to Bridport £1 1s. 0d. The following year the Vestry agreed to have an engine-house built on a piece of land purchased from Thomas Conway (this was next to No. 21 The Square), the cost to be met from the poor rate. Benjamin Hoskins, cooper, was to receive 'One Pound and One Shilling to keep the Engines cleane & to have them Playd at least Four times & to keep the water belonging to the Towne in its proper Course' during the forthcoming year. The town pump and the water courses were repaired, and in order that sufficient water should be available in case of fire, a large reservoir was constructed beneath the roadway in the market place.[21]

Another fire-engine was purchased in 1764, apparently identical to the one bought ten years earlier; the cost came out of the poor rate, apart from £10 contributed by Thomas Strode and £21 given by the managers of the Sun Fire Office.[21] In London all the fire insurance companies had their own brigades by now, but in the rural areas they usually contributed, in proportion to their business, to the fire-fighting services provided by the local authority or by voluntary effort. After the fire in East Street in 1786, a memorial was sent to the Sun Office, signed by 14 leading inhabitants, in which the following remarks were made on the subject of fire-fighting:

> Are sorry to say at the said Fire we observ'd some Men very inactive, the reason we since find was their being disatisfied in the Distribution of some Monies gave by your Office and other-wise Collected in the Town at late Fires. We think, was there a Select Number of Men (Viz) 100 paid an Annual Sum of 1s. each to be under the directions of some of the Principal and Active People of Property would be more likely to extinguish Fires than by the common Rabble.[22]

In 1824 the Sun Office gave one dozen leather buckets, and in 1833 £10 towards the upkeep of the engines. In 1837 the West of England Fire Insurance Company gave one dozen leather buckets and three guineas towards the repair of the engines.[23]

In 1783 an order was given by the overseers to 'put the Town Pump in repair and . . . place it against the new market house wall and employ a plumber to add as much pipe as may be wanting, and a carpenter to new timber it'.[24] In 1831, 77 inhabitants subscribed £28 15s. 6d. to pay for 'the New Prison, for the Repair of the Fire Engines and the Town Pump'.[23] Anthony Toleman was put in charge of 'the several fire engines' in 1833.[25] One of these small manual engines is still kept in the care of the Dorset Fire Brigade at Beaminster. It is only 3 ft. long and 18 in. wide, and has four solid wheels; a pole fixed to each side enabled it to be carried like a sedan chair. In 1845 '1 doz. Fire Crooks with handles 20 ft. long' were purchased[23] — examples of these massive iron hooks, which were used for tearing down thatch from the roofs of burning houses, can be seen in the porch of Bere Regis church.

Law and order

In the late 18th century and earlier 19th century, night watchmen used to patrol the streets of the town. The 'Bellman', who carried a bell attached to his waist by a cord, was paid a regular salary 'to walke the towne at night from 12 of the Clock until 5 in the morninge the somer time, and . . . untill 6 in the morninge the winter time'. He also received a quantity of free beer, and in 1789 a coat was made for him. [26] An account rendered to parish officials in 1831 reads 'Making two Great Coats with flaps & Capes for the Watchmen, 18/-'. [27]

In 1789 it was reported in Vestry that the town had been 'greatly burthened of late years by divers Beggars belonging to divers remote Places, solliciting Alms from House to House . . .';[24] it was the job of the overseers and the constable to see that such vagrants were moved on. The stocks, which had been placed near the wall of the new market house in 1783, were broken up about 1835. [28] Before 1831 the 'Blind House' at the East Street workhouse was used to confine disorderly people for the night pending prosecution. The 'New Prison' or lock-up, known as the 'Round House', which was built in 1831 at a cost of £40, adjoined the parish pound on the south-east of the church; it disappeared when the churchyard was enlarged in 1841. [29] In 1830 there were two Beaminster constables, together with a tithingman of Beaminster and a tithingman of Langdon. Richard Hine tells us that he had in his possession a truncheon belonging to a Beaminster constable, inscribed in gold letters 'IV W.R.'[30]

Shops and services

Just what repairs were carried out to the town hall or market house after the fire of 1684, in which it was virtually destroyed, is not clear. According to J. B. Russell's MS. of the later 18th century, the west part of the building had been turned into a market house, and there had been shambles on the west side and on the north side towards the main road, while the south part was entirely disused. It was obviously a very inferior building compared with the earlier one, as Russell goes on:

> The Market House was a very shabby Building, being on the Top patched up with Boards, and thatched, & for a long Time the Arches there were walled up: but Certain People being of late very solicitous for the Beauty of the Town, have pulled it down. The South Walls belonging to the Hall are down also & the remaining part is very ruinous . . . [31]

There seems to have been a market bell, to give notice of the opening and closing of the market, for in 1765 when the church bells were being recast, an entry in the churchwardens' accounts reads 'paid 6d. to the Crier, giving Notice, the Market Bell will ring for Prayer'.[32]

About 1780 a new market house was erected on the site of the one which had been pulled down; the north and south walls each contained five hamstone arches in which butchers' stalls were set. Some time before 1818, John Warr, builder (to whom the lessees of the manor of Langdon subleased the market house, flesh shambles, and the tolls of the market) built a room known as 'the Town Hall' over the original market house; this room was approached from the road on the south side by wooden stairs. A house and shop were also added at the western end of the building; about 1850 a licence was obtained for the sale of cider and beer in part of the house, and it acquired the name *Market House Inn*. For many years before the building was pulled down in 1886, the occupier and licensee was Samuel Poole, who also collected the market tolls.[33]

Although Thursday was the official market day in Beaminster, Sunday seems to have been observed as a universal market day until the 19th century. The main traders in the Beaminster market were the butchers, and in 1798 one of them (John Keech) stated that he had kept the market on Sundays without interruption for more than 50 years.[34] Markets gradually became less important as permanent shops increased, and road connections to larger towns improved. Some markets faded out: for instance we are told in 1798 that at Evershot, a large village about eight miles north-east of Beaminster, the weekly market which was formerly held for corn etc. had been disused 'for upwards of 50 years'. The Beaminster market continued in being until after the middle of the 19th century. In 1830 it was said to be well supplied with corn, butchers' meat, etc.[17] About 1857 the tolls taken 'for the standing for sale of all manner of Live Stock and Agricultural produce and Merchandize and Exhibitions or Shows' varied in amount from £7 to £50 a year; the average for the last eight years had been £18 18s. 1d.[35] (This sum must have included any fair tolls.)

The original grant of an annual fair was for three days in September (7th, 8th and 9th); after the new calendar was adopted in 1752 (with the loss of 11 days) the fair was held on 19 September. In 1793 there were also public sales for cattle, cheese, etc. on 4 April and 9 October.[17] The cattle sale on 9 October seems to have started with a sale held at Beaminster in 1786; farmers wished to avoid a toll which was being imposed on cattle coming to the fair at Bridport in order to obtain funds for building the new market house there.[36] The sale of sheep is mentioned in 1824.[17] Before the middle of the century the numbers of animals were small; the sheep were penned in North Street, and the cattle tied up in Hogshill Street. In 1844, in order to relieve the increasing congestion, it was arranged for the horse, sheep and cattle fair to be held in the field called Hams off the Bridport road.[37]

In the earlier 18th century such information as we have about craftsmen and retail tradesmen in the town comes from insurance policies, lists of freeholders, deeds, rate books and wills. In 1737 Samuel Cox, shopkeeper, had a workshop in the 'Back Street' to make soap and candles.[38] In 1755 freeholders owning property worth £10 a year included seven butchers; in the list also were Samuel Cox (grocer), Joseph Symes (mercer), William Chick (shoemaker), George Eveleigh (cutler), and John Hallett (tailor) — the Hallets were owners of No. 18 Hogshill Street for nearly 150 years from 1722.[39] From wills of the same period we can identify a saddler (Samuel Banks, 1742), a mason (John Canterbury, 1748), and several shoemakers: Joseph Hoskins (1733), Arthur Lush (1736), John Oliver (1732), and Charles Warren (1724).[40]

The earliest commercial directory in which Beaminster appears is dated 1793.[17] We find some of the rural craftsmen ancillary to agriculture: saddler (James Fowerackers), and wheelwrights (John Pearce and William Hoare). For the general needs of the population, the list includes a grocer (William Oliver), two 'merchants' (Samuel Cox and Robert Barfoot), a tailor (William Hallett), a shoemaker (James Daniel), three mercers

(Thomas Abbett, Henry Hart and Thomas Hine), two ironmongers (William Gerrard Eveleigh and William Clift), and a cabinet-maker (John Warr). Butchers were not listed, and other trades seem to be under-represented.

By the mid-19th century a great expansion of facilities had taken place in shops catering for general household needs — it must be borne in mind that over the previous 50 years the population of the parish had increased from about 2,000 to nearly 3,300. In 1831, 313 out of 725 males of 20 years and over (43 per cent.) were employed in retail trades and crafts.[41] In 1842 there were about 20 bakers, grocers, and general shop-keepers, seven or eight butchers, and three wine and spirit merchants. There were nine tailors, a hatter (Mary Slade), four linen drapers (including George Brough at 21 The Square, previously occupied by Thomas Hine and Robert Conway), five milliners and dressmakers, 13 boot and shoe makers, and no fewer than five hairdressers. To cater for the house and household, there were two builders, two carpenters, four masons, three painters and plumbers, and two ironmongers:[17] Benjamin Seymour, ironmonger, was now occupier of the old Eveleigh premises (formerly the *King's Arms*),[42] and Emanuel Pester Davy was at the Fleet Street shop (No. 7), probably established by the Pester family who lived there in the late 18th century,[2] which became Pines, the grocers.

Professional services continued, and some expanded over the period. The number of doctors remained the same: John Daniel, James Dunning and Hermon Hodge in 1793, and J. W. Daniel, T. P. Daniel and Joachim Gilbert in 1842. So did the number of lawyers: in 1793 we find James Daniel, John Russell and Baruch Fox (who married Hannah, daughter of Theodore Levieux, a Huguenot), while Peter Cox, Thomas Russell and another Baruch Fox were the solicitors in 1842.[17] The number of private schools increased.[43] Among the earliest boys' schools of which we know are J. Adam's in St Mary Well Street and William May's in Fleet Street which existed in 1824.[17] A grammar school run by G. A. Henessey & Son from at least 1824 had been taken over by William Gardner by 1832;[44] Alfred Hine was a pupil there in 1838. Both boarders and day scholars were taken, and the curriculum included, as well as English Language, Reading, Writing, Arithmetic, Composition and Geography, the optional extra subjects Greek, Latin, Merchants' Accounts, Drawing and Landsurveying.[45] The Tithe Award shows that in 1843 Gardner's school, later known as Beaminster Classical and Commercial School, was held at the house now called Shadrack House in Shadrack Street. There were several private girls' schools: one was conducted in Hogshill Street in 1835 by Mrs. John Warr, and Elizabeth Nicholls ran a ladies' boarding school at Barton End, Fleet Street, in 1842.[17]

In 1793 a regular daily post came from Bridport. In 1842, while letters from London and the South and East came from Bridport, those from the West arrived by the Taunton coach. There were two banks in 1842: a branch of Williams' Bank, and a branch of the Bridport Bank.[17] In November 1847 the banks ran into some trouble: Arthur Hull of Chard recorded in his diary, 'Bridport Bank suspended . . . Many are totally ruined lost all they have, most people thought the Bridport Bank was as safe as the Bank of England, many in Chard got all their money in the Bridport Bank'.[46] So had many people in Beaminster, no doubt.

In addition to the principal inns, some of which were mentioned earlier, there were numerous alehouses in Beaminster at this period. It is difficult to say where particular taverns were at the various times, because a name was so frequently transferred to another building. Soon after 1700 the names of alehouse-keepers begin to be recorded: each had to give two sureties for good behaviour. The names of the public houses are not given in the earlier records, but in 1754 each landlord's name is followed by the name of his alehouse, and we find the following: *Naggs Head, Red Lyon, New Inn, Half Moon, Shoulder of Mutton, White Horse, King's Arms, Fountain, White Hart, Bull, George, Swan, Crown & Grayhound, Hare & Hounds, Rising Sun, Lace, Three Horseshoes, Green Dragon, White Dog, Blew Ball* and *Valiant Soldier.*[47]

The *King's Arms*, as we saw earlier, was in the Fore Place, at the south-east corner of Hogshill Street. The *White Horse* was apparently also in the Fore Place in the later 18th century; it was an inn of some consequence, as it was insured for £150 in 1763.[48] It seems as if at one time this was the name of the *King's Arms*, as there is a reference in manor court records to the 'King's Arms, formerly White Horse'.[49] After the fire of 1781, which destroyed a great part of the premises of the *King's Arms*, its position as chief coaching inn and meeting-place was taken by the *White Hart* in Hogshill Street. The existing building at the *White Hart* dates from the earlier 19th century. At a public meeting held in 1846 regarding the 'proposed alteration in the front of the White Hart', plans and specifications for rebuilding were presented: the front then had bay windows.[50]

In 1737, when it was insured by Samuel Cox for £225, the *Red Lion* (Fore Place) was described as in the 'Pigg market'.[38] The *Greyhound* was already in the Fore Place by the middle of the 18th century, but the present building dates from the early 19th century. In 1718 Robert Richards was paying church rates on the *Crown*; the *Crown* in 1842 was at the western corner of North Street, an 18th-century building still standing, with the date 1789 on a door. The *Swan* was near the Fore Place; earlier on it may have been in North Street, but by 1830 it was on the east side of Fleet Street (present Town Offices).[17] The *Nags Head* was also in the Fore Place in the later 18th century, when it appears to have incorporated Nos. 18 and 19 The Square.[2, 47]

In 1763 the *Green Dragon* was insured for £80.[48] It was then near the Fore Place, probably at No. 6 Prout Bridge.[51] After the fire of 1781, Susannah Symes acquired the sites of three properties in Hogshill Street which had been burnt down. On these was erected a 'new dwelling house with other buildings called the Green Dragon being a common inn or alehouse'; No. 15 Hogshill Street bears a sign 'Green Dragon'. In 1818 the *Green Dragon* became the property of John Hearn Barratt, owner of the *New Inn* next door, which he had acquired from the Harris family in 1807;[52] the *Green Dragon* seems to have been closed before 1830.[17] The *Eight Bells*, on the corner of Church Street and St Mary Well Street, must have changed its name from the *Five Bells* when the church bells were recast in 1765.[47]

Houses in the Town

The few surviving 17th-century houses illustrate the progress made in the three-roomed house typical of this area (elsewhere in Dorset two-roomed houses were more common in the 17th century) towards a more symmetrical plan, with centrally-placed door-ways, and gable end instead of central chimney-stacks; these houses are mostly on the fringes of the town. The central part of Beaminster today presents a largely 18th-century and earlier 19th-century appearance, and only a detailed examination of

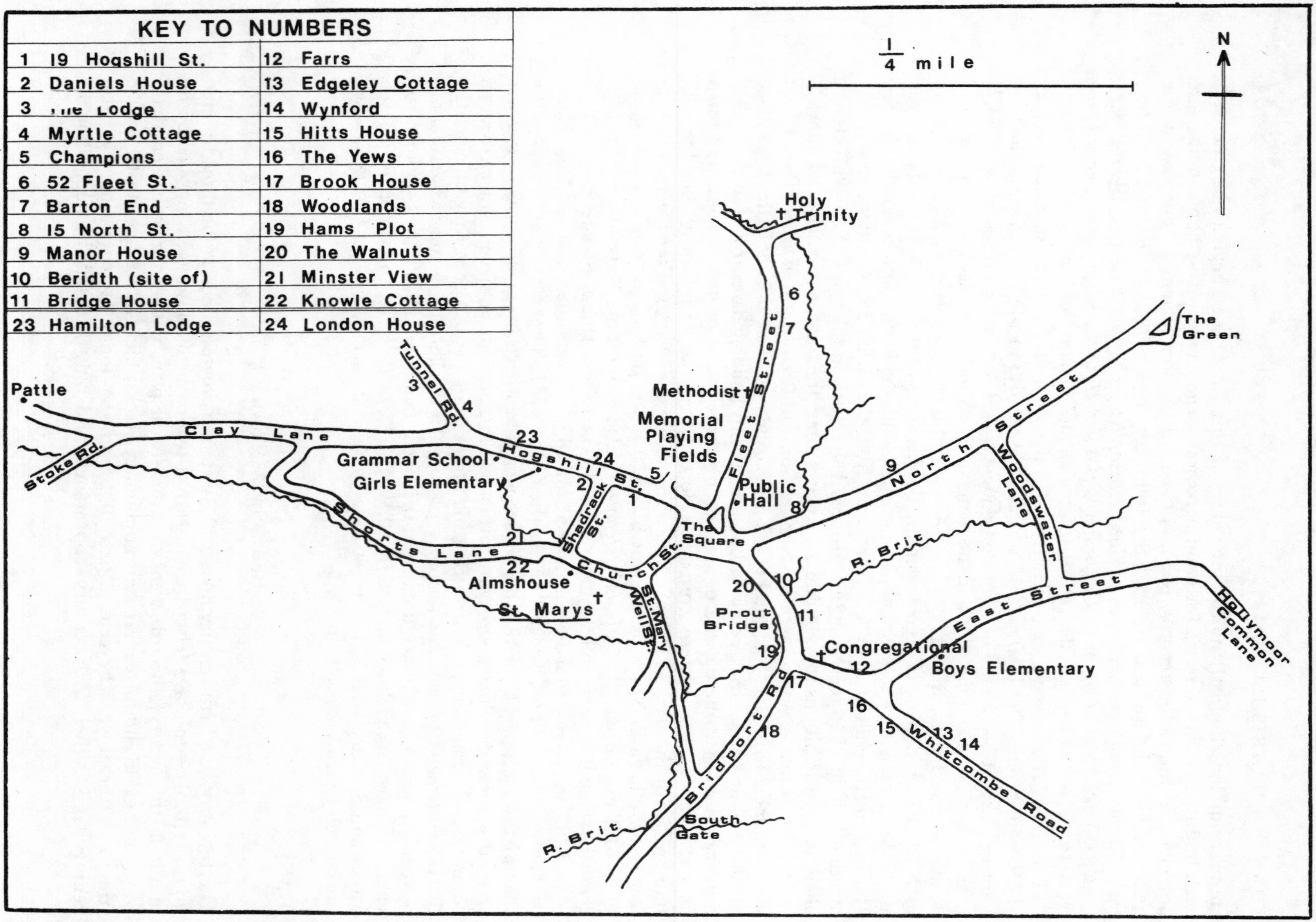

KEY TO NUMBERS

1	19 Hogshill St.	12	Farrs
2	Daniels House	13	Edgeley Cottage
3	The Lodge	14	Wynford
4	Myrtle Cottage	15	Hitts House
5	Champions	16	The Yews
6	52 Fleet St.	17	Brook House
7	Barton End	18	Woodlands
8	15 North St.	19	Hams Plot
9	Manor House	20	The Walnuts
10	Beridth (site of)	21	Minster View
11	Bridge House	22	Knowle Cottage
23	Hamilton Lodge	24	London House

Fig. 9. Plan of town of Beaminster (about 1950) indicating houses described in Chapter 6 (Nos. 1–22) and some of the other buildings of interest.

individual buildings would disclose how much earlier work behind the facades survived the three disastrous fires of 1644, 1684 and 1781, which mainly affected the central areas.

Between 1700 and 1850 there was an increase in the number of larger houses, partly by new building of 'town houses' and partly by additions and improvements to existing houses. In 1793 there were three clergy, three doctors, three lawyers, and seven other 'gentlemen' listed in the directory, as well as three members of the Cox family under 'traders'.[17] In 1831 we are told that 29 capitalists, bankers, and professionals lived in the parish;[41] the 1830 directory gives 17 addresses of gentry and clergy in the town, and names two doctors, four law firms, two schools, and two other members of the Cox family.[17] Many of the houses connected with professional people had similar associations going back into the 17th century.

It has been possible, from the commercial directory of 1842 and the Tithe Award and map of 1843, to identify most of the better houses and their inhabitants at this time. About half these houses were in what was then called East Street, which included – as well as the present street of this name – Prout Bridge, Whitcombe Road, and the near end of the Bridport road. This section describes such 'gentlemen's houses' – the owners and occupiers of which are taken from the Award – in a sequence which provides a continuous walk round the town, starting from The Square and finishing at the church.[53] (See Fig. 9).

19 Hogshill Street (formerly known as 'Devonia'), owned by William Baker Hine of London, hosier. The house has an ashlar stone north front, with stone quoins, modillion cornice and parapet; the sash windows have architraves and projecting keys. There is no entrance on this side. The rear wing has dressed stone walls to about nine feet, and brick walls above in Flemish bond; possibly remains of earlier buildings were incorporated. The house was built by Jeremiah Whitaker Newman, surgeon of Beaminster, in 1783 on three pieces of land which he had just acquired. Two of them were the sites or part of the sites of houses burnt down in the fire of 1781: one had belonged to the Sergeant family, and the other to Kenaz Keech, baker. In 1797 Newman sold the house to Thomas Hine, the clothier. After the death of Thomas Hine in 1817, the house continued in the ownership of his descendants until 1886; it was usually let in the latter part of the period.[54]

29 Hogshill Street (now Daniels House), owned and occupied by J. W. Daniel, surgeon. The rear wing of the house is early 18th century; its front in Shadrack Street is in header bond brick with stone quoins. The front range on Hogshill Street was built in the late 18th century, replacing the part of the building burnt in the 1781 fire, which may then have been the older section: the Daniel family had a substantial house in the street, presumably on this site, since at least 1647.[20] The front has a central doorway, set under a Greek Doric stone portico with fluted columns of 19th-century date and flanked by two-storeyed canted bay windows.

The Lodge (Tunnel Road), owned and occupied by Edward Fox. The house was known in 1842 as 'Beaminster House', and can be traced back under this name to 1830, when it was the home of Mary Clarke;[17] her father, William Clarke, had a house in 'Hogshill Street' in 1775,[2] and it may have been on this site. The present building, which has stuccoed stone walls, stone plinth with rusticated quoins, and moulded cornice, is early 19th century. The symmetrical facade has sash windows and a central doorway with fluted pilaster capitals, set in a stone portico with Roman Doric columns and pilasters.

Myrtle Cottage (Tunnel Road), owned and occupied by James Rendle, veterinary surgeon. The house was built *c.* 1800 and extended in the earlier 19th century.[55]

Champions (10–14 Hogshill Street), owned and occupied by Henry Steele. The house was built in the late 17th century, and refaced in the 19th century. It has an ashlar stone facade, with moulded cornice and parapet, and a central doorway with Tuscan pilaster surround. At the rear the windows are 2-light stone mullions, with continuous labels over. This is one of the three 'neat houses' mentioned by Hutchins, the house 'in the centre of the town', built by Silas Symes, attorney, but 'now [late 18th century] the property of Mr. Russell'.[56] After John Russell, the solicitor, the house was lived in by his son John Banger Russell, one of whose daughters married Captain Steele. The house was known as 'The Elms' from the mid-19th century to the 1920s, when it was called 'Champions' by Claud Streatfeild, whose middle name was Champion. There was however a family named Champion who owned property in Hogshill Street in the mid 17th century, and there was a Champions Lane in 1842.[20, 57]

52 Fleet Street, owned and occupied by John and Richard Read, woolstaplers. The house dates to *c.* 1700. It has walls of coursed lias stone, and 2-light stone mullions. The front doorway, left of centre, has stone pilasters, and over the door is a plain open pediment. Both this house and No. 50 belonged earlier to members of the Willmott family, who had property in Fleet Street from the 17th century.[20] Thomas Willmott, who seems to have lived here in 1775,[2] was a tanner.

Barton End (50 Fleet Street), owned by Samuel Cox (whose 'Yarn Barton' stretched up the street behind the houses), but occupied by Elizabeth Nicholls, who ran an academy for young ladies.[17] This consists of a 17th-century stone house at the rear at right-angles to the street, and a front block of *c.* 1730. The old block has stone mullions with labels over, and a 2-storey porch with depressed doorway. The front range is symmetrically designed, and has brick walls with burnt headers, stone rusticated quoins, and a stone cornice and parapet. There are sash windows with stone architraves and projecting dropped keys, and the doorway has a part-open stone pediment. In 1775 the owner was Henry Willmott, a woolstapler.[2]

15 North Street (The Red House), owned and occupied by George Cox. This is an early 18th-century stone house, with a brick front in Flemish bond with stone dressings, and a brick dentil cornice. The windows have stone architraves and flat-section stone mullions, and they hold sashes with crown glass; the central upper window has stone shaped side-pieces carved with open flowers. The doorway, at the centre, has a moulded architrave with scrolled flush-feet and a carved pediment. The house seems to have belonged in the 18th century to the Harris family,[2] who were maltsters; there was a malt-house attached on the right rear in 1843.

Beaminster Manor House (North Street), owned and occupied by Samuel Cox, with a residential estate of about 20 acres. The stables adjoining the house have mullion windows with architraves and pediments, and have been dated to *c.* 1670; they must have been built by either John Hoskins or his daughter Mary Gifford, who rebuilt part of the Hoskins family house after she inherited about 1683. The manor house itself is late 18th century, remodelled in the early 19th century. Samuel Cox, merchant, acquired the property about 1767 from William Buckler, a descendant of the Gifford family.[56] After the death of Samuel Cox in 1801 his nephew Samuel, who inherited, made additions to the house under the direction of John Schofield, a London architect. It was further considerably altered and enlarged by Samuel's son Samuel soon after 1822, the plans being drawn by George Underwood.[58] The existing house has stone walls, stuccoed, and rusticated quoins with moulded cornice and plain parapet. The porch, which is early 19th century, has coupled Doric columns. The north-east face of local lias stone has recently been exposed by the removal of some Victorian additions. The gardens and pleasure grounds were described as 'of interest' in 1793;[17] a Tudor gateway from Clifton Maybank (a house pulled down in 1786) was erected in the garden, and an ornamental lake made to the north of the house, while a double avenue of elms nearly a mile long led north-east to the 'Pinnacles', a gateway on White Sheet Hill.[58]

Beridth (Prout Bridge), owned and occupied by Thomas Russell. On the site next to the *Red Lion* (now belonging to Aplin & Barrett) stood a house later known as 'Beridth'. This house, on the west side of the river Brit, was another of the three 'neat houses' mentioned by Hutchins in the later 18th century.[56] When a property here was bought by Henry Samways in 1648, it was described as 'one dwelling house, one barn, one house then lately burnt down called the kitchen'. In 1699 the Samways acquired three roofless cottages named 'Red Lyon Cottage', 'Baker's Cottage', and 'Webb's Cottage', which were between the *Red Lion* and the Samways' house and had been burnt down in the fire of 1684; the site of these was converted into an orchard.[59] In 1719 Joan Samways sold the property to Giles Merefeild, who had been married to her only daughter Mary.[60] Thomas Cook, Merefeild's grandson from a second marriage, sold it to Thomas Brown, innholder of Beaminster, in 1778.[59] Giles Russell, solicitor, leased the property in 1792, when it was specified that he should have the use of four 'Bath Stove Grates now fixed in the Parlour & Chambers'.[61] (Presumably the reference is to 'Bath metal', an alloy of copper and zinc.) Russell purchased the house in 1801 for £525, and by 1804 he had acquired three other properties which stood somewhere between his house and Prout Bridge: two of them were at a place called Island, which must have been between the North Street stream and the main river. These three properties were then either pulled down, or used as outbuildings, or incorporated in the main house, which appears from photographs to have had an early 19th-century facade. The estate passed to Thomas Russell, son of Giles, in 1840;[59] the house was pulled down about 1960.

Bridge House (3 Prout Bridge), owned and occupied by Joachim Gilbert, surgeon. This was the other 'neat' house; it was next to Beridth, but on the east side of the river.[56] It is a large early 17th-century house with stone mullions, and a small 2-light blocked window low down on the left of the front. The plan is still asymmetrical, with off-centre entry; the doorway has a Tudor-arch head. The house has two gable end chimney-stacks, but there is evidence for a central rear lateral stack, which usually denotes gentry status in the 17th century.[62] In the mid-17th century the house belonged to the Abington family of Over Compton; a Thomas Abington was Steward of Prima and Secunda 1651–66. It was acquired early in the 18th century by Henry Dunning, a doctor;[20, 56] he left it to his kinsman Bishop Dunning in 1762,[56] and in the late 18th century the house was occupied by Dr. James Dunning.[63] In 1824 there was another doctor, Richard Phelps.[17]

Farrs (3 Whitcombe Road), owned and occupied by Peter Cox, solicitor. The house is L-shaped, consisting of a 17th-century rear part, extended later towards the north, and an early 18th-century south range at right-angles, with ashlar stone walls. The symmetrical south front has 2-light mullion windows, and a central doorway with architrave and plain open pediment. There are two staircase wings: an 18th-century stair-wing at the rear with canted oriel window, and a 17th-century one at the rear of that part of the house. The house was known as 'Farrs' in 1809;[51] it seems to have been occupied by a Robert Farr in the later 17th century,[20] and a Robert Farr acted as Deputy Steward for Prima and Secunda in 1715. In 1775 the owner and occupier was Richard Symes, barrister,[2] whose daughter Ann married Samuel Cox in 1790.

Edgeley Cottage (9 Whitcombe Road), owned and occupied by Mary Read. The house was built in the mid-17th century, and seems to have consisted of three rooms in line, with cross passage, and a chimney-stack at the upper end of a central hall, a variation of which a few examples are found;[62] the entry is right of centre. There is a continuous integral outshut, probably 17th century, at the rear. The house may have been associated with the Read family (wool-staplers) from the later 18th century;[63] it was known as 'East Road Cottage' in 1885, when James Read was the occupier.[17]

Wynford (11 Whitcombe Road), owned and occupied by John Meadway. Dating from the later 18th century, the house has a brick facade in Flemish bond, with brick dentil-cornice, and stone gable walls; there are gauged brick voussoirs over the sash windows. The front door is central. About 1900 the house, then known as 'Whitcombe Cottage' and occupied by the Congregational minister, was acquired for a manse;[64] it was so used until the 1950s.

Hitts House (14 Whitcombe Road), owned and occupied by Phillis Dunning. The house, which has coursed lias stone walls, dates from the late 17th century, but was remodelled in the 19th century. It has gable end stacks; the front door is central, but the plan is asymmetrical, with two stone mullion windows to the left and one to the right. The doorway has a very depressed-arch head, surmounted by a *c.* 1700 wooden shell-hood with carved scallop-shell. The gate-piers to the garden are 18th century, with ball-finials. Phillis Dunning no doubt inherited the house from the Hitt family who built it; the marriage of Thomas Hitt to Mary Dunning is recorded in 1765. When the house was sold by auction in 1847, it was acquired by Philip Hine, the wine merchant,[65] and passed to his son John.

The Yews (6 Whitcombe Road), owned by John Hitt and occupied by the Rev. James Woodward Scott, curate at Beaminster. The house is late 17th century, with lias stone walls. It has three rooms in line, and the east front has 2-light mullion windows; the front door was formerly to the right of centre. The property was once known as 'Niles tenement';[66] the Nile family appear in many records. The Hitts later became the owners. Edward Hitt was a maltster in 1750 when he went bankrupt;[67] in 1763 the house was described as a malt-house, but it was in use again as a dwelling-house by 1832. Robert Leigh senior, solicitor, lived here in the 1880s and 1890s.[66]

Brook House (1 and 3 Bridport Road), occupied by Frances Way. The house has rendered and red brick walls, with rusticated stone quoins and modillion cornice on the gable end to the road. It was erected for Thomas Fox, solicitor, at the beginning of the 19th century on the sites of five properties acquired by him and largely pulled down; these included a building which had been used as an office by his cousin Baruch Fox, and a slaughterhouse belonging to the Guy family, butchers. The house was let to Frances Way in 1824.[68]

Woodlands (9 Bridport Road), owned and occupied by Thomas Fox. This house consists of a 17th-century north range with some mullion windows, and a south block built in the early 19th century, with sash windows and a large square porch. On the garden front are French windows and a glass-topped verandah on iron columns. According to a sale brochure of 1881, water was raised from the brook which formed the southern boundary of the property by means of a water-wheel and a double-action pump, and conveyed to an iron storage cistern;[69] the site of the wheel can still be seen.

Hams Plot (6 Bridport Road), owned by Thomas Fox and occupied by Alexander Ramsay. This is a 17th-century house, with mullions on the north side, which was considerably altered *c*. 1830. The south facade with french windows, verandah and ironwork balcony is similar to the garden front at Woodlands, and suggests that Thomas Fox was concerned with both rebuildings — he was also involved with Nos. 5 and 7 Bridport Road. The house, which was formerly known as 'Brook Lodge' and 'Brook-lands', was described by Percy Codd (in the later 19th century) as 'a nice enough house, but damp and unhealthy, owing to the water-courses around it'.[70]

The Walnuts (2 Prout Bridge), owned and occupied by T. P. Daniel. The front part of the house was built *c*. 1820, and the facade has lias ashlar walls with incised cement-stone pilasters at either end; the central doorway is flanked by Doric pilasters. The house next door (4 Prout Bridge), built in the early 19th century, and also 6 Prout Bridge, were at one time owned by the Daniel family, and Dr. John Daniel was living at a house on the site in 1775.[2] The back part of the house was built on for Dr. A. Pim in 1909, and it was at this period that it received its present name.[71]

Minster View (6 Shorts Lane), owned and occupied by a Mrs. A. Curtis. The house is of stone, with a red brick facade in Flemish bond; there is a decorative band of four courses of alternating burnt-headers between ground floor and first floor, and a dog-tooth brick eaves-cornice. The windows are sash, and the central doorway has a flat wood canopy. On the side wall there is a plaque with the date 1781 and the name J. Brown. A John Brown, serge-maker, is listed among freeholders in Beaminster in 1755, and was paying rates on a property here from 1760;[72] perhaps he built himself a new house. The property became the home of the Keech family (monumental masons, Hogshill Street) in the late 19th century.

Knowle Cottage (Shorts Lane), owned by William Bishop Eveleigh and occupied by Thomas Bishop. The house today consists of two separate parts linked together, a cottage fronting the road and a house behind it, both 19th century. The field adjoining the churchyard here was called 'Millers Hay' in 1776,[73] and in 1830 Rev. T. R. Coles (who may have been the curate at Beaminster) was the occupier of 'Millershay Cottage',[17] probably the front cottage. The attractive garden front (south) was depicted in a painting of the area by Abel Bugler about 1845. The garden entrance on the road has square stone gate-piers with squared ball-finials. James Rawlins, who married Barbara, daughter of W. B. Eveleigh, lived here between about 1863 and 1883.[74]

Parnham House

After the death in 1731 of Anne, granddaughter of the Sir John Strode who made the survey of 1628, her cousin George Strode came into the property;[75] he improved the family estate by 'enlarging and fitting-up the rooms in the south-west wing, and re-building the stables and garden walls'.[76] Entries in George Strode's 'Waste Book'[77] show that he consulted John Bastard, one of the two brothers well known for their work in rebuilding Blandford Forum after the great fire of 1731. An entry in October 1732 reads:

> Agreed with John Miller To lay the Stonework under the Joyces of the Great Parlor for finishing the Chimney of the same & the dore from the Starecace to enlarge the Starecase as Mr. Bastard has designed it & for finishing the Chimney in the Chamber over the Great Parlor & the Arch to the Starecase & the Doore to the Hall Chamber and for finishing the front to the Garden for all am to pay him £14 by agreement.

In May 1733 an account for 'Marnell' stone (a coarse but serviceable off-white lime-stone quarried near Marnhull, north of Sturminster Newton) was received from John Bastard. In August 1733 Purbeck stone was used for paving in the back yard, wash house, dairy court and fore porch. In November 1734 William Hallet was to 'lay the flores of the Chambers . . . loose for the present and to nail them down the next year'.

Meanwhile work to the stable and garden walls is indicated by the large quantities of brick and tile being made at kilns set up at Fonthill near Hindon (Wilts.) and carried to Parnham by the waggons of George Strode and his farmers. In 1734 the stable was to be glazed 'with the best Bristoll Glass'.[77] In 1735 we hear from Bishop Secker that 'Mr. Strode . . . worth nearly 2000[li] a year, hath improved his house & garden much'.[1] George Strode died in 1753, and with the death of his brother Thomas in 1764, the Strode family of Parnham came to an end.

The estate passed to Sir John Oglander of Nunwell in the Isle of Wight. Although Sir John's son William evidently lived some of the time at Parnham, he probably spent most of his money on the large family estates on the Isle of Wight. It was not until Sir William died in 1806 that his son William, born at Parnham in 1769,[78] was able to take the neglected Parnham house and estate in hand. The alterations to the house are understood to have been carried out under the direction of John Nash, who had earlier built East Cowes Castle on the Isle of Wight for his own occupation, and so was a neighbour of the Oglanders.

A book of accounts which covered the years 1807 to 1811 has all the pages after 1809 torn out; the amount of money expended up to the end of 1809 was £14,550.[79]

The accounts consist simply of day-by-day entries of sums paid out for work done —
in November 1807 beer was supplied to 'upwards of 50 workpeople'. The south front
of the house, and the wall between the old dining room and the library on that side,
were pulled down in 1808, and new floors laid in library and 'drawing room'. Ground
was dug out under the 'New Dining Room' which was built to the west of the great
hall, the west windows of the hall being blocked up. The missing pages in the book
would have covered the next stages of work in the house — the last entry is 'Treat for
London carpenters & plasterers by Sir William's order'. Work was done at a spring
'intended to supply the house with water', and many hundred feet of new drains
were laid.

One of the first items in the accounts, early in 1807, concerns building a brick kiln,
and 'by Sir William's order' money was expended for 'Drink for the Brickmakers when
burning the first kiln'. Between May and October 1808 there was a series of payments
for wheeling a total of 276,000 bricks from the kiln 'to Garden Wall' or 'to Garden
Wall & Building'. What was done with over a quarter of a million bricks? Brick — and
some Bothenhampton stone — was used to build new stables and a new coach house.
Much of the extensive and high walling around the kitchen garden must have been
built or rebuilt: there are some mentions of digging foundations for a garden wall, and
innumerable entries 'building Garden Wall'. Flues in the north wall must have enabled
it to be heated so as to grow fruit on the south face; a hot-house was also erected.
Steps — still there today, with the iron railings put up by Charles Coombs — were
made to an entrance in the wall at the north-west corner. Kennel Orchard was railed
against the river, and fruit trees planted. It was in the orchard that a brick ice-house
was built: a pit and drain were first dug, and when the ice-house was completed, it was
covered with a mound of earth, and a stone wall built round it.[79] The ice-house can
still be seen today, though it is unsafe to enter; in 1945 the owner was told that it
had been used within living memory.[80]

A great deal of landscaping was carried out in the grounds; by this time the 18th-
century fashion for landscaping had spread to the smaller estates. There are references
to 'making New Road' and 'Making road through the avenue of trees', planting thorn
hedges, and making gravel walks with gravel taken from the river. Many shrubs were
planted, some of them 'taken up at Slape', and borders made.[79]

We know from a footpath diversion order that it was in 1809 that the old path to
Netherbury, which ran across the park 'beginning at the entrance to the field called
Parnham Walk [near South Gate]', and went over the river not far from Kennel Lane,
was stopped up. The footpath which was substituted began near the same spot as the
old one, but crossed the river almost immediately and continued on the west side
through the 'Mill Barton' to Kennel Lane.[81] (Parnham Mill stood near the present Mill
Ground Cottages.) The accounts mention the making of a road by the mill, and
'Putting in Posts & Rails & Hanging Gates in the New Path Way leading to Netherbury
through the Mill Yard'.[81] (This path too has been altered.) The water was drained from
the mill pond, the head of which was pulled down, and clay was brought to fill in the
pond and level up the area.[79]

In 1843 Sir William Oglander's residential estate comprised, in Beaminster parish,
some 44 acres; another 17 acres of coppice at Hewstock were in hand. Sir William, who
gave to parish charities and lent money to the turnpike trust, died in 1852. His widow,

Maria, who died in 1855, supported the National School (see Chapter 15), and was well loved for her generous help to those in need. A poem written by William Gardner 'On the death of Lady Maria Oglander'[82] concludes:

> The poor, the aged, the infirm — her care —
> An earthly friend have lost beyond compare.

Sir William's son Henry, born at Parnham in 1811,[78] did not make any great changes; he seems to have preferred the estate in the Isle of Wight.

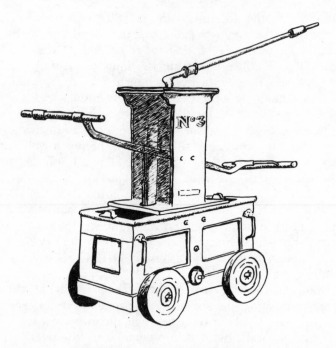

An old Beaminster fire-engine

CHAPTER SEVEN

AGRICULTURE 1700-1850

Land Use

MOST OF THE LAND in West Dorset was grassland in the 18th century, and William Marshall found in 1796 that it had been 'from time immemorial a Dairy District'. Formerly cheese had been the chief product, but more recently 'Butter, for the London market, to which it is sent in tubs . . .'. The size of the farms was small, and dairies consisted of about 30 or 40 cows, but the same man might own two or three farms. The local practice of letting out the dairy, whereby the farmer provided cows, pasture, winter fodder, and a house for the dairyman, who made his profit from the sale of milk, butter and cheese, was condemned by Marshall. He considered it to be bad for buildings and fences, which the under-tenant had no interest in maintaining.[1]

George Strode, in his 'Waste Book No. 5', gives details of the letting of dairies on several farms in the neighbourhood which he owned and ran from Parnham. In 1735 he agreed with William Waygood of Horne to provide 11 cows at £3 a cow per annum, together with 33 acres of pasture for summer leaze and 10 acres for after-grass. An inventory of George Strode's cattle made at Lady Day 1744 showed that he then had 16 cows at Horne, 24 cows at Parke (for Horne and Parke farms, see under Farms and Farmhouses), and 10 cows at Parnham itself. These 50 cows were worth £200, and there were 15 bulls, heifers, steers etc. worth a further £60. In 1747 there were five dairies out on lease: Horne, Parke, Chantmarle, Mosterton and Bilshay; in 1749 George Strode purchased four bulls (for the four largest dairies) for just over £10 at the weekly market at Frampton, near Dorchester.[2]

As well as cattle, there were considerable numbers of sheep in West Dorset in the 18th century. George Strode also went in for sheep farming, and an inventory of his sheep at Lady Day 1744 showed a total of 632. This was made up as follows: 63 wethers, 60 old ewes, 127 flock sheep, 182 hogs (hoggets), 10 rams, 180 lambs, and 10 old wethers. The value of the flock was £297. In 1747 the sheep kept at Parnham and Horne numbered 402. The wool was sold on more than one occasion to John Bishop of Beaminster, clothier. George Strode records that, in September 1748, 100 ewes from Chantmarle and 100 ewes from Parnham were driven to Weyhill Fair, near Andover.[2] Daniel Defoe described Weyhill as 'the greatest fair for sheep . . . that this nation can show'; he was told by a grazier that as many as 500,000 sheep were sold there in one fair.[3] According to George Strode's calculation, the Parnham ewes, sold at 11s. each, made £54 19s. 6d., from which he deducted for the expenses of driving them £4 0s. 1½d.[2]

A list made in 1759 by the vicar of Netherbury and Beaminster of all the payers to the small tithes in the parish of Beaminster shows that nearly all the farms then kept both cows and sheep.[4] The table gives information for the main farms; the identification of some is not absolutely certain.

Farm	Farmer/Owner	Cows	Young beast	Sheep and lambs
S. Buckham	Wm. Clarke	29	—	200
N. Buckham	Thos. Harris	3	2	180
Buckham Mill	Robt. Watts	18	7	—
Chapel Marsh	John Gill	19	7	102
W. Axnoller	John Bowring	18	—	—
W. Axnoller	Wm. Pope	17	2	—
E. Axnoller	Lancelot Milles	30	3	400
Higher Meerhay	Thos. Caddy	15	2	112
Lower Meerhay	John Newman	8	3	60
Shatcombe	John Godsole	18	4	102
Shatcombe?	Henry Fowler	6	—	40
Stonecombe	John Conway	14	2	130
Northfield (Mr. Bucklers)	Wm. Canterbury and Robt. Chilcott	15	—	88
Langdon	Eliz. Soper	30	8	480
Storridge	Wm. Wade	18	—	90
Marsh	John Strong	36	4	320
Coombe Down	James Gale	6	10	290
Coombe?	Robt. Conway	—	—	30
Whitcombe?	John Painter	7	2	33
Whitcombe?	Thos. Pittman jun.	4	—	60
Whitcombe?	Nich. Pittman	3	2	48
Parnham	Thos. Clift	15	—	110
Horne	John Pope	10	—	20
Knowle	James Daniel	17	—	160
Barrowfield?	Isaac Daniel	16	—	—

The herds of cows ranged from six to 36, the flocks of sheep from 20 to 480, but there were also a number of people who kept just two or three cows or a few sheep. The total numbers of animals were: dairy cows 448, young beast 63, sheep and lambs 3,103, pigs 79.

In 1738 George Strode noted that he began to reap his wheat on Foxholes Hill (part of Horne farm) on 31 July and finished on 5 August. There were 17 acres of wheat, but his yield was only small, being 15 bushels to the acre, whereas 'a Great Crop of Wheate is 30 bushells per acre'.[2] Marshall reported (in 1796) that many of the farms in West Dorset had little if any arable, though near Bridport the soil in the valleys was a rich loam, well suited to wheat, beans, flax and hemp; farther inland wheat and oats were grown.[5] Returns made during the Napoleonic wars show that arable farming here was fairly backward, farmers being slow to adopt the new ideas in cultivation, such as the inclusion of pulses and cattle crops in the courses;[6] the crop returns made in 1801 of land sown since the previous year's harvest with specific crops have not survived for Beaminster.[7] Wheat was being grown in Beaminster in the early 1800s; the sowing season was 5 October.[8] Mr. Bridge of Langdon sowed white oats between 24 March and 5 April, producing 40 to 60 bushels per acre.[9] A rare mention of a course of crops in Beaminster occurs in connection with Tucker's Charity Marsh farm in 1826, when a

new lease being granted: the arable field called 'Rocks' was to be 'laid down to
pasture — the next Spring to be sown with Turnips to be followed with a crop of
Barley — with Seeds — to remain as a permanent pasture'.[10]

Stevenson suggested in 1812 that where the soil had sufficient fertility to bear good
crops of hemp and flax, there was little reason for regular courses of crops. Flax or
hemp was sown frequently as a fallow crop, and succeeded by wheat, barley, oats and
seeds. 'Seeds are often broken up for flax, and in many cases the clover is sown with
the flax crop.'[11] The Parnham accounts for 1809 refer to 'clover & trefoil seed sown
with the flax near the House'.[12] By the end of the 18th century the growing of hemp
and flax had become concentrated in West Dorset, and particularly on the light well
drained brown earths (foxmoulds) of the Greensand slopes above the rivers Brit and
Char and their tributaries. When grown, the flax would be laid out on the ground,
often in pits, to be retted or rotted, that is softened by dew and other moisture. An
Act of 1787 provided for a bounty (3d. a stone for hemp, and 4d. a stone for flax) to
be given to encourage the growing of these crops; in 1794 Netherbury was the leading
parish in flax production, with 2,319 stones.[13] Some flax must have been grown in
Beaminster, for instance at Marsh farm where there was a field called 'Flax Plot' in
1843, and probably on south and west facing lynchets by the streams at 'Linhams';
lynchets at Higher Meerhay are also said to have been used for flax. The growing of
flax declined in the 19th century, owing to foreign competition, and in the latter
part of the century, the scarcity of labour. Beaminster was included among the 13
hemp-growing parishes in 1812.[14]

Potatoes, which were also grown as a fallow crop on the rich loams, must have
helped to take the place of hemp and flax where the growth of these was discontinued.
According to William Stevenson, the growth of potatoes had 'extended very rapidly
and appears likely to be further increased'.[15]

Gentlemen farmers were normally in the forefront with agricultural improvements
such as field drainage to increase production: Stevenson mentions that among gentlemen managing their own estates were Mr. Cox of Beaminster and Mr. Richard Bridge
of Langdon, both of whom had drained many acres of pasture with drains 2 ft. deep,
filled with stones. Mr. Bridge believed the value of Langdon farm 'is more than
doubled by the great exertions he has made in chalking, liming and draining'.[16] The
sheepfold was considered by most farmers to provide manure which was not only
useful but indispensable in the culture of the arable, though Richard Bridge found
folding on seeds not so useful as on fallow.[17] He kept 18 asses, 12 of them employed
in the carriage of marl, chalk, lime and stone for draining; in this hilly country, where
it was difficult to use wheeled carriages, asses could carry their loads in paniers. He also
used donkeys to convey turnips to the sheep in their pastures.[18]

At Langdon, Richard Bridge had a two-horse threshing machine: 100 bushels
of barley or oats, 48 bushels of wheat from the sheaf or 80 bushels from the ears,
threshed twice over, could be procured in a day of eight hours, employing one
man and two women. Threshing machines had been invented by 1786, but were
not yet in general use. The machine at Langdon, which cost £60, had been built
by Mr. Coombs of Beaminster, who had also made a four-horse machine for Mr.
Bryant of Berwick in the Bride valley.[19] Coombs and Son are shown as millwrights in 1811;[20] millwrights — and wheelwrights — might be called in to repair

farm machinery, and sometimes branched out into designing their own implements. Coombs seems a very early example.

Inclosure of common fields and commons 1809

In 1796 Marshall reported that all the lower land in West Dorset was enclosed, mostly in small fields, only the hilltops being still open.[21] In the parish of Beaminster the two large common fields, the common land on Beaminster West Down, and the commons of Beaminster Wood, Shortmoor and Hollymoor (see Fig. 3) then remained open. The idea of inclosing the common fields caused no trouble, as virtually all the holdings had already come into the ownership of the larger farms. There were, however, differences of opinion about the commons.

A proposal to divide and inclose the commons and downs belonging to the manors of Prima and Secunda had been made at the Easter vestry meeting of 1789. A pamphlet published in 1790 contained copies of four letters addressed to the tenants of the manors, two against inclosure and two in favour. The letters were anonymous, but those against were understood to have been written by Baruch Fox; his argument, which he claimed was supported by quite a number of tenants, was based on the expense involved in getting an Act of Parliament, and putting up fences and hedges, and the amount of common land which would be wasted in hedges and roads. The poor cottager, he suggested, would gain only a quarter of an acre, while losing his right to pasture on the whole extent of the commons. The proposal was 'fraught with the most baneful consequences to the tenants in general, being a measure that must unavoidably distress the inhabitants to a very great degree, and bid fair in a few years to depopulate the town . . .'. John Banger Russell, author of the letters in favour, pointed out that at present the commons and downs were very marshy in places, and overrun with ant-hills, furze and heath, and that sheep pastured on the downs suffered from sheep-rot. If inclosed, the land was capable of great improvement. With proper drainage, sheep would be able to graze safely, and if cattle were also allowed to graze the downs, they would consume the grass now wasted. With manuring, corn could be grown in abundance on the downs 'which would afford Employment for the Labourer, and Bread for his Family'. It was suggested that landowners in general, who had no rights in the commons, would benefit from an inclosure because the additional quantity of cultivated land which would be rated to the poor would reduce the liability of individual ratepayers.[22]

An Act was passed in 1804, whereby the common fields and about two-thirds of the commons — the 235 acres at Beaminster Wood, Shortmoor and Hollymoor — were inclosed. The total number of rights to pasturage (geldings and oxen only) on these commons was found to be 420, and the rights belonged to about 70 owners of 203 copyhold properties in the two manors. (Every 'tenement' had three rights and every 'cottage' two rights: how far these rights were actually exercised is not known.) Under the Award made in 1809, the commons were divided into enclosures, rather more than half-an-acre being allotted in respect of every commonable right. Beaminster West Down (131 acres) was left open and uninclosed, every tenement having the right to pasture four sheep there and every cottage two sheep. The poor of the parish retained the right to cut and carry away furze, heath and fuel from the common down for their own use.[23]

The common fields, East Field and South Field, were parcelled out in 21 allotments, varying in size from 1¼ to 66 acres, between the persons entitled to the foreshare in (or right to crop) these two fields. They had to pay compensation to the owners of the aftershare or right to run a certain number of sheep (20 for a tenement, 10 for a cottage) over the fields after harvest; the total number of sheep which the copyholders had a right to run was 2,620.[23]

The Tithe Award and map show the use of land in the parish about 1840. Out of 5,119 acres altogether, pasture and meadow accounted for 3,606 acres, just over two-thirds. The acreage of arable was 1,137, which is a little under a quarter of the total. Most of the arable was on the Chalk and Greensand of Beaminster Down; some areas of the Bridport Sands and Inferior Oolite formations were also under cultivation, and parts of the former commons had been turned over to arable. There were 136 acres of orchards, and 124 acres of woodland most of which consisted of plantations. The balance was taken up by houses and gardens, roads, water and waste.

Farms and Farmhouses

By 1700 the larger farms in Beaminster were already owned by major landlords and farmed by substantial tenant farmers. During the 18th century, a process of absorption and amalgamation — more important in West Dorset than inclosure — led to the disappearance of many of the remaining small units and the creation of some more large farms. In 1831, out of 725 males of 20 years and over, 170 (23 per cent.) were employed in agriculture in the parish. Of these 170, 124 were labourers employed by 23 of the 46 occupiers of farm land; the other 23 occupiers did not use any labour outside their own families.[24]

Some 55 occupiers of land (five acres and over) can be identified on the Tithe map (and Award) of 1843. Some of the smaller units which were owner-occupied belonged to upper and middle class residents, for example landowners with woods and plantations in hand, and owners or occupiers of houses with paddocks and orchards attached. Local tradesmen and manufacturers were also part-time farmers: they included John Hearn Barratt, maltster (about 54 acres), Thomas Frampton, sail-cloth manufacturer and maltster (about 39 acres), and Thomas and John Guy, butchers (about 58 acres between them). There were four 'farm units' of about 25 acres near the town; some of the land was owned, some rented, and the farmers were John Strong, Benjamin Cox, Thomas House and William Sprake.

Twenty-six occupiers held 29 farms, each of which was attached to what is described in the Award as a 'homestead'; to these farms names — or at least labels — can be given, though the names by which they have been identified may not all have been in use during the period. The 29 farms ranged in size from 25 to 500 acres. There was only one 500-acre farm, that of Langdon; three farms — Mapperton Marsh, Coombe Down and Higher Meerhay — were about 250 acres. There were 13 farms of between 100 and 200 acres: Tucker's Charity Marsh, Shatcombe, Northfield, Barrowfield, Storridge, Chapel Marsh, East Axnoller, West Axnoller I, South Buckham, North Buckham, Wellwood, Hewstock Dairy and Parnham 'home farm'. Seven farms had an acreage of between 50 and 100 acres: Knowle, Whitcombe, West Axnoller II, Lower

Meerhay, Stonecombe, Whatley and Chantry. A further two holdings with a similar acreage (Buckham Mill and Coombe I) were part of larger farms in other parishes. The remaining three farms — Bowgrove, Coombe II and Coombe III — were under 50 acres.

The order in which the 29 main farms are now described is based roughly on geographical location (see Fig. 3) and on ownership links. The acreages quoted comprise the lands in the parish of Beaminster which seem to be farmed by the individual farms at the time of the Award; some farms may have had land in neighbouring parishes.

Northfield—153 acres, owned by Samuel Cox and farmed by Theophilus Gould. The farm adjoins the residential grounds of Beaminster Manor House on the north, and came in the same way from the Hoskins family to their descendant William Buckler, from whom it was acquired by the Cox family. The name North Field House occurs in 1799, and in 1831: the Bishop family were the occupiers on both occasions.[25] The house is of L-shaped plan, with lias dressed stone walls.[26]

Barrowfield—111 acres on both sides of the Broadwindsor road, mostly owned by Samuel Cox, but including about 15 acres north of the road owned by T. P. Daniel; both areas were farmed by Henry Paull. The farm was amalgamated from smaller holdings: in 1738 two of the people who paid rates on 'Barrowfield' were Samuel Cox and Henry Daniel.[27] The name Mary Cox and the date 1745 are on a slab of Ham stone inset on the wall of one of the barns at (Higher) Barrowfield farmhouse, but there was no house on this site in 1843. (The house at Lower Barrowfield, with about 17 acres, was in separate occupation.)

Whitcombe—80 acres, owned by George Cox and Peter Cox, and farmed by Henry Paull. A farm at Whitcombe previously owned by the Hitt family was acquired by Samuel Cox, merchant, in 1788.[28] The Painter family — which was linked by marriage to the Cox family, Mary (daughter of William and Sarah Painter) having married a Samuel Cox — also had land hereabouts in the mid-18th century. This came to John Cox, brother of Samuel the merchant, in 1774; 'Painter's Batch' was part of the Whitcombe estate in 1809.[29] Some Whitcombe land owned by the Hitts was previously farmed by the Nile family — part of a field named 'Earth Pit Meadow' in 1783 was earlier called 'Niles Great Backley'[30] — and it is possible that the farmhouse was once The Yews (Whitcombe Road), formerly 'Nile's tenement'.[31] The present Whitcombe Farm may have been erected in the 1770s or 1780s, though some features suggest a date nearer 1700. The house has brick walls in Flemish bond with stone dressings, square-section stone mullion windows with 19th-century casements, and a doorway with simple open stone pediment. Contemporary wings at both ends constituted dairy (with granary over) and workshop.

Knowle—71 acres, owned by J. W. Daniel, and farmed by Theophilus Gould. The farm had been in the Daniel family from at least the Tudor period, and probably well before this,[32] and it is possible that in early times all the land behind the family house in Hogshill Street belonged to it, and was farmed from a farmhouse on this site. The name Knowle or Knole is probably a reference to Edmundcoombe Hill.

Parnham farming estates

'*Home farm*'—113 acres, owned by Sir William Oglander and farmed by Clement Davy, apparently from Yondover Farm, Netherbury. A transcript of a MS. book kept between 1760 and 1800 shows that at this period the farm, which is described as 'formerly part of the demesne', consisted of 83 acres;[33] some land was probably acquired from Knowle.

Hewstock—117 acres, owned by Sir William Oglander and farmed by Francis and John Davy. Mention has already been made of about 100 acres at East Hewstock within the parish of Beaminster which belonged to Parnham. In George Strode's time this farm was known as Horne, and consisted of 179 acres,[2] which must have included some land in Broadwindsor. There was then a separate farm at Parke in Broadwindsor, but after the Oglanders took over, the two farms were united under the name Horn Park.[34] A map made about 1800 has the words 'New Dairy house' on the site of the present Hewstock Dairy.[35]

Coombe Down—250 acres, owned by Sir William Oglander and farmed by Edward Legg. The core of this farm was the land on Coombe Down Hill described in the 1628 survey, but it was added to subsequently. In 1734 George Strode agreed with 'Farmer Conway' a new seven-year lease of Coombe Down farm: Conway paid £100 a year, together with a further £80 for West Leaze, Bowling Green, The Warren and part of Edmundcoombe, all of which were later part of the home farm.[2] The farmhouse is later 17th century, with subsequent additions: it has coursed lias stone walls. The windows are stone mullions and there are two small triangular-headed windows each side of a central front door.

Coombe

In the 17th century land at Coombe was owned by the Horsfords, Halletts and Conways.[36] In 1843 there were three tenements here. Coombe Cottage, situated at the point where Coombe I and Coombe II join, is now derelict; it was built in the early 17th century, and has a later extension on the west.

Coombe I—66 acres, owned by H. C. Compton of Mapperton Manor, and farmed by John Furmidge with Mapperton farm in Mapperton parish. In 1684 we find Richard Brodrepp of Mapperton paying rates on 'Coombe'.

Coombe II—42 acres, owned and farmed by James Conway. Robert Conway of Mapperton was the owner of property here, which was described in 1789 as a house and about 30 acres; it passed to his son James Conway of Netherbury in 1813.[37] In the meantime three closes nearby (later called 'Higher Broad Hatch', 'Lower Broad Hatch', and 'Little Mead'), together with two small 'nurseries', passed from the Hallett family and through various hands before they were acquired by James Conway in 1823.[38]

Coombe III—25 acres, owned by Samuel Cox and farmed by Henry Symes. The tenement formerly belonged to the Russells, and came to the Cox family by marriage.[32]

Whatley—74 acres, all rented from various people, mostly in the general area of Newtown and Chantry Lane. John Swaffield, who was described as a farmer in the directory of 1855, lived in the old farmhouse at Whatley, a 17th-century building with some stone mullion windows.

Chantry—61 acres, owned by William Eveleigh and Silvia Eveleigh, and farmed by William Eveleigh.

Bowgrove—56 acres, land owned by William Cox and Samuel Cox, and farmed by William Genge. Before it was bought by Samuel Cox, merchant, in 1795, the farm is said to have belonged to the Conway family.[39] The house on the east side of Stintford Lane called Bowgrove Farm bears a panel with the date 1704, the initials W.H., and a text; the initials may be for William Hoare, who in 1736 was renting an estate from the Mildmays of Higher Meerhay.[40] In 1843 this building was owned and occupied by Richard Hoare, wheelwright; the 'homestead' attached to the land was then on the opposite side of the lane.

The two Meerhays

Lower Meerhay or Meerhay Manor—83 acres, owned by Mary Clarke and occupied by Richard Tolley. The Hillary family were at Meerhay from at least early Tudor times. The house, which has rubble-stone and ashlar walls, is 16th century. It was rebuilt in the early 17th century: at the north-east end, in the former kitchen, the windows have fragments of painted glass, one with the initials J.R. and a crown (James I), and another with the initials H.H. (Henry Hillary) and the date 1610. A north-west wing was added later in the 17th century. There are three chimney-stacks in the south-east elevation, one at each gable and one right of centre; the front doorway, which is slightly left of centre, has a Tudor-arch head. The living room (original hall), at the south-west end, has a stone fireplace with Tudor arch, with spiral steps set in to the left of it. The roof, which is of jointed-cruck construction with collar-beams, is probably 16th century, tie-beams being inserted when a bedroom floor was created. Lower Meerhay passed from the Hillarys to the Milles family by marriage; it remained in that family until 1784, when it was acquired by William Clarke, father of Mary.[41] Field names include 'Puddymore', still an apt description today!

Higher Meerhay—244 acres, owned by Lady Steele and farmed by David Short. The Hillary family were also the owners of a farm at Higher Meerhay as far back as can be traced. After the death of Henry Hillary about 1666, the farm passed to Sir William Stevens, who had married an Elizabeth Hillary. It was owned by a Mr. Eastmond in 1718,[36] and in 1723 his daughter Dorothy, wife of C. H. Mildmay, acquired various lands here.[42] By this time some fields which had belonged to the Newman family, together with land in the common fields, had been added to the farm. Higher Meerhay was acquired by William Clarke, father of Lady Steele, in 1779.[4]

The three Buckhams

According to Hutchins, the Gerards of Sandford Orcas, who held the manor of Buckham, divided it into three parts in the reign of Elizabeth.[43] All three parts, which became known as West (Lower or South) Buckham, Larder's (Higher or North) Buckham, and Buckham Mill, in the early 17th century were owned by the Hillary family. Land at Buckham linked on to Lower Meerhay property on Buckham Down, and a John Hillary of Buckham was cousin to a John Hillary of Meerhay in 1634.[44]

West or South Buckham—173 acres, owned by James Notley and farmed by John Gale. The farm was conveyed by John Hillary to Robert Mohun on his marriage to Elizabeth, daughter and heiress of John Hillary, in 1634.[43] In 1650 it was purchased by Henry Browne of Mappercombe, and came to his son Nicholas, whose daughter Elizabeth brought it to her husband Thomas Dibben *c.* 1725;[45] a survey made in 1810 for William Clarke, who had acquired the farm by 1759,[4] shows 23 acres called 'Dibbin's Cowleaze'.[46] James Notley presumably became owner by his marriage to Clarke's daughter Rachel. The farmhouse is late 17th century with rendered stone walls; there is a chimney-stack at the right-hand gable, and another one bay in from the left-hand gable. The front door is at the centre and the windows have stone and wooden mullions.

Larder's or North Buckham—176 acres, owned by James Notley and Lord Rolle, and farmed by Thomas Elliott. This farm continued in the ownership of the Hillarys of Meerhay until 1681, when it was acquired by George Keate.[36] In 1690 it passed from Keate to Anthony Larder of Loders,[47] and when the Larder family died out without a male heir, it descended on the female side to Lord Rolle.[48]

Buckham Mill—78 acres, owned by William Maskell and farmed by Jonathan Goaring; a further three acres containing house, mill and pond was in the occupation of Charles Podger, and there was other land in the parish of South Perrott. The farm passed to Hugh Bennett in the early 17th century,[32] and in 1639 there was a Chancery suit between John Bennett, complainant, and Robert Mohun and Henry Hillary, defendants, concerning a watercourse supplying the mill, which flowed through grounds belonging to the defendants.[49] Early in the 18th century the property was acquired by the Sweets of Bruton,[32] but by 1759 it had passed to Edward Gerard of Beaminster, and in 1772 it was owned by his grandson Edward Eveleigh.[4] The house was built in the early 17th century, and has dressed stone walls, a central doorway, and one chimney-stack left of centre.

Wellwood—129 acres, owned by John Meliai and farmed by Jane Newman. This farm passed from the Mynternes to the Milles of Meerhay, and about 1790 to William Devenish of Up Sydling.[28]

Chapel Marsh—152 acres, owned by Phillis Dunning and farmed by Thomas Chapman. The farm passed from the Moors of Melplash through the Paulets to William Gibbs of South Perrott.[32] In 1648 Gregory Gibbs was paying church rates on the property, but by 1655 it had come into the ownership of John Richards of Abbotsbury,[36] who had married Mary, daughter of Henry Garland of Chapel Marsh. (A crossing of the infant river Axe north of the farm was at one time known as 'Richards Ford'.) John Richards died in 1684,[50] and in May that year his son Garland was one of the witnesses to the nuncupative will of Lancelot Mills of Chapel Marsh, the farmer.[51] The estate was subsequently sold by the Richards of Warmwell to William Dunning.[32]

The farmhouse is late 17th century, with lias stone and rubble banded walls and stacks at either end; a continuous 17th-century outshut at the rear includes the cheese room. Inside the house there is plank-and-muntin partitioning both sides of the entrance, and a fireplace with large Ham stone lintel with Tudor arch.

West Axnoller

The land here was held copyhold by a number of small farmers in the 17th century, when we find the names of Ireland, Ewens, Fowler, Damett and Gudge.[36] This explains why the fields of the two farms into which it had been amalgamated before 1843 were so intertwined; in 1775 there were still six houses with 34 inhabitants.[52]

West Axnoller I—130 acres, owned and farmed by Robert Phelps. Several tenements had been combined into one large farm by the Bowring family. John Bowring had a farm here in 1759,[4] and in the 1780s his son Joseph was in possession of the following:[53]

> two tenements containing 60 acres, and three closes called Thessells; a tenement, a close of pasture called Broadmead, and two houses; a house and four closes called Common Closes alias Marsh (no doubt enclosed earlier from Axnoller Moor).

In 1833 the farm, then owned by John Quantock, was of approximately 102 acres.[54]

West Axnoller II—68 acres, owned by William Phelps and farmed by William Stickland. William Pope, woolstapler, inherited from John Ewens, whose daughter he married, a house and a number of fields: Yards, Langditches, Rodwell, Middle Furlong, Pit Close, Greenfields, Middle and Lower West, Hookedland, Broadmead and Sherwells. In the 1760s he acquired from the Fowler family a second house, and closes called Bickens, Longcraft and Stills. The property passed to his son Thomas in 1790;[55] he also owned three closes called Common Close, Millcroft and the Backside.[30] The farm was sold by the Pope family to William Phelps in 1809.[43]

East or Higher Axnoller—193 acres, owned by John Adair Hawkins and farmed by Daniel Akerman. The land here was freehold; the owner in 1630 was John Good[43] who was still paying the rates in 1664. By 1688 the farm had come into the Ridgway family, and they sold it about 1724 to Lancelot Milles of Beaminster.[36] The farmhouse has banded flint and lias stone walls and stone mullion windows; the facade is symmetrical, and the front door, at the centre, has the date 1709 and initials J.R. over it.

Stonecombe—87 acres, owned by George Maxwell and farmed by Joseph Bishop. According to Hutchins, the farm was earlier owned by the Willmotts of Beaminster;[28] from at least 1762 to 1778 it belonged to the Bryant family.[4]

Shatcombe—182 acres, owned by Daniel Bishop and farmed by John Bowditch. In medieval times there was a common field at Shatcombe, and the land was once divided among a number of owners — we find Gudges and Fowlers paying church rates here in the 17th century.[36] By 1775 it had been amalgamated into one farm, the property of George Eveleigh.[52]

Langdon—501 acres, leased from the Ecclesiastical Commissioners by George Roberts and farmed by John Furmidge. After the Hoskins and Giffords, the lease came to their descendant William Buckler; early in the 19th century the lessee was Richard Bridge. The house was built in the later 18th century. The west part has rendered stone walls, rusticated quoins, and dentil cornice; the door between two sash windows was formerly the front door. The present front door is in the rear wing.

The two Marsh farms and Storridge

On the Tithe map of 1843 there were three farms here, extending on both sides of Whitcombe Road: two of them, Storridge farm, and the farm which we will call 'Mapperton' Marsh farm, belonged to the owners of Mapperton Manor (Mapperton), while the third, Marsh farm, belonged to Tucker's Charity. All the land in the manor of North Mapperton was held in Tudor times by St Maur and Drury, lords of Wraxall and Rampisham, passing from them to the Stawels and the Bampfields, who held a moiety each. We are told by Hutchins that two farms at North Mapperton had been created by a division of land:[56] in the early 17th century these belonged to the two families Hoskins and Tucker. Probably because the lands were intertwined (as they were in 1776[57]), the two owners seem to have leased them to each other: for example in 1584-5 the 'South moiety' of North Mapperton (which was later inherited by William Tucker) was leased to John Hoskins, father of Peter Hoskins, for 'ninety nyne yeares if the said John Hoskins ... and ... Peter Hoskins or either of them should soe longe live'. This led to disputes and Chancery lawsuits in the early 1630s about who had the right to cut down what trees, and what land should be put under tillage.[58] In 1647 we find Peter Hoskins' son John and William Tucker both paying church rates for 'Mapperton'.[36]

When Frances Tucker, William Tucker's daughter and heiress, made her will in 1682, she left the lands which she then owned in two parts.[59] The part of her farm called South Mapperton, 'by estimation ninety pounds per annum', went to endow a school for poor boys; this became known as Tucker's Charity farm or School Lands. The part of her farm called North Mapperton, 'by estimation one hundred pounds', was left in four parts as separate legacies, but they all ended up in the possession of the Brodrepps of Mapperton Manor;[60] in 1718 Richard Brodrepp was paying rates on 'part of Tuckers'. The Hoskins family were still paying rates on their own farm ('Mapperton' Marsh) which they sold a little later to Edward Hitt,[36] and we can only conclude that Frances Tucker's 'North Mapperton' was in fact the farm we know as Storridge. The early history of this farm is obscure, but according to Hutchins Storridge had also belonged to the lords of Wraxall and Rampisham, and it was owned by John Luttrell in 1630;[28] poor rate entries suggest some connection between Luttrell and William Tucker. The name Storridge, as applied to the farm, has not been traced in any original document before 1759;[4] it does however occur as a field name in 1700, when land conveyed as 'the north part of North Mapperton Farm' included three closes called Storridge, which lay 'above Backley' (Brackley),[61] and must be part of the land on the opposite side of the road from the farmhouse. Land called Little Downe, which was part of Storridge farm c. 1800,[62] was also included. Richard Brodrepp bought 'Mapperton' Marsh farm about 1751,[36] after Edward Hitt went bankrupt, so Mapperton Manor then owned both farms.

Storridge—191 acres, owned by H. C. Compton and farmed by Jonathan Dowdeswell. The farmhouse, which is 17th century, has a symmetrical facade with central doorway and two gable-end chimney-stacks. The original house seems to have been built in the early part of the century — there is evidence for a newel stair beside the E. fireplace — with rooms one behind the other. A double-depth plan is unusual as early as this, though it has appeared in gentry-status houses, but as the rear service rooms were apparently narrow, it was not a full double-depth plan. The windows are ovolo mullions, and the house was altered in the late 17th century; there is an 18th-century addition on the east.[63]

'Mapperton' Marsh—255 acres, owned by H. C. Compton and farmed by Absalom Chick.

Tucker's Charity Marsh—168 acres, also farmed by Absalom Chick. The affairs of the Charity were not settled until about 20 years after Frances Tucker's death (1685). The trustees' account book, which begins in 1708, shows that a great deal of repair work had to be carried out to the house on their farm in the early years; in 1743 it was 'rebuilt' at a cost of £135. A lot of hedging was done, and more or less new hedges were planted in places; sums were paid for gathering plants for the hedges, presumably on the woods of the estate.[10]

The present range of buildings at Marsh Farm comprises a 17th-century north block with 2-light stone mullions, and a farmhouse attached on the south, which has been virtually rebuilt, replacing an earlier house burnt down in the mid 1970s. Early this century the 17th-century block provided a cottage at the north end for a farm-labourer, a dairy, and a dairyman's house, and this was probably its use from at least 1800 when the two Marsh farms usually had the same tenant farmer. The original use is not so clear: in 1776 the northern part seems to have belonged to Tucker's Charity Marsh, and the southern part to 'Mapperton' Marsh,[57] and on the Tithe map there are two 'homesteads', No. 544 (Tucker's) and No. 547 ('Mapperton' Marsh).

Wheel of West Mill, Sherborne, made
by Coombs of Beaminster, 1877.

CHAPTER EIGHT

INDUSTRIES AND COMMUNICATIONS 1700-1850

Woollen-cloth Industry

A CERTAIN AMOUNT of wool cloth continued to be made in Beaminster during the 18th century and earlier 19th century. In 1793 the trade was 'still in a thriving state', but not long afterwards it began to decline. In 1824 the industry was 'still considerable, though much declined', and in 1830 'of little importance to the place'. By 1842 it was almost extinct.[1]

In the earlier part of the 18th century the bare information that certain people were engaged in the trade comes from their wills: Richard Hart (1708) and Thomas Keate (1719) were clothiers or cloth-weavers, John Sillwood (1702) was a wool-comber, and Richard Hoskins senior (1739) and Henry Cox (1748) serge-weavers or makers.[2] The registers of the Sun Fire Insurance Company show that quite a number of men engaged in the woollen trade insured their premises in Beaminster with that Office between 1727 and 1771. Richard Hoskins junior, William Pope, John Jessop, John Brown, John Bagg senior, Philip Bond, John Wheadon, John Wheadon junior, John Barter and Thomas Hine were all described as clothiers in their policies. Henry Willmott and James Wheadon were wool-staplers, while Richard Gollop was a wool-comber. Theodore Levieux, John Hallet, Thomas Bozie, Richard Read and John Barfoot were serge-makers.[3] John Brown lived at Minster View in Shorts Lane, and Thomas Bozie probably had premises south of the church bordering the stream,[4] but it is not possible to identify most of these mills today. Many would have been buildings temporarily converted for the purpose, as for example two houses described in 1836 as 'lately converted into a Mill for driving Machinery employed in the Woollen Manufacture ... but lately pulled down and destroyed'.[5]

None of the amounts insured is comparable with those of clothiers in the other West Country clothing counties — Wiltshire, Gloucestershire, Somerset — for Dorset was really only on the fringe of the cloth-making area.[3] John Jessop was insured for £300 in 1767; all his property was thatched, and was possibly in Fleet Street. His dwelling-house, weaving shop and press shop all under one roof were valued at £200, with household goods therein being worth £20, and utensils and stock £60. His drying-house and stable, which were separate under one roof, were valued at £10, and utensils and stock therein also at £10.[6] John Barfoot's dwelling-house, which was part tiled, was valued at £100 in 1766; the household goods were worth £60, but stock-in-trade amounted to £300. The press shop and stable adjoining, thatched, were valued at £30, and the utensils and stock therein at £20. John Barfoot also had a comb shop, shear shop, and dye-house, all under one thatched roof, which were assessed at £40, with the utensils and stock at £30. This property may have been in North Street; together with two dwelling-houses elsewhere, the total amount insured was £600.[7]

Members of the Wheadon family continue to occur in directories as wool-staplers and cloth-makers up to 1811;[1] they supplied the workhouse with men's and women's plod, a material used for trousers, jackets and gowns. The Wheadon factory was in East Street. Thomas Hine & Sons, who were broadcloth makers in 1807, supplied the workhouse with a great variety of materials, not only serge, flannel, blanketing, drugget and lindsey (linsey-woolsey, a coarse material of wool and flax), but also ticking, tape, sheeting, dowlas, Irish linen, thread, yarn, handkerchiefs and buttons.[8] Thomas Hine's mill (and shop) was probably in the Fore Place at No. 21 The Square, a property belonging to the Conway family,[9] where there was once an 'extensive textile manufactory'.[10] In 1843 the Read family had a factory at the top of Fleet Street,[11] Simon Read having become about 1806 owner of a 'water grist mill, fulling mill or clothing mill' which had previously belonged to Henry Willmott.[12] John Read supplied blue cloth and serge to the workhouse in 1831.[8] From about 1800 to 1830 John Hamilton was a woollen manufacturer with a factory in Hogshill Street, on the site of Hamilton Lodge;[10] he provided blanketing, lindsey, canvas, sheeting, ticking, dowlas and laces for the workhouse.[8]

Hemp and Flax Manufactures

Many different items were made from hemp and flax in the neighbourhood of Bridport and Beaminster in the late 18th century; they included twine, string, packthread, netting, cordage, ropes — 'from the finest thread used by saddlers . . . to the cable which holds the first rate man of war' — as well as sails for shipping, and sacking for hammocks, bags and tarpaulins. Some of the flax and hemp used was, as we have seen, grown locally, but about two-thirds was imported from Russia and America.[13] The process of separating the flax or hemp fibres was called swingling; the material had then to be combed or heckled to remove the tow or broken fibres before spinning into yarn. Before 1800 swingling was done by hand, often by women and children. In 1803 Richard Roberts of Burton Bradstock opened a swingling mill which he claimed was 'the first in the South West of England': a plaque to this effect can be seen on the building, Grove Mill, which still stands on the river Bride a little way east of Roberts' house, Grove House. Roberts, who also had two spinning mills, employed many boys and girls from workhouses;[14] Elizabeth Crabb of Beaminster was apprenticed to him in 1812.[15]

Samuel Cox was already making sackcloth in Beaminster in 1737, when his insurance policy covered a weaving shop in 'the Back Street'.[16] Daniel Cox agreed to employ two workhouse girls in 'The Spinning Way' in 1760.[17] In the late 18th century 'upwards of 2,000 people' were employed by Cox and Co. and other firms in and about the environs of the town; Samuel Cox junior, who was a manufacturer of sailcloth in 1793, employed 'upwards of 600 people' in his business.[1,13] A number of other firms in Beaminster were also making sail-cloth at this period. Richard Hine was a sail-cloth manufacturer with a factory in Hogshill Street between 1797 and the 1830s.[18,1] Matthew Gifford (North Street) and William Curtis (Church Street) both made sail-cloth in 1824. David Bugler was making sail-cloth in Church Street in 1830, and Thomas Frampton & Son, sail-cloth makers, had a factory in the Fore Place, but we are now told that the manufacture 'is here carried on to a small extent'.[1]

Three water mills on the river Brit in Beaminster were being used in 1830 for spinning flax for the yarn required for sail-cloth;[1] in 1838 46 people were employed in these spinning mills.[19] Spinning was done by women and girls: Thomas Fox, solicitor, giving evidence before the Royal Commission enquiring into the employment of women and children in agriculture, said that whenever a spinning mill was erected in the area, the young women all sought employment there and 'cannot be prevailed to take any out-door work'.[20] One of the three mills must have been that of Samuel and George Cox whose premises extended on the east side of Fleet Street from the present Public Hall building, behind the houses to Barton End;[11] the allotments here were once a large green, used for bleaching yarn and known as Yarn Barton.[21] Another mill may have been that of Charles Clay, flax spinner in North Street in 1842;[1] his premises were down by the Brit opposite the Manor House, where there was a saw mill later in the century.[11] Charles Coombs, millwright and flax spinner in 1840,[22] had a work-shop on the site of Aplin and Barrett's factory at the bottom of North Street in 1843;[11] he also had a twine and thread factory at Hooke.[23]

In 1831 the census report shows that 87 men (out of the 725 men in Beaminster aged 20 and over, that is 12 per cent.) were employed in manufacture. Weaving was still carried out by hand, and in 1838 the sail-cloth trade employed 120 looms in Beaminster and the adjoining villages.[24] The Cox factory in Fleet Street was taken over by Thomas Frampton & Son, who were also owners and occupiers of a flax mill at Whatley, which they had built (or acquired from Cox) in 1836.[11, 25] ('Bucking House' is shown near Whatley on the 1st edition O.S. map of 1811 — 'bucking' was a process for bleaching yarn by steeping it in lye.) In 1837 a list of persons summoned for offences against the Factory Act included Thomas and William Frampton, who were indicted for employing a child under 13 years of age for more than nine hours a day, and for employing the same without a school certificate.[26] Framptons were still making sail-cloth in 1842, but by then the manufacture had 'almost become extinct'.[1]

Some of the other items which were listed in the late 18th century continued to be manufactured. William Bugler of St Mary Well Street and David Bugler of East Street were making bags in 1824;[1] David Lane was a sack and bag maker in Church Street between 1830 and 1840.[1, 22] In 1824 a number of hands in Beaminster were employed in spinning twine and pack thread and in making fishing nets.[1] Robert Conway, a direct descendant of the William Conway who issued a Trade Token in 1667,[27] was a twine and shoe-thread manufacturer in Shadrack Street in 1842,[1] probably at a building still standing. Edwin Woodbury made rope and twine at Prout Bridge, and Joseph Tite was a rope and twine maker in the Bridport road.[1, 11]

Other Industries and Crafts

Paper-making. An industry which had an indirect connection with the manufacture of flax and hemp was that of paper-making: among the chief materials used in the production of hand-made paper were linen rags and discarded ropes and sail-cloth, and often mills were sited near towns yielding such materials. There was a large increase in the number of paper mills in the 18th century, but such mills were usually quite small with only one or two vats. Good supplies of water were essential, both as a source of power and in the manufacturing process itself, and as cleanliness was important, mills were often sited upstream above other factories. In 1729 a list of prisoners in the Fleet prison (London) included the name of William Northam, late of Beaminster, paper-maker. There were two paper mills in Beaminster in the 18th century. One of them was at Whatley, beyond the top of Fleet Street, and may have been on the same site as the mill used in the 19th century for processing flax. A deed of 1742 refers to the paper mill and nearby close called Whatley Coat, but does not contain evidence that the mill was then working.[28]

The other paper mill, described as in East Street, was in fact near Prout Bridge. The site was probably a stone building on the west side of the Bridport road, part of which has been converted into a house (No. 8); at one time water was diverted here from the river at Prout Bridge and conducted back again by a watercourse running to the old weir at Hams Bridge. In the 1790s there are references to a 'Dwelling house with the Grinding House and Dyehouse thereunto belonging lately called the Paper Mill, formerly Richards since Symes'.[12] This mill seems to have been working in 1738, when Robert Richards paid poor rates on his mill.[17]

Printing. The first printer of whom we know is William Oliver who printed the circular asking for contributions in aid after the fire of 1781;[29] he had an office in the market place. William Oliver's two sons, Isaac and James, were both printers.[30] In 1830 Isaac was printer, bookseller and stationer in East Street;[1] in 1843 his printing-office was in the cottage next to the Congregational church.[11] James was also a surveyor — he drew a plan for the new approach roads to Horn Hill tunnel in 1829 — and he had an office in Church Street in 1842, presumably at premises which he occupied on the corner of Shadrack Street.[1, 11] William Sherring was printing in Beaminster in 1823.[30] In 1830 his office was in East Street, but in 1842 he was printing in Church Street; he was still engaged in the trade in 1867.[1] Edwin Coombs printed in Hogshill Street in 1842, in an office at the rear of his drapery business, later Reynolds (London House), outfitters.[1, 30]

Potteries. The Fullers Earth Clay, on which much of the town is situated, is suitable for the making of bricks and tiles, pottery, and drainage pipes, but the clay is of too poor quality for first-class products. The Hearn family were potters in the late 17th and 18th centuries; the inventory of Alice Hearn, widow, made in 1695, lists in the 'workeing house' the item 'Boards to dry earthen Weares on'.[2] John Hearn, potter, seems to have been on the north side of Hogshill Street in 1775.[9] Another family of 18th-century potters were the Chicks: James Chick was a potter in 1755.[31] In 1812 there were two potteries making coarse ware.[32] In 1830 George Hallett was an earthenware manufacturer in Hogshill Street,[1] and in 1843 Robert and George Hallett were owners of the premises on the south side of the street[11] where pottery continued to be made until later in the century.

In 1767 a tile makers company was floated in Beaminster, but the enterprise proved a failure. Nineteen members originally contributed £10 each, but this was lost in trade, and in 1781 Richard Symes's share of the debt was £1 5s. 0d.[33] The whereabouts of the yard is not known.

Metal-working. We have the names of workers in metal in Beaminster from the mid-18th century. George Eveleigh was a cutler in 1755;[31] in 1764 he was engaged to make all the ironwork in connection with the new church bells.[34] In 1793 his son, William Gerrard Eveleigh, was not only ironmonger, cutler and locksmith, but tinman, brazier, maker of edge tools (such as scythes), and finisher of Bath and Pantheon stoves. John Meech and Charles Canterbury worked in tinplate in North Street in 1842, and Charles Canterbury continued in the business in 1855.[1]

In the earlier 19th century there was an iron foundry at South Gate, established by Richard Waygood, an ironmonger in the market place in 1830.[1] The massive iron entrance gates to the churchyard, erected in 1837, were designed by Charles Coombs and supplied by Waygood and Seymour; they cost £37 10s. 0d. The iron railings round the new burial ground, added at the east end of the church in 1840, were provided by Waygood and Porter.[35] Richard Waygood removed to London in 1840,[22] leaving Benjamin Coombs Porter to carry on at the mill. In 1855 James Hunt had a brass and iron foundry on these premises.[1]

Clockmaking. The earliest clocks were made for ecclesiastical buildings, but big technical advances during the 17th century led to the making of reliable domestic clocks and watches. From the later 17th century to the earlier 19th century, Beaminster craftsmen were responsible for quite a number of modest handmade clocks. We know of three good clockmakers connected with the town in the latter part of the 17th century.[36] John Mintern, 'a clever maker of lantern clocks', may be the gunsmith of this name whose goods were listed for probate in 1693;[2] at this period, clockmakers came under the ironmongers' companies, which included also smiths, braziers and gunners. Richard Pinney, who died in 1696, must have been one of the earliest Dorset makers of the 30-hour longcase brass dial clock, the sort of clock which was then the cheaper end of an expensive market. Ralph Cloud, born in 1663, became well known as a clockmaker: Broadwindsor church clock bears a nameplate 'Cloud fecit', and Stoke Abbott and Netherbury clocks are attributed to him or to his son. In 1709 Ralph Cloud received £10 11s. 6d. for work about the bells and chimes at the church at Beaminster; his son Ralph (1692–1764) made the church clock, which has a nameplate 'Ra. Cloud the Maker 1739'. William Clift, blacksmith and ironmonger, who died in 1794, is known as the maker of an 8-day clock and a 30-hour clock (both with brass dials) which are still owned in the Beaminster area.[36]

Painted faces were introduced during the 18th century, and by the end of it they had superseded brass dials; specialist firms supplied the dials, and the country clock-maker assembled a movement. George Eveleigh, who died in 1784, made both 8-day and 30-hour brass dial clocks; his son William Gerrard also made 30-hour clocks with painted faces. Two prolific makers were the Drake family and the Peach family. A Richard Drake apparently made a longcase clock about 1750;[36] another Richard Drake, an ironmonger in Hogshill Street, made a number of 8-day and 30-hour clocks with painted faces between 1811[1] and his death in 1844. Matthew Peach, who died in 1750, was a clockmaker, and a Henry Peach made an 8-day clock *c.* 1800.[36] Another Henry Peach, ironmonger in the Fore Place in 1843,[11] made many 8-day and 30-hour clocks in the earlier 19th century. The making of handmade clocks declined as factory-made products came along to meet the increased demand.[36]

Tanning. The tanning business, with allied trades, continued to be one of some importance in Beaminster. In 1793 we are told that 'The conveniency of water has afforded great encouragement to the tanning business'.[1] Some processing was being carried on at Hams near Prout Bridge in the later 18th century when mention is made of a 'convenient way to come from the river' and the 'liberty to set up poles or forks in or near the Foot Path Way . . . to dry leather thereon . . .'.[12] The Willmott family went in for tanning: Thomas Willmott was a tanner in 1775,[31] and Samuel and Henry were tanners in 1793.[1] There was also a family of Daniels who were in the business. Isaac Daniel was a tanner in 1755;[31] in 1793 Henry Daniel was a tanner, while James, currier and shoemaker, processed the leather after it had been tanned and made shoes with it.[1] Some time in the earlier 19th century the actual process of tanning in the tan-yard (Shadrack Street), by use of tannin made from bark, seems to have stopped. John Bartlett of St Mary Well Street was a tawer in 1824 — he made hides into leather using a solution of alum and salt to whiten them.[1] He was described in 1828 as a fell-monger, leather breeches maker and glover; an insurance policy on his dwelling-house valued the stock and utensils in it at £100, with further stock in the warehouse worth £40.[37] The only other connection with the gloving trade of which we know is that George Tucker, a Beaminster fellmonger in 1811, was supplying William Bidel, a Yeovil glover, with skins.[1, 38]

Two other firms had meantime entered the currying trade in Beaminster. In 1830 Richard Dunn was a currier in East Street; by 1836 the business was being carried on at No. 15 Hogshill Street, formerly the *Green Dragon*.[33, 11] J. O. Bowditch was a currier in Shadrack Street in 1836.[33]

Malting and brewing. Up to the mid-19th century many of the innkeepers continued to brew the beer they sold, and there was a demand for considerable quantities of malt. The maltster was often a man of wealth and importance in the town, and malting was usually combined with other activities. Two members of the Hitt family — Samuel Hitt senior in 1731,[39] and Edward Hitt in 1750[40] — were maltsters. Richard Hoskins junior in 1738, and John Wheadon in 1752, seem to have been both clothiers and maltsters.[3] The Harris family were in this trade, and we find a Ralph Harris in 1740,[39] and a Thomas Harris in 1793;[1] they were connected with the *New Inn*. Other maltsters in 1793 were Daniel Cox and William Coward.[1] In 1830 there were four different malting concerns in the town: John Hearn Barratt at Pimlico (Fleet Street), Bishop & Waygood in the market place, William, John Garrett, and Joseph Tite in Church Street, and Thomas Frampton (owner of the *Red Lion*) in Fleet Street. Thomas Frampton and John Barratt were still malting in 1842, when other maltsters were William Eveleigh and William Swatridge.[1]

Roads and Transport

All these commercial activities must have involved a great deal of travel and transport. The more important roads in the neighbourhood were improved, but only slowly, by the introduction of turnpikes and tolls. The lesser routes remained very hard going: in 1796 Marshall commented that Dorset roads 'in the more recluse Vallies, are nearly in a state of Nature . . . crooked, narrow, numerous and full of sloughs'.[41] (A good description of bridleways in West Dorset today!) Although the distance was much the same either way, it is probable that people travelling from London to the Beaminster area mostly used the southern route from Salisbury (via Dorchester) in preference to the northern one (via Yeovil). Well-to-do folk still travelled mainly on horseback or in their own carriages, and unless they hired fresh post-horses every 10 to 15 miles, they were limited by the distance a horse could go in the day, between 25 and 50 miles.

In the 1730s George Strode used to come down to Parnham every year in early April, and return to spend the winter at his London house in late November or early December. The journeys down normally took him four days, travelling about 30 to 35 miles a day, in three stages of 10 or 12 miles. In 1733 and 1734, for example, on the first day he had breakfast at Egham, dinner at Bagshot, and supped and spent the night at Basingstoke. The second day it was breakfast at Sutton Scotney, dinner at Stockbridge, night at Salisbury, and on the third day the stops were at Woodyates, Blandford, and Dorchester or Cerne Abbas. The trip cost him round about £20, including expenses of 'selves' and servants at inns, hire of horses and their food and sometimes coach hire, and turnpike tolls.[42]

About 1739 the 'Fly Coach' from London to Exeter slept at the *Ship Inn* at Morecombelake on the fifth night from London;[43] as the roads and the construction of coaches improved, the time taken on such journeys was reduced. Travellers were still comparatively few before the coming of the railways, but people must have appreciated the swifter transit of news and goods. In 1793 there was a mail-coach daily through Bridport on the great west road, and Beaminster got a regular daily post. In 1824 the 'new Auxiliary Mail' of the Royal Mail, running from Bridport to Taunton, left Beaminster at 2 p.m. daily; on the return journey from Taunton, the Mail left Beaminster for Bridport at 11 a.m.[1] By 1840 the Royal Mail, which left the *White Hart*, Beaminster, daily for Taunton at 6 a.m., and for Bridport at 8.30 p.m., was no longer the only coach. The Victoria Coach left the *White Hart* for Taunton and Bridgwater on Tuesday, Thursday and Saturday at 1.30 p.m., and for Weymouth on Monday, Wednesday and Friday at 3 p.m. Two other daily coaches also stopped at Beaminster on their way to Bridport, one from Bath, and another from Bristol.[43]

Beaminster was linked by goods carriers not only with local markets, but also with larger more distant ones. In 1772 a carrier which left the *Saracen's Head*, Friday Street, London, on Monday, Thursday and Saturday, called at Broadwindsor and Beaminster on its way to Bridport; another carrier, from the *Bell*, Friday Street, also called at Beaminster.[44] In 1793 Russell's waggon from Exeter to London passed through every Thursday, and two waggons from Bristol to Bridport passed through every Saturday.[1]

The number of carriers calling at Beaminster increased during the first half of the 19th century. In 1830 there was a veritable network of carriers on the road:[1]

— To London. Whitmash from Hogshill St. every Monday & Friday
— To Axminster. Robert Gill from the *Red Lion* every Wednesday
— To Bridport. John Perry every Tuesday & Saturday, Thomas Chaffey every Tuesday, and Tapscott every Thursday from the *White Hart*
— To Bristol. Whitmash from Hogshill Street every Monday, John Perry from the *White Hart* every Tuesday & Saturday, James Webber and Robert & William Gange from the *Red Lion* every Saturday
— To Haslebury. John Perry from the *White Hart* every Tuesday & Saturday
— To Ilminster. Tapscott from the *White Hart* every Thursday
— To Maiden Newton. Bridge from the *White Hart* every Wednesday
— To Yeovil. Whitmash from Hogshill St., and Thomas Chaffey from the *White Hart* every Friday, and Hawker from the *Red Lion*, days uncertain

In 1842 Whitmash and Co. were making three journeys a week to Yeovil and London, and three to Ilminster and Bristol.[1]

By the earlier 19th century all the larger market towns in the vicinity were accessible from Beaminster by turnpiked roads. Bridport, whose population (borough and parish) was 6,333 in 1841, and Dorchester, with a population of 6,186 (including Fordington), could be reached by roads of the 1st and 2nd Bridport Trusts, and Dorchester could also be gained direct by roads of the Maiden Newton Trust. Crewkerne, which had a population (parish) of 4,414 in 1841, was accessible by the turnpike of the 2nd Bridport Trust as far as Misterton, and from there by the road of the Crewkerne Trust. Before the building of Horn Hill Tunnel made this route easier, there were alternative turnpike routes to Crewkerne: one by the Maiden Newton turnpike over Catsley Down, and another from Broadwindsor through Drimpton by the Bridport and Broadwindsor Trust, joining the Lyme Regis turnpike at Clapton Bridge. Chard was reached from Drimpton, through Winsham and Forton, by roads of the Chard Trust, which had granite milestones with curved tops marking the distances between Beaminster and Chard;[45] the population of Chard parish was 5,788 in 1841, and there was a market for corn, beans and potatoes on Monday, and for meat on Thursday and Saturday. There were several ways to Yeovil, which had a population of 7,043 in 1841: by roads of the Maiden Newton Trust via Holywell, by Misterton, or through the lanes to Corscombe and Halstock.

Brief mention must be made of the only canal to have any effect on Beaminster and its neighbourhood: this was the Chard Canal, one of the last canals to be built, and one of the shortest lived. A scheme was put up in 1833 to link the Chard area to Bristol by means of a canal (13½ miles long) from Creech St Michael on the Bridgwater and Taunton Canal; the canal was opened in 1842. Welsh coal and culm (for lime-burning) were brought, together with stone and other building materials, for distribution to Crewkerne, Lyme Regis, and the Beaminster area,[46] the last-named now more accessible as a result of the building of the tunnel in 1832. It was anticipated that the canal would 'prove extensively beneficial not only to Chard, but to Crewkerne, Axminster, Beaminster... Lyme and the circumjacent villages by affording them increased facilities of traffic with Bridgwater, Bristol, Gloucester, Liverpool and all ports on that coast'. The reduction in the price of coal and other articles of staple consumption was, it was stated soon after the opening, 'already very considerable'.[47] The trouble was that there was little return traffic from this largely agricultural area; the Chard Canal never paid its way and lasted only 25 years before it succumbed to the railway.[46]

Bridport and Beaminster (Bridport 2nd District) Turnpike Trust

The first turnpike trusts were set up in the later 17th century, and most of the routes from London to the major provincial cities had been turnpiked for nearly their whole length before the middle of the 18th century. The great west road to Exeter via Salisbury was the last to be taken in hand; the first Act was passed only in 1728. The Harnham, Blandford and Dorchester Trust was set up to look after the southern route from Salisbury via Dorchester: an Act of 1753–4 dealt with two parts of the main road, from Askerswell through Bridport to Penn Inn in Whitchurch Canonicorum, and from Penn Inn through Axminster to Honiton. A further Act covered the road from

Harnham, on the outskirts of Salisbury, through Dorchester to Askerswell.[48] The Act of 1753-4 also dealt with the road from Bridport to Beaminster which, like the other roads, was said to be 'in a very ruinous condition'. The same trustees were appointed for this road as for the road from Askerswell to Penn, but the tolls collected at the turnpikes to be set up on the two roads were to be separately applied to repairs in the appropriate district.

The only surviving minute book which covers the Bridport to Beaminster road is for the period 1754-1812.[49] A meeting held on 27 August 1754 at the *White Hart* in Beaminster discussed the places where turnpike gates should be set up. It was agreed to put a gate at the Bridport end 'between Great Conniger lane and Stake lane'; Stake Lane was the name given earlier to Barrack Street and St Andrews Road. This was the south gate of the turnpike. The north gate was to be set up between 'Parnham Stile and Mr. Baruch Fox's dwelling house': this was at the south entrance to Beaminster, and was later called Beaminster South Gate. The Act empowered the trust to erect side gates, that is gates across roads leading into the turnpike road which might be used for the evasion of tolls. It was decided to erect one side or 'stop' gate on the road from Bridport to Netherbury (Watford Lane), and another at Clampits (near the former gas-works) across the 'Halter Path' road leading from Netherbury to Beaminster. Tolls were being collected soon afterwards at South, North, Watford and Clampits Gates. Side gates in Clampit Lane and Pig Lane (North St., Bridport) were specified in an Act of 1764-5,[50] and in the same year tolls were being collected at Pig Lane Gate; probably the Watford gate had been replaced by one in a more strategic position.[51] Clampits Gate was repaired in 1794, and was still in operation in 1811;[49] it was again authorised by an Act of 1818-19,[52] but must have been removed at some time thereafter. In 1872 the four gates were Bradpole Gate, Pymore Lane Gate, Beaminster South Gate, and Tunnel Gate at Horn Hill.[53]

The trustees were very busy in late 1754 and early 1755, and met many times. At Beaminster a 'new erected dwelling house adjoining to a late publick house known by the sign of the Bottle' was rented for a toll house; the chimney wall of this building is incorporated in the present South Lodge. Parishes along the line of a new turnpike road were still required to supply statute labour, and stone for repair of the road. Much effort and money was spent in hauling stone, though it was of course brought from the nearest available site: for example, all the stones wanted for repairing the road from Beaminster to 'Hope gate' (Hope Farm, Netherbury) were to be taken from Mr. Strode's quarry on Coombe Down Hill.[49]

There is a gap in the minutes between July 1755 and February 1775, except for a few short notes entered with the accounts. Between 18 June 1758 and 26 February 1759 £44 18s. 8½d. was collected at the North Gate and £27 10s. 6¾d. at the South Gate; Clampits Gate was losing money in 1759, but made a small profit in 1760. In November 1759, instead of men being paid to collect the tolls, the North and South Gates were let together at 100 guineas a year, and in 1765 Robert Oliver was leasing all four gates at a year rent of £153. In 1777, when the tolls were auctioned for three years, they fetched £166 a year, William Newbury being the best bidder; in 1795 the tolls were let to Richard Smith for £255, and they fetched £401 from John Woodbury in 1811.[49] Meanwhile some of the tolls originally laid down, which had been found 'ineffectual', were raised, so that a waggon drawn by five or more horses paid 1s. 6d.

(instead of 1s. 0d.), and one drawn by three or four houses 1s. 0d. (instead of 8d.).[50] Milestones were set up along the road at some date, as in 1777 it was ordered that the milestones were to be cleaned and blacked;[49] the milestone which is now built into a wall, not far from the turning to Colfox School, may be one of these.

The Act of 1765 designated the road between Askerswell and Penn, together with that from Bridport to West Bay, as the Bridport 1st District. The Bridport to Beaminster road became the 2nd District. The Act added to the 2nd District the roads from the 'North Turnpike Gate at the South End of the Town of Beaminster to the Entrance into the Common called Beaminster Wood, otherwise Wood Common, and to Lenham's Water . . . which several Roads are in a ruinous Condition, and in many places narrow and incommodious'.[50] (Lenhams Water is the small stream which crosses the Beaminster to Broadwindsor road at Horn Park Farm.)

The surveyors appointed by the trust were local men of varying occupations, none of them experts, and it is doubtful how well the road was actually kept up. In May 1775 John Crabb, gardener, was appointed surveyor for seven years to put the road from Bridport to Beaminster in 'complete good repair'. He was to cover it 'with good Gravel or at least as much thereof as Gravel can be procured to do the same and will do and repair the Rest with the best Stone and materials he can get . . .'. During the seven years he was to keep in repair the road from Bridport Town to the end of Spring Lane (off Tunnel Road, the beginning of Wood Common). The new stretch of road had not yet been made up all the way because it was further ordered that the 'New Road added to the Turnpike Road . . . be new made from the White Hart Sign Post in Beaminster where the Road at present made Ends to the end of Spring Lane the Extremity of the said Turnpike . . .'. John Crabb cannot have done much because his appointment was followed in 1776 by that of John Hallet, glazier, with exactly the same instructions, but this time for 14 years. Hallet was to receive a yearly salary of £59, and the yearly sum of £7 out of the statute labour or the composition money which was paid in lieu. The trustees were also to pay him the sum of £118 15s. 6d. for the purpose of putting the road in immediate repair. John Hallet was not very conscientious, at any rate after the first few years, and the road got into such a bad state that in 1790 the trustees considered prosecuting him for neglect; two independent surveyors advised that £100 was needed to put the road in proper repair.[49]

In March 1778 it was ordered that the road from Beaminster to Lenhams Water should be repaired forthwith;[49] this must have been prompted by the passing of the Act of 1777-8 setting up the Maiden Newton Turnpike Trust, which was made responsible for the road from Furzemoor (Birdsmoor) gate to Lenhams Water.[54] The road between Beaminster and Broadwindsor seems to have been virtually a new construction, as Taylor's map of Dorset (1765) shows the route as either over Horn Hill or round by Stoke Abbott. The two sharp double bends in the road at Lenhams — smoothed out quite recently — suggest that the two trusts worked on slightly different alignments; they each paid half the cost of a bridge over Lenhams Water.[49]

There were several changes of surveyor after John Hallet's term, and then in 1799 a new scheme was proposed to the 'gentlemen of the different parishes adjoining this turnpike road'. Under the arrangements agreed, separate surveyors were appointed for the sections of the road in Bradpole, Melplash and Beaminster. There is no reference to 'salaries': the 'gentlemen' surveyors were allowed certain sums of money out of the tolls plus additional amounts from the highway rates, which they were to expend on the section of road, accounting for the total advanced at the end of the year. Henry Willmott, for the part of the road within Beaminster parish, was allowed £25 4s. 0d. plus £12 12s. 0d. In 1802 John Banger Russell, attorney, was appointed surveyor in Beaminster; he was re-appointed every year up to and including 1811[49] and he was still taking care of this stretch of the road in 1822.[55]

Horn Hill Tunnel. A plan of Horn Park farm *c.* 1800 shows the upper part of Horn Hill Lane, as the road was then called; the turnpiked road at that date went of course only as far as the south end of Beaminster Wood Common, and beyond this the road was gated in places.[56] The common was enclosed in 1809, and under the 1819 Act a stretch of turnpiked road was made from the south end of the former common right to Misterton Water, where it met the Dorchester to Crewkerne road of the Maiden Newton Trust; land was taken to widen the road.[57] The road went right over the top of Horn Hill at a height of about 650 feet above sea level — its course can still be traced, with a considerable embankment (see Fig. 3). In less than ten years it was decided that what was really wanted was a tunnel through the hill. In the words of Giles Russell, the Beaminster solicitor who more than any other person was instrumental in getting the tunnel built, the hill constituted, at a time when the horse provided the sole means of transport, 'a barrier which cut off Bridport and Beaminster from the interior of Somerset'.[58]

The plan which the turnpike trustees deposited in 1829 was for a new line of road between Beaminster and Whetley Cross, involving the diversion of certain parts of the existing road and the construction of a tunnel, and also a new approach road from north of the tunnel to the Dorchester road over Beaminster Down. The Act of 1830, largely obtained through the efforts of Giles Russell, also added to the trust the road which ran from Whetley Cross through Littlewindsor to the turnpike road from North Allington to Clapton Bridge.[59] The plan of roads in Hine's *History of Beaminster*[60] must represent a variant on the scheme which was not carried out: it shows the new road north of the tunnel on a different line from the road actually made, and at West Dibberford, the junction between the old and new roads, a further new road to Broadwindsor which was never constructed.

Most of the money borrowed by the turnpike trustees on the security of the tolls (£10,940 between September 1829 and September 1833) came from Beaminster people. Giles Russell himself put up £2,000, and so did Samuel and Peter Cox. Other sums ranging from £50 to £500, lent by local people, included advances from John and Richard Warr (builders), J. W. & T. P. Daniel (doctors), Richard Waygood (iron-monger), Robert Conway (draper), John Purchase Frampton (builder), Richard Hine (grocer), and Richard Hine (linen manufacturer). Two firms of Bridport bankers — Williams, Pattison & Co., and S. & W. E. Gundry — also put money into the project.[61] It is no wonder that the people of Beaminster regarded it as *their* tunnel, since much of the work was carried out by craftsmen and labourers from the town: according to the census report (1831), 50 out of the 70 non-agricultural labourers in the parish were then excavating a tunnel.

The ceremony of cutting the first sod was performed on 12 April 1830, when 'About 12 o'clock, a great number of gentlemen and most respectable tradesmen met near the market-house and forming themselves into pairs, proceeded to the hill with banners flying, and a band of music . . .'.[62] The construction of the tunnel itself, which is 115 yards long and 20 feet wide, was commenced in August 1831 and finished only 10 months later in June 1832. The walls are 3 ft. 6 in. thick, built of solid brick, and the arch likewise is 2 ft. 9 in. thick; it has been calculated that 1½ million bricks must have been used in the construction.[63] The bricks may have come from the Bothenhampton brickworks; their peak annual production (earlier 20th century) was one million bricks, and radius of supply about 10 miles.[64] South Petherton has also been suggested as the source of the bricks: a brickyard there, which would have been operating in 1830, was situated to the west of the Pitway to East Lambrook road (ST 437180).[65]

No detailed accounts survive for the construction, but the annual statements of account of the 2nd District Turnpike Trust show that the total cost of the tunnel and the new roads immediately adjacent to it, over the four years of heavy expenditure, was in the region of £13,000. For the year covering most of the building of the actual tunnel, the expenditure was over £6,000.[61] Horn Hill Tunnel is an unusual piece of early road improvement (only a few similar tunnels are known) and a most impressive achievement for its date. The two stone portals are listed as of special architectural or historic interest, and it has been described as 'a remarkable foretaste of railway architecture'.[66] The engineer was Michael Lane, then aged only 29; he had worked under Mark Brunel (father of Isambard Kingdom) on the Thames Tunnel at Rotherhithe in 1825, and he went on to work on the railways.[67]

There was a great procession from Beaminster on the day of the opening of the tunnel, 29 June 1832. It was led by the Bridport and Taunton mail coach, bearing the Clerk to the Turnpike Commissioners, the engineer and the surveyor. Next came, in an open carriage, Giles Russell and Samuel Cox, treasurer of the Trust. They were followed by several hundred gentlemen on horseback and as many more on foot (both visitors and inhabitants of Beaminster), and then by about 60 carriages. Finally there were the skilled workmen and the labourers employed on the tunnel, all carrying their working tools. The procession was nearly half a mile in length, and there were great crowds of spectators along the road and on the slopes of the hill; it was estimated that as many as 9,000 people were there at the time, and one can imagine them coming from miles around to be present at this great spectacle.[58] Shortly after the tunnel was opened, turnpike gates and house were erected on the Crewkerne side, at the junction with the new approach to the Dorchester road. The tolls of all four gates of the Trust fetched £993 in 1835.[61]

The main object in building a tunnel was to improve communications between Bridport 'Harbour' — West Bay, 1½ miles from the town — and the towns and villages of south Somerset; at this period most of the flax and hemp used in the many small industries of this area was imported through Bridport. The *Dorset County Chronicle* commented as follows:

Commerce will be greatly benefitted by the measure, as the conveyance of heavy goods, timber, etc. will be rendered at much lower rates; the kind feelings of humanity are promoted, as the steepness of the hill previously was most toilsome and painful to horses; and the general convenience of the public is vastly augmented . . .'.[58]

Great hopes were entertained of the prosperity to come to Beaminster from the

1. Beaminster from the south-west early this century.

2. St Mary's church, with the almshouse built by Sir John Strode. From a drawing by Abel Bugler c.1845.

3. (*top*) Figures on the west front of the church tower: *centre left* Resurrection, *centre right* Ascension. The figures on either side are thought to be those of donors.

4. (*centre*) Inscription on the south side of the almshouse. It reads: ' God's House. Sit Honos Trino Deo. Anno Dom 1630'.

5. (*left*) Plaque on the gable of No. 12 The Square. It reads: 'This Towne/ Burnt in 1684/ Howse rebuilt/ in 1687. W.L.' The initials are for William Lacke, a clothier.

6. (*top*) Bridge House at Prout Bridge, built in the early 17th century. Houses on the outskirts of the town escaped the great fires.

7. (*centre*) Barton End, Fleet Street. The symmetrical early-18th-century front range has brick walls with stone doorway, architraves and dressings.

8. (*below*) Farrs, East Street, in 1897. It was from this house that Ann Symes eloped to Gretna Green with Samuel Cox in 1790.

9. The Red House, North Street, built in the early 18th century, is brick-fronted with stone mullions. Attractive detail of central upper window with side-pieces carved with open flowers and doorway with scrolled flush-feet and bracketed pediment.

10. (*below*) Minster View, Shorts Lane. An inscription on the gable end shows that it was built for John Brown, serge-maker, in 1781.

11. Manor House, North Street, c.1900. The house was built in the later 18th century but was altered and enlarged in the early 19th century.

12. East Axnoller Farm on the northern slopes of Beaminster Down overlooking the sources of the river Axe. The plaque over the door bears the date 1709 and initials J.R.

13. (*below*) Storridge Farm, Whitcombe Road, dating from the 17th century.

14. Whitcombe Farm, built in the 18th century.

15. (*left*) Whitcombe Farm: steps up to the old granary with dog kennel underneath.

16. (*below*) Whitcombe Farm: 18th- or 19th-century sheep dip under a cart-track, still in use in the 1920s — the entrance (east) is rebated to take a blocking plate.

17. Horn Hill Tunnel, south entrance, c.1900. Opened in 1832, it is a very unusual example of an early road tunnel.

18. Turnpike lodge and gate at South Gate, Bridport Road, Beaminster, from a water-colour by H. Codd. Tolls were abolished and the gate removed at the end of 1880.

19. Tomb in Daniel's Knowle burial ground commemorating John Daniel (d.1829), his wife Betsy and their descendants.

20. Dr. A.A. Pim in his Rover, the first motor car in Beaminster, acquired in 1909. He used to travel some 60 miles a day on the rough unmade roads, visiting patients.

21. (*above*) Philip Hine (1810-67) of Conway and Hine, wine merchants. A deacon in the Congregational church at Beaminster, he lived at Hitts House from about 1847.

22. (*top right*) Richard ('Dicky') Hine, chemist. Author of *A History of Beaminster*, published in 1914, and great-nephew of Philip Hine.

23. (*right*) Peter Cox (1800-92), son of Ann (née Symes) and Samuel Cox, and according to Percy Codd 'a true bit of English oak'. His law firm later became Kitson and Trotman.

24. Fore Place looking west on south side of market house, c.1870. Parmenas Galpin, grocer and ironmonger, and John Cox Williams, draper.

25. Fore Place looking east, c.1870. North side of market house — pulled down in 1886.
26. Fore Place, north-west corner c.1870 with Stembridge, saddler, and Toleman, ironmonger.

27. Hay-maker made by Robert Bugler, founder of the firm Francis Bugler Ltd., about 1870. An advanced model, with improved rising action, which turned a wide swath.

28. Brick kiln at Hogshill Street potteries, c.1890.

29. Benjamin Brinson Chambers, builder of the Public Hall opened in 1903. The Chambers family were masons and builders in Beaminster from the 1840s.

30. Henry Crocker, draper (d.1920). A leading Methodist and a parish and district councillor for many years, he was described as 'a man who always tried to improve and forward all progressive movements for the Town's benefit'.

31. Fiennes Trotman (d.1935). Chairman of Beaminster Parish Council from 1900 to 1915. 'He was a friend of all and always ready to give his services in any way possible for the benefit of the Town'.

32. John Lane Kitson who joined Peter Cox's firm in 1868. In Percy Codd's opinion 'a great acquisition to Beaminster, being a cheery disposition and a good hand at games'. For many years a district councillor and chairman of Beaminster Water Supply and Sewerage Committee, he died in 1924.

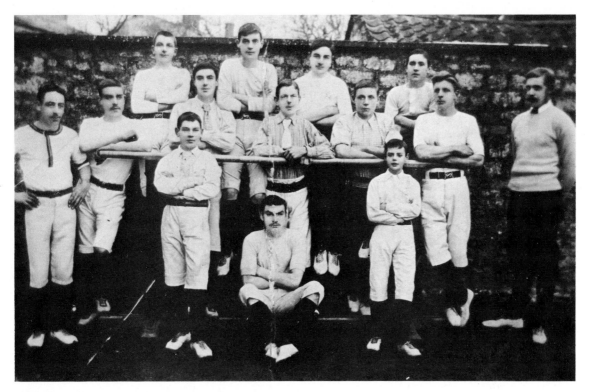

33. Boys at the elementary school, 1894.

34. Girls' and Infants' Elementary School, Hogshill Street. Top class of infants 1924: *Fourth row (l to r)* Arthur Bugler, Edgar Rendell. *Third row (l to r)* Ronald Thomas, Olive Barter, Charles Satchell, Edwin Woodbury, Dorothy Hiscock, Betty Hinton. *Second row (l to r)* John Hodder, Kathleen Watts, 'Banger' Smith, Leslie England, Peggy Wakely, Daisy Greening. *Front row (l to r)* Pauline Biles, Zillah Swaffield, Donald Swaffield, Ron Ackerman, Alec Walbridge, Phyllis Hayward.

35. Grammar School staff, 1930. *Back row (l to r)* J.F.H.S. Mussell, Lès L. (French, 1924-30); L. Skyrm, M.A. (Headmaster); A.H. Habbitts, B.A. (Latin and English, 1926-43); A.W. Graveson, M.A. (Natural Sciences and Agriculture, 1919-59). *Front row (l to r)* D.S. Peters, B.A. (Maths., 1921-59); F.S. Hann, L.L.A., A.C.P. (Drawing and Music, 1914-45); E.M. Hastings, B.A. (History and Geography, 1927-37).

36. Grammar School pupils (Oxford and Higher Oxford School Certificates), 1930. *Back row (l to r)* R.A. Paulley, G. Randell, W.W. Bugler, Rd. J. House, H.E.C. Biggin, G. Wyatt, R.M. Perry, C.F. Buckland, R.C. Travers, H.J. Clarke, E.R. Wakely, H.C. Gould. *Middle row (l to r)* E. Mildred Barrett, E. Mary Barrett, Peggy Frampton, L. Skyrm (Headmaster), L. E. Rockett, M.L. Miller, N.L. Wakely. *Front row (l to r)* F. Gregory, Robt. J House, B. Wyatt, T.J. Yeatman, D.W. Bugler, L.J. Miller.

37.   Beaminster Board of Guardians and Rural District Council, 1911-12. *Back row (l to r)* Messrs. C.M. Meech (Relieving Officer), S.M. Wrixon, Freeman Roper J.P., W. Manfield, Rev. R.T. Parker, Mr. J.G. Kitson, Mr. S.R. Baskett, The Earl of Ilchester, J.P., Com. Hon. G.F. Digby, R.N., Messrs. W. Budden, G. Bugler, G. Johnston, Mrs. Andrews (Matron), Nurse Peskett. *Middle row (l to r)* Sir H. Peto, Bart., Messrs. J.L. Kitson, M. Dawbney, H.S. Studley, S. Gillingham, Rev. F. Williams, J.P. (Chairman), Messrs. W.W. Sampson (Vice-Chairman), J.T. Holloway, A.B. Dawbney, W.J. Major, Frank Bugler (Assistant Clerk), T.D. Andrews (Master Union House). *Front row (l to r)* Messrs. C.C. Hann (Inspector of Nuisances), F.G. Wakely (Surveyor of Highways), J.M. Meech (Relieving Officer), F.H. Studley, Canon J. Pulliblank, Messrs. T.B. Hardy, E. Masters, B. Bussell, W.P. Stephens (Porter), S.R. Meech (Master's Assistant).

38.   East Street, 1910. On the right the gates of the Boys' Elementary School opened in 1875.

39. Beaminster Rural District Council, September 1947. *Back row (l to r)* Mrs. Ellis (Staff), Mr. H.R. Newgass, Mr. F.H.E. Moorhouse (C.F.O.), Mr. L. Samways (Housing Foreman), Mr. C.L. Perry, Mr. A.C. Lambert, Mr. R.C.H. Studley, Adm. Sir Dudley North, G.C.V.O., C.B., C.S.I., C.M.G., Mr. C.S. Coram, Mr. R.C. Travers (Clerk of the Council), Mr. E.D. Jones (Collector of Revenues), Mr. C.C. Rundle (Sanitary & Building Inspector), Mr. J.W.R. Newman (Manager, Beaminster Water Supply), Mr.W.R. Riglar (Staff), Miss G. Travers (Staff). *Middle row (l to r)* Dr. A. Armit (M.O.H.), Lt. Col. T.A. Headlam, Hon. J.W. Best, O.B.E., Rev. O.R. Powell-Evans, S.S.F., Col. W.F.S. Casson, Adm. Sir V.A. Crutchley, V.C., K.C.B., D.S.C., Mr E.J. Henson, Mr. J.C. Shoobridge, M.B.E., Mr. R.E. Ashford, Mr. L. Skyrm, M.A. (Beaminster), Mr. E.J. Bailey, Mr. M.A. Pinney, Mr. J.S. Bugler, Mr. S.J. Stenhouse, Comdr. Sir Francis Peto, Bart., R.N., Mr. S. Chaffey. *Front row (l to r)* Capt. G. Walker, Lt.Col. C.J. Troyte-Bullock, D.S.O., Mrs. le Poer Trench, Mr. T.A.Case, Lady Lilian Digby, Mr. J.C. Davy, Capt. N.H. Carter, R.N. (Former Chairman), Col. G.A. Pinney, D.L., J.P., (Chairman), Mr. Robert Leigh (Former Clerk), Mr. J.R. Wyatt, Mr. E.J.S. Holloway, Mr. R. Pease, Mr. Robert Hine (Beaminster), Mrs. E.F. Holden, Mr. F.T. Bugler (Beaminster).

40. The Square, south-west corner, early 1900s, with Hine (chemist), Hill (grocer), and Moore (baker) in Church Street.

increased trade. A poem by William Gardner (proprietor of Beaminster Academy), which was sung at the dinner held at the *White Hart* to celebrate the opening of the tunnel, includes these lines;[68]

> When, ever studious of thy weal,
>   Thy commerce to promote,
> A Russell's patriots zeal
>   Shall live when we're forgot.
>
> In swelling streams may cheering wealth
>   To Beaminster descend;
> And ever joy-inspiring health
>   Her social sons attend.
>
> May patriots successive rise,
>   This peaceful town to grace,
> And future ages richly prize
>   Her enterprising race!

Maiden Newton Turnpike Trust

The turnpiking of the northern route from Salisbury to Exeter via Yeovil was completed in 1762; the Maiden Newton Trust was set up in 1778 to improve a number of roads in the Yeovil area. One of the lengths of road for which it was made responsible was the one to Beaminster from Holywell, the junction of the Dorchester to Yeovil road with the road to Evershot.[54] Professor Good says that at first this turnpike (having run along the old line of Benville Lane, which originally joined the Maiden Newton to Crewkerne road at the Hore Stones) came down into Beaminster by White Sheet Hill,[69] but this cannot be correct. There *are* references in the minutes to a road between the Hore Stones and 'White Sheet gate'[70] — the writing is so bad as to be virtually illegible for long stretches — but this may be the other White Sheet Hill just outside Maiden Newton on the Crewkerne road; the Trust was also responsible for this road. (A sketch map of roads near Beaminster *c.* 1800 describes White Sheet Hill, Beaminster, as 'as good as a turnpike'.[71]) As early as January 1779 it was decided that the road between Catsley (Toller) Down and Buglers Corner (junction of Whitcombe Road and Bridport Road in Beaminster) should 'be made and carried through part of the ground belonging to Bennett Coombe called Little Down': this is land bordering the side of Whitcombe Road at Dirty Gate. As a through route to Toller Down this road is largely a turnpike creation; in 1776 it was known as Hackthorn Lane where it climbed Hackthorn Hill past Storridge and the two Marsh farms, and it was repaired at the expense of these three farms which it served.[4] Between Little Down and Beaminster, the road lying against the lands of various owners, including Tucker's Charity Marsh farm, was widened by the turnpike trust, hedges being taken down where necessary and part of the lands 'thrown to the road'. The accounts show expenses in 1779 in connection with 'forming road on Hackthorn', 'forming road from Hart Hill [Catsley Down] to Dirty Gate', and 'hedging at Storredge'.[70]

Following on the making of the turnpike road, Tucker's Charity spent just over £50 in 1783 'making the New Road through the Cowleaze', no doubt the present one to Mapperton past Marsh Farm known as Knapps Lane. It was stated that 'all the then

roads through Hackthorn and the sheep slight were to be stopt up and disused'.[72]
Several tracks from Mapperton and Ramsmoor came out on to Hackthorn Hill near
Dirty Gate where they met the Crabb Barn Lane route from South Perrott and Broad-
windsor.[4] In 1813 authority was apparently given for setting up a turnpike gate near
Dirty Gate, possibly to prevent the use of Crabb Barn Lane to evade tolls, but this
did not materialise.[73]

A turnpike gate had been set up on the Maiden Newton road at Catsley Down, and
in 1779 it was ordered that a gate for receiving tolls be set up between a place called
Earthpit and Beaminster Town. In 1788 Samuel Cox was to build 'a convenient
dwelling house . . . by the side of the gate in Earthpitt Lane';[70] there was a field called
Earthpits on Whitcombe farm, not far from the cottage in Whitcombe Road still
known as 'Toll Bar'.

Cross near Horn Hill Tunnel marking the spot where a workman was killed by a fall of earth

CHAPTER NINE

THE POOR 1700-1850

The Parish Workhouse

BY THE 18th CENTURY we can begin to see something of the working of the Beaminster Parish Vestry. All the ratepayers could attend, but it was only the gentry, farmers, manufacturers and leading tradesmen who did so, any lesser folk who did pay rates preferring to leave the management of affairs to their betters. There are no actual vestry minute books before the mid-19th century, but account books of parish officials, especially overseers' accounts, contain quite a number of minutes in between the financial items. Although other matters do crop up from time to time, most minutes concern the operation of the poor law — the most important civil function of parish vestries — as increasing demands were made on poor relief.

In earlier days, any able-bodied paupers who were set to work by their parish remained as domestic outworkers in their own cottages, but in 1722 an Act was passed permitting parishes to buy or rent workhouses and to refuse relief to any who declined to enter. At a vestry meeting held in Beaminster in May 1739, it was decided to consult with the trustees of the Gilbert Adams Charity in order to rebuild 'the House in Beaminster called Gilbert Adams Alms House, so as to make it capable and fitt to receive all the poor of the parish'. The almshouse in East Street had apparently got into a very poor condition, and the trustees had not sufficient funds to repair it. Furniture and equipment were purchased by the Vestry during the year 1746–7, one of the items being three dozen trenchers — William Barnes mentions 'wooden trenchers, square, wi' zalt-holes at the rim'. A pound was put up for the pigs which were kept to supply the workhouse with bacon. Garden tools were also bought, and no doubt the inmates grew the 'garden stuff' on the diet sheet. In 1748 the overseers were told to collect 12 poor rates to be applied towards the 'furnishing repairing and compleating the workhouse'.[1]

On the night of 24 May 1766 the workhouse was burnt to the ground. The building was reduced 'to Aishes together with all the Furniture belonging to the Same and the materials there in contained for setting the Poore . . . to Worke'. It was agreed at a vestry meeting held on 4 June that the workhouse should be rebuilt on the same spot, and of the same size as the former building. There was one important difference: all the new buildings were to be roofed with Cornish slate instead of thatch.[1]

An inventory of all the household goods and furniture in the workhouse, made in 1785, lists the following accommodation: vestry room, inner garret, middle garret, outer garret, men's chamber, women's room, little room, dining room, work house, coal house, kitchen, pantry, wash house, hospital under room, hospital chamber, second hospital chamber, scale house, yard and spinning path. The bedrooms contained

35 bedsteads and there were 11 more in the hospital rooms; each was furnished with a dust bed (stuffed with chaff), sheet, bolster cloth, blanket and rug. The dining room furniture consisted of two long oak tables and four long forms.[2] In 1822 there were some additional rooms, for example a governor's room or parlour and a school room; in 1827 there was a separate 'Married men & women's bedroom' with six bedsteads. Some poor people brought their own furniture, bedding etc., into the workhouse, taking it out again with them if and when they left. In 1827 one old lady brought the following:

> 3 Feather Pillows, Bellows and Cards, Iron Kettle, Brass Kettle, Back Crook, Iron Bolt, Tongs, Poker & Grid Iron, Bed Tick, Bag and a Little Wool. Dresser and shelves, two aprons, one gown, one shift, two caps, two handkerchiefs, one pair of old stockings, six pieces of Earthenware, one tea spoon, knife & fork, one tea caddy.

After her death, some of the goods were sold and the rest divided between two sons and a daughter.[3]

What were conditions like inside? In 1775, when the total population of the parish was 1,955, there were 77 people in the workhouse: seven husbands, eight wives, six widowers, 12 widows, two single males, 15 single females, 17 boys and 10 girls.[4] By 1790 the number had risen to about one hundred, two-thirds of them old people. In April 1801 the peak was reached with 196 in the workhouse, 92 old people and 104 young people.[5] The poor were distinguished from the rest of the inhabitants, first by the wearing of a badge (from 1753), and later on (1766) by the adoption of a uniform of 'parish clothes'. In 1753 it was expressly forbidden to go out of the workhouse without consent of the overseers; the penalty for the first offence was the loss of 'one Meal's Victuals', and the penalties were increased until at the fourth offence the person was to be put in the 'Blind House' (a small room with no windows) with only bread and water for 24 hours.[1] Rules laid down in 1785 permitted the poor to go out of the workhouse only on a Sunday, when they might attend church morning and afternoon, but they must come straight back and be in the workhouse within a quarter of an hour after the end of the service.[2] By 1834 the rules were rather kinder, and have something of an air of Victorian paternalism.[6]

A weekly dietary table was laid down in 1774. The diet varied day by day, the meals consisting of breakfast, dinner and supper. Each adult person was to receive 96 oz. of bread together with 12 oz. of bacon (or 18 oz. of cow beef or 24 oz. of bull beef) per week; in addition oatmeal was served 11 times, milk nine times, 'garden stuff' twice and peas once.[2] When the price of bread was very high in 1795, special arrangements were made for supply. The overseers were told to buy wheat and barley at the lowest prices, to be ground at mills in the parish nominated by the Vestry, sufficient being ground at one time for a month's consumption. Loaves of two-thirds wheat to one-third barley were to be made at the workhouse and baked at a bakehouse approved by the monthly vestry meeting. Nothing was to be wasted, the coarse bran separated out from the meal being fed to the workhouse pigs. A revised diet sheet reduced the weekly bread ration to 50 oz. and included large quantities of potatoes, which were to be served twice a day on some days.[5]

Methods of workhouse management under the old Poor Law varied. The care of the poor might be farmed out entirely to a contractor. An alternative was for the overseers themselves to buy from local traders the supplies needed for the workhouse, and employ a salaried workhouse master who would live in the workhouse. In 1746, when the house was first taken over, John Bussel of Netherbury, clothier, was appointed 'to take care of and set the Poor in the Work House to work'; he was to receive £12 for a year, and a shilling out of every £1 the poor in the workhouse earned. This arrangement cannot have proved satisfactory, for in November 1747 it was decided to run the workhouse directly. Twelve principal ratepayers were chosen as annual trustees, two of them to act as managers each month, dealing with ordering and paying for the goods required. Richard Hoskings and his wife were appointed as master and mistress, to be paid £8 a year and receive 2s. 6d. out of every £1 earned by the poor.[1]

In June 1748 a number of regulations 'for the better Management of the Workhouse and the Accounts thereof and the other Concerns of this parish' were agreed by the Vestry and entered in the overseers' account book. One of these regulations involved the setting up of a Select Vestry or committee, to be appointed annually and consisting of seven persons besides the two 'acting' workhouse trustees, who were always to be members. The purpose of this was 'the better Management & speedy Dispatch of any emergent Affairs of the parish that require immediately to be transacted', and so the Select Vestry was to meet at the workhouse every Wednesday afternoon. It was to have power to admit persons into the workhouse, regulate their diet and clothing, and 'on any sudden occasion to direct & order what they shall judge to be most conducive to the good of the parish'. It was laid down that, 'when any Accident or Hurt shall happen to any poor person', immediate notice should be sent by the workhouse master to the Reverend Thomas Fox (the curate at Beaminster, a member of the Select Vestry), who would get in touch with the other members to decide what should be done.[1]

This is an interesting anticipation of the 1819 Vestry Act, which authorised the appointment of Select Vestries. There is, however, no further reference to a Select Vestry in the Beaminster records. The appointment of 12 workhouse trustees continued for a time, the general vestry meeting of April 1749 voting to continue the 12 previously chosen, and the appointment of 12 trustees being again recorded in 1753, but this arrangement seems then to have also lapsed. Management of the day-to-day affairs of the workhouse was left to the overseers elected each year, of whom there were three in the earlier part of the period and four later on. The overseers were of course unpaid, and in Dorset it was quite common, in order to relieve them and to improve administration, to appoint a 'perpetual overseer' who would hold office year after year and be paid a small salary; the practice had no legal basis before paid assistant overseers were authorised by the 1819 Act. Some examples are recorded in Beaminster. In 1752 Thomas Harris was appointed to transact all the parish business for £10 a year: he was to allow himself to be elected as one of the overseers every year, to collect the poor rate, keep the overseers' accounts, carry out orders made at vestry meetings, and deal with binding out apprentices, settlement examinations, and so on. In 1756 James Daniel agreed to accept the office of overseer 'although it is not . . . come to his turne', and to perform the same duties as Thomas Harris; he was allowed £5 5s. a year, but was to receive horse hire and expenses at five shillings a day in addition, whenever he had to attend Quarter Sessions.[1]

William Clift was perpetual overseer for 24 years from 1810. Early in May that year, it was decided on account of the 'great Expenditure in the Parish Workhouse which has lately been increasing in an excessive degree' to appoint a special overseer to manage the workhouse and the concerns of the poor. William Clift was appointed, for one year to start with, at a salary of £50, and his appointment appears to have had an immediate effect on the numbers admitted to and kept in the house. In the month ending 29 April 1810 the number of people inside had been recorded as 41 old and 58 young (usually under 16); four weeks later the number had been reduced to 38 old and 17 young people, and this lower level was maintained, although there was no noticeable increase in the number relieved outside.[7, 8] It was not until 1816 that the number in the workhouse began to rise again; it reached 118 on 29 March 1822,[8, 9] but fell thereafter and remained in the 60s and 70s over the period to 1834. The Vestry passed a vote of thanks to William Clift in March 1834 for 'his exertions as overseer' over the previous 24 years.[10] In the early 1830s the average annual cost of maintaining the poor of the parish was £1,437;[11] on a population of 2,968 in 1831, this is 9s. 8d. a head, compared with an average for the area of 11s. 0d.

The Beaminster Vestry kept a strict control over the management of the workhouse, and scrutinised and passed the accounts at a monthly meeting. In 1774 it was ruled that 'the workhouse is the properest place to hold the monthly vestory, on account of seeing the House kept in order and to hear the Complaints of the Poor'.[2] Among the rules made in 1748 was one to the effect that 'no monthly Trustee for the workhouse during the time he acts as such supplys the Workhouse with any provision cloaths or any other Necessarys whatsoever of his own property', and when James Daniel agreed to carry out the duties of assistant overseer, he promised not to supply the poor with any goods of his own.[1] In 1773 it was decided that for the future no overseer should buy any provisions or clothing for the workhouse, but these items should be contracted for monthly at a vestry meeting held for the purpose. This developed into a regular system whereby any person wishing to contract for goods had to put a ticket — a separate one for each item — in a box at the workhouse; on the ticket he stated the price at which he was willing to supply.[2] Goods offered, for example cloth, must be as good as the workhouse pattern. In 1796 there is a record of the quantities of various kinds of cloth which were bought by the yard from local manufacturers and representatives, and then made up in the workhouse into items of clothing for the inmates (all listed), and also into sheets, bolster cloths, and blankets. Leather was bought by the butt from James Daniel and Thomas Carter, Beaminster curriers, and made into shoes; in 1827 there were in the boys' schoolroom 18 lasts for shoes, one shoe hammer, one pair of shoe nippers and one pair of shoe pincers.[3]

Among the 12 rules laid down in 1785 were several concerning the workhouse master or governor. One of the rules was that a note must be kept of what was consumed and by whom; if the consumption was greater than that authorised under the scheme laid down by the Vestry, the governor would have the extra cost deducted from his salary.[2] By 1810 the governor's salary had risen to £20 a year.[7] In 1834 the duties of governor and governess were set out in elaborate detail.[6]

One of the parish doctors was engaged at an annual salary to take care of the poor, and before 1760 this included the poor outside the workhouse as well. This must have been a lot more economical than paying for specific visits and medicine. From 1748 until 1753 (when John Cox was brought in) the appointment alternated between Oliver Hoskins and John Daniel;[1] in 1778 James Dunning was engaged in place of

Oliver Hoskins.[2] Later workhouse doctors were Hermon Hodge and John Daniel (probably a nephew) who commenced duties in the late 18th century,[5] and James William Daniel (son of John) who was appointed in the early 1820s.[9] The salary paid was £10 in 1750;[1] by 1827 it had risen to £40.[10]

Surgery, and innoculations against small-pox, were paid for separately. In 1758 it was agreed to allow the three doctors five shillings a head for innoculating all poor parishioners who were willing.[1] Beaminster Vestry complained in 1780 that people were being brought into the parish to be innoculated who were not legal inhabitants, and the doctors were requested not to carry out such innoculations.[2] After 379 poor people had been treated in 1791, the Vestry ordered that all innoculation should cease; any surgeon acting in defiance would be considered 'as an improper Person to have the Care of the poor at any future Time'.[5] Innoculations were recommenced at a later period.

It was the hope — largely a delusion — of 18th-century poor law authorities that workhouses could be made to pay for themselves. From this point of view, Beaminster was one of the two more successful workhouses in Dorset, the other being the work-house at Broadwindsor.[12] The rural workhouses of West Dorset were able to economise by growing some of their own food, and Beaminster paid close attention to manage-ment. But the poor had also to work to earn their keep as far as possible, and the success of the workhouse at Beaminster was doubtless due in part to early adoption of a policy of 'no relief outside the workhouse'. In 1760 it was unanimously agreed that 'the Poor of this Parish shall be relieved in the Work House, and no person to be relieved out of the House unless in case of sickness, and then not for more than One Month unless the Parish Doctor do certifie they are not fit to be removed into the House'.[1] This policy, which was maintained until the last few years of the 18th cen-tury, prevented the workhouse becoming solely the refuge of the old and incapable, though it is unlikely that the able-bodied represented more than a fairly small pro-portion of the inmates.

The availability of traditional crafts, such as the separation of fibres of hemp and flax, and the spinning of yarn, contributed to the comparative success of the work-house at Beaminster. When it was first equipped in 1747, eight turns (spinning-wheels) were purchased;[1] in 1771 three further spinning-wheels were acquired, and a turnhouse (spinning shed) was erected by Mr. Warr, a Beaminster builder, while the spinning path was fenced. The 1785 inventory of goods details equipment used for making yarn. There were then 21 turns in the 'Work House', and seven more turns, a post, 10 reels and seven bolts in the spinning path. In the 'Scale House' were one quilling turn and swift (a swift was a revolving frame for winding yarn on), and three balling stocks for making yarn into balls.[2] In the 1790s spinners earned 18d. a dozen runs of flax (a run was a measure of yarn) and were allowed to keep 2s. 6d. in the £ out of these earnings as a 'salary'. Oakum (loose fibre got by picking old rope to pieces) was also spun at 4½d. a run.[13]

The introduction of water-powered mills reduced the demand for work done by hand in the workhouse. In 1812 it was reported that 'Mr. Russell of Beaminster does not seem to entertain a very favourable opinion of workhouses, for he believes it is less expensive to relieve the poor at their own homes. They are not so capable of earning money in workhouses, as was the case previous to the introduction of machinery'.[14] In 1822 the spinning shed at Beaminster workhouse held only two spinning turns and four reels.[3] In 1818 it was decided to establish a 'Knitting School and School of Industry'; the 'knitting children' too were allowed to keep a small sum out of their earnings, and there are entries in the accounts of sums paid each month to knitters.[9] Socks and stockings were made, many being supplied to inmates and some occasionally sold 'in the market'. This experiment seems to have come to an end by early 1822.[3]

Sometimes the poor were allowed to go outside the workhouse to work. In 1760 it was agreed that Daniel Cox should employ Mary Gundry 'in the Spinning Way & pay her Six pence per week for One Year', while Susanna Serjeant was to be similarly employed for two years, and to receive a shilling a week the second year.[1] In 1774 the Vestry ordered that no person should work out of the house, except for children under 12, who were to be contracted for monthly; by 1784 however it had become an established rule 'to let out such poor as are not employed to work by Auction', the system being the same as that of contracting for supply of goods.[2] Contracted men out-of-doors worked on the highways or on farms, and like the spinners in the workhouse were allowed a 'salary' of 1½d. in the shilling in 1796. The total amount earned for parish funds by all the poor employed during the year 1796–7 — round about 20 people each month — was just over £225,[3] but for the reason already given, and no doubt because there were fewer able-bodied people in the house, earnings dropped after 1800.[13, 15] (The setting up of the new Poor Law Union in 1836 is dealt with in Chapter 13).

The Poor Outside

At an early stage in the operation of a parish workhouse, the Beaminster Vestry, as we have already noted, adopted a policy of refusing to grant relief outside the workhouse. This policy was reaffirmed in 1774, an exception being made for blind people, who were to be allowed 1s. 0d. per week. In 1783 the Vestry protested against charges in an overseers' account for outside relief, 'the same being contrary to, and in defiance of a standing order of Vestry', and the rules of 1785 stated that only people incapable of being moved to the workhouse, or suffering from some infectious disease, were to receive outside relief. The Vestry had been forced to make an exception to its own rule in the winter of 1784, when in February it was agreed 'on account of very inclement weather' to relieve the poor out of the workhouse 'whilst the severe Weather lasted and the Snow lay on the Ground...'. There is an entry in the accounts for payment made 'to a number of parishioners out of imployment sent to Beaminster Down to throw up the Road... in the Frost & Snow' — cold comfort indeed at a height of 700 feet![2] In 1795 the Vestry was obliged to relax its rules to a more significant extent.

General opinion had been swinging round towards giving outdoor relief, and Gilbert's Act of 1782 legitimised a policy already being practised by many parishes. The outbreak of war with France, and several poor harvests in the last decade of the 18th century, led to shortage of corn and a steep rise in the price of bread. This forced even men who were in employment to seek assistance for their families, and it was better to help them outside — the workhouses could not in any case accommodate them all. In 1792 the J.P.s at Dorchester passed a resolution to the effect that relief should be given to supplement an applicant's pay in order to achieve a comfortable standard; they did not make any specific recommendation like that of the Speenhamland justices, who laid down a scale based on the price of bread. A meeting of the gentlemen, clergy and freeholders of the county of Dorset held in 1795 agreed to raise a county subscription from which to subsidize the price of bread sold to the poor.[16]

Beaminster decided to raise its own fund 'exclusively for poor inhabitants of the parish, without any participation with the general subscription raised in the County'. On 14 June 1795 a meeting of the subscribers to the Beaminster fund 'for reducing the Price of Bread to the necessitous poor' resolved that a list should be made of those who were to have the benefit of buying the subsidized bread. The amount of the subsidy given varied. For the first two weeks the half-peck wheaten loaf was sold at 1s. 3d. and from 28 June to 26 July the price was 1s. 4d. For the next week the subsidy was 4d. a loaf, reduced to 3d. for the week beginning 2 August. At this point the subscribers' fund seems to have been running out. However, in the meantime, Robert Barfoot, merchant, had arranged to sell to the bakers 24 bags of flour per week for five weeks at 69 shillings per bag, and was proposing that the bread should be retailed to inhabitants of the parish only at 1s. 10d. a loaf. On 9 August the Vestry (no longer the 'subscribers') agreed that this bread should be sold to the necessitous poor at 1s. 7d. and to those not on the list at 1s. 10d., the 3d. allowance to be debited in the overseers' accounts. Supply of subsidized bread continued until 6 September, the allowance being reduced to 2d on 23 August; the total amount debited 9 August–6 September was £15 9s. 2d. in respect of 1,532 loaves, or 383 loaves a week.[5]

The accounts show that outside relief continued, and indeed tended to increase from this time. For various reasons the period between the end of the Napoleonic wars (1815) and the accession of Victoria (1837) was a very difficult one for the rural labourer. This led to riots in the countryside in parts of southern England: these do not seem to have affected Beaminster, but it was never again possible to maintain a policy of not granting relief outside. In 1834 D. O. P. Okeden, the Assistant Poor Law Commissioner, stated that the system of relieving in workhouses had been almost abandoned in the county, the only inmates of the Dorset workhouses being the aged, the infirm, and orphans.[17]

In the Bridport Division of West Dorset the administration of the poor outside the workhouse in the earlier 19th century was based on a system of family allowances to bring family earnings up to an agreed level. In Beaminster records exist of the earnings of poor families over the period 1820 to 1836. These show the man's name and the weekly amount earned if employed — this was left blank if unemployed, and sometimes 'ill' was inserted. Underneath are entered the wife's earnings (if any), and the children's names, ages, and amounts earned; sometimes the name of the employer or place of employment and the occupation of the children are given.[18] Another volume, covering the period March 1835 to July 1836, contains accounts of money and food given to labourers out of work. On the first page is a scale laid down on 12 May 1834, indicating the daily level to which wages were to be made up:

Single man	8d.	Man, wife & 3 children	13d.
Man & wife	9d.	Man, wife & 4 children	14d.
Man, wife & 1 child	10d.	Man, wife & 5 children	15d.
Man, wife & 2 children	12d.	Man, wife & 6 children	16d.

Underneath is a note that the earnings of the family were to be deducted. The lists of men show day by day the days out of work, the entitlement as above, and the relief given weekly. Part of this was in bread and potatoes, the quantity varying with the size of the family; the remainder was in a cash allowance. The number of men out of work varied: usually there were about 12, but sometimes only four or five, and sometimes up to 20, depending on the time of year.[19] The numbers seem low, considering that in 1831 there were 725 males of 20 years and over in the parish.

In order to keep down the number of pauper children in the workhouse, it was the custom of the Beaminster Vestry to apprentice them out, usually until they reached the age of 24 for boys and 21 for girls. In most cases this did not mean that the children learned a trade, but merely that they worked as domestic servants or farm labourers for the gentlemen, farmers and craftsmen of the parish. (An Act of 1696 gave overseers the right to compel a master to accept an apprentice in his own parish.) Out of 122 apprenticeship indentures covering the period 1697 to 1821, 105 were to masters either living in Beaminster or owning estates there, and of these 93 were apprenticeships to husbandry or housewifery. Of the remaining 12 apprenticeships within the parish, four in the early years were to weaving, one at the end of the period to twine-spinning, and the other seven (spread over the period) to fishing, chairmaking, fell-mongery, potting, butchery and baking. Although children who were apprenticed in another parish gained a settlement (giving the right to assistance from the rates) after 40 days, only 17 Beaminster children were apprenticed away. Three went to husbandry or housewifery in Netherbury and Mapperton, and one to carpentry in Netherbury. One girl was apprenticed to a clothier in Whitchurch Canonicorum in 1731; nine girls were apprenticed to twine-spinning and thread-spinning in Bridport, Bradpole and Burton Bradstock between 1805 and 1818, and three boys over the same period to flax-combing and bag-making in Bridport, and to shoethread spinning in Whitchurch Canonicorum.[20]

Some assistance was given outside the poor rates, in various ways, to the less fortunate members of the community. In 1816, for instance, a small fund was set up 'for employing such industrious Labourers and Manufacturers of the Parish of Beaminster as are out of work'. The total subscribed by 28 people was just over £141; Sir William Oglander gave £30, Samuel Cox £20, and a collection taken at the 'Meeting House' (Congregational Church) raised £1. A further £50 was contributed by the London Association for the Relief of the Industrious Poor. The money was expended on the wages of labourers who were employed on the Horn Hill road and in removing earth for widening the turnpike road at Melplash Farm.[21]

The Assistant Poor Law Commissioner reported in 1834 that in most parishes in Dorset the farmer gave or leased an allotment of land to the labourer, the size depending on the size of his family. The farmer ploughed and manured the land and carried the crop to the labourer's cottage, so that all the man had to do was to put the crop in and house it. The beginnings of the system whereby garden grounds or allotments were provided for labourers at a low rent can be traced back to the late 18th century; after the agricultural riots of 1830 the practice became very common, two Acts being passed (in 1831 and 1832) to facilitate the provision of allotments. Okeden stated that wages in the Beaminster district were the highest in the county overall: 'indulgencies' such as fuel, potato-ground, house rent and cider brought up a money wage of 7s. 0d. a week to 11s. 6d.[17]

Aid was also given by the friendly societies, whose purpose was to help their members in sickness and unemployment. In 1796 there were only 12 such societies in Dorset, but by 1855 the number had grown to 167. The first Beaminster Friendly Society, one of the earliest in Dorset, was started in 1762. About 1780 the number of members was 248; in 1853 the membership was 341, but not necessarily all Beaminster residents.[22]

Charities

Sir John Strode's almshouse. In 1775 there were five female residents in the almshouse.[4] This had been kept up by later members of the Strode family, and by the Oglanders who followed them at Parnham, regardless of the amount of income actually received from the endowment, which was by then inadequate to meet expenses. Repairs to the farmhouse at Bilshay (two-thirds of which constituted part of the endowment) and to the almshouse itself were paid for by them, and the inmates maintained.[23] In 1786 Sir William Oglander stated in a letter to the Beaminster parish officers that the total revenue did not then exceed £20 a year.[24] The houses on the chantry lands, the rents of which had been settled on the almshouse, had since disappeared, though the site of one of them, on the west of the almshouse, was let. Sir William detailed his expenses over the year in connection with the almspeople as follows:

6s. a week [1s. to each inmate]	£15 12s. 0d.
Apothecary	£ 2 0s. 0d.
2s. 6d. each to fire at Xmas	£ 0 15s. 0d.
Shoes	£ 1 1s. 0d.
6 pr. of Shoes	£ 0 6s. 4d.
4 gowns & two coats	—

The inmates were chosen 'from distressed persons of a better class, who have not generally received parochial aid'.[23]

Hillary's Charity. By his will of 1712, William Hillary of Minstead in Hampshire left his estate called Ernley Wood in Corscombe (approximately 50 acres), after the end of a term of 99 years, to 12 of the poorest distressed families of the parish of Beaminster for ever. People in receipt of parish relief were to be excluded, and assistance was confined to older married people who had brought up large families.[25, 26]

Keate's and Champion's Charities. There were two bread charities by which loaves were distributed at certain times to poor people who did not receive any other relief. Thomas Keate, mercer, designated one acre of land called Woodswater in 1709, and Francis Champion alias Clark, butcher, designated two acres called Culverhays in 1741, from the profits of which a specified number of loaves was for ever to be provided.[27, 26] In 1837 the Charity Commissioners appointed the minister and church-wardens of Beaminster to administer these two charities, there being no existing trustees.[28]

Tucker's Charity. In the early 1730s the school endowed by Frances Tucker, which had met in the church, was transferred to a building on the south side of the church-yard. The new school premises were bounded by the churchyard on the north and by orchards on the other three sides. The approach to the school house was through the churchyard, and the path ran on from the front of the house to the stream;[29] the position is shown on the plan of Charity lands dated 1776.[26] The school house was rented at first, but the trustees of Tucker's Charity purchased it in 1746. The building, which was thatched, was burnt down in the fire of 1781. (A tombstone to the memory of Betty, a daughter of William Pavy the schoolmaster, who died in the fire, stands on the west side of the churchyard.) The school house was rebuilt by Joseph and Richard Warr at a cost of just over £150, and tiles replaced the thatched roof.[30] In 1814 the school premises, which were then 'in an extremely dilapidated state, and no longer fit for the purposes of instruction',[29] were sold for £200, and were pulled down. The trustees bought a dwelling house and malt-house at Shortmoor from Samuel Cox for £500; repairs were carried out to the master's house, and the malt-house converted into a school house, at a further cost of about £150.[30]

In 1784 the trustees resolved that the schoolmaster should in future be chosen yearly at their annual meeting, when they would make out a list of boys from which he was to fill the vacancies arising in the school during the coming year. Boys were not to be admitted until they were between eight and ten years of age, and were not to continue at the school longer than four years. (By the time they were 11 or 12 years old, their parents would want their help in agricultural work.) The salary of the school-master was still £20 a year; from 1786 £4 was allowed for providing the boys with paper, pens and ink.[30] In the earlier 19th century the rent of the estate at Marsh Farm increased considerably: in 1836 it was £160.[31] It was no longer necessary to limit the number of poor boys to the 20 prescribed in Frances Tucker's will, and there were 111 boys on the books, 80 of whom attended regularly; the salary of the master had been raised to £50. Reading, writing and arithmetic, and the Church of England catechism, were taught, using the system of 'monitors' pioneered in Madras by the Reverend Dr. Bell.[29] The actual number of boys apprenticed out depended on the state of the charity funds, the average being four or five each year.[23] The trustees did not always find it possible to bind two boys to a master mariner (as provided in the will), owing to 'a general dislike to go to sea prevailing amongst the youths' of the district.[29]

In 1872 Tucker's Free School ceased to exist as such, though the former malt-house continued in use as a school for some years (see Chapter 15). The building was demolished in 1883.[32]

Another part of the funds was being used to supply coal to the poor at a reduced price. In 1789 the Vestry had been forced to take steps to stop poor people stealing wood for fuel, a complaint being made that the 'Trees, Hedges, Coppices, and other Wood growing in this Parish have been of late Years greatly injured by divers poor Persons unlawfully cutting lopping and destroying the Same . . .'.[2] Under Frances

Tucker's will there was a legacy of £20 a year which eventually fell to be devoted to 'pious uses',[31] and in 1798 the trustees ordered that £10 should be advanced out of this fund to lay in a stock of wood and coal, which would be kept in a coal-house at the workhouse for re-sale to the poor;[30] in 1837 the £20 was being regularly expended in the purchase of coal for this purpose.[23]

Tucker's Charity schoolhouse at Shortmoor

CHAPTER TEN

PEOPLE AND SOCIETY 1700-1850

Anglicans and Nonconformists

AFTER THE PERIOD of steady growth which nonconformity experienced in England in the later 17th century, the cause suffered a considerable decline during the earlier part of the 18th century. It was only after a fresh impetus had been given by the work of John Wesley and his followers, leading to the establishment of Methodism, that the older forms of dissent also took on a new lease of life by 1800. By the mid-19th century nonconformity had established itself as about equal in terms of attendances with the Church of England over the country as a whole. The county of Dorset was however among the more Anglican counties: in 1676, of inhabitants above 16 years old (59,000), only 1,600 were known to be dissenters,[1] and in 1851, when the one and only religious census was taken, the total sittings were 65 per cent. Anglican and 35 per cent. Nonconformist.[2] The sittings in the parish church at Beaminster on 30 March 1851 represented about 60 per cent. of the total, the Congregational and Methodist churches providing the other 40 per cent.,[3] but the nonconformist percentage was to be considerably reduced with the opening of Holy Trinity church only a couple of months later. The actual attendance figures in any case suggest a rather lower proportion of nonconformists.

Congregational church

From the time of its formation up to 1900 the records of the old 'Protestant Dissenting Congregation' in Beaminster were held by private persons; most of those from before 1781 were lost at the house of James Daniel in Hogshill Street in the great fire of that year. Richard Hine the historian said in a lecture given at the chapel at the end of the 19th century:

> I am pleased to state that a few papers & books of immense value to this Church & Congregation have been passed down from generation to generation by my ancestors to me, but are now safely deposited in this building.[4]

The account which follows is based mainly on these documents.

Up to the middle of the 18th century, the nonconformists were still meeting in private houses; J. B. Russell tells us: 'Of late years the Dissenters here have been united, which I imagine is owing to their numbers diminishing — but formerly they had separate Ministers & held different meetings'.[5] In 1738 the Rev. Josiah Bradshaw of Beaminster was ordained at Bridport, at what was almost certainly a Presbyterian ordination.[6] In 1745 the Rev. John Bryant succeeded him as minister of the meeting-

124

house in East Street, and remained 30 years. At the time Mr. Bryant took over, there were about 200 people attending the meeting-house, 'consisting without exception of all the principal people in the town'.[7] Perhaps the decline came later in the rural communities than elsewhere: at Beaminster they were sufficiently confident of the future to decide to build a more commodious meeting-house.

In 1749 the existing building 'or such other meeting house or Building as shall hereafter be built . . .' was made over to John Daniel, apothecary, and Samuel Cox, ironmonger, on trust 'to be resorted to and made use of for and as a publick presbyterian meeting house, in such manner and as the same now is and for severall years last past has been so resorted and made use of . . .'. At the same time a plot adjoining the house was acquired, the intention being to pull down the meeting-house and rebuild it farther back from the street; the 'new' meeting-house was tucked away behind a row of cottages which then occupied the front part of the site of the present Congregational church, and was approached by a narrow passage.[8] According to a later note in one of the minute books (1801), it was built under the direction of Samuel Cox, and he probably paid much of the cost.[9] Entries in an early account book show that it was originally thatched, 8s. 5d. being paid in 1762 for reed, spars and two days' work by thatcher and boy; the roof was tiled, at a cost of £22 2s. 8d. in 1778. There was a gallery, as the seats in it were repaired in 1776. Frequent sums for mending windows, and for new locks to doors and gate, suggest that damage was constantly being done by people unsympathetic to the cause.[10]

The few records which have survived from before 1781 do not suggest a very large community. A list of members dated January 1760 contains 33 names, including those of Edward Hitt senior, Mrs. Catherine Hitt, Dr. John Daniel and his wife, Edward Gerrard, Stephen Hallett of Melplash; 19 members had died or left the chapel since 1747. Two-thirds of the names on a list of 45 subscribers (dated 1761) do not seem to be those of members, and it is here we find the 'three Mr. Cox's'. Between 1761 and 1775 the annual sum collected for the minister's salary and the upkeep of the building was £25 to £35. From the midsummer of 1775 new increased subscriptions were agreed on 'by the Members and others of this Congregation', and these amounted to £55 to £65 (including £10 from Messrs. Cox), with a further subscription for the minister's rent from the better-off; there were only 38 subscribers.[10]

From the earlier 18th century Arianism had been a feature of West Country Presbyterian communities, and the Rev. Samuel Fawcett (minister 1776–90) was eventually forced to resign owing to his preaching being coloured by Arian attitudes.[11] This doctrinal dispute was to lead to the break-up of the old English Presbyterianism, those who wished to retain the orthodox Calvinistic theology usually forming Independent Congregations, which were in due course inherited by the Congregationalists; in the earlier 19th century Beaminster described itself as an Independent Congregation.

After several ministers who only stayed a short time, the Rev. John Rogers was invited to become the minister in 1796, and he remained for 13 years. During his ministry Beaminster came under the influence of the Evangelical Revival, Mr. Rogers holding prayer-meetings and being very active in the neighbourhood. Nonconformists had begun to realise that a rigid independency was not helpful to further evangelism, and that it led also to great disparity in the resources of congregations and in ministerial emoluments. Among the many county-based associations formed was one set up by

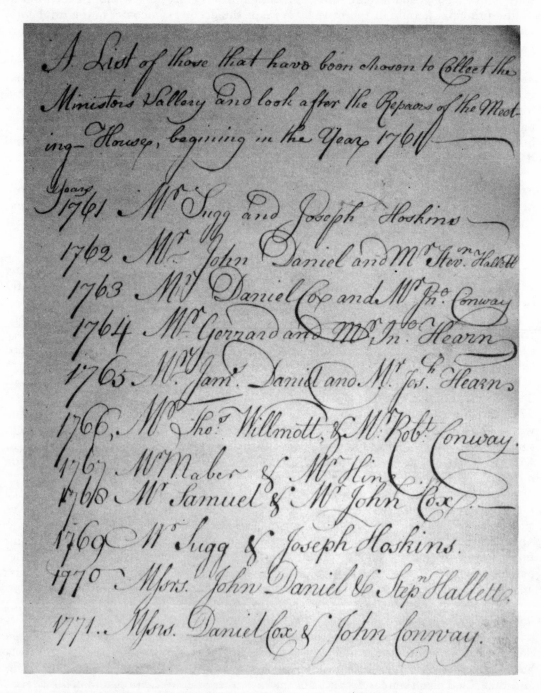

Fig. 10. Page from Congregational chapel account book, later 18th century.

the Independent ministers in Dorset in 1795; this met at Beaminster in 1798 and again in 1803. In 1807 the Sunday school, which had been started at some earlier date but which had then not met for a year or more, was re-established, a room being rented from Ann Tuck next door to the meeting-house.[9]

Mr. Rogers only received a salary of some £70, but the Rev. William Judson, who succeeded him, was promised 100 guineas a year free of taxes, and a house. The Rev. Alfred Bishop was offered £105 to £110 in 1828, with the pledge that it would 'most probably be increased', and 81 people signed the letter of invitation. This represents a financial high-water mark in the records of the church, which seems to have taken on a fresh lease of life, with quite a number of new members in the first 30 years or so of the 19th century.[9] Some 260 baptisms are recorded between 1796 and 1836, though this figure would include children of adherents from the neighbourhood.[12]

After the death of Samuel (the last of the 'three Mr. Cox's') in 1801, the family ceased to be regular subscribers and indeed were held by Mr. Rogers to be 'no Friends to Religion'. Samuel Cox himself had not been a member, but a 'constant Hearer'. The Daniel family must have adhered to the Church of England after the death of James in 1797, though they continued to be buried at Knowle; there were no Daniels among the 36 members and subscribers of church and congregation who invited Mr. Judson in 1810.[9] The Hines were now the most prominent family: Thomas Hine, broadcloth maker (deacon in 1796), had been one of the subscribers from 1764; he collected the funds from 1775 to 1814.[10] Richard Hine, linen manufacturer (a son of Thomas), and Richard Hine, grocer, who was Thomas's half-brother and also became a deacon, subsequently took a very active part in the chapel's financial affairs.[13]

The prospects of the community must have seemed bright, and as the general atmosphere had improved, it was decided to enlarge the chapel by extending it to the road, the cottages having meantime disappeared. A plaque on the present building states that it was built in 1749 and enlarged in 1826, but whether the new building actually incorporates part of the old one is not known — there is no obvious structural evidence to suggest it does. The early 19th-century chapel is very lofty, and it is most improbable that the 1749 building soared over the adjacent cottages in this way. The documents relating to the enlargement are missing, but a list of subscribers entitled 'Inhabitants of Beaminster and members of the congregation' includes the names of several prominent people who were not Congregationalists.[14] A letter sent to the Rev. Alfred Bishop shows that £600 was still owing to the builder in 1828, and assistance was being sought from neighbouring communities.[13] In 1846 the house adjoining was purchased, and both a Sunday school and a day school were conducted in part of the premises.[15] No fewer than four deacons — Benjamin Seymour (ironmonger), Robert Conway (rope and twine maker), Joseph Tite (flax-spinner) and George Brough (linen draper) — were appointed in 1840.[9]

On 30 March 1851, there were 452 sittings in the chapel (180 free seats and 272 others); the congregation on that morning consisted of 150 general congregation together with 50 Sunday school scholars. The afternoon congregation was the same, and the evening attendance consisted of 150 general congregation. Some people would have attended more than once in the day. Mr. Bishop added the remark 'The number regularly attending either one part of the day or another abt 200'; he was a powerful and popular preacher, and the congregation was probably augmented by visitors from the surrounding area.[3]

A number of Independent communities had in fact been started in the villages of the neighbourhood. In the parish of Broadwindsor, Venn near Stoney Knapp had apparently been an Independent chapel from 1816, although by 1851 it had been taken over by the Baptists; an Independent chapel was opened at Blackdown in 1821.[3] In 1838 a new Independent chapel was built at Stoke Abbott, where the community had met at Wood Mill from the late 18th century; the land was given by Robert Conway of the Beaminster chapel.[16] Other chapels were opened at Marshwood (1832), Salway Ash (1842), and Rampisham (1849); at Rampisham the preacher on 30 March 1851 was Benjamin Seymour from Beaminster.[3]

Congregational support was however already beginning to decline in Beaminster by the 1830s and 1840s as the textile industries died out. The main supporters had always been families in the manufacturing trades in the town: in earlier days the Keates, Coxs and Willmotts, and more recently the Hines, Conways, Giffords and Tites. These were the very people who were leaving the town for London and other parts of the country, or in some instances to emigrate to the United States, as is clear from numerous entries in the membership lists.[9]

Wesleyan Methodist church

The earliest reference to Methodism in Beaminster is made by J. B. Russell, who wrote (about 1797) 'In North Street is a Methodist Meeting House'.[17] Our main source of information, however, is a manuscript book written by the Rev. John Stevens (Wesleyan Supernumerary Minister of Bridport) in 1856–7. He tells us that a Wesleyan Society was formed at Bridport in 1808 as part of the South Petherton circuit.[18] A missionary effort was made in the vicinity, and in 1811 the Rev. William Flint, accompanied by William Tutcher of Bridport, preached at a house in Beaminster; the Vicar of Netherbury and Beaminster, Rev. W. J. Brookland, 'came in to complain of their intrusion into his parish'. It was not until a few years later, in 1815, that a small society was formed which met for a time in the house of a Mr. Bunt.[19] From 1813 Bridport had belonged to a new Axminster circuit,[20] and although the society in Beaminster faded out, preachers from Axminster preached regularly once a fortnight on a Wednesday evening, and local preachers conducted a service on Sunday evenings.[21] These meetings were held in Fleet Street, in a loft at the back of a house then occupied by John Hallett, baker.[22] After 1823 the society (re-formed in 1821) again broke up and Beaminster was abandoned by the Methodists for quite a number of years.[23]

Bridport, where the cause had flourished, became the head of a circuit in 1834,[24] and in 1837 the Wesleyan Methodist ministers stationed there obtained permission to use the 'Town Hall' at Beaminster for meetings; 'the attendance generally was large'.[25] One hundred years after John Wesley 'felt his heart strangely warmed', a chapel was built in Fleet Street, next door to the house where meetings had once been held; an inscription on the building reads 'Wesleyan Centenary Chapel 1839'. The mason's work was carried out by Robert Chambers, and the carpenter's work by Richard Warr; the building cost about £470. Beaminster subscriptions amounted to £100, but £253 was subscribed from Bridport and other places in the circuit.[26] We are told by the Rev.

John Stevens that no chapel had been erected in the circuit to which Methodists in Bridport had not contributed, and he goes on to say 'Of some of these country chapels a few individuals have to bear the whole burden', and that this was the case with Beaminster.[27]

We have the names of some of the people connected with the chapel in its earlier days. George Chambers, to whose memory a plaque was later erected in the chapel by his family, must have been its first Society and Chapel Steward, as he was appointed to these offices in 1839. He was also made a class leader, and superintendent of the Sunday school. He died in 1852, but while he lived 'The Wesleyan cause in Beaminster lay near his heart, and he took an earnest interest in promoting its prosperity to the best of his ability'.[28] Mrs. Hannah Guy also joined the society in 1839, and was leader of a women's class for 10 years.[29] Other names which have come down to us are those of Francis Nossiter (chapel steward 1844), William Clare (leader 1851), and Charles Lawrence (Society Steward 1855).[30]

A number of new chapels had been opened at places in the vicinity of Bridport and Beaminster, including Uploders (1827), Netherbury (1828), Netherhay (1838), Mosterton (1842), Nettlecombe (1843), Salway Ash (1846) and West Bay (1849).[3, 31] (Societies were in existence at most of these places some years before special chapel buildings came into use.) The membership of the Bridport circuit began to rise from 1838, when it was 208; the peak — in 1850 — was 425.[32] For a while things in Beaminster 'appeared very promising'.[33] On 30 March 1851 there were in the morning 53 people in the general congregation at the Beaminster chapel, together with 54 Sunday school scholars, while in the evening the congregation numbered 105. The number of sittings was 210, 114 free seats and 96 others.[3] The Methodists, however, for the same reasons as the Congregationalists, were beginning to suffer from a decline in both membership and congregation.

Anglican churches

Apart from the building of galleries (referred to elsewhere), the only significant alterations to the parish church in this period were the rebuilding of the north porch in 1830,[34] and the recasting of the bells. It was agreed in 1764 that on account of their poor condition 'the five bells be taken down and new cast into eight . . . and that new chimes be made to go on the said bells'. The bells, which were recast in a weaving shed that adjoined the churchyard, were made by Thomas Bilbie of Cullompton.[35]

The sittings in the church in 1851 were 980 (426 free, 554 other), and attendance on 30 March was as follows: in the morning general congregation 512 and Sunday school 222, in the afternoon general congregation 474 and Sunday school 221, and in the evening a congregation of 627.[3]

In 1849 Beaminster was separated from Netherbury and became a distinct benefice with its own vicar.[36] The new district church of Holy Trinity, which was built at Shortmoor between 1849 and 1851, had 404 sittings; it was in Early English style, of flint or random stonework with Ham stone dressings, quoins and buttresses. The architects were Carver and Giles of Taunton, and the builder John Chick was assisted by William and Robert Chambers, all Beaminster men.[37]

Some Leading Families

Men from all walks of life, and all religious beliefs, joined together in the community for sport and the celebration of national events. Cricket would certainly have been played, and J. B. Russell notes that on 21 September 1780 there was horse-racing for the first time on Hollymoor Common.[38] The church bells were rung for the military victories of the Duke of Marlborough in the early 18th century, and at all coronations. When William IV was crowned in 1831, the town band paraded the street, playing 'God save the King' and 'Rule Britannia'. The 'gentlemen' dined at the *White Hart*, while the 'humbler inhabitants were gladdened by a distribution of about seventy score [a weight of 20 or 21 lbs.] of fat beef ...'. Captain Bishop of Northfield Farm regaled his labourers and their families, nearly a hundred people, with 'two fat sheep, roast beef, plum pudding, etc.'[39] The coronation of Queen Victoria in 1838 was celebrated 'by a distribution of beef and beer to upwards of four hundred poor families in the parish'; the school children were given tea and cake on Thomas Frampton's factory green at Yarn Barton.[40]

In 1798, under the threat of Napoleonic invasion, the men of Beaminster united to form a corps of infantry known as the Beaminster Loyal Town Volunteers. An assembly was sounded one night, probably in 1799, but it proved to be a false alarm; the force was disbanded in 1814. The captain was Samuel Cox junior, and the lieutenants J. B. Russell and Baruch Fox; Giles Russell was a sergeant, while the ensign was Joseph Bishop and the sergeant-major Henry Willmott.[41] There are many other familiar names among the 86 volunteers.[42]

Among the families of importance during this period were those of Cox, Russell, Daniel and Hine; the leading families of Hoskins and Hillary had disappeared before 1700, and the Oglanders, who replaced the Strodes in 1764, were often absent from Parnham during their first 40 years there.

Cox. This family, descendants of Lancelot Cox, had emerged as the leading family of the town soon after the middle of the 18th century. When Samuel Cox made his survey of the parish in 1775, the family had properties all over the town, many of them owned earlier by the Hoskins family; they had land at Barrowfield and Whitcombe. There were then three brothers: Samuel and Daniel, who were merchants and manufacturers of linen cloth, and John, a doctor. They were the sons of Samuel Cox (died 1741) and his second wife Mary, daughter of William Painter.[43] It seems to have been Samuel the merchant, not his brother Daniel, who bought the manor house and Northfield farm from William Buckler, a descendant of the Gifford family, about 1767,[44] though the estate may have belonged jointly to him and one of his brothers. At any rate Samuel outlived the other two (Daniel died in 1778, John in 1783), and was responsible for the fine monument commemorating the three brothers which is in the north aisle of St Mary's church. (The family were now Anglicans, though remaining 'on the Low Church side'.[45]) In 1797 Samuel became lord of the manor of Beaminster Secunda, as lessee of the prebendary.[44] He apparently had no children, for his heir was his nephew Samuel.[46]

Samuel junior, sail-cloth manufacturer, was married in 1790 to Ann, daughter of Richard Symes, barrister-at-law, then living at Farrs; it was a runaway match at Gretna Green. Three of their sons became well known in Beaminster: Samuel (1790–1860),

Peter (1800-1892), and George. Samuel, who married Virtue, daughter and co-heiress of John Banger Russell, in 1816, inherited the manor house estate on the death of his father in 1822;[46] he and George carried on the sail-cloth factory. Samuel was very prominent in all local affairs: he was Deputy Lieutenant of the County and Chairman of the local Board of Guardians. He took an active part in the erection of Holy Trinity church, giving the land for the site and the sum of £150, the third highest amount.[47] Peter Cox became a solicitor, joining John Banger Russell in 1822; he married Anne, daughter of William Leigh of Bardon, in 1826, and in 1830 his office was in East Street adjoining his house (Farrs).[48]

Russell. In 1756 John Russell, attorney, who had been practising at Dorchester with a Mr. Willis, came to Beaminster to set up on his own, and so became the founder of the firm later known as Kitson & Trotman.[49] In 1775 he was living at Champions in Hogshill Street;[50] he died in 1808. The Beaminster historian John Banger Russell, son of John and his wife Virtue, was born in 1760; he married Mary, daughter of Daniel Cox, in 1782,[49] and in 1824 he was in Hogshill Street,[48] no doubt at Champions. He died in 1827 and there is a mural tablet to his memory in the north aisle of the parish church. His only son became a clergyman, and so he took Peter Cox, to whom he was related through his wife, into the practice. After John Banger Russell's retirement in 1826, the business was carried on by Peter Cox under his own name until 1851, when he took James Warden into partnership.[51]

We can only suppose that the reason the firm did not perpetuate the name 'Russell' was that there was another firm of solicitors of this name in Beaminster at the time, that of Giles (1768-1839), a younger son of John and Virtue.[49] In 1792 Giles — no doubt in anticipation of his marriage in January 1793 — took a lease of the house near Prout Bridge later known as Beridth, and in 1830 Giles and his son Thomas were solicitors there.[48] Giles Russell was prime mover in getting the tunnel built at Horn Hill. Thomas Russell, who gave £150 towards the building of Holy Trinity church in 1848,[52] practised as a solicitor on his own at Beridth until at least 1867;[48] he died in 1872. (His son, also Thomas, went into the army.)

Daniel. In the mid-18th century there were living in Beaminster two prominent descendants of the James Daniel who fought at the Battle of Sedgemoor: their names were James and John. Like his grandfather, James went in for the law; in 1793 he was one of the coroners of the county.[48] He died in 1797, and is buried in the earliest tomb at Knowle.[53] The relationship between James and John — 'celebrated surgeon of this town' — who died in 1781 and is buried with his wife Hannah on the south side of St Mary's churchyard, is not clear. (They could have been brothers or cousins: James of Sedgemoor had two sons, named of course John and James.) In 1775 the farm at Knowle was on lease to a tenant, and the Daniels had two houses in Beaminster; the old family home on the corner of Hogshill Street and Shadrack Street was occupied by James, while John lived on or near the site of the house later known as The Walnuts at Prout Bridge.[50]

The John Daniel who died in 1829, and is buried at Knowle with his wife Betsy, was the first (apart from the 'celebrated surgeon') in a line of doctors. He was probably James's younger son; by 1809 he owned the property at Prout Bridge, from now on usually occupied by the younger member or branch of the family. Both his sons,

James William (died 1859) and Thomas Palmer (died 1853), also buried at Knowle, were surgeons;[54] in 1843 James William was at the house in Hogshill Street, while Thomas Palmer owned the house at Prout Bridge.[55]

Hine. Thomas Hine of Powerstock, yeoman, whose will was proved in 1780,[56] seems to have been married twice, and had two families. His eldest son Thomas, the broad-cloth maker, married Elizabeth Daniel, daughter of James the coroner, in 1761, and was buried in the Knowle burial ground in 1817.[53] Thomas and Elizabeth had 11 children; baptisms of the five youngest are recorded in a Congregational chapel register:[57] In 1797 Thomas Hine bought No. 19 Hogshill Street; the house belonged to his son Richard, sail-cloth maker, from 1818 until his death in 1837.[58] Another son, Thomas, born in 1775, emigrated to France in 1792 and later gave his name to the firm which became Hine's Cognac.[56]

Richard Hine (1768-1844), a younger son of Thomas of Powerstock, was apprenticed in 1782 to Thomas Fisher, a grocer in Dorchester. Later on he worked for a Mr. Butt at Warminster, and planned to open a grocery business of his own in Beaminster. In a letter dated 3 December 1791 Mr. Fisher advised him against doing this, because so many people had gone in for that line of business recently and Beaminster was 'so near Bridport, where every article in the whole Grocery trade is in fact given away owing to a spirit of opposition . . .'.[59] However, Richard Hine carried out his intention, and his business went well, for we learn from an entry in a Congregational chapel minute book (1797) that 'the Lord having blessed him with prosperity in his secular business' he gave a building in Powerstock to be fitted out at his own expense as a place of worship.[9] He appears to have owned the whole property in The Square now occupied by the pharmacy (No. 23) and the grocers (No. 24), having acquired it from Henry Hart, mercer.[60]

The second Richard Hine (1803-1878), one of the sons of the first, was in 1821 apprenticed for three years to Ambrose Larkworthy, druggist, of Weymouth;[59] he is often distinguished in records from his father (grocer) and from Richard (sail-cloth maker) by the addition of 'druggist' after his name. When Richard (grocer) retired, the present pharmacy premises became (in 1838) the property of another son, Philip, wine merchant (1810-1867); yet another son, Benjamin, was then running the grocery business next door.[59, 61] Richard, druggist, probably had his shop at No. 12 The Square, which he or his father owned in 1843.[55]

In 1844 — the year that Richard (grocer) died — the grocery premises were leased to George Stocker, grocer, who bought the stock; presumably the younger Richard preferred to concentrate on the drug trade. In March 1852 Richard took into partnership his son Alfred (1826-1882), who had trained with Randall & Son, chemists of Southampton, and gave notice that the tea and grocery business was to be commenced 'in the old established shop in the market place where the above trade has been conducted by his family for more than a half-century'; the drug business was to be kept quite distinct, and to be transacted in the same shop as it had been for the past 20 years, although both would be conducted under the name Hine & Son.[59] A photograph taken about 1865 shows 'Hine and Son' over No. 12 The Square.[62] Richard, druggist, retired in 1868,[63] and No. 12 was occupied from at least 1874 by the printer T. Patten Coombs.

Meanwhile Philip Hine, who had purchased Hitts House about 1847, seems to have carried on the wine business there; his shop in the market place (No. 23) was empty in the 1850s. A photograph of 1874 shows 'Hine and Son' over the grocers (No. 24), but in 1876 Alfred Hine was occupier of Philip's former premises next door as well.[64] In 1880 Alfred appears as chemist only, and the grocery was probably in other hands; by 1899 Henry Herbert Hill was the grocer at the corner shop.[48] (Philip's son John, who came from Stalbridge to take over the wine business when his father died in 1867, and remained in Beaminster until 1880, presumably ran it from Hitts.[65])

Inscription on a barn at Barrowfield

PART FOUR — 1850-1950

CHAPTER ELEVEN

TOWN AND PARISH 1850-1950

Population

ALTHOUGH THE DECLINE in industries was beginning to be felt by the 1830s, it was not until 1851 that the census showed an actual fall in the population of Beaminster parish. After reaching its peak in 1841 (at 3,270), the population suffered such a severe fall over the next 40 years that in 1881 it was back again just below the total for 1801, at 2,130. During the 40 years following it fell again, so that in 1921 it was only about half what it had been in 1841, at 1,651.[1] Between 1841 and 1921 the population of England and Wales rose by 138 per cent. Some time after 1931 the population of Beaminster began to rise again, but we do not know exactly when, as no census was taken in 1941.

The census reports show that the fall in population did not proceed at an even pace throughout. Between 1841 and 1851 there was a sharp fall of 13.4 per cent., and in the following 10 years a fall of 7.7. per cent., while between 1861 and 1871 the fall was quite small. The main cause of the dwindling population over the period to 1861 was the decline and eventual disappearance of virtually all the small industries; the census reports refer in 1861 to emigration, and in 1871 to the closure of two flax mills. Dorset had no large centres to encourage the railway developers, and the routes taken by the railway lines were both a result of the lack of attraction of the smaller towns, with their decaying industries, and a cause of the further decline of many such centres. In both 1861 and 1871 there is a reference to houses having been destroyed by fire or pulled down: the number of inhabited houses in Beaminster fell from 642 in 1841 to 571 in 1871.[1] The galleries in the church were taken down in 1860-1;[2] the north and south galleries then standing had only been built in 1828.[3]

Between 1871 and 1881 Beaminster had another sharp fall in population, by 17.6 per cent., and there were further falls of 10.1 per cent. (1881-91), and 11.1 per cent. (1891-1901). The number of inhabited houses had dropped to 459 by 1891.[1] Although by no means all those who left the countryside were agricultural labourers, the decline in rural populations at this time is mainly attributed to the movement from the land, which by the 1870s had spread to the south-western counties.

Between 1901 and 1911 there was a distinct rise in the population of Beaminster, which went up by 9.3 per cent., from 1,702 to 1,860. This feature, like the smaller fall of 1861-71, is common to all rural areas, and indeed in some parishes an actual rise occurs in the earlier period as well. In the case of Beaminster, the large number of skilled workmen brought into the town in connection with extensive alterations going on at Parnham contributed to the increase.[4] Between 1911 and 1931 the population was again falling, unemployment probably causing further movement from the rural areas.

The populations of most of the larger parishes in the Beaminster Poor Law Union dropped significantly after 1841; the only exceptions were Misterton and Evershot, where railway stations were opened. The census report of 1851 mentions emigration as a factor at Netherbury, Halstock and Corscombe. At Mosterton (1851), and at Netherbury, Hooke and Stoke Abbott (1861 and 1871), falls in population were linked to the closing or burning down of flax mills, or to 'a decline in the flax and hemp trade'.[1]

The Town

It has been suggested that small towns like Beaminster which were bypassed by the railway 'virtually ceased to be towns at all'.[5] I have found no real evidence for this, although in the late 1860s we are told: 'As a place of business and bustle, Beaminster has no great pretensions, and it suffers from the want of direct railway accommodation ... Its staple is agriculture, and the trades associated therewith'.[6] This was probably more true of the town from the latter part of the 19th century up to the Second World War than it had been for some hundreds of years before, while many of its inhabitants worked part-time in a number of industries. The sense of isolation and dependence on its own 'neighbourhood' is brought out in speeches made by Charles Toleman (iron-monger) at the Tradesmen's and Agricultural Dinners held in 1908. He said that they were a long way from anywhere 'and the tradespeople had to depend a good deal upon each other for business ... they were so well supported by their friends the farmers that it was a pleasure to do business in the town'.[7] The first hint of yet another change was seen between the wars when 'outsiders' moved in to build the odd bunga-low or renovate a cottage. In 1925 Vickery & Kyrle of London approached the parish council for permission to produce a town guide which 'had been found a most bene-ficial form of propaganda for Towns desirous of bringing their claims before Visitors'.[8]

We are of course back on the old argument of what does or does not constitute a town. Maybe the final arbiter is what the actual place considers itself to be: 'if the inhabitants of a settlement believe it to be a town then it is a town'.[9] Beaminster was regarded as a town by contemporary people throughout this period. In 1836 it had been chosen as the focal point of the new Poor Law Union: 24 Dorset parishes and two Somerset ones, forming nearly a parallelogram 16 miles long and 10 miles broad, were included in the union, with Beaminster placed 'as nearly as possible in the centre of its incorporation'[10] This same area, with only minor changes, became that of the Beaminster Rural District Council, and also the Registration District for births and deaths. Petty sessions were held at Beaminster once a fortnight in the 1830s; in 1867 special and petty sessions were held every alternate month, and petty sessions for magisterial and criminal business every fortnight. A police station was established in Beaminster after the Police Act of 1856 which set up the Dorset County Constabulary, and Supt. P. W. MacHale of the Bridport Division was appointed to Beaminster; in 1899 the force of Supt. G. Brooks consisted of four sergeants and 20 constables.[11]

In the early 20th century, with the building of new premises, including boarding houses, for Beaminster and Netherbury Grammar School, the school became important as an educational centre for a wide area: in 1914 Richard Hine mentions the splendid work which it was doing 'not only for the boys and girls of the immediate neighbourhood, but for the whole county of Dorset'.[12]

In 1906 Sir Frederick Treves described Beaminster in the following terms:

> . . . a clean, cheerful, self-respecting county town, without pretensions, without offensively modern houses, and without red-brick suburbs. There are a few thatched cottages in the streets, but Beaminster mostly affects a cosy, yellow-brown stone and ruddy tiles for its dwelling-places. No two houses in the town are alike. They . . . are much given to stone porticos and ample bow windows, full of red geraniums. Beaminster is never puffed up, and never obtrusive . . . [13]

The market cross in the Square was erected in 1906 by Vincent Robinson of Parnham as a memorial to his sister Julia; it is constructed of local and Ham stone, and has finials of Portland stone brought from Christ's Hospital in London. There was comparatively little new private building in the town between 1850 and 1950. Houses were erected to replace ones damaged or destroyed by fire, which affected property in most of the streets at one time or another during the later 19th century.[14] After serious floods in 1894, some cottages at Prout Bridge were demolished; Dover House there bears the date 1897.

London House, an imposing building on the north side of Hogshill Street, was erected in 1862, and Hamilton Lodge, another notable dwelling nearby, also seems to be of the later 19th century. In Church Street a brick building (King's Villa) bears the date 1901 and initials T.H.; Martock Cottage in Clay Lane has the date 1852 and initials T.G.M., while the cottage next door has the same date and initials J.T. (for John Trevett). A pair of semi-detached houses was built in 1913 on the former site of the pound, at the corner of Stoke Road, by builder Edwin Bailey. A few houses went up here and there on the outskirts for retired tradesmen and professional people.

Many of the streets seem to have had more than one name. The eastern end of Hogshill Street was at one time White Hart Street, while East Street was known as High Street. Early this century Whitcombe Road was called East Road, and the hill down to Prout Bridge was for a time Bank Hill. The Fore Place or Market Place was already referred to as Market Square or The Square before the First World War.

Shops and services

Tradesmen in the town were experiencing difficulties in the 1840s. In 1845 an appeal was made to the 'Monied and Influential Classes' in Beaminster to support local shops and craftsmen. The printed notice read:

> It is thought that the practice, on the part of the more opulent inhabitants of this town, of expending their custom in London or in some larger town in the vicinity, is rather on the increase, and it is felt to be both unneighbourly and unkind, not to say *unjust* . . .

The notice went on to say that although Beaminster was not large, there were sufficient dealers to produce competition, and that to take away custom was a poor encouragement to them to furnish their shops well.[15] Rate books show that a number of properties were 'void' in the 1850s.[16] In 1867 the 'Depressed state of Town as regards Trade' was one of the reasons for asking Government help in the building of a new girls' school.[17]

In 1836 Beaminster could still be described as 'a market town of some repute'.[10] As other larger towns came to be served by the railway and increased their market business, so the smaller local markets were killed off; the market at Beaminster had probably already stopped some years before the market house was pulled down. The building, no longer used by the butchers, had degenerated into a lumber store, and had become an eye-sore. A public meeting held in November 1884 petitioned the Ecclesiastical Commissioners (in whom the property was now vested) for its removal, and in return for the sum of £200, which had been raised by public subscription, the Commissioners made over to trustees all the property and the franchise for a market and fair. The market house was taken down in 1886, and by early 1887 three further premises in the market place, including two former flesh shambles, had also been acquired and pulled down. The management of the property and income arising was vested in a 'Market Place Improvement Committee' whose powers were transferred to the parish council in 1896.[18] Directories go on referring to a Thursday market right through to the 1920s; attempts were made on more than one occasion to revive a regular cattle market, but with only limited success.

The September cattle and sheep fair continued to be held at the field called Hams off the Bridport road until about 1870, when it was moved to a field on Whitcombe Road. In 1893 some leading farmers and townsfolk rented the 'Fair Field' off Tunnel Road, and several thousand sheep were regularly offered for sale here; Morey & Sons, auctioneers of Bridport, used to hold a spring cattle fair in the same field. After the First World War, the cattle and sheep fairs dwindled, though Moreys continued to hold one.[19]

Beaminster was still pretty self-sufficient in the 1870s. Percy Codd, son of the vicar, says:

> I rather fancy that with three butchers . . . to choose from, the Beaminster shops sufficed very well for most of our modest household wants, and it was some years before my mother took to driving into Bridport now and then for special shopping, while for us boys at any rate everything required in the way of clothing and boots could be had in the town.[20]

The traditional self-sufficiency of such centres began to decline towards the end of the 19th century with the availability of factory-made goods, and their wide distribution by means of the nearest railways; on the other hand, the general increase in the scope of retail shops and services brought in new kinds of shops.

There was certainly a fall in the number of small general shopkeepers, grocers and bakers; in 1855 there were 18 shops of this kind, but a progressive reduction led to there being only nine in 1915, of which one of the most important was Pines. The shop of Thomas Pine, grocer, in the Fore Place was burnt down in 1844, and reopened in Fleet Street, where it now stands; it was run by Alfred Pine in 1880 and 1899, and by his son Reggie in 1915, but it went out of the family in the 1920s. The number of butchers declined after 1842, from seven or eight to only four or five; in 1915 there were four in the centre of the town — Hine Bros. in North Street, Frampton & Sons in Fore Place, Benjamin Froome in Hogshill Street, and J. H. Bugler in Church Street. Alfred Gibbs, butcher and slaughter-house owner, had premises at Newtown.[11]

An increasing variety of ready-made goods led to a fall in the number of tailors, of whom there were still as many as 10 in 1867; by 1880 there were only four. In 1899 the Brooks family were master tailors in the Fore Place. Josiah Brooks came to

Beaminster in the 1830s and worked (in Hogshill Street) as a journeyman, first for John Goldsworthy and then for William Hallett, to whose business he succeeded; he died in 1912, and was followed by his son Richard ('Danny') and grandson Frank.[11, 21] There were a dozen boot and shoe makers in 1867; by 1899 the number had fallen to five.[11]

The number of firms engaged in the building and allied trades was maintained. The Chambers family were masons and builders from at least 1842 (Robert) to 1903 (Benjamin). The Hanns were builders from at least 1867 (David) to 1923 (Albert). In 1923 there were three building firms, Hann, Symes and Bailey.[11] The largest business was that established by Edwin Bailey in Broadwindsor Road in 1905, which employed nearly 200 people in the 1930s; it is still going strong today. Thomas Crew & Son (builders, Gerrards Green and The Square, 1935) had a regular force of a dozen or more.[22] There were usually two firms of ironmongers and plumbers; further reference to Newmans and Tolemans is made below.

Richard ('Dicky') Hine (1860-1939), author of *A History of Beaminster*, succeeded his father Alfred at the pharmacy in 1882; he sold out to J. W. Sill in 1925. The Hine family had been in business in the town as grocers and chemists for nearly 135 years.

There was an eventual decline in the crafts ancillary to agriculture. James Everett (at No. 4 Hogshill Street in 1842) was followed as saddler by Jeremiah Stembridge who appears in directories from 1855; his shop (and post office) was probably at No. 2 Church Street by 1885. Thomas Warren was a saddler in 1880;[11] Bill Warren, at No. 19 The Square in 1899 and the early years of this century, is still remembered as one who was 'never too busy to talk to boys, let them come in and watch the work, and give them a bit of leather on which to practise'.[23] Ernest Hussey still had a saddler's shop in Hogshill Street in 1935. There were several wheelwrights and the firm of Buglers is mentioned below. Shiners, wheelwrights from 1855, were cart and carriage builders and timber merchants with their own saw mills in 1899; in 1915 they supplied planks, felloes, spokes and wheelstocks.[11] The craft did not survive after the First World War, when surplus army vehicles flooded the market with factory-made trailers with pneumatic wheels, killing off the businesses of the remaining wheelwrights.

The increasing use by the 1880s of the new items of agricultural machinery brought more work to the blacksmith for some time, but owing to a drastic reduction in the number of horses employed in agriculture and on delivery vans, and to later mass production of farm machinery and spare parts, the demand for the blacksmith's skill declined from the 1930s. For most of the period under review, there were two or three blacksmiths in the town, and in the later 19th century the Watts family were smiths at Beaminster Bottom, where they kept an inn, the *Three Horseshoes*. From at least 1855 the family of Weaver were blacksmiths: Robert Weaver had premises off Hogshill Street (now Tolmans) in 1923. Thomas Hull was a blacksmith in 1867, and in 1915 John Hull was in Shorts Lane, where he was followed by Herbert Neller. Thatchers were kept busy thatching hay and corn ricks, and repairing roofs on the many farmhouses, cottages and barns which were still thatched. Moses Tuck & Son (William), thatchers of Gerrards Green in 1923 and 1935, were the latest of a long line of thatchers.[11]   .

Manchester House (No. 21 The Square) continued to be occupied by drapers, Henry Virgint succeeding George Brough by 1855, and being himself replaced by Henry Crocker by 1885.[11] The new large general outfitters had virtually replaced the tailors and bootmakers by the end of the 19th century. A. Reynolds, drapers and boot and shoe mercers, occupied the site of Edwin Coombs' drapers shop in Hogshill Street (London House) from 1892;[24] in 1915 the shop, of which there was a larger branch in Bridport, was described as 'outfitters, tailors, dressmakers, milliners, hosiers, glovers, drapers and boot & shoe mercers'. By 1935 the shop had moved to Crocker's former premises.[11]

An important new kind of business was that connected with mechanised transport. As early as 1903 John Hunt of South Gate built a motor car with an engine supplied by Edwin Chard of Bridport.[25] In 1915 Cecil Hann ran the Beaminster Garage Company at Prout Bridge and was sole district agent for 'G.W.K.' light cars; Albert Hann was the proprietor in 1923. George Symes ran the Fleet Street Garage Company, and Frank Bridle, motor engineer in Fleet Street in 1923, had set up Bridle's Garage in Tunnel Road by 1935. S. W. Gibbs, motor engineer, was at Prout Bridge by 1923.[11] George Perry first started up in Beaminster in 1920 as a coal merchant with a horse and cart; having got into the coaching business, he turned his attention to local haulage needs of sand, gravel and stone, using convertible charabancs in the early days. In 1961 the firm had over 60 vehicles engaged in supply and haulage of road-making materials, and owned four quarries, three of them within 30 miles of Beaminster.[26]

Other new services included dentists: William Palk & Son were in Hogshill Street by 1915.[11] Before the advent of Mr. Palk, teeth were extracted by Richard Hine in his chemists's shop with the help of some ether and Mr. W. T. Bugler.[27]

It would obviously be impossible to mention all the tradesmen and shopkeepers who served the town and neighbourhood, but we cannot leave this section without a brief account of four family firms which were operating for the whole century under review, though some modified the nature of their business in response to changing demands. These firms were Buglers, Framptons, Newmans and Tolemans; the first three are still here today (1984).

The firm of Francis Bugler Ltd., agricultural engineers, originated in 1851 when Robert Bugler (who died in 1907 and was the great-grandfather of the present managing director, Ralph Bugler) commenced business on his own account. He used a field in North Street opposite the Manor House, with a sawmill by the river Brit, and made simple agricultural machines such as hay-makers. The business was carried on by his two sons, William and George: in 1899 they were timber merchants, cart and waggon builders, wheelwrights and blacksmiths. They made waggons, hay-making machines, rollers and gates — straightforward wheelwrights' work in ash and elm with iron tyres bonded on to the wheeled items; as time went on they used a water-wheel on the river for sawing power. When a wider range of new agricultural machinery began to come on the scene, they became agents for that sort of equipment, and in the 1930s the firm was dealing in tractors, by then in fairly common use. William Bugler's son Francis trained as an engineer at Petters of Yeovil; in 1935, at a period when engineers tended to dabble in all kinds of mechanical and engine-driven items, he was — as well as agricultural implement dealer — motor, hydraulic and general engineer at the present premises in Hogshill Street. Between 1939 and 1949 the firm sold new motor cars, but found this business did not mix too well with the farming world. In the 1930s there were about 10 employees, but in the 1940s some 35 men were employed.[27, 11]

The firm of Frampton & Son, butchers, can be traced back to at least 1842, when Giles Frampton was a butcher in Fleet Street; at that time Thomas Frampton (sail-cloth maker) was owner of the present premises in The Square, then occupied by Henry Peach, clockmaker. In 1867 Giles Frampton (great-grandfather of the present owners of the business) was farmer and cattle dealer at Whitcombe, and in 1880 his son Giles (born about 1852) also had the shop in the 'Fore Place', which is today run by his descendants.[11, 28]

The firm of J. W. R. Newman & Co., water, heating and electrical engineers, was founded by Thomas Newman, plumber and brazier, who in 1836 laid the service pipes for the first public gas supply in the town, and made the street lamps and brackets. The business was carried on by Thomas's son W. B. Newman, manager of the gasworks from 1872 to 1910.[29] His son (also W.B.), who was made manager of the new water-works and collector of water rates in 1908,[30] looked after both gas and water from St Mary Well Street until his death in 1923.[31] W. B. Newman junior was not only a trained plumber but also a very expert worker in iron: he devoted five years to making new iron gates for the Manor House to an elaborate design.[32] J. W. R. Newman, his son, was described as plumber, water and heating engineer in 1935; he continued in the business until his death in 1965.[31]

The first reference to Tolemans occurs when Anthony Toleman, who was a plumber in 1830. By 1855 Anthony & Edward Toleman had become ironmongers as well, having taken over the premises formerly occupied by Benjamin Seymour at No. 4 The Square; in 1867 they were also described as tin plate workers, locksmiths and bell-hangers.[11] By about 1900 tin plate working and plumbing were carried on at the original premises, while the ironmongery business was at the corner of Fleet Street. The firm employed between 20 and 25 men before the First World War; the tin-smiths made dairy equipment for the local farms.[33] The last of the family, Charlie, died in 1946, and the business was sold, becoming Colsons.

J. W. Daniel and T. P. Daniel were followed as doctors in the later 19th century by their respective sons, William James (died 1909) and Thomas Palmer (died 1925); in 1894 A. A. Pim came as assistant to T. P. Daniel and married his younger daughter Ethel in 1896.[34] Other doctors over the period were John Staines Webb (who died in 1899[35]) and his partner, Francis Parsons Kitson, who later joined the partnership of Daniel and Pim. Dr. Kitson died in 1919, and Herbert Lake came as his replacement; Robert Hope Simpson took the place of Dr. Pim when the latter retired at the beginning of 1933.[34]

As regards solicitors, Peter Cox, now on his own again, took into partnership in 1868 John Lane Kitson, who married his niece Charlotte, daughter of George Cox. Fiennes Trotman, grandson of Peter Cox, became a partner in the firm in 1890, and after the death of Peter Cox (1892) it became known as Kitson & Trotman, with offices in Fleet Street; the firm continued with Henry Lane Kitson (from 1901) and Fiennes Trotman junior (from 1928).[36] Robert Leigh senior, whose mother was Charlotte, sister of Peter Cox, was articled to his uncle on coming to Beaminster in 1858; by 1863, however, he had set up in business in Beaminster, at first in association with Sherring Keddle of Bridport, but soon afterwards on his own.[37] Robert Leigh died in 1917, but his son Robert carried on the business at No. 6 Church Street until the 1960s.[34]

In 1855 the only bank was a branch of the Dorchester & Dorsetshire (Williams' Bank), but by 1867 the Wilts & Dorset also had an office in Beaminster.[11] In 1872 the

Dorsetshire moved from its premises at Prout Bridge to a new building erected in the Fore Place; James Andrews, who was appointed manager, was a well-known figure in the town for 40 years or more. The old premises at Prout Bridge were later occupied by the Wilts & Dorset;[38] this bank took over the Dorsetshire by the 1890s, and was itself taken over by Lloyds early this century. In 1921 the London Joint City & Midland Bank first opened an office in the Fore Place, under the supervision of its Bridport branch;[39] there was a branch of the Midland in 1935.[11]

All the principal inns of the mid-19th century survived into the earlier part of the 20th century, and the *Red Lion* (rebuilt in 1892), *White Hart, Greyhound* and *Eight Bells* are with us today. The *New Inn* was open in Hogshill Street in 1923, and the *Crown* in North Street in 1935; the *Swan* was still in Fleet Street in the early 1930s. The *Bell & Crown* (in existence in 1867) was in 1935 near the corner of East Street. The *Sun*, then opposite Farrs, was burnt down in 1861, and the sign was transferred to the top of East Street, where the pub still stands. The *Star*, at one time in Hogshill Street, was by 1867 at the house next door to the Methodist chapel in Fleet Street, formerly the *Baker's Arms*; it was not closed until well after the Second World War. The *Mason's Arms* was once in Hogshill Street; the *Royal Oak*, in Hogshill Street in 1914, and the *Knapp* in Clay Lane (William Harris, 1915) are still open.[11, 40] In 1914 Richard Hine listed a number of other beerhouses which had then recently closed: *Market House Inn* (Fore Place), *Alma* (Prout Bridge), *Royal Oak* (Gerrards Green), *Smith's Arms* (Hogshill Street), *Lamb & Flag* (Shadrack Street), *Manor Arms* (North Street) and *King's Arms* (St Mary Well Street).[40]

Hats in Crocker's window in the Square

CHAPTER TWELVE

AGRICULTURE AND OTHER OCCUPATIONS 1850-1950

THE CHANGING FORTUNES of farming, in which the 'high farming' of the 1850s, 1860s and early 1870s was followed by a period of depression which lasted up to the First World War, did not affect the pastoral farmers of West Dorset quite as much as farmers in some other parts of the country. There was a fall in the value of livestock and in the price of wool but at the same time the demand for pasture products — liquid milk, butter and cheese — was rising. All farmers then had some corn and during the war more land in Beaminster, as elsewhere, was turned over to arable. The National Farmers' Union, recently set up, became a political force, with the increasing need for extra food production. The Dorset Farmers' Union was founded in 1918. The Beaminster branch was the first to be organised and at an annual dinner held in January 1921 Dr. A. A. Pim, proposing the toast 'The National Farmers' Union and Agriculture', said that the 'dark cloud' which had hung over agriculture for so long had at last begun to lift.[1] A number of tenant farmers in Beaminster bought their farms about this time. But there came another slump, and it was not till the mid 1930s that government policies led to an improvement.

Most of the larger farming units remained much the same over the century under review, though there were some changes.[2] From at least 1855 South and North Buckham were farmed together, first by William Elliott,[3] and then (from 1893) by the Dunell family;[4] Buckham was divided into three farms (South, North and Buckham Down) in 1920.[5] The two parts of West Axnoller were being farmed together by William and James Stickland by 1855; the present farmhouse was built about this time. The Compton estate was split up in 1919. Mapperton Marsh farm and Tucker's Charity Marsh farm were both bought by the tenant B. L. Cox; Storridge — which had been rented by the Guy family from the mid-19th century (Thos. Guy, junior, 1855) to the First World War — was bought by Robert Hine.[6]

Over the whole period, the most noticeable change in local farming was the decline in the number of sheep, which in Dorset generally fell from a peak of 500,000 in 1850 to only 46,000 in 1949. Increased labour costs demanded more remunerative returns than could be obtained from sheep at the prices prevailing, and at the same time there were fewer men with the old shepherding skills.[7] Percy Codd comments that whereas 'in olden days' every farm in the Beaminster area carried a large flock of sheep, 'now' (about 1918) there was only one farm so stocked.[8] At Buckham in the early 1900s Richard Dunell would lamb about 200 ewes,[4] and when James Sprackling came to Northfield in 1915 his flock numbered about 120,[9] but by the 1920s it did not pay to keep sheep on Beaminster farms, and they had virtually disappeared.

Throughout the period the main occupation in the area was dairy farming; the size of the herd probably did not change between the mid-19th century and the 1920s, remaining about 30 to 40 cows. The practice of renting out the dairy to a dairyman was still common in Dorset, especially on the larger farms where the farmer concentrated on corn and sheep. For men who lacked the capital to start up in farming on their own, renting a small herd of cows could be an important first step on the way to becoming a farmer. We may have a couple of instances of this in Beaminster. In 1855 John Woodward was dairyman to John Bowditch, the farmer at Shatcombe; in 1880 John Woodward was the farmer there. Similarly William James, who was dairyman at Langdon and Shatcombe farms to the then farmer (William Pile) in 1899, is in 1915 shown as farmer at Shatcombe; Benjamin Ryall, now farmer at Langdon, was letting the dairy there to William Gale.[3] The rent paid by a dairyman would then have been about £9 or £10 a cow per year. At Buckham, on the other hand, the dairyman was an employee, who lived and carried out his milking and cheese-making at North Buckham, which at that time was the dairy house for South Buckham.[4]

Of 118 dairy farms in Beaminster Rural District in 1908, 14 of the larger ones sent their milk to London, and these were the best in the area because the dairy companies insisted on high standards of buildings and hygiene. Sixteen dairies with much the same conditions — though the buildings were not so good — sold their milk locally. A further 18 sent milk to factories like the one set up by the West Surrey Central Dairy Company in Beaminster in 1904, where the milk was processed and the dried milk marketed as 'Cow and Gate Pure English Milk Powder'. But as many as 70 dairies in the Rural District still converted their milk into butter or cheese, in many cases the cows being let to a dairyman; in these the buildings were often bad, and conditions not very hygienic.[10] (As late as 1926, Dr. Pim, then Medical Officer of Health, commented that many of the cowsheds required complete reconstruction — 'or the torch of the incendiary'!)

At Storridge, where land left in arable after the war was turned over as soon as possible to grass, the herd consisted in 1920 of about 50 cows, and 10 men were employed. By 1931 milking machines were in use, and the herd had grown to 70 cows. The disposal of the milk varied: it might be sent to London, or sold either to the milk factory or to Nestlé, whose representative would come down to buy.[11]

There was a great extension in dairy farming and cattle production in Dorset from the 1930s. Herds could now be built up quickly by artificial insemination, and their quality improved. The yield of milk went up, but the labour costs connected with larger herds were kept to a minimum by the introduction of the milking machine. There were only a few machines in Dorset in 1929, but by 1940 there were 259, and in 1949 there were 1,360.[12] With the great interest in new agricultural techniques, and the encouragement of new government policies, Young Farmers' Clubs were started and Beaminster Y.F.C. was one of the first in Dorset, being inaugurated early in 1935.[13]

The rural labourer

The plight of the rural Dorset labourer was particularly bad in the 1840s, owing to periods of unemployment on the farms and fewer alternative opportunities in small industries. In *The Times* of 10 July 1846, the newspaper's own correspondent wrote:

> Since my arrival at Beaminster, I have had an opportunity of visiting several places in the neighbourhood . . . Here as in other places, the same scarcity and inadequate rate of wages 'mock the useful toil' of the labourer, and the same comfortless and dirty abode awaits his return . . . .

At a vestry meeting held at Beaminster on 14 November 1844, the farmers were asked to consider the expediency of each farm having 'one, two, or more labourers allotted to them for support'. It was suggested at a subsequent meeting that it was desirable 'that employment be given to all those able-bodied persons now receiving relief from the Poor Rate', and a motion was carried that the farmers should form a committee to take the agricultural labourers into employ, while the highways surveyor was to employ the other labourers on the part of the town; a subscription was to be raised among the inhabitants to pay for this. Nine farmers were named for a committee, and eight gentlemen were to represent the town.[14] The notice of a further meeting to be held on 5 December declared its object to be that 'occupiers of farms and lands do form themselves in Committee to consult on the subject of the employment of the Able bodied Poor of the Parish who now are, or during the Winter Months shall be out of employ, at adequate Wages; and Secondly, on the subject of raising a fund by way of subscription, with a View to the renting a convenient Field or Fields to be allotted and cultivated by and for the benefit of and towards the maintenance of such of the Poor . . . as they the said Inhabitants may think fitting'.[15] No proposition was however put to the meeting, which was adjourned *sine die*.[14]

Allotments were still regarded at this period as a form of poor relief: a House of Commons Select Committee had reported in 1843 that in places where allotments were let to farm workers there was less distress. In April 1847 it was proposed at a Beaminster vestry meeting that land should be rented in the parish for the use or employment of the poor. About 20 acres of land were allocated: four at Cockroad, six at Earthpit, seven in Portway Lane Meadow and three at Stokewater Pucketts.[14] These lands would be capable of employing 16 men wholly in the year or 'doing a great benefit to 76 famillys by letting it out in ¼ parts of an acre'. In addition, five acres of land at Cooks Knowle, 'good dry loam capable of being dug at any time of year', if divided into parts of an eighth of an acre each, would give employment for 45 families. It was said that 'The great evil in some of our garden allotments in this parish is that [they] are let out for profit and get extravagant prices'.[16]

Emigration was a feature of the 'hungry forties'. In 1849 the Beaminster Vestry approved the emigration plan of the Poor Law Commissioners and asked for information about families anxious to emigrate to Australia. Three families were accepted for emigration at the expense of the parish: George Daw and his wife and six children, Thomas Bugler and his wife and six children, and John Newberry and his wife and five children.[14]

Many young men from Beaminster families must have moved a shorter distance in the late 1840s and 1850s in order to take advantage of jobs offering on the railways. Fred Oliver, one of the six children of James Oliver (the printer), was born in Beaminster in 1823; he became a railwayman and was at one time gatekeeper at Moreton, near Dorchester, on the Southampton line opened in 1847.[17] William Frampton, whose parents lived on a farm in Beaminster, was probably already working on the railways when in 1857 he married a girl from Bincombe near Weymouth; he was later a ganger on Portland.[18]

In the 40 years between 1871 (when the flight from the land was everywhere in progress) and 1911, the proportion of the working population of the country which was engaged in farming was nearly halved. Men had left the land partly because of the reduced demand for labour as the use of machinery on the farm increased, but also because of the attraction of higher wages and better conditions in areas of growing industry. The railways had broken down the old rural isolation and unawareness, and men now wished to be more 'in the stream of life'.

For those who remained on the land after the great exodus, wages rose substantially and conditions improved. Joseph Arch, founder of the first agricultural trade union (1872) came to Beaminster on one occasion: a Mr. Paul, born and brought up in the parish, who died in 1935 aged 87, recalled how Arch's visit 'raised our wages two shillings all round'.[19] Wages were however still pretty low in the low-wage counties (of which Dorset was one) even in the early 20th century: at this time a dairyman or shepherd in Beaminster earned only about 12s. 6d. a week, and an ordinary labourer 10s. 0d. With the thinning down of the agricultural labour force, a shortage of labour was felt when many of the men left to fight in the First World War.

Industries

In the 1850s manufactures from flax and hemp had almost died out in Beaminster — Percy Codd was told by Miss F. O. Cox that she remembered only one loom at work then.[20] The mention of Thomas Stembridge, miller, at Whatley Mill in 1855[3] suggests that it had turned over to milling corn. There was some revival in the preparation of flax and the sail-cloth business in the 1860s, but we are told that Beaminster 'is not a manufacturing town'.[21] In 1865 Toby and Hayward were making sail-cloth, twine and thread at Whatley Mill,[22] but by 1868 it had definitely been converted to a flour mill. The Cox factory in Fleet Street did not apparently close down entirely until about 1870; some of the buildings used for weaving still stand, beside the entrance to the car park. Flax mills in the neighbourhood continued to employ Beaminster people. Clenham Mill in Netherbury, Horsehill Mill in Stoke Abbott, and Mosterton Mill were working until at least 1880. Sail-cloth was being made at Broadwindsor in 1895, and Slape Mill at Netherbury was still working in 1915.[3] In the First World War some flax was grown in Beaminster and Whatley Mill was used again for manufactures up to the 1920s.

The only industries of any consequence in the town in the 1850s were the potteries, and what Percy Codd called the tannery.[20] In 1867 John Barratt Dunn, son of Richard Dunn, was currier, leather seller & machine-upper manufacturer at the old premises, No. 15 Hogshill Street; the firm was still in existence in 1899. Oliver Bowditch, another currier, was still in business in 1885. In 1867 Abraham Meech made green and coarse ware, drainage pipes, tiles, chimney pots etc., at the Beaminster pottery on the old site in Hogshill Street. Robert Chambers was the last potter in the 1880s;[3] the kilns were removed in 1890. A certain amount of metal working (iron, brass, tin plate) continued until the early 1900s.

In 1867 Thomas Patten Coombs was managing the printing-office in Hogshill Street for his uncle Edwin Coombs.[3] T. P. Coombs commenced business for himself at No. 12 The Square in 1874, and continued until 1883; he employed several men and apprentices, and had the first steam-engine to drive machinery in the town.[23] He printed the early numbers of the parish magazine which was started in February 1877.[24]

We must here go back a little in time to describe the gas industry: gas was introduced into Beaminster at a pretty early date, and was a private venture. Towards the end of 1832 Benjamin Coombs Porter, iron founder and engineer, set up a gasometer and works in the old tan-yard in Shadrack Street. A company known as the Beaminster Gas, Coal and Coke Company was formed, pipes were laid, and shopkeepers and residents were supplied with gas for lighting purposes. In 1833 gas was taken into the Congregational chapel – the first public building to be lighted with gas – and in 1839 into the parish church.[25] In 1849, the shareholders of the Gas Company having suffered considerable loss, the company decided to discontinue manufacture. The works, tendered at a public meeting 'to any party or parties, for the sum of One Hundred Pounds', were purchased by a new 'Beaminster Gas Association', with Samuel Cox as treasurer and Charles Coombs, John P. Frampton and Anthony Toleman as a committee of management. A new company, the Beaminster Gas Company Ltd., was registered in 1868.[26]

In 1860 the gas-works were transferred to the old quarry at Clampits and a new gasholder was erected, supplied by John Smith of Chard. In 1869, the consumption of gas having increased, a new and larger gasholder was set up by Edward Cockey and Sons of Frome: the two holders together contained about 10,000 cu.ft. of gas. The thatched cottage occupied by the manager of the gas-works was demolished in 1896 and replaced by the red brick house still standing. The consumption of gas went up steadily. Receipts for private lights increased five-fold between 1850 and 1913, while the price of gas fell from 12s. 6d. to 4s. 7d. per 1,000 cu.ft.[27]

In 1924, because of a noticeable falling off in sales, the gas company decided to go in for the installation of pre-payment meters and cooking stoves etc. on hire. This policy, which 'appeared to be the only way in which the undertaking could be saved for the town', proved to be a wise one: in 1926–7 nearly 60 per cent. more gas was supplied to customers than in the year 1923–4. However, this meant that in 1927 the provision of a new gasholder became absolutely essential: the old ones, which had been in use for 60 years or so, had 'never been really adequate for the needs of the town', and there was now no reserve of gas, the works operating on a 'hand-to-mouth' basis. A gasholder with a capacity of 18,000 cu.ft. was erected.[28] The gas-works had been taken over by the Crewkerne Gas & Coke Co. Ltd. by early 1938.[29]

Transport

The confidence expressed at the opening of Horn Hill Tunnel in 1832 that it would be the means of encouraging increased trade through Beaminster proved to be unjustified. In 1854, some twenty years after his poem in honour of Giles Russell, William Gardner was bewailing the departure of trade, and pinning his hopes on the coming of a railway:[30]

> See Gen'rous Horn, what care displayed
> To welcome back departed trade!
> Op'd her once beauteous, verdant side,
> T'admit a tunnel, high and wide,
> For Trade and Commerce, sisters twin;
> OH! would their presence she could win!
> . . . . .

Lift up thine eyes — a patriot son!
Yes, Fox — replies the ready tongue,
May he a prosp'rous journey run,
And trade lured back, HIS praise be sung!
May Rail-trains shout our hills between,
And wake the echoes with their din.

'Fox' is probably Baruch Fox, the third of that name, a Beaminster solicitor who died in 1863 aged 54. The reference may be to the scheme for a GWR line (Dorset & Devon) from Maiden Newton to Axminster, serving Bridport with a branch from Netherbury, which would have brought the railway within a mile or so of Beaminster. The plans, deposited in 1852-3, fell through:[31] Russell's tunnel was not succeeded by Fox's railway.

The Southampton & Dorchester (London & South Western) Railway had reached Dorchester in 1847, but that town was never made into a through station on to the south west. The main route to Exeter was made by the Salisbury & Yeovil (London & South Western) Railway, which went via Crewkerne, Chard and Axminster; this line was opened in 1860. Meanwhile Dorchester was linked to Bristol in 1856 by the Wilts & Somerset (Great Western) Railway via Yeovil and Frome. In 1857 Bridport acquired a single track running north-east to connect with the latter line at Maiden Newton, the 'Bridport Branch'. (See Fig. 1.)

There were several further attempts to improve connections between Bridport and Chard or Crewkerne between 1860 and 1914, and one of them might well have provided Beaminster with a railway. On 16 November 1863 an enthusiastic meeting held at Beaminster approved the project for a railway from Bridport Harbour through Beaminster, to join the London & South Western at Clapton, about three miles south-west of Crewkerne; the route, it was said, would embrace a rich agricultural valley with several mills, and a large water power which would need to be supplemented by steam power and cheap coal. This scheme was withdrawn owing to opposition but was revived in 1864 in the truncated form of a railway from Crewkerne to Beaminster only — 'the Beaminster Railway', which was to pass in front of Horn Park Farm under the road leading to the farmhouse. Captain Flower, engineer to the company, was received with acclaim at a meeting in Beaminster on 22 December 1864; he urged the towns-people not only to vote in favour of the scheme, but to give it financial backing by taking up shares, for 'if the inhabitants did not encourage this scheme, Beaminster would never have a line of railway'. This project too failed because of opposition.[32] In 1878 a railway was being promoted from Bridport to Chard Road through the Marsh-wood Vale, and it was suggested in the *Dorset County Chronicle* that at a little more expense the line could be made to serve Beaminster, Broadwindsor and Winsham, and 'a country would be opened up abounding with factories'; this line was never proceeded with.[33] In 1903 the whole route was mapped for a light railway from Bridport to Crewkerne via Pymore, Netherbury and Beaminster, but this also fell through.[34]

The nearest railway stations to Beaminster remained Crewkerne on the main SWR line, and Bridport on the branch GWR line to Maiden Newton. In 1855 one coach only, the Royal Mail between Bridport and Taunton, called daily at Beaminster in each direction.[3] When this coach stopped in 1860, the Bridport, Beaminster and Crewkerne station horse omnibus service was inaugurated.[35] This was one of three such services operating in West Dorset before the motor era: the others ran between Bridport and Lyme Regis, and between Charmouth and Axminster.[36] In 1880, the horse bus left Bridport daily at 9.30 a.m. for Beaminster, whence it departed at 10.15 a.m. for Crewkerne. The return journey left Crewkerne at 11.50 a.m. and Beaminster at 1 p.m., arriving at Bridport about 2.00 p.m. In 1899 there was a similar service and also a Royal Mail waggonette, carrying passengers, which did the double trip between Beaminster and Bridport every day.[3] In November 1910 the mails between Bridport and Ilminster (via Beaminster and Crewkerne) first began to travel by motor transport.[37] From 1904, when it was finally realised that a train service for the district was out of the question, many attempts had been made to persuade either the LSWR or the GWR to put on a motor passenger service for Beaminster, but without success.[38] In May 1912 Cecil Hann of the Beaminster Garage Co. inaugurated a service by motor brake carrying 14 passengers between Bridport, Beaminster and Crewkerne; it did not receive the anticipated support, and was discontinued after less than a year.[39]

Regular goods carriers still plied between Beaminster and the nearest towns. John Slade, Crewkerne carrier, was agent for goods for the SWR in 1867. Goods were taken to Bridport daily by E. Woodbury in 1867 and Alfred Woodbury in 1885; the Woodburys were agents for parcels for the GWR. Andress & Son, coopers and basket makers in Hogshill Street, were the GWR agents in 1899 and 1915.[3]

Most journeys had to be made on foot or on horseback (later by bicycle), or in a pony trap or larger waggonette. Jim Hine (son of Robert Hine of Storridge) recalls how in school summer holidays during the First World War, Mr. Tuck's waggonette would be hired to take family and friends on a day trip to West Bay:[40]

> We set off early taking all our food, picnicked on the beach, often lighting a fire from drift-wood to boil a kettle for tea. On the homeward journey the older children had to get out and walk up the hills, and push to help the horse, especially going up 'Crooked Oak' Melplash.

In 1899 William Gibbs at Prout Bridge was offering apartments and refreshments to 'visitors & cyclists'. Thomas Macey, men's hairdresser at No. 18 Hogshill Street, let out bicycles on hire, and was a cycle agent.[3] It was from Macey that in 1917 Miss Kathleen Pim, daughter of Dr. Pim, bought her first bicycle — a second-hand model that was to do her excellent service for the next 50 years. So quiet was the stretch of the Bridport road past Parnham at this time that the 14-year-old girl and her sister learned to ride their bicycles there!

In 1904, when compulsory registration was introduced for that other new invention, the motor car, cars were still a rich man's luxury, and although by the end of that year 162 cars were registered in Dorset, there were very few indeed in Beaminster until after the First World War. The first motor car in the town was purchased in May 1909 by Dr. Pim, and caused so much excitement that the police had to be called to disperse the crowd. In 1923 'smart cars' were available for hire from Albert Hann at Prout Bridge.[3]

At a meeting held by the County Council in November 1918 to discuss the extension and improvement of rural travelling, either by road transport or light railways, reference was made to 'the absence of almost any form of [public] transport' in the Beaminster Rural District.[41] In March 1919 Hann's garage started a service between Beaminster and Bridport, and in the summer of 1921 a service was running to Bridport and West Bay twice daily on Monday, Tuesday, Thursday and Friday, and three times daily on Wednesday and Saturday; the trip cost 2s. 6d. return.[42] In 1923 the National Omnibus & Transport Co. Ltd., which had opened a depot at Yeovil in 1921, also passed through Beaminster from Yeovil to Bridport, and vice versa, every Wednesday.[3, 43] In 1933 the local omnibus firm, then Edwards & Hann, was acquired by the Southern National, which had taken over the more southern portion of the National in 1929.[44]

Chimney erected at their milk factory by West Surrey Central Dairy Company

CHAPTER THIRTEEN

PUBLIC SERVICES 1850-1950

The Local Authorities

The Beaminster Vestry. BETWEEN 1836 AND 1894 the activities of parish vestries were increasingly affected by the setting up of new *ad hoc* bodies. The first change came when the Beaminster Vestry lost direct responsibility for the parish poor to the Board of Guardians of the Beaminster Poor Law Union. From 1863 parish roads came under the Bridport Highway Board, and in 1872 the Beaminster Guardians became a Rural Sanitary Authority with responsibility for sanitation and water supplies. We have vestry minutes from 1842 to 1886,[1] but the final book, to 1894, is missing. The Vestry was attended mainly by the gentry and the professional classes, and by the more important farmers and shopkeepers. Meetings were held sometimes in the vestry room at the church, and sometimes in the 'New School Room' in the former workhouse in East Street; after 1868 they were held in the new girls' school in Hogshill Street.

The unpaid overseers of the poor still collected the rates in the earlier part of the period. At a meeting held on 8 December 1842 to consider the appointment of a permanent paid Assistant Overseer, Samuel Cox 'strongly recommended the measure as one which was found to be of real use in a neighbouring Parish'. Isaac Daniel was appointed in January 1843, from four applicants for the post. His duties were to be present at meetings relating to parish matters, to attend the Relieving Officer of the Beaminster Union at the pay table, and to investigate the circumstances of applicants. In 1845 tenders were asked for the office of Collector of Rates and Assistant Overseer, which was now to 'include the whole duties of the Overseers and their Assistant Overseer'. None of the candidates was thought suitable, and Isaac Daniel remained until 1857.

Between 1857 and 1863 the posts of Assistant Overseer and Waywarden were combined. (The post of paid surveyor or waywarden — to look after roads in both Beaminster and Langdon tithings — had been held by John Cox from 1843 to 1857.) The duties were to make out and collect the poor, highway and lighting rates, devoting the whole time to the office. In December 1858 (John Cox, first holder of the combined post, having resigned) there were three applicants for the position, and such a large attendance at the vestry meeting that it had to be adjourned to the 'town hall'; Samuel Miller of Hawkchurch was appointed after a special poll had been held. When the post fell vacant in April 1869, it was advertised in the *Bridport News* and *Pulmans Weekly*, and David Hann (builder) was chosen out of five applicants; the assistant overseer was now no longer required to devote his whole time to the job. In April 1876 Albert Hann became assistant overseer, and he was followed by his brother Edwin in September 1879.

The Vestry appointed one waywarden to the Bridport Highway Board from 1863, though it was said more than once that there ought to be two waywardens, one for each tithing. John Furmedge of Langdon was the first Beaminster waywarden on the board; he was followed by David Symes of Langdon (1867), Moses Gillingham of West Axnoller (1871), John Pile of Marsh (1875), William Way of Langdon (1879), and Mr. Pile senior of Langdon (1882).

Board of Guardians of the Beaminster Union — 26 parishes were included in the Beaminster Union, which was the last of the 12 Dorset Poor Law Unions to be formed. The Assistant Poor Law Commissioner responsible for Dorset said in February 1836 that he was persuaded that the Union would not be far behind 'in reaping the benefits enjoyed by its fore-runners'.[2] The surviving records of the Beaminster Board of Guardians are patchy, and there are no minutes between 1865 and 1916. At the first meeting held in April 1836 at the *Red Lion*, Samuel Cox was appointed chairman,[3] a position which he was to hold for nearly a quarter of a century. On his death in 1860, a letter of condolence from the board to his son, Samuel Symes Cox, contained the following tribute:[4]

> . . . how much more severe will be the blow on the Poor, by the withdrawal from them of their tender hearted protector, whose chief delight and constant practice it was, to lessen their privations and increase their comforts.

Samuel Symes Cox was himself chairman from 1871 to 1878.

Voting papers issued to ratepayers for the election of three guardians to represent Beaminster parish in 1838 show that only about two-thirds of those qualified to vote did so. There were six candidates: Joseph Bishop (of North Field, gentleman), Jonathan Dowdeswell (of Storridge, yeoman), Thomas Chapman (of Chapel Marsh, yeoman), James Rendle (veterinary surgeon of Beaminster), Thomas Frampton (innkeeper of the *Red Lion*) and Clement Davy (of Yondover, yeoman); the first three were elected.[5] In 1868, 1869 and 1870 recommendations made at vestry meetings included Richard Swatridge (miller), Edward G. Legg (farmer, of Coombe Down), John Paull (farmer, of Barrowfield), John Hine (wine merchant) and William Trask (farmer, of Marsh). In 1885 the nominations were Edward Legg, Francis Toleman (ironmonger) and George Squire (innkeeper of the *White Hart*).[1]

Samuel Cox's younger brother George became Clerk to the Union in 1836.[3] He was succeeded in 1876 by Robert Leigh senior; Robert Leigh junior was appointed in 1910.[6] The area was divided into two districts, each with its own Relieving Officer, and four (later five) districts were established for medical attendance. J. W. Daniel was appointed Medical Officer to No. 2 District which was based on Beaminster.[3] After his death in 1859, his son W. J. Daniel became responsible for medical attention in this district.[4] T. P. Daniel junior, cousin of William James, followed him in the post in 1890, and was himself succeeded by A. A. Pim in 1909.[7] One of the medical officers was appointed separately to take care of the inmates of the workhouse.

Bridport Highway Board. Set up under the Highways Act of 1862, this covered a large area, from Burton Bradstock to Lyme Regis (excluding Bridport borough) and as far north as Halstock and South Perrott. Meetings were held alternately at Bridport and Beaminster. Benjamin John Cox of Beaminster was appointed Surveyor in 1863;

in August 1864 he was also made Sanitary Inspector, after some discussion with the various boards of guardians within the highway district as to who was responsible for the appointment. Benjamin Cox was dismissed in 1877, following a vote of censure on his expenditure, and was succeeded by Richard Rendell.[8]

The J.P.s ordered in 1863 that contributions should be paid by the board towards the upkeep of the turnpike roads. From 1872 onwards turnpike trusts were in process of being wound down. Roads were taken over by parishes, or by highway boards where these existed; half the cost of repairing former turnpike roads declared 'main' roads was paid by the county between 1879 and April 1889 when the new Dorset County Council became wholly responsible for them. Roads other than main roads were taken over by rural district councils in 1895.

Beaminster Rural Sanitary Authority. At the first meeting, in September 1872, of the new body set up under the Public Health Act of that year, it was resolved that the entire Beaminster Board of Guardians should constitute the 'Sanitary Committee'. In August 1873 however, it was decided that in future the rural sanitary authority should consist of eight members in addition to the chairman and vice-chairman of the board of guardians. The Clerk to the guardians became Clerk to the sanitary authority. In March 1873 it was resolved that the four Medical Officers of the Beaminster Union should become Medical Officers of Health under the sanitary authority. The Local Government Board asked for this to be reconsidered, preferring the appointment of one medical officer of health for the whole area, but the view was maintained that 'exceptional circumstances strongly apply to this Union' and the Local Government Board reluctantly agreed to this arrangement being continued year by year; it was not until 1879 that John Staines Webb was finally appointed sole medical officer of health. Charles Hann was appointed Inspector of Nuisances to the sanitary authority in 1873 for three years; when he was reappointed in 1876, his salary was reduced, his duties 'now being very light', but it was raised again the following year.[9]

Beaminster Rural District Council. Rural district councils set up under the Local Government Act 1894 superseded rural sanitary authorities, whose powers they inherited; they were concerned not only with water supply, sewerage, refuse collection and disposal, and housing, but also with roads (other than main) up to 1930. The area of Beaminster Rural District Council was virtually the same as that of the former sanitary authority. Rural district councillors were elected by democratic suffrage, and not by voting based on property qualifications, but for the first few years the Beaminster Rural District Council looks rather like the sanitary authority continuing under another name. It merely carried on with the meetings for sanitary purposes, following them by meetings for highway purposes; as a matter of convenience, meetings continued to be held on the same day as those of the Beaminster Board of Guardians, and at the Union workhouse, which remained the venue even after it became a Public Assistance institution of Dorset County Council in 1930. Many of the first members of the rural district council were the same people as had been serving on the sanitary authority; its first chairman was E. G. Legg, the former chairman of the authority.[10, 11]

In 1920, when there was already one lady member of the district council, Miss Edith Ward, a comparatively new resident, stood as a candidate for one of the three

Beaminster seats; she was nominated by the Women's Institute, of which she was president. Miss Ward pointed out in her election speech made in The Square that in Beaminster women electors outnumbered men. Several hundred people gathered outside the school in Hogshill Street where the poll was declared, to hear Miss Ward's opponent Charles Toleman, a native of the town, declared the winner by 295 votes to 155; Mr. Toleman was chaired through the main street to his house.[12]

The same officers who had served the sanitary authority were appointed by the district council in 1895: Robert Leigh (Clerk), J. S. Webb (Medical Officer of Health), and Charles Hann (Inspector of Nuisances).[10] The former clerk to the Bridport Highway Board was employed for highway matters for the first two years, but in March 1897 Robert Leigh took over.[11] When Robert Leigh resigned because of illness in March 1910, his son Robert became Clerk, and Frank Bugler (his clerk) was appointed Assistant Clerk.[13] Under the Rating and Valuation Act 1925 the rural district council became the rating authority in 1927; Frank Bugler, then Assistant Overseer of the parish of Beaminster, was retained as Rating Officer by the district council, and in his capacity as Assistant Clerk became Accounting Officer. The Clerk received an additional salary which covered the provision of further accommodation at his office in Church Street, Beaminster.[14]

John Staines Webb resigned from his position as medical officer of health in June 1898 and was succeeded by Francis Parsons Kitson.[15] When Dr. Kitson died in 1919, A. A. Pim became medical officer of health;[16] his annual reports, which are quoted from elsewhere, make lively reading, being written in a highly individual style and imbued with a delightful sense of humour. On the resignation of Dr. Pim owing to ill-health, Herbert Lake was appointed from 1 January 1933, but in May 1936, by the request of the Ministry of Health, a new post of Joint Medical Officer, covering several other local boroughs and rural districts, was created.[17] The first holder of this post, J. D. Mackay, resigned after only a year, and was succeeded by Dr. Adam Armit.[18]

Richard Rendell, Road Surveyor to Bridport Highway Board, continued with the district council, but resigned after a few months. The post was advertised in the *Bridport News* and the *Western Gazette* in May 1895, and 10 applications were received, F. G. Wakely of Stoke Abbott being appointed.[11] In 1923 difficulties arose in connection with the work: Mr. Wakely was now 69 years of age, and with only a pony and trap he was no longer able to supervise the contractors efficiently. As from April 1924, A. E. Orledge was appointed Assistant Surveyor; he was to provide a motor cycle and side-car and take the surveyor around. When he left after a year, the opportunity was taken of appointing a fully qualified, full-time man to take over as surveyor from Mr. Wakely, and W. V. Fryer was appointed in 1925. In April 1926, on the recommendation of the new surveyor, premises were rented for office and store for five years at £30 a year,[14] but the post of surveyor disappeared in 1930 when repair of roads passed to the County Council.

Charles Hann, who had been inspector of nuisances for nearly 40 years, resigned in December 1910 owing to ill-health. His son Charles C. Hann was appointed in his place;[13] when he volunteered for the Forces in August 1914, an allowance of half his salary was made to him and the other half was paid to the surveyor, who agreed to carry out the duties of inspector of nuisances jointly with the medical officer of health. Mr. Hann having resigned in August 1918, the surveyor was made temporary inspector of nuisances and continued to share the work with the medical officer whose salary was increased.[16] In May 1922 the Ministry of Health objected to the permanent sharing of the duties, and recommended the engagement of a certificated officer to perform all the duties of a Sanitary Inspector whole-time. Permission was however secured to maintain the existing arrangement in the interests of economy, 'this being an entirely Agricultural District'.[19] Mr. Wakely in fact continued to act as inspector of nuisances until January 1931 when he resigned because of old age; he had been in the service of the district council for some 36 years.[20] Thirteen applications were received in response to the advertisement for a fully qualified sanitary inspector; C. C. Rundle was appointed in July 1931.[17] From April 1938 the sanitary inspector used a room at the new offices in Fleet Street.[18]

In 1934 the annual parish meeting asked the district council to provide public conveniences in the town, and approval was given in September 1935 to purchase from Messrs. Palmer property in Fleet Street (formerly the *Swan Inn*) and adjoining premises.[17] The buildings were converted by G. Symes & Son to provide not only toilets but also parish council room and offices, fire station, and store for refuse collection equipment. The 'Town Offices' came into use in April 1938.[18]

A review of Rural Districts was made following on the Local Government Act 1929. It was at one time proposed that the Rural Districts of Bridport and Beaminster should be merged; this was resisted by Beaminster Rural District councillors, and no change in fact took place.[20, 17] In anticipation of an increase in its post-war responsibilities, Beaminster Rural District Council took over the town offices as from April 1946, and moved there in July 1947 with a permanent full-time staff. Frank Bugler, assistant clerk, resigned on account of illness. Robert Leigh resigned as from 30 September 1947, after 37 years as Clerk of the Council, and R. C. Travers was appointed in his place.[21]

Beaminster Parish Council. For all parishes with a population of over 300, elected parish councils were also set up under the 1894 Act, and to them were transferred the rights and duties of vestries in connection with the appointment of overseers, management of parish property, and the provision of allotments, public lighting etc. At the first elections for Beaminster held in December 1894 there were 33 nominations for 11 seats, and the following were elected: Rev. A. A. Leonard (vicar of Beaminster), F. P. Kitson (doctor), F. Trotman (solicitor), R. Toleman (ironmonger), J. Shiner (timber merchant), H. Gillingham (farmer, West Axnoller), A. V. Pine (grocer), W. Andress (cooper), H. J. Sherring (painter), O. M. Beament (carpenter) and J. Rogers (beer retailer).[22] It was generally understood that two of the 11 councillors should normally be farmers, and of the other nine representing the town two should be working men in receipt of a weekly wage – though there were not always two, for lack of nominations.[23] There was less competition for seats as time went by, but 1907 was a particularly lively election. More than usual interest was taken in it, 16 men being nominated at the annual parish meeting, where there was a large attendance. A show of hands was taken, but a poll was then demanded. A great deal of amusement was caused by somebody issuing a printed 'race-card', entitled 'The Parish Council Handicap', but only about half the electorate – 213 people – voted.[23, 24] It was not until 1934 that the first lady member, Miss F. H. Ramsden of Lower Meerhay, was elected.[25]

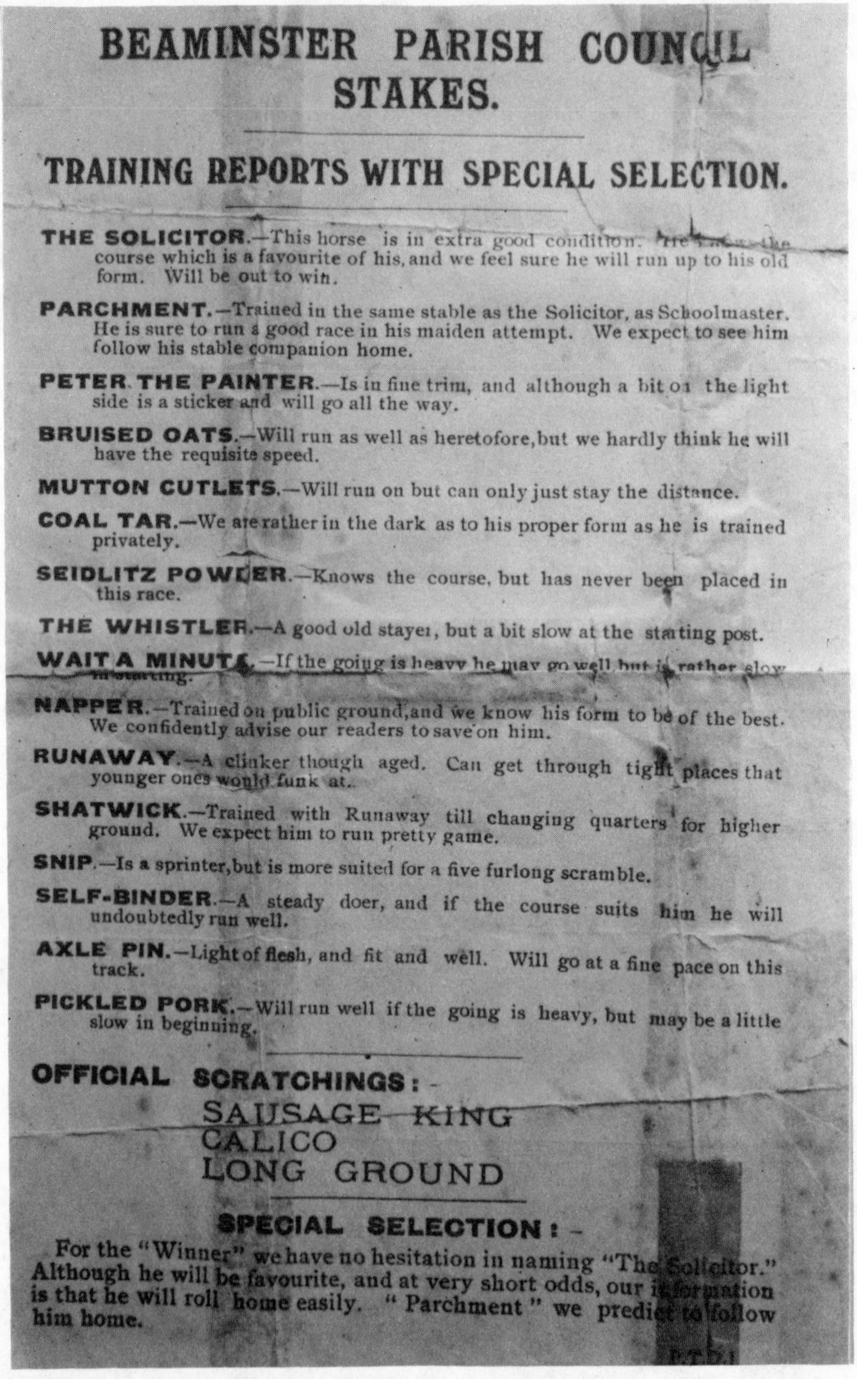

BEAMINSTER PARISH COUNCIL STAKES.

TRAINING REPORTS WITH SPECIAL SELECTION.

THE SOLICITOR.—This horse is in extra good condition. He likes the course which is a favourite of his, and we feel sure he will run up to his old form. Will be out to win.

PARCHMENT.—Trained in the same stable as the Solicitor, as Schoolmaster. He is sure to run a good race in his maiden attempt. We expect to see him follow his stable companion home.

PETER THE PAINTER.—Is in fine trim, and although a bit on the light side is a sticker and will go all the way.

BRUISED OATS.—Will run as well as heretofore, but we hardly think he will have the requisite speed.

MUTTON CUTLETS.—Will run on but can only just stay the distance.

COAL TAR.—We are rather in the dark as to his proper form as he is trained privately.

SEIDLITZ POWDER.—Knows the course, but has never been placed in this race.

THE WHISTLER.—A good old stayer, but a bit slow at the starting post.

WAIT A MINUTE.—If the going is heavy he may go well but is rather slow in starting.

NAPPER.—Trained on public ground, and we know his form to be of the best. We confidently advise our readers to save on him.

RUNAWAY.—A clinker though aged. Can get through tight places that younger ones would funk at.

SHATWICK.—Trained with Runaway till changing quarters for higher ground. We expect him to run pretty game.

SNIP.—Is a sprinter, but is more suited for a five furlong scramble.

SELF-BINDER.—A steady doer, and if the course suits him he will undoubtedly run well.

AXLE PIN.—Light of flesh, and fit and well. Will go at a fine pace on this track.

PICKLED PORK.—Will run well if the going is heavy, but may be a little slow in beginning.

OFFICIAL SCRATCHINGS:-
SAUSAGE KING
CALICO
LONG GROUND

SPECIAL SELECTION:-
For the "Winner" we have no hesitation in naming "The Solicitor." Although he will be favourite, and at very short odds, our information is that he will roll home easily. "Parchment" we predict to follow him home.

Fig. 11. Parish council election 'race-card' 1907. Among 'starters' who can be identified are: The Solicitor (Fiennes Trotman), Parchment (J. R. Bridle), Seidlitz Powder (Richard Hine), Wait-a-minute (W. D. Bishop).

In the early 1900s it was commonly remarked that the parish council had nothing to attend to but the allotments, and that all it could do was to complain and ask the other councils to do something. It was pointed out by 'Beaminsterian' in the *Bridport News* that the council was 'very useful seeing that much that has been done, would not have been carried out probably, but for the persistency of our local parliament'.[23] In the years immediately following the First World War the parish council was asked for advice on some important matters, such as the housing of the working classes and refuse disposal; no fewer than 26 meetings were held over the three years to March 1922, compared with the statutory twelve.[22] In June 1924 W. H. Bugler enquired as to the steps necessary to obtain urban powers for the parish. The Clerk explained that the Ministry of Health was not in favour of the constitution of urban district councils for small rural parishes, and the matter was allowed to stand over.[26]

Under the provisions of the 1894 Act, Albert Hann, then assistant overseer (to which post he had first been appointed in 1876), became the first Clerk to the Parish Council. In 1901 his salary was increased, the work having 'very much increased from year to year since the Council came into office'.[27] He resigned in 1911 and Frank Bugler was appointed Clerk and Assistant Overseer out of 12 applicants for the post.[28]

Up to January 1920 the parish council met at the girls' elementary school in Hogshill Street, but a change was then made to the library at the Institute (Fleet Street).[28] From July 1938 meetings were held at the town offices until the war necessitated their transfer to the Clerk's house. In March 1946 a return was made to the Institute.[25]

Union Workhouse

The first problem which faced the Beaminster Guardians in 1836 was that of suitable workhouse accommodation. There were three parish workhouses in their area: Beaminster, Broadwindsor and Netherbury. The buildings at Broadwindsor and Netherbury were too small for the purposes of the Union, and Broadwindsor was besides 'inconvenient in distance'. The Assistant Poor Law Commissioner thought that Beaminster workhouse might be utilisable for the whole Union, but there was a difficulty in that the building had been erected by the Gilbert Adams Charity,[2] and it was decided in May 1836 to built a new workhouse instead. In the meantime rent was paid to the parish authorities for the use of their workhouses, and a committee visited them at least once a month to report on the condition of the paupers. When the committee went to Beaminster for the first time, it obviously felt that discipline was lax, and in order to provide more occupation for the inmates it recommended that the following items should be obtained:

Three spinning turns
Old rope or junk, to set the female paupers to work (this was picked to produce oakum, a loose fibre used in caulking)
About ten loads of flints to be cracked
Bones to be pounded

In June 1836 land was purchased for £315 at Stoke Water in the parish of Stoke Abbott, a mile or more from Beaminster. Richard Warr, Beaminster builder, agreed in October 1836 to build the workhouse for £4,120; the plan was one of two standard

'New Poor Law' designs. In May 1838 the Clerk was instructed to visit the workhouses at Dorchester, Chard and Yeovil to gain information with regard to furnishing the kitchen; a tender from E. P. Davy, a Beaminster ironmonger, was later accepted. The building was opened in June 1838 and the inmates of the parish workhouses were transferred there.[3]

The whole idea behind the new Poor Law was that relief should not be given to the able-bodied outside the workhouse (though individual boards did not strictly adhere to this principle), and that at the same time conditions inside should not be such as to encourage the able-bodied to seek admission. The new Beaminster Union workhouse had accommodation for 230 paupers but it is unlikely that there were ever quite so many inmates. At the time of the 1841 census the number actually inside was 141; in 1849, during a period of severe depression it had risen to 218,[29] but by 1858 it had dropped to 87. In the six months ending 25 March 1850, 141 poor people from Beaminster parish were relieved in the workhouse — they were not of course all inside the whole time — at a cost of approximately £155; in the six months ending 25 March 1857 the number was only 40 and the cost approximately £94.[30]

Although the union workhouse is often regarded as the symbol of mid 19th-century poor law administration, it must be remembered that only a fairly small proportion of the poor ever saw the inside. Those who did might actually find themselves better off in accommodation and diet than those who got a meagre dole of out-relief and scraps from charity. The accounts made up on 25 March 1850 show that as many as 727 Beaminster paupers had been relieved outside the workhouse during the previous six months at a cost of £741; on 25 March 1857 the number (over a similar period) was 435 and the cost £610.[30]

Most workhouse inmates were in the event drawn from the young, infirm and aged; by the mid-1860s the buildings were no longer workhouses so much as asylums and infirmaries. The number of people inside the Beaminster workhouse when the census was taken in 1891 was 67; in 1911 there were 100 people. Old age pensions had been introduced in 1908, but it was reported in the *Bridport News* that 'Not a single inmate . . . has elected to leave the house [Beaminster Union] in order to obtain an old-age pension. Many could do so if they liked, but they know too well where they are best off . . .'.[31]

Street Lighting

The first public gas lamps (18 in all) were erected in the town for the winter of 1836. At a poll taken in September that year, over two-thirds of the parishioners had voted against adoption of the Lighting and Watching Act and the levying of a rate; a committee was therefore set up, which resolved to collect subscriptions immediately 'for the purpose of providing Lamps and Erecting Lamp Posts'. A contract was entered into with the Beaminster Gas Company for laying down iron pipes, and supplying and furnishing the lamps with gas for one year — 161 nights at nine hours a night — at £3 a light.[32] The service pipes were laid, and the street lamps and brackets made, by Thomas Newman, brazier and plumber.[33]

Subscriptions for the first year amounted to £67 10s. 6d., but they gradually decreased until in 1841 the lighting had to be suspended owing to lack of funds.[32] A voluntary subscription was again assessed on individual ratepayers from 1844,[34] but in 1853 the management committee of the Gas Association advised that unless contributions could be raised to £46 annually, a rate should be levied, or the public lights would have to be extinguished altogether.[35]

The Lighting and Watching Act was adopted in 1854; the company contracted to supply public lighting at £75 for the year, nine more lamps being ordered.[35] Six Lighting Inspectors were appointed, the first being J. Gilbert, W. Gardner, G. Swaffield, B. Seymour, H. Virgint and G. Squire. The 'Gas Lighting District' comprised the Fore Place and the following streets: Hogshill, Shadrack, Church, St Mary Well, Clampits, Fleet, North, High and East, together with houses within 350 yards in a straight line from any of these streets. At an annual meeting of ratepayers of the Lighting District held each year in June, the amount of money needed for the coming year was voted, and the inspectors gave an order to the overseers of the poor to raise this sum.[36] The inspectors put an advertisement for tenders to light the area in the local paper (*Dorset County Chronicle* over the period 1867-79 and *Bridport News* 1894-1914), but invariably the only tender received was from the Beaminster Gas Company. The amount of the contract varied very little from the 1870s onwards, being round about £100.[37]

The lamps were lighted one hour after sunset and extinguished at midnight from the beginning of September to the middle of May. Over the period to 1914 two extra lamps are recorded, one in 1875 in The Green, and one at Hams in 1901. Soon after the parish council was set up, it complained about 'the bad lighting of the Town generally', and in March 1900 a resolution was passed by the annual parish meeting that the town 'should be better lighted especially at the outskirts'. Miss Charlotte Keddle of St Mary's Cottage had been pressing for lamps in Clay Lane since 1897, but the inspectors would still not agree in 1903, having found the road 'perfectly straight & of good width & without any bend or obstacle of any kind on either side thereof to obstruct the light'. In 1902, in reply to a letter from the Local Government Board about the area of the lighting rate, the inspectors expressed the view that 'to extend the Area so as to include land not hitherto rated would meet with considerable opposition'.[37]

The question of the parish council taking over lighting was raised at the annual meeting of the lighting area in 1904,[22] but the council was not willing because the extra duties devolving on the Clerk would be so onerous that his salary would have to be increased.[27] (The Lighting Inspectors were of course unpaid.) In 1912 the District Auditor commented that the continued appointment of inspectors was very unusual, parish councils normally undertaking lighting, as envisaged in the 1894 Act.[22] Responsibility was transferred in June 1914.[28]

In August 1914 a tender was accepted from the Beaminster Gas Company to light all the existing public lamps (now 37) from 1 September 1914 to 14 May 1915 from one hour after sunset until 11.30 p.m. for £103.[28, 33] No sum was voted in 1915 on account of the war, a proposition that £30 be allowed for partial lighting (five lamps, widely spaced) being lost. No sums were voted in 1916 and 1917,[22] but in March 1918 J. R. Bridle, one of the parish councillors, referred to the inconvenience caused by the town being entirely dark during winter months, while towns nearer the sea had many subdued lights in their streets. It was agreed to spend a sum not exceeding £35, and it was arranged to light six lamps, but only to 10 p.m.[28] In September 1922 the Gas

Company's offer to light 10 lamps from 1 October to 1 April at only £5 per lamp was accepted; any smaller number would have been charged at £5 10s. 0d. In June 1925 the number of street lamps to be lit during the coming winter was doubled to 21, in response to the offer to light not less than 20 lamps from sunset to 10.30 p.m. for £4 per lamp.[26]

In May 1926 the Lighting Meeting — the date of the meeting had been put forward a month in order to get a better attendance — approved a proposal to extend the lighting area to take in Shorts Lane and the further part of Clay Lane including the new council houses at Pattle.[22] The number of lamps was added to steadily, with new ones well spaced over the town streets; by 1932, 34 lamps were being lit from 14 days before to 14 days after the official winter time. The were situated as follows: [26, 25]

Tunnel Road and Clay Lane (5) — at Dannemora, on Mr. Skyrm's workshop, opposite the *Knapp*, the junction of Stoke Road, the top of Pattle Road.
Hogshill St. (4) — the corner of Shadrack St., Grammar School, *White Hart*, *Royal Oak*.
The Square (2) — at Eddoll's and Carter's shops.
Fleet St. (4) — Pine's, Wesleyan Chapel, near Barton End, Luggs.
North St. (4) — Milk factory, opposite the Manor House, top of street, in The Green.
Prout Bridge (3) — opposite The Walnuts, Hanns, 'Prout Bridge'.
Bridport Road (2) — at Woodlands, South Gate.
East St. (4) — Parsons' cottage, middle of the street, *Sun Inn*, junction of Woodswater Lane.
East Road (2) — at Hitts, Whitemore's.
St Mary Well St. (2) — opposite Rogers', Hams.
Church St. and Shadrack St. (2).

Electricity reached Beaminster in 1932, Bridport Corporation having obtained an Order allowing them to supply the surrounding district, and in June 1933 a quotation was received from the corporation for lighting Beaminster street lamps by electricity. The quotation was £1 lower (at £119) than that of the Beaminster Gas Company, but the parish council resolved to accept the tender for gas, 'the Company having served the Council very well in the past'. In the years following the gas tender was always lower than the one for electricity, and the price steadily reduced. In July 1935 it was resolved to light 39 lamps for £100 10s. 0d.; the extra lamps were in Fleet Street, on Vicarage Hill, and in Shorts Lane, with two at the latest council houses at Pattle. By now the lighting period was from 7 September to 14 days after the end of winter time and all the lamps were kept alight until 11 p.m. For the first time there were again as many street lights as before the First World War.[25] (Two of the old lamp-posts are still standing, one at Prout Bridge and the other outside Knowle Cottage.)

In August 1938 an agreement was entered into with the Crewkerne Gas & Coke Company, which had purchased the Beaminster gas works, to light the street lamps (now 41) for five years, at the lower price of £2 8s. 9d. per lamp per annum. A proposal to extend the lighting area to all the streets within one mile of The Square was to be put at the lighting meeting in 1940, but meantime public lighting had been discontinued on account of the war. Street lighting on a small scale was again permitted in October 1944, and 20 lamps were lit, a return to the full number being made the following winter. In May 1946 the parish council asked for a quotation for seven additional lamps, and for the period to be extended to run from 21 August to the end of May; Crewkerne Gas Company was not prepared to meet the expense of new lamps for an agreement lasting only one year, and the quotation of £3 7s. 0d. per lamp for a longer lighting period was not found acceptable. In October 1946 a sub-committee was set up to consider a change from gas to electricity.[25] The lighting area was extended to cover the whole parish in 1947.[21]

Fire Brigade

The upkeep of the fire-engines, and the proper way to pay for it, continued to worry the Vestry. In 1857 the churchwardens were told to confer with some competent person as to whether the fire-engines, the engine-house and the town pump were repairable, and to get an estimate. The Vestry could not agree however whether to raise a rate for the repairs — it was uncertain if the poor rate could properly be used — or whether to ask for voluntary subscriptions. In the end a tender was accepted (in 1860) from Shand & Mason in London to repair one of the engines for £11 10s. 0d.[1]

In September 1870 a proposal that the overseers should be authorised to raise the sum of £20 to keep the engines in repair failed to be carried. A public meeting held on 10 November 1870, for the purpose of forming a Volunteer Fire Brigade, appointed a Fire Brigade Committee (Edwin Coombs, John Hine, J. L. Kitson, J. S. Webb and Richard Swatridge) to which the Vestry agreed to entrust custody and control of the engines, appliances and engine-house.[1,38] The records of this committee have not survived and there are no further details about the formation of the volunteer brigade. In May 1877 a motion put to the Vestry that the engine-house was 'property which the Parish is interested to hold and keep in repair' was carried, and the assistant over-seer was instructed to put it in repair to the directions of the fire brigade committee.[1]

It was not until April 1896 that the new Beaminster Parish Council decided to take over the fire-engines. In October 1897 approval was given for the sale of two old engines,[27] one of which was probably the small engine still kept on the premises of the Dorset Fire Brigade at Beaminster; in 1911 this fire-engine belonged to Charles Toleman, and had 'long been in disuse'.[39] The parish council drew the attention of the district council in March 1899 to the fact that there was insufficient water available in the town in case of fire.[27] When the water supply was eventually laid on, £30 was voted in April 1909 for better equipment; it was decided to buy new canvas hose and four scaling ladders from Shand & Mason, but to have a hose cart made locally as this would be cheaper. The council's fire brigade committee felt the premises then in use were inadequate: the shed (next to No. 21 The Square) measured 11 ft. by 10 ft., and there was hardly room to clean the engine, let alone dry the additional lengths of hose. The old weaving shed in the Yarn Barton would be very suitable, and in December 1909 the parish council passed a resolution to purchase the shed for £100.[28] A special parish meeting held in February 1910 approved, but a complaint was later made that few parishioners were aware that this meeting was to take place, and that there was some feeling in the town about the whole thing; at another parish meeting held in May the previous resolution was rescinded.[22] A bracket was fixed outside the public hall for drying the hose, a cement floor was put down at the engine-house and water laid on, and a hand cart was finally ordered from Hunt & Son.[28]

The fire brigade was of course still entirely voluntary, and was not paid by the parish council for any services rendered at a fire; the captain was however paid a small salary for cleaning the engine, etc., and members received a small sum for each fire practice. In March 1914 James Poole retired; he had been captain since 1872, and must have been appointed soon after the formation of the brigade. John Trump, who had been deputy captain since 1898, was appointed captain, the other eight members being John Bowditch, J. I. Newman, James Poole junior, George Trump, Arthur Brooks, Alfred Winter, Percy Paull and W. A. Poole. In November 1919 it was agreed that the brigade should be summoned by maroon signals sent off by Richard Hine, and the fire brigade committee suggested that shafts with a bar should be provided to draw the fire-engine in place of the pole.[28] It has not been possible to find out the type and make of engine in use at this period, nor when it was purchased. Presumably it was one of the larger manual engines which were developed during the 19th century, for Richard Hine writes (in 1914) of a pair of horses being harnessed to the lumbering fire-engine, and after men and equipment had finally been got together, a start being made for the scene of the outbreak, 'with the firemen aboard the engine holding on for dear life'. 'If only', Hine says, 'a fire burns long enough for it to arrive on the scene, the time-honoured machine can still be relied upon to render good service!'[40]

In January 1926 the fire brigade committee reported that all premises in the neighbourhood of water mains or hydrants were reasonably well protected by means of the existing appliances; it recommended however that, for the outlying areas, some arrangement should be made with a neighbouring town or towns with efficient fire brigades. Evidently an agreement had been come to with Bridport by 1928, for necessary adjustments were provided to enable Bridport's appliances to be connected up to Beaminster's hydrants. In June 1931 it was agreed that the present manual fire-engine was useless; it was sold later for £1 2s. 6d., and this made room for drying the hose in the engine-house.[26]

During 1935 the parish council debated whether to continue the fire brigade, spending a considerable sum in bringing it up to date, or whether to scrap it and rely entirely on the Bridport or Crewkerne brigades. In April 1936 — the parish meeting having decided that the brigade should be revitalized and approved an additional rate of up to 2d. in the £ — the decision was made to purchase an electric siren, two chemical extinguishers and a hook ladder. However, before these purchases were actually made, a conference of local authorities owning fire brigades (held at Dorchester in April 1937 in connection with air-raid precautions) took the view that Beaminster ought to have some form of *mobile* appliance. Beaminster Parish Council estimated the sum required to be spent at £700, including the purchase of a mobile trailer pump for £400, and in October 1937 approached the rural district council for financial assistance. In the meantime a siren (3 horsepower) was purchased at a cost of £62, and was erected in July 1938 on the new town offices in Fleet Street where accommodation had been provided for a fire station.[25]

It now became known that under new legislation (Fire Brigades Act 1938) rural district councils were to become the fire authorities in place of parish councils, and would have a statutory obligation to make provision for fire appliances. Agreements were made by Beaminster Rural District Council with neighbouring authorities to cover groups of parishes in its district, and it was decided to continue the Beaminster Fire Brigade as at present, the parish council acting as agents from 29 January 1939, the date of transfer. In August 1941 all duties were transferred to the newly formed National Fire Service.[18]

Allotments

As the situation of the farm worker improved during the later 19th century, allotments ceased to be regarded as a form of poor relief, and were made available to all who wanted them, sometimes in larger portions of land. A requisition signed by 52 persons in Beaminster, requiring that allotments should be provided under the Allotments Act 1887, was made to the Beaminster Rural Sanitary Authority in March 1888. More than 20 acres were then let privately in the parish — a similar acreage to 1847 — but a well attended public meeting complained subsequently of the rents being too high, and the size of the allotments unsatisfactory. Twenty-two people gave in their names as having no allotment ground, but not a single response was received to a notice issued inviting applications.[9]

One of the first decisions taken by the new parish council in January 1895 was to implement the provisions of the Local Government Act 1894 regarding allotments, which it had power to supply to working men at a reasonable rate. Notices were issued to the public that the parish council would be glad to interview them on the subject; '18 working men and others' came and stated their needs. It was found that about 17 acres were either let as allotments or had been so used during the past five years, but this would probably be reduced shortly as some of the fields were grassed down. Arrangements were made without delay to rent several fields of two to three acres: at Furlands and Hollymoor from Miss F. O. Cox, at Peasehill from J. R. Cox, at Hollymoor from Mrs. Tuck, and off Broadwindsor Road (at Cockroad) from Peter Meech. All these fields, some of which were already being let privately to allotment holders, were measured, pegged out, and let to applicants in allotments of an eighth of an acre. In March 1896 the chairman was able to report that since the parish council came into office, the number of allotments had been increased from 36 to 83,[27] and in March 1901 to claim that the allotments had not cost the ratepayers a penny over the past six years.[22] There were still some allotments rented out privately: the 25-inch O.S. map (revised 1901) shows allotments also at Yarn Barton, Clampits and opposite the manor house in North Street.

At the end of 1901 the Broadwindsor Road allotment was given up at the request of Peter Meech,[27] but it continued to be let privately for the purpose until late in 1909 when 10 allotment holders there were given notice to quit; most of the men were accommodated elsewhere. Only seven further applications for allotments were received in response to a public notice in July 1910, and it was decided that further action was not warranted, there being an 'insufficient number of applications from men of stability'.[28]

In June 1920, it having become known that the Yarn Barton allotments were to be put up for sale at public auction, the parish council tried to purchase this field so as to ensure that it remained in use as allotments; the price limit set was £200, and Yarn Barton went for £290 to another purchaser.[28, 26] When the Furlands and Hollymoor allotments were about to be auctioned in September 1924, the council moved quickly to secure a purchase by private treaty; owners offered to sell for £250 and the purchase was completed in June 1925.[26]

CHAPTER FOURTEEN

MORE ABOUT PUBLIC SERVICES 1850-1950

Roads

A HIGHWAY RATE was raised by the Vestry to pay for the upkeep of parish roads,[1] but no record of expenditure has survived; the two main roads through the parish, the Bridport-Crewkerne road and the Dorchester-Broadwindsor road, were in any case the responsibility of turnpike trusts. When Bridport Highway Board took over in 1863, the miles of road in each parish for which it was responsible were measured; in Beaminster there were 12 miles. In the later 1860s reference is made to improving the road at The Green, and to widening the road from Beaminster to the Union workhouse and reducing the gradient.[2]

The Maiden Newton Turnpike Trust expired 31 December 1872, and the Bridport 2nd District Trust 1 November 1881. In October 1880 the Bridport Highway Board agreed with the Bridport trust to take over the repair of the road and the lighting of the tunnel at Horn Hill as from 1 January 1881. Tolls were abolished; the toll collector was to be allowed the use of the tollhouse – the building was only pulled down in 1963 – and to be paid 2s. 0d. a week for lighting the lamps at each end of the tunnel, 'he to find the oil'. The tollhouse at South Gate was sold.[3] Both the former turnpike roads were classified as 'main' roads, so becoming the responsibility of Dorset County Council. In 1892 the average width of the carriageway was 19 ft. in the case of the Bridport road, while the Dorchester road was 16 ft. wide from Dirty Gate to Beaminster and 18 ft. wide between Beaminster and Lenhams Water.[4]

Beaminster Rural District Council became responsible for the other roads in 1895; from 31 March 1930 the repair of all roads was assumed by Dorset County Council under the Local Government Act 1929. (Beaminster District Council applied in March 1929 for delegation to it of all functions in connection with unclassified roads, but withdrew the application when the county council would not agree.[5])

The upkeep of its roads was effected by the district council by means of separate contracts, normally for three years, made with local people in the various parishes; the contracts covered (a) scraping the road and keeping it and the drains free of earth, brambles, grass etc. and (b) quarrying and spreading flint, stone or gravel, and keeping it well raked afterwards. Other contracts were agreed with hauliers for loading and hauling the materials. County roads were steam-rolled, but this was not done on Beaminster District roads before the 1920s. Dorset County Council pointed out in August 1910 that steam-rolling was both desirable and economical, and was being done in the northern and eastern divisions of the county,[6] but in February 1914 Beaminster District Council would not even consider steam-rolling because of the enormous increase it would mean in the rates.[7] There were constant complaints about the dangerous state of the roads, and in July 1911 it was proposed that a permanent 'Road Committee' should be set up to supervise, but the motion was lost.[6]

One of the problems connected with the advent of the motor car was the dust it created. The weather was very dry in the summer of 1908, and Beaminster Parish Council tried to get the streets watered, but without success. J. G. Kitson suggested (October 1908) that as regards the main road through the town, the best solution would be to get the county council to treat it with tar: 'he had seen many roads so treated and it was successful'. When it was found in March 1909 that the parish would have to pay half the cost — which was estimated at £46 17s. 6d. even if some parts of the streets were omitted — the matter was left in abeyance. Tar-spraying was carried out at county council expense in July 1911, and in subsequent years.[8, 9]

Responsibility for the repair of pavements was the subject of discussion from time to time. In 1859 the Vestry decided that each person ought to repair the pavement along the frontage of his own house, but that the tithing would repair 'the curb stones, crossings and gravelling as heretofore'.[1] (Crossings were paved with stone and provided firm smooth places for pedestrians to cross the otherwise miry or dusty rough gravel street.) In March 1873 Bridport Highway Board called the attention of the Vestry to the need for repairing the sidepaths or causeways; a motion to the effect that causeways in the principal thoroughfares were the responsibility of the highway board was lost, and it was agreed that owners of house property should be called upon to repair those adjoining. In March 1876 the Vestry set up a committee to confer with the waywarden and the board and, if expedient, to solicit subscriptions; the following month the board authorised its surveyor to repair the pavements.[2] In October 1890 the board agreed to pay half the cost of repairs, provided owners and occupiers paid the other half.[3]

Beaminster Rural District Council at first tried to make occupiers pay half the cost of repair of pavements, but later accepted sole responsibility;[10] most of the pavements in Beaminster were in a bad way in the early years of this century. After the laying of the water mains in 1908, a ratepayer complained in a letter to the *Bridport News* that the pavements in Fleet Street were 'in a most disgraceful condition and notwithstanding that they lead to two places of worship, and consequently are more used on the Sabbath day than any other street in the town'. Parishioners, he said, waded through water in the roadway in preference to splashing through the puddles which in places lurked beneath the loose stones: 'What is more annoying than a sudden "douche" from beneath a paving stone, shot with unexpected vigour and volleys of mud half way up one's legs?'.[11, 6]

The First World War brought difficulties owing to shortage of both men and materials, and from 1916 tenders for repairing the roads were only invited for one year at a time. In an application made to the Road Board in March 1919 for a grant for District roads, Beaminster District Council stated that although the rate for maintenance had been collected regularly during the war it had been impossible to spend all the money, and the roads were now in such a bad state that it would take more than the sum saved to put them back into their pre-war condition.[7] The problem got worse in the early 1920s as roads were increasingly used by heavy traffic for which, this being an entirely rural district, they had not been designed.[12]

In October 1919 the district council, which had briefly considered the purchase of its own horses and waggons, or a steam or motor lorry, for the haulage of materials, decided to stick to using a contractor. In November 1920 the decision was reaffirmed not to steam-roll roads, except any previously steam-rolled and those in respect of which a special grant was received. In March 1922, however, a committee was set up to consider the use of a steam-roller and to investigate comparative costs. Sturminster Newton Rural District Council was reported now to be steam-rolling its roads, having purchased its own steam-rollers, and the scheme there was considered 'an extra-ordinary success'. It was decided in September 1922 that as an experiment that season roads would be steam-rolled where granite and picked flint were to be put down, but that the machine would be hired.[7, 12] Gradually the steam-roller was used on more and more roads. In October 1925 the chairman commented that councillors had doubtless observed the improvement to the roads, and the surveyor was instructed to steam-roll any road which he thought would benefit.[13]

The two main roads had been classified under the new scheme of Class 1 and Class 2 roads set up the Ministry of Transport, but a census taken had not revealed sufficient traffic on any of the District roads for them to be classified and thus automatically attract a grant. However, from 1924–5 onwards, grants were received from Road Fund revenue to enable selected roads (the more important unclassified ones) to be improved by the use of harder materials and tar-spraying, and the removal of dangerous corners. For 1927–8 a new improvement scheme was introduced, giving in addition a grant in respect of ordinary maintenance of all roads of more than local importance.[12, 13] (In February 1926 pavements in Beaminster were taken up and replaced with granolithic concrete.[13])

Tenders for road repairs for three years were again invited in February 1925, but in January 1928, on the suggestion of the surveyor, it was resolved that all manual work should be done by direct labour for one year initially as a trial.[13, 5] In 1930, 21 men were being employed regularly on the roads, but other work had continued by contract.[14] A Llewellin & James bitumen-spraying machine (160 gallons) was purchased in July 1928 for £150; this was later taken over by Dorset County Council.[5]

Sanitation and Sewerage

Investigations made by the Poor Law Commissioners in the early 1840s found that the main causes of disease among the poor were inadequacies of drainage, water supplies and facilities for disposal of refuse. In 1846 a Nuisance Removal Act recognised the boards of guardians as authorities for sanitary matters in rural areas; under the Public Health Act 1848 and the Local Government Act 1858 local boards of health could be set up in defined urban districts.

In December 1853 Beaminster Board of Guardians issued a circular letter drawing the attention of parish officers to a resolution which it had passed in connection with an outbreak of cholera. This called upon the parish officers to take immediate steps for the appointment of a board of health, to consist of the clergyman, parochial officers and principal inhabitants, and where possible the medical officer having charge of the sick poor. A vestry meeting held at Beaminster in January 1854 — attended by only nine people, among them Joachim Gilbert, one of the doctors in the town — carried a resolution to the effect that there was no necessity for the establishment of such a board.[15] In September 1866, during another cholera scare, it was resolved at a vestry meeting 'that with a view of making a thorough house to house visitation throughout the parish . . . preparatory to the removal of existing nuisances, the following Gentlemen do form a local Board of Health . . .'. The list of 16 names included those of the vicar, curate, parish officers and four doctors: W. J. Daniel (Board of Guardians' M.O. for the Beaminster district), R. W. Broster (Marshwood district), T. P. Daniel and J. Gilbert.[1] There was no formal adoption of the Local Government Act, which would have required a special meeting of ratepayers.

The Bridport Highway Board carried out some cleansing of the rivers and watercourses running through Beaminster, but once Beaminster Rural Sanitary Authority had been set up (1872), the board instructed its surveyor in October 1873 to discontinue this work,[2] which became the responsibility of the new authority. Some of the watercourses were covered over: for example, in 1880 the Inspector of Nuisances was instructed to obtain estimates for repairs to the bed of the stream at the bottom of Little (Shadrack) Street, and for 'arching same over below the Road Bridge there to that part farther down already arched in'.[16]

In July 1878, on the request of Beaminster Rural Sanitary Authority, W. J. Daniel (M.O.H. for Beaminster district) made a thorough investigation into the state of drainage of the town;[16] he reported that it was very bad in some parts, 'more especially perhaps at the lower part of St Mary Well St., where at times when the water is stagnant it is really quite unhealthy'. He thought the various slaughter-houses were a great source of trouble, and it would be better if a common one were erected out of the town. This report was laid before the Beaminster Vestry with the comment that 'They [the sanitary authority] in no way waive their powers and it is only in a spirit of courtesy they leave this matter for the primary consideration of the Ratepayers . . .'. A vestry meeting held in August considered that the main problem could be dealt with by placing hatches to raise a flush from the two streams which flowed into the river at the bottom of St Mary Well Street.[1]

However in January 1880 a further and 'very lengthy' report made by J. S. Webb on the sanitary condition of certain parts of Beaminster was referred to the Vestry. The covering letter read: 'feeling that this Report is but the precursor of other Reports affecting this Town they [the sanitary authority] consider the matter now brought forward may well be considered by a Vestry who may perhaps offer some suggestions on matters of detail'. The vestry meeting, while agreeing to some of the proposals, passed a unanimous resolution that 'the drainage leading from the top of Fleet Street down to the bridge in North Street is sufficient for sanitary purposes provided it can be kept properly flushed'.[1] In March 1893 a committee recommended 'one good drain thro' the middle of Fleet Street instead of the two existing drains'.[17]

Meanwhile in November 1883 a vestry meeting, held to consider a letter from the authority about the 'insufficiency and bad condition of the drain between the Bell and Crown [East Street] and Prout Bridge', passed a resolution that it should be made into an efficient sewer,[1] and the sanitary authority accepted a tender from Robert Chambers to construct the sewer for £52. In April 1886 a tender was accepted from George Gale for construction of a sewer along the Fore Place from Framptons to the bank (now Lloyds) for £17 7s. 6d. Later that year the Local Government Board asked how the sewage of Beaminster was treated but the reply is not recorded.[16]

Regular annual contracts were now being made with Trump & Poole for cleansing of watercourses, drains and stench traps,[16] and similar arrangements were continued by Beaminster Rural District Council with Edwin Bugler and later W. J. Boon.[18, 6] In October 1901 the Local Government Board, which seems to have been silent on the subject of Beaminster sewage since 1886, asked the council to state without further delay the position regarding drainage of the town. The Clerk was instructed to reply that arrangements for improved drainage and a scheme for water supply were being carried out 'hand in hand', and both were awaiting the result of experimental water works. When the Beaminster Water Supply Committee (set up by the district council) was reconstituted in 1902, its terms of reference were extended to include sewerage.[18]

The sanitary condition of the town came to the fore again in August 1906: the Local Government Board, which had asked for a special report from the M.O.H. owing to the prevalence of diphtheria, was now enquiring what steps were proposed, especially as regards an improved system of water-closets and the removal of pollution from the river. A parish meeting was held in May 1907 at which Mr. J. L. Kitson (chairman of the water supply and sewerage committee) explained that the most satisfactory way would be to drain the town in a thorough manner, but this would cost between £4,000 and £5,000 exclusive of purchase of land; furthermore, of the 400 houses then occupied in the town, less than 100 had water-closets, and the other 300 house owners would have the expense of converting their present closets into water-closets and connecting to the public sewers. In the discussion which ensued, it was stated on behalf of Vincent Robinson of Parnham that he would oppose a water-borne system which would place a sewage works at a spot immediately south of the town or involve pipes through his grounds. Dr. F. P. Kitson (Medical Officer of Health) and Dr. A. A. Pim both spoke in favour of a conservancy system; it was by no means clear to all those present how such a system worked, but it was explained that for one thing water-closets connected with a drain or river would be cut off and cesspools would have to be constructed. A resolution in favour of a conservancy system was finally carried, though by then 'many had left the room'; 10 people voted for it and one against![9, 19]

A plan prepared by a Bridport surveyor was submitted to Beaminster District Council by its water supply committee in September 1907. The town was to be drained in sections: No. 2 section (Hogshill Street, The Square, Prout Bridge, Church Street and St Mary Well Street), being the worst area, would be dealt with first by conducting the sewage by means of new sewers to a large tank constructed in a field near Hams, which would be emptied periodically.[6, 20] The council told the Local Government Board that it believed this to be the only practicable method 'without incurring expenses far beyond what the Parish would be able to bear', but in December 1907 the board rejected the proposals outright, urging the council to obtain the advice of an engineer with wide experience of schemes for sewerage and sewage disposal, and pointing out that the question of a scheme for the town had been before the council since 1901.[6]

The matter seems to have remained in abeyance for another 20 years. In May 1927 representations about the pollution of the river were made by the owners of Parnham, who offered financial assistance if a sewerage scheme was undertaken, and the district council engaged an engineer, A. J. Martin, to advise. In October 1927 he submitted a scheme which would cost £11,000 excluding the purchase of the land: £7,300 would be required for sewers, and £3,700 for purification works for which he suggested the best site was at Millground on the Parnham estate. The plans were sent to the Parnham trustees, but in the meantime the estate changed hands.[13, 21]

When Beaminster Debating Society debated whether a sewerage scheme should be undertaken, the vote was 50 for and 61 against,[22] but Dr. Pim (M.O.H.) pointed out in his report for 1928 that the bringing of a water supply to Beaminster in 1908 had made a sewage disposal scheme inevitable in the long run.[23] The sewage which had previously received 'innocuous burial in garden middens' was now swept, as water-borne sanitation became the norm, into the streams and culverts and so carried to the river. The Brit used to be 'comparatively unpolluted, and it was no unusual thing to see numerous trout in the river, well within the area of population'. Now not only sewage but quantities of rubbish were deposited in it, owing to the increased consumption of tinned food. As Dr. Pim so graphically described:[23]

> The river struggled manfully against its numerous persecutors, but when the Milk Factory came and poured its noxious effluent into its waters, it gave up the struggle and ceased to be a stream and became a sewer. At the end of 1927, the stream had reached, both literally and metaphorically, its blackest point.

Early in 1929 representatives of Beaminister Water Supply and Sewerage Committee visited Crewkerne, where similar sewage works to those proposed had been operating successfully for over 20 years, and the district council decided in May to proceed with the scheme if a grant could be obtained from the central government Unemployment Grants Committee. However, the Yeo Vale Country Club, new owners of Parnham, objected to the site suggested for the outfull for the purification works; they proposed other sites (for example Clenham) which were found unsuitable because of the additional expense involved. In October 1929 the scheme was postponed for six months, and in February 1931 it was reported 'in abeyance'.[5]

Apart from special arrangements for the council housing schemes, the sewage problem was not tackled again until after the end of the Second World War. In spite of all the efforts of sanitary enthusiasts, the stone culverts (open under the pavements), which did duty as sewers, remained unaltered except for the piping of a small portion. When proper sewers were finally laid down in the 1960s a veritable network of these culverts was found in the central part of the town.

Water Supply

Before about 1850 people living in the Fore Place would have used the town pump near the market house, the filling of buckets giving opportunity for a good gossip. In his verses 'Lament of the Beaminster Town Pump, 1871',[24] William Gardner imagines the pump saying:

> Well I remember happy, social days,
>   When empty vessels hither came,
> And freighted full, accorded me due praise:
>   Ah! then I gloried in my name!

In 1857 the question of repairs to the pump was raised at a vestry meeting, but it is unlikely that anything was done. By 1871 the town pump no longer functioned:

> My choler — would't were water! rises high,
> Wrapt in thick darkness there it lies;
> Like Tantalus, myself I can't supply;
> No sparkling drops from thence arise.

The derelict pump was removed with the market house building in 1886.[25] A large proportion of the drinking water was obtained at this time from 'Flatter Chute' at the bottom of St Mary Well Street; we also hear of 'dipping wells' in Hogshill Street and Fleet Street, and public pumps in Clay Lane and The Green.[26, 10]

In March 1885 Beaminster Rural Sanitary Authority referred to the Beaminster Vestry part of the annual report of the Medical Officer of Health dealing with the town's water supply. The vestry meeting only suggested that 'where the Water Supply is proved to be insufficient or unwholesome notice should in the first place be served on the Owners to make good the supply'. The Inspector of Nuisances was appointed Surveyor for matters affecting water supply and in September 1885 was authorised to get samples of water from public wells analysed, and to prepare an estimate of the cost of bringing water from Shatcombe. The M.O.H. (in a further report made in May 1886) detailed the source from which each house got its water, and S. Cox (auctioneer and estate agent) was subsequently paid for ascertaining the distance of the houses in the town from a water supply. The Clerk was instructed to call a public meeting in order to find out the general feeling about establishing a water company. In March 1887 the Clerk reported that he had written to the Local Government Board to the effect that 'the inhabitants of Beaminster and the Authority were generally of the opinion that the town was sufficiently supplied with water', and he had asked 'to be clearly informed of the powers of the Board to enforce a supply in the face of determined opposition'. The Local Government Board asked for a further report from the Medical Officer of Health, which was duly sent in July 1887.[16]

Nothing more seems to have been heard of the subject for about 10 years. In September 1897 the Local Government Board enquired again what was being done about a water supply for the town. The Clerk of Beaminster Rural District Council was told to say in reply that Beaminster was 'one of the healthiest towns in England', but the Board pointed out that this did not relieve the council of its duty under the Public Health Act to see that every dwelling house had a sufficient supply of wholesome water within a reasonable distance.[18] Beaminster Parish Council was asked to hold a parish meeting, and in July 1898 a resolution was passed by the parish that the district council should take steps to provide a supply of pure water.[9] Preliminary expenses of an experimental adit in a field off Stintford Lane were sanctioned, but this proved unsuccessful.[18]

A fresh start was made in April 1902 with a committee composed of the Beaminster councillors on the district council and three representatives nominated by the parish council;[10] over the years powers were delegated to this committee in connection with the town's water supply and related problems. In March 1903 the chairman of the committee (J. L. Kitson) commented at the annual parish meeting on the 'slow pace' at which the matter was proceeding; he explained that the engineers, Messrs. Beesley, Son, and Nichols, had now examined all the springs in the hills and had recommended water from a spring on Langdon farm. In March 1904 Mr. Kitson reported that the Ecclesiastical Commissioners, owners of Langdon, were prepared to sign a 99-year lease covering land for a reservoir and powers to tap springs and lay pipes. A year later the annual meeting was told that although the committee had done an immense amount of work and had held 51 meetings, the consent of some of the riparian owners had still to be obtained.[9]

The engineers reported in September 1906 that an 'eminently satisfactory' supply of water had been met with.[18] After an enquiry had been held by the Local Government Board at the *White Hart* on 14 February 1907, sanction was given to borrow the sum of £3,420, and the work was commenced. An adit cut into the side of the hill at Little West Woods produced a daily discharge of 92,000 gallons, while the daily requirement, on a population of 1,700, was only 25,000 gallons. Near the adit a covered service reservoir was constructed with a capacity of 76,000 gallons; water was conducted to the town by a main 4 in. in diameter. Rates to be charged for water varied according to the rateable value of the property, but the rate was the same whether the water was drawn from a tap inside the premises or from a standpipe in the street. Ten standpipes were initially ordered, to be set up at various points for the use of cottagers.[21]

At the annual parish meeting in March 1908, J. L. Kitson was able to congratulate the parish on the long-awaited water supply being now an accomplished fact. Almost every cottager in the town would have a supply of thoroughly good water within 200 feet of his house; keys would be given to all who asked, and everyone within 200 feet would be bound to pay the rate whether he used the water or not, unless he had a right of access to some other supply within the same distance. Householders within 200 feet of the 'Flatter Chute' or a public pump could continue to use this water provided it was not condemned, and would not be liable for the water rate.[27]

It had been a source of grievance that the water supply did not extend to the 18 or so houses at Newtown and Shortmoor, and the parish meeting carried a resolution to the effect that this was desirable.[9] At a second Local Government Board Inquiry held on 23 September 1908, application was made for consent to raise a further loan of £718 to cover the extensions and the cost of standpipes and additional hydrants. The extensions were completed in June 1909.[21]

In the later 1920s the water supply became insufficient for growing requirements. In his report for 1928, the medical officer of health pointed out that when the supply had first been brought there were only two bathrooms in the town, and the possessors of water-borne sanitation were so few as to 'occupy a position of dignified isolation'; since then bathrooms had multiplied — there were now 100 — and water-closets had become the rule. It had been necessary to turn off the supply at night during 11 weeks in the year and there was only a 10-minute supply available at such times in the event of fire.[23]

Beaminster Water Supply Committee recommended in May 1929 that an auxiliary water supply should be obtained by driving another adit at Shatcombe above the reservoir. An agreement was made with the owners of Shatcombe granting water rights under a lease for 77 years, and another with the owners of Langdon allowing pipes to be laid across their land to the reservoir. Work started in the spring of 1930 with local labour under the supervision of the manager of the waterworks (J. W. R. Newman), but owing to slips at the site, in October the workmen refused to continue. A firm of experts, George Stow & Co. of Newport, had to be engaged to complete the work; their bill amounted to £989 8s. 0d. and the total sum involved in the project was a little over £1,500. The auxiliary supply was available by early 1931;[5] it was further augmented in 1934 by collecting additional springs into the reservoir.[28] There were still a number of houses without a piped supply of water in 1946, the householders taking their water from standpipes; the water at 'Flatter Chute' continued to be used although it had been condemned.[29]

Under the Rural Water Supplies and Sewerage Act 1944 all water undertakings vested in rural district councils and were in future to be a charge on the general rate fund of the district, and not as in the past a parochial charge. Beaminster District Council had commissioned a preliminary survey for a water supplies (and sewerage) scheme for the whole rural district in August 1943, but this was subsequently absorbed into a much larger regional scheme for West Dorset.[30, 29]

Refuse Collection

In April 1910 Beaminster Parish Council drew the attention of the district council to the want of a place for the deposit of refuse and some means of collecting it and carting it away. The district council offered the site in Stintford Lane originally purchased for experimental waterworks, but this was obviously no use because of its inaccessibility. The parish council set up a sub-committee, which included Beaminster district councillors, to find a suitable site near the town, but all the suggestions put forward met with difficulties.[8]

At the annual parish meeting in March 1914, Charles Toleman said it was a 'disgrace' that the town was still without any arrangements for refuse disposal,[9] and the matter was again brought to the notice of the district council. In July 1914 the district council agreed to rent a suitable piece of the Peasehill allotment from the parish council, and to employ men to make a collection of domestic refuse once a month, convey it to the site and attend to it as necessary. Collection was to start in September; to begin with, it would be made only from the 'lighting area' of the town.[21] The advent of the First World War put a stop to the scheme: it was not the time, explained the chairman of Beaminster Water Supply and Sewerage Committee in March 1915, to launch out into fresh expenditure and besides labour would be scarce.[9]

The question was raised again at the annual parish meeting in 1919. The water supply committee thought it would be impossible to get anyone to collect refuse and that in any case it would involve heavy expenditure; in March 1920 the parish meeting passed a resolution that the district council should provide some place near the town to which refuse could be taken by the inhabitants.[9, 21] The district council agreed to rent the north-eastern corner of the Peasehill allotment from the parish council. In January 1921 Beaminster District Council was vested with urban powers under the Public Health Act 1875, enabling it to provide a refuse site, and the land at Peasehill became available for the deposit of refuse.[31]

In 1927 the question of collection of refuse came to the fore again when Mrs. Edward Moorhouse of Parnham complained of people throwing rubbish in the river

Brit. At a special parish meeting held in July 1927, the chairman explained that while many people availed themselves of the dump at Peasehill, many did not. A resolution was carried that a system of collection was necessary but that it should be a voluntary one, not rate-aided; a committee was set up.[9] The committee reported in October that a circular had been delivered to 282 householders, asking whether they desired a regular collection and what sum they were prepared to contribute weekly. Of the 172 replies collected, only 144 actually answered the questions asked; of these, 55 were in favour of a refuse collection and 89 were not, while the total weekly sum promised was 14s. 0¼d. A voluntary system was obviously impossible![32]

There the matter rested until August 1928 when complaints from new owners at Parnham, and from the Ministry of Agriculture and Fisheries, about house refuse and trade waste being thrown into the river, led to a decision on the part of the district council to institute a system of regular collection and disposal in the town, where nine-tenths of the population of the parish lived; the cost would be a special charge on the parish. A Refuse Disposal Committee was set up (including two parish councillors) and this committee suggested that, as the quantity of refuse was bound to increase, the Peasehill allotment should be purchased by the parish council in order to obtain security of tenure. The parish council wanted the district council to effect the purchase and rent back the portion which would continue in use as allotments, and in March 1929 the parish meeting refused to sanction the raising of the necessary loan.[5]

Collection of refuse had meantime been going on since December 1928 and it was necessary to make some proper arrangements because of trouble with rats at Peasehill. In April 1929 the refuse disposal committee recommended that another site should be obtained and an incinerator provided. The plan to put the incinerator in the same Parnham field as the proposed sewage works had to be abandoned, and the district council resolved in November 1929 to purchase a field just north of Whatley; a Meldrums incinerator (capable of dealing with four tons of refuse a day) was to be bought for £286. The Ministry of Health recommended the alternative of controlled tipping, although it was pointed out that Beaminster Rural District Council, unlike some councils, did not employ regular staff to deal with refuse as it was brought in and cover it with soil as required. The purchase of an incinerator was postponed indefinitely and for some time the council toyed with the idea of a comprehensive scheme for the whole District.[5] In the end the Peasehill dump continued to be used, and in April 1932 a tender was accepted from J. Boon & Sons not only to collect the refuse and haul it to Peasehill but also keep the dump in order.[28]

In June 1937 approval was given to purchase a large disused quarry at the top of Stintford Lane as a site for the disposal of Beaminster refuse; the site was in use by June 1938 and dumping ceased at Peasehill. Refuse from Corscombe, South Perrott, Mosterton and Netherbury was also collected and deposited here for a time under a joint scheme.[30] After the war Beaminster Rural District Council purchased a lorry and engaged a driver and assistant. Collections of indestructible refuse were started over the whole District, the cost being charged to General Expenses from 1 April 1946.[29]

Housing

Not long after the passing of the Housing of the Working Classes Act 1890, Dorset County Council suggested (June 1892) that Beaminster Rural Sanitary Authority should carry out a house-to-house visitation in order to provide information about the housing of the working classes in the area, but as the county council had no funds to pay for it, the sanitary authority did not feel able to take the job on.[17] The Local Government Board asked Beaminster Rural District Council in August 1910 whether it had considered the advisability of adopting the 1890 Act; in its reply of May 1911 the district council pointed out that there were as many as 201 uninhabited houses in the District, and that during the last few years 'landowners have built & are still continuing to build'.[6] (In 1891 there had been 327 unoccupied houses, of which 72 were in Beaminster.[33] The medical officer of health said in his report for 1906 that the housing of the working classes 'has much improved owing to the decline in the population; many of the worst houses have either been destroyed or have become ruins'.[34])

After the war the general shortage of decent cheap houses was acute. The Housing and Town Planning Act 1919 stated for the first time that it was the duty of local authorities to consider the housing needs of their areas; they should submit a housing scheme to the Local Government Board and the Treasury would bear all the losses they incurred in excess of a penny rate. In September 1918 Beaminster Rural District Council instructed the special Housing Committee which it had recently set up to go ahead and prepare a scheme in the light of the forthcoming legislation; in December 1918 the committee was strengthened by the addition of a further six members, in view of the 'important work to be undertaken'.[7]

The housing committee sought the opinion of parish councils. Beaminster Parish Council drew attention to the fact that the condition of many of the existing 'uncon- demned' working class houses in the parish (244) was unsatisfactory, these houses only continuing to be occupied for want of better ones; in view of demobilisation, the development of agriculture, and the hoped-for increase in trade, there would be an increased demand for more modern dwellings.[8] A special meeting of the parish council and the district councillors for the parish was held in January 1919 to consider sites. The first thing to be decided was how the cottages should be built: in one block, or distributed over the parish. Henry Crocker suggested that the whole 24 houses (the number then proposed) should be built on Dickie's Field at the end of Shorts Lane; he envisaged 'a little garden city – a model place'. In the end it was resolved that the houses should be constructed on a number of different sites.[35]

In April 1919 the Regional Housing Commissioner visited the area and explained that the Government's intention was that the new houses should not be 'scattered over the farms' as in the past. The aim was to get the population housed in better social conditions and together in communities, hoping thereby 'to cure the dullness of country life'; the problem of people being farther from their work could be overcome by use of bicycles.[36] The district council continued to support Beaminster Parish Council in its desire to limit the number of houses at any one site. In July 1919 the parish council, in conjunction with Beaminster district councillors, approved a dis- persed scheme for 30 houses in Beaminster: Half Acre 6, Hogshill Street 4, North Street 4, Newtown 4, The Green 4, and 8 in Whitcombe Road. The majority of the houses were to be 'non-parlour', with a large kitchen and a scullery, while a minority would have a parlour as well as kitchen and scullery; all the houses were to have earth closets.[8] Although the Housing Commissioner exerted pressure for the houses to be more 'concentrated' in accordance with central Government wishes, the housing committee stuck to the previous decision, and in June 1920 asked for Orders for compulsory acquisition, which were required for certain Beaminster sites, to be expedited.[36]

A new problem now arose: it proved impossible to get the Builders' Federation to agree prices in the District which were acceptable to the new Government department concerned, the Ministry of Health. At a meeting attended by the Regional Housing Commissioner in March 1921, the chairman of the housing committee stated that they were 'getting sick of continually meeting and getting no more forward'. It had already been agreed that virtually all the houses would be non-parlour, but further economies were now made. In June 1921 Beaminster Rural District Council was ready with a contract; as soon as the builders' representative had signed, it was to be rushed to Bristol for the approval of the Housing Commissioner, upon which the Clerk would call a special meeting of the council to seal the contract in order that building could commence. It was then that the final blow fell: the Government was running out of money and would not accept any more tenders for rural houses, priority being given to industrial areas. Since the inception of the scheme more than two years before, the housing committee had been meeting regularly every fortnight, and as the chairman said in July 1921, they had 'worked their hardest, and now when they had overcome numerous difficulties and were in a position to start building' the Government abandoned the scheme. What was more the district council had incurred a liability of over £5,000.[36] (The sites acquired had to be sold, and it was not until 31 March 1927 that the accounts of this scheme were finally cleared with the ministry.[12, 13])

The housing problem became even more difficult as time passed. The wealthy philanthropic landlord had virtually disappeared, and the main reason why cottages were in a bad state of repair was that many of the owners were poor people who would be quite unable to carry out, with the rents allowed (then only 1s. to 2s. a week) the costly repairs which the Sanitary Inspector might order.[37] Under Chamberlain's Housing Act 1923 new subsidies were to be granted for all houses — built by local authorities or private enterprise — which could satisfy certain conditions as to size and amenities. Beaminster Rural District Council decided in February 1924 to put up a scheme under the Act to provide assistance to private enterprise; a number of houses were built in the District, including some by W. J. Bailey in Clay Lane.[13]

Wheatley's Housing (Financial Provisions) Act 1924 provided a larger subsidy for houses built by local authorities for letting only; for this new subsidy restrictions were placed on the average rent which could be charged. In February 1925 the district council resolved to build 20 houses in Beaminster. On this occasion there seems to have been no reference to the parish council and no question of building on more than one site, for in March the housing committee recommended the purchase of 2½ acres at Pattle for £250. In April, with Ministry of Health approval, the council passed a resolution to purchase Pattle and to accept the tender of W. J. Cooper of Bridport (the lowest) to build the cottages for £8,990 plus £824 for layout of roads and water mains. By February 1926 the first eight houses were not only completed, but occupied; eight of the remaining 12 were still unlet, and these were advertised.[13] The houses (Pattle No. 1 scheme, Nos. 1-20) which were in four blocks of four and two blocks of two, were of a superior type for the time, with parlours; rents to be charged were set at 6s. 6d. weekly, plus 3s. 0d. rates.[38] The first occupiers were skilled workers at Bailey's (builders) and the gas works, assistants at Pine's (grocers), a postman, a policeman, and people connected with Perry's, the developing haulage company.[39] The medical officer of health referred in his report to the success of the Pattle scheme, which was 'evidenced by the happy and healthy community which has arisen at its door'.[40]

The first houses at Pattle were quite beyond the means of the agricultural worker. In June 1931, when the Housing (Rural Authorities) Bill was before Parliament, Beaminster District Council's housing committee considered the new scheme for houses to be built to let at a rental within reach of persons in agriculture or in other work at a similar wage.[28] Beaminster Parish Council asked for 30 houses, eight for agricultural workers, 12 for other working class people and 10 to replace unfit houses.[31] In March 1932 the district council allocated to Beaminster four of the 20 houses which the Ministry of Health had agreed to for the whole District. A two-acre site in Broadwindsor Road, not far from the first council houses, was selected in June, the four houses to be erected in one block on half-an-acre. A tender from Universal Housing Company of Rickmansworth for £5,780 for the 20 houses in the District (including septic tanks, wells etc.) was accepted in October 1932. The Beaminster houses (Pattle No. 2 scheme, Nos. 21–24), which were of non-parlour type, were completed in September 1933; rents were fixed at 4s. 0d. weekly inclusive of rates.[28, 38]

A letter to the district council from Beaminster Parish Council in October 1933 said that the four houses just completed were 'greatly appreciated' and there had been a large number of applicants for them; it pressed for further houses, pointing out that the rest of the site was already in council ownership.[41] It was decided to build 12 more houses there, and a tender from Universal Housing for £3,950 was accepted in August 1934. The houses, again non-parlour, were to be let at an economic rent of 7s. 6d. weekly exclusive of rates; no grant was obtained for these houses. In October 1934, after a visit to the site by the County Medical Officer, it was found that a further £600 would be required in order that the filtration system should cover not only No. 2 and No. 3 schemes, but also the 20 houses of No. 1 scheme, which would be converted from earth-closets to water-closets. The houses (Pattle No. 3 scheme, Nos. 25–36), consisting of one block of four and one block of eight, were occupied in April 1935;[28, 38] six of their first tenants were employees of Perry's and a further three were skilled workers employed by Bailey's.[39]

In the first half of 1936, a survey made under the Housing Act 1935 (which dealt with overcrowding) established a need for at least six more houses in Beaminster; land at Pattle (between schemes 1 and 2) was compulsorily acquired in August 1937, and in April 1938 a tender from J. Loving of Birdsmoorgate to build two blocks of three houses (non-parlour type) for £2,275 was accepted. An economic rent of 9s. 0d. weekly, exclusive of rates, was fixed in February 1939;[28, 30, 38] the houses (Pattle No. 4 scheme, Nos. 37–42) were occupied mainly by skilled workers and drivers employed by Bailey's, Newman's and Perry's.[39]

Beaminster Parish Council had been exerting continuous pressure for more houses,[41] while a survey made by the new joint medical officer of health and the sanitary officer found in February 1938 that 12 houses in Beaminster were unfit and ought to be demolished. The old 'Fair Field' off Tunnel Road was acquired for £575 by August

1938, and it was resolved to build 34 houses on this site, 10 in 1938-9 and a further 24 in 1939-40.[30] But then came the war. Towards the end of it Beaminster Rural District Council began to prepare its post-war housing programme. A decision was taken in January 1946 to proceed with the development of the Fairfield site and soon afterwards the first houses were under construction here.[29]

The Crewkerne carrier's cart

CHAPTER FIFTEEN

PEOPLE AND SOCIETY 1850-1950

Churches

IN THE LATER 19th CENTURY there were still some occasions of dissension between the Anglican and Nonconformist communities in Beaminster, but by the early part of this century harmony seems to have prevailed. This was no doubt largely due to the wide sympathies of the Rev. A. A. Leonard, a man 'beloved by all classes and creeds', who was vicar of the parish for 21 years from 1890. The Rev. R. B. Goodden (assistant curate at Beaminster), speaking at an Agriculture and Trade Dinner held in 1912 not long after Mr. Leonard's death, said that they and the other denominations in the town were all 'a very happy family'.[1]

St Mary's Church

The exterior of the church has not changed much since the large-scale rebuilding was completed early in the 16th century. The porch is early 19th century, and when the tower was restored in 1877–8 six new figures were placed in the then vacant niches on its north and west fronts.[2]

The interior of the church has however been much altered. The fine 17th-century three-decker pulpit of carved oak, comprising pulpit, reading desk, clerk's desk and clergyman's pew, which stood in the nave, was taken down and mutilated in 1851 and re-erected in the chancel. Although the pulpit and patched-up reading desk were returned to their place in the nave in 1856, the reading desk was taken away again in 1862 and the pulpit set on a modern base. During 1861 and 1862 a drastic restoration was carried out to the interior at a cost of about £3,000. It was at this time that the present roof of the nave was installed – the 17th-century roofs of the aisles were retained. The unsightly galleries went, and the removal of rough stone-work enclosing the mort-house (now the choir vestry) exposed the fine panelled arch on its north side.[3] However, much old work of interest and value disappeared at the same time; one of the most important items, the square 12th-century font of Purbeck stone, was fortunately found a good deal later in the stonemason's yard (Keech's) and restored to its place.[4] The old vicarage in Clay Lane was built for Canon Alfred Codd (vicar 1857–90) in 1859–61; it was designed by William White, and is High Victorian Gothic.[5]

Congregational church

In 1855 the Rev. G. Waterman (who followed Rev. Alfred Bishop) found the church at Beaminster 'in a weaker state than it had been for many years'.[6] This was partly due to the fact that many nonconformist families in the manufacturing trades had left the town, but nonconformity as a whole was depressed in the 1850s before the Second Evangelical Revival which took place between 1859 and 1865. Very few new members had been entered in the record when Mr. Waterman left in 1857 and he penned a sad note: 'I most earnestly pray that my successor may be enabled, by God's grace, to make many more such entries than it has been my privilege to do'. The chapel was so badly off that it remained for two years without a pastor. Philip Hine, who was made a decon in 1856, wrote:[7]

> In April 1858, the sum of £45 having been raised by 3 individuals, an appeal was made by the Deacons to the congregation for their assistance and co-operation to get a Pastor; that appeal was not responded to, excepting by a few of the smaller subscribers, together with the poorer members of the church, who have always cheerfully contributed to the extent of their means . . .

In October 1859 a decision was taken to apply to the Home Missionary Society for aid;[7] when this was promised, a finance committee was formed which in January 1860 pledged the society that a sum of £50 would be raised by the congregation during the forthcoming year.[8] The Rev. John Thomson became the minister, and the town 'was canvassed in districts that subscribers might be supplied with cheap pure literature, & an opportunity kept up of visiting the people'. By 1863 the chairman of the Good Friday tea-meeting was able to report 'a very great change'. The church was 're-established' in September 1863, and a system of weekly offerings commenced,[7] but it remained dependent, to make ends meet, on the aid which continued to be received from the Dorset Association and the Home Missionary Society. In January 1872 a finance committee meeting blamed the inability of the church to keep up the level of the minister's salary on a reduction in these grants and 'lessened subscriptions arising from diminished attendance'. Although the invitation to Rev. Thomas Sheldon in Januar 1873 contained 90 names of 'members of the Church and congregation', the church was able to promise for that year only £70 plus £25 from the two societies. A letter to Mr. Sheldon explains: 'As you are aware from the peculiar circumstances of the place there is no probability of any very large increase in our members or resources'.[9] The circumstances referred to were probably the declining population, of which, according to the vicar's calculations in 1872, dissenters represented only one eighth,[10] and the fact that much of the renewed support came from the less well-off members. In 1878 weekly offerings amounted to £44 10s. 9d., quarterly subscriptions £24 7s. 5d. and aid from societies £25, while four quarterly collections brought in £5 10s. 3d., and rent of the schoolroom to bodies such as friendly societies £4; the minister's salary was £100. In 1883 the pastor was asked to state from the pulpit the 'urgent need for greater help of funds which had greatly fallen off during the past year'. The interior of the chapel was modernised and rearranged in 1878, the old high pews and the organ gallery on the south wall being removed. The cost of this restoration (approximately £280) was however raised by contributions from other Beaminster citizens as well as members of the church and congregation.[9]

The leading people in the Congregational community were the owners of the more prosperous businesses in the town, and certain of the farmers. The Hine family continued to be prominent supporters. A brass tablet at the chapel commemorates Richard Hine, grocer (a deacon), his son Richard, druggist (treasurer of the finance committee formed in 1860) and grandson Alfred, who was continuously involved in chapel affairs in the 1860s and 1870s.[8, 9] There is another tablet in memory of Philip Hine, wine merchant. Philip's son John was elected to the general committee in 1870; during the time he was superintendent of the Sunday school 'there ensued some of its most prosperous days'. After he left Beaminster, John Hine returned every year for the anniversary services on Good Friday.[9, 11] Others holding the office of deacon were George Whitty (farmer at Higher Meerhay) who was elected in 1856, and Henry Virgint (draper) elected in 1869; in the 1870s and 1880s the office was held by John Cox Williams (draper), Samuel Chambers (builder), Isaac Orchard (grocer), Isaac Trevett (carriage builder of Melplash) and Charles Ebdon (coal dealer).[7]

The Rev. Uriah Randall, who became the minister in 1873, remained for nearly 17 years. Rev. William Bevan became pastor in 1890; no records can now be traced covering the period from then to the 1930s, but Richard Hine the historian, who like his forebears attended the chapel, says that for some time before Mr. Bevan left in 1895 there was a considerable decline in the congregation. He states that 'several Nonconformist families severed their connection with their old place of worship', but does not tell us what families or why.[12] It was round about 1900 that nonconformity in England reached the apex of its strength, but even in the industrial areas where the new chapels were built in the late 19th century, increases in membership were small in comparison with the rapid population growth; in rural areas of falling population, a congregation which maintained its numbers would have been doing very well. A decline was already setting in before the First World War, and was very evident by the 1920s.

In the early 1930s there were some 80 children in the Congregational Sunday school at Beaminster, and in 1936 several new children were enrolled, but by 1955 numbers of scholars had fallen off. In 1964 the church building was divided into two by the erection of a partition wall, the galleries being removed; the accommodation was turned around, putting the communion table on the east wall instead of the north wall as previously.[13]

Wesleyan Methodist church

In 1853 the Methodist church at Beaminster still had 21 members in the society,[14] but at the end of March 1856 the number of members was only 10, with a quarterly income of just £1. The total income of the Bridport circuit from all sources was only £50. Part of this consisted of 'The Circuit Collection', made in the town and the country congregations; it had recently been introduced 'to prevent an inconvenient increase of debt, and the too frequent appeals to the principal friends . . . The collection is not popular; a large proportion of the people give very little, and many of them nothing'. Circuit stewards seldom had a balance in their hands; 'in this [Bridport] Circuit, we believe, it has never been the case'.[15]

A sum of £200 had been borrowed towards the building of the chapel at Beaminster in 1839 and in 1856 the debt on the chapel was just over £235.[16] In 1876, a bequest of £45 to the trustees encouraged them to appeal for further help from friends to clear the debt. The amount needed was soon over-subscribed, and the surplus was used to put the building in thorough repair; Charles Lawrence, still serving the chapel, was chairman of the collectors' committee.[17] It seems that a gallery had been built in

1846; in 1884, because of increased attendance at the Sunday school, it was decided to enclose the gallery for a schoolroom.[18]

Few of the original records of the chapel seem to have survived. Circuit preaching plans for 1859-72 and 1881-90 show that W. B. Swatridge was accepted as a local preacher in 1871 and Benjamin Chambers (builder) in 1881. Henry Crocker, who was now the proprietor of the draper's shop at No. 21 The Square, also appears on preaching plans in the 1880s,[19] and was for many years superintendent of the Sunday school.[20] An article on Methodism in the Bridport area (1902) described Crocker, 'our genial circuit steward', as one who had 'done much to further the interests of Methodism in the circuit'.[21]

Renovations carried out in 1924 cost almost £335. Four years later there was no outstanding debt, but in 1935 an appeal had to be made to friends throughout the circuit in order to wipe out an adverse balance of about £43. In 1938 the advisability of discontinuing the evening service was under discussion so attendances must have dwindled.[22] The church was closed temporarily during the Second World War.

Schools

In the early years of the 19th century the only 'public' schools in Beaminster were Tucker's Charity school for boys, a 'School of Industry' run for a time at the parish workhouse, and a Sunday school. The Sunday school reported in 1818 was probably the one attached to St Mary's, which is known to have been formed before 1836.[23]

National school for girls (later girls' elementary)

A voluntary school for girls was established in 1830 and affiliated to the National Society for Educating the Poor in the Principles of the Established Church in November 1831. A note concerning the need for a school, in the handwriting of the then curate (Rev. Thomas Evans), appears in a school account book:

> The extreme idleness and ignorance of Needle-work which prevails among many of the children of the Parish of Beaminster . . . makes it desirable that a School should be established by Subscription, for the instruction of Girls in common needle-work, knitting, reading, and their moral and religious duties.

All the girls in the workhouse were to be admitted.

In its early days the school was entirely dependent on voluntary subscriptions, which amounted to about £15 annually; the 20 or so subscribers included Sir William Oglander of Parnham and his wife, Mrs. Samuel Cox, the solicitors or their wives, the doctors' wives and a few other gentry. In 1835 children's pence were collected, the charge being one penny a week or twopence if taught writing.[24] From 1848, and probably until at least 1860, an annual grant of £5 was received from Betton's Charity, a fund run by the Ironmongers Company of the City of London.[24, 25] Items such as baby linen, knitted socks and blankets were made and sold for school funds. In 1850-1 the income consisted of: subscriptions £16 15s. 0d., children's pence £15 1s. 3½d., Ironmongers Co. £5 0s. 0d. and sale of goods 8s. 5d. This amounts to £37 4s. 8½d., as compared with an expenditure for the same year of £35 11s. 1½d.[24]

Between 1830 and 1836 the number of scholars varied between 54 and 67. In 1854 there were 80 children and, in 1860, 71 girls and 33 boys were taught in a mixed girls' and infants' school.[25] The school was conducted in a room adjoining the parish work-house in East Street; after the paupers had been transferred to the new union work-house, the school also used in summer a larger room in the main building of the former workhouse. The buildings were also used for St Mary's Sunday school.[25, 26]

A subscription list circulated by the Vicar of Beaminster (Rev. Alfred Codd) on 8 November 1865 set out a proposal to erect a new school building with three rooms: one room to accommodate 120 infants (boys and girls) and be used for a boys' Sunday school, another for 120 girls for both Sunday and weekday use, and the third (a good sized class-room) to serve as an infants' Sunday school.[27] A meeting of subscribers held in June 1866 decided to build the new school on a site in Hogshill Street offered by Mr. Andress for £225.[28]

Before the Elementary Education Act 1870 the State had nothing to do with a large number of schools of this kind run by religious organisations which either did not welcome State participation or were unable to conform to State requirements; grants were however available for building from 1833, and for teaching purposes from 1846, when State inspection was made a condition of all grants. There is no record of a grant being received by the National school at Beaminster before the building of the new school in Hogshill Street, but the Rev. Alfred Codd's diary shows that the school was the subject of annual Government inspections from at least 1857.[29] In August 1866 an application was made to the Committee of the Privy Council on Education for assistance towards the cost of building a school for 20 boys, 80 girls and 100 infants, together with a house for the mistress. Among the special grounds given for asking for help were the bad state and inconvenience of the present building, and the great want of a proper infants' school and mistress's residence; the number of families of the 'labouring poor' (chiefly farm workers and artisans) within the area who were said to be members of the Church of England was 150. In reply, the Education Committee asked (September 1866) 'on what grounds the Managers propose to erect a Strictly Church of England School for so many as 200 children', as the number of C. of E. families would suggest accommodation was needed for only about 125 children, par-ticularly as there was another Anglican school (Tucker's) near by with accommodation for 100. Detailed reasons were required as to the necessity for a new school building, no complaint having been made by H.M. Inspector about the existing buildings; a subsequent letter asked for the number of dissenting families in the labouring popula-tion. Mr. Codd's answers must have satisfied the Education Committee because the plans were approved and a grant of £307 2s. 6d. was subsequently made.[27]

Other grants towards the building were made by Gilbert Adams' Charity (£300), National Society (£100) and Salisbury Diocesan Board of Education (£40). A note to the vicar from a representative of the Diocesan Board commented that it had 'made a most liberal grant — in fact the highest ever yet made . . .' and went on to say that 'this grant was prompted by a consideration of the large sum required for the school, the large sum locally raised for this & other church objects, & the wish to meet the generous spirit manifested in Beaminster'.[27] Most of the rest of the money was pro-vided by local subscriptions, Samuel Symes Cox giving £200, Sir Henry Oglander £105 and Peter Cox £100.[30]

The total cost of construction amounted to £1,885. The architects were Slater and Carpenter of London, and the builders William and Robert Chambers, masons, and John Chick and David Hann, carpenters; Edward Toleman, ironmonger, supplied furnishings and laid on the gas.[27] The building, of random stonework with Ham stone dressings, was opened on 3 September 1868 by the then Bishop of Salisbury, the ceremonies being followed by a 'splendid *dejeuner*' at the *White Hart*.[31]

When it was opened, the school contained a schoolroom and a smaller class-room for girls, and a schoolroom for infants.[32] In 1871 it was decided to add a class-room for 35 or 40 children at the north-east corner of the infants' schoolroom;[28] the architect chosen was William White. Grants were again obtained from the National Society (£12), Diocesan Board (£7 10s. 0d.) and Education Department (£51 13s. 4d.). It was made a condition of the government grant that the managers should execute an undertaking that the school would be conducted as a public elementary school within the meaning of the 1870 Act, until such time as a decision were taken to repay the grant.[33]

In 1872 the annual maintenance grant being received from the Education Department amounted to £90; by 1882 it had risen to £151 5s. 0d. The sum total of the children's pence likewise increased, from £40 to £56 11s. 10d., but subscriptions decreased from about £38 to £23 over the same period.[33, 34] The committee of management, which was set up in 1867 to conform with government requirements, was keen to raise the level of attendance; it decided to charge 2d. a week, but to repay 1d. at the end of the year to children who had attended at least 200 times. In 1872 it was laid down that the charge for two children of the same family should be 3d. a week only, further children attending free, provided that attendance was regular. In 1876 a premium of 1s 0d. was given to children who passed in all three elementary subjects at the time of government inspection, and 6d. to children who passed in two subjects.[28] Under Acts of 1876 and 1880, school attendance became compulsory for children under 13 years, but there were some exceptions. In Beaminster the children of labourers continued to pay at the rates laid down in 1872, but under a new scale of fees, farmers and substantial tradesmen paid 9d. for the first child and 6d. for the second, 'Dairy people and small Tradespeople' 6d. for the first child, 4d. for the second, and 2d. for the third, and artisans paid 2d. for each child.[35]

In 1902 Dorset County Council became responsible for the general expenses of the girls' school, which were paid for out of the rates and the government grant. As the buildings were not provided out of the rates, six local managers (including the Vicar of Beaminster) remained responsible for keeping them in repair, the annual outlay having to be raised by subscription. Religious teaching, the appointment of teachers and the control of the building out of school hours were left in the hands of the managers.[35] In 1906 average attendance was 206, accommodation being available for 291.[36]

Boys' elementary school

Under the Elementary Education Act 1870, the funds of charities such as Tucker's Charity were no longer allowed to be applied to elementary education, and it became necessary to make new arrangements for the elementary education of Beaminster boys. Where sufficient accommodation for the children of an area was not made available by voluntary organisations, the Act provided for the setting up of a 'School Board' with power to levy a rate on owners and occupiers for the purpose of elementary education; in order to avoid the necessity for this in Beaminster, a voluntary scheme was promoted. Gilbert Adams' Charity offered to convey the old site and buildings in East Street for the purposes of a boys' elementary school, and Tucker's Charity was permitted to make available the sum of £1,000 to provide accommodation which would satisfy the requirements of the Education Department.[37]

A circular letter issued by a committee of management of a boys' elementary school – comprised of the Beaminster members of the governing body elected for the new scheme for Tucker's Charity[38] – was distributed in the parish in November 1872. The letter appealed for voluntary annual subscriptions: at least £80 a year would be needed to maintain the school in addition to the boys' pence and the government grant which could be obtained.[37] In 1886 the annual sources of income were boys' pence £32, subscriptions £65 and Education Committee £82.[39] The scale of fees was the same as at the girls' elementary school.[35]

The school was first established in the old schoolhouse at Shortmoor in January 1873. New buildings were erected on the site in East Street and opened in 1875; the architect was J. M. Allen of Crewkerne, and the builders David Hann and George Gale of Beaminster, the accommodation consisting of a schoolroom and a class-room.[37] In 1906 there was accommodation for 129 boys, with an average attendance of 77.[36] When the school came under the control of Dorset County Council in 1902, the governors of Beaminster and Netherbury Grammar School continued to nominate one of the school managers because of the financial contribution made by Tucker's Charity at its foundation.[37]

Beaminster and Netherbury Grammar School

It was proposed by the Endowed Schools Commission, which dealt with charitable foundations, that the Tucker endowment should in future be used to support a higher grade school for a wider area. Such schools, which were described at that period as 'middle' or 'middle class' schools, were intermediate between the great public schools and the elementary schools, and were largely intended for the sons of farmers and tradespeople, whose education would continue until 14 or 15 years. (The leaving age at Tucker's school in 1870 was 11 years.) By 1870 there were eight middle schools in Dorset.[40]

In November 1871 the Endowed Schools Commission produced a draft scheme whereby boys of seven to 15 years were to be taught reading and spelling, writing, arithmetic, algebra and geometry, mensuration and land surveying, English grammar, composition and literature, history, geography, drawing, vocal music, at least one branch of natural science, Latin or French or both. The Beaminster school was to be combined with Netherbury Grammar School at a future date, once a similar scheme had been established for that charity also. The draft combined scheme published in 1879 covered boys up to the age of 16, and the governors were to provide proper buildings for 50 boys as soon as possible. The subjects were much the same, except that no provision was made for mensuration and surveying. The two schools were amalgamated in 1881, Netherbury Grammar School being closed.[41]

The appointment of a body of governors to manage these schemes aroused some friction in Beaminster. There were to be five co-optative governors, the first three of whom, already named in the draft scheme of 1871, were Anglicans. Both the existing schools (Tucker's and National) having been firmly under church control, the Congregationalists sent a memorial to the Endowed Schools Commission asking for Alfred Hine, a member of the chapel, to be the fourth co-optative member. At the same time an amendment was inserted in the draft scheme by the commission whereby the eight representative governors, instead of being five nominated by Beaminster Vestry and three by Netherbury Vestry, should be three only for Beaminster Vestry, two for Netherbury Vestry, and three from Beaminster Board of Guardians.[41, 10]

Neither of these proposals pleased the vicar, but J. G. Fitch of the Endowed Schools Commission (with whom Mr. Codd had been conducting a copious correspondence throughout 1870 and 1871) pointed out (letter of 22 February 1872) that the memorial appeared to be 'respectably signed', one of the signatories being the Congregational minister. Mr. Codd then wrote officially to the Education Department (draft copy 3 April 1872) asking for approval of the scheme to be withheld until there had been an opportunity for proper consideration; the proposal to include guardians in the governing body had been made, he said, unknown to the parish at large, at the suggestion of a small body of memorialists representing only about one-eighth of the population. The vestry meeting which he then called was attended by leading members of the memorialists but, perhaps not surprisingly, 'an influential body' of parishioners carried by more than two to one a motion to the effect that no part of the governing body of 'our parochial charity' should be transferred to the board of guardians. In a letter to the Education Department dated 13 April (draft copy), Mr. Codd stated that the election of three guardians as governors 'would probably throw too much weight into the hands of one Class — the Farmers', whereas the farmers of the district were 'only too glad to avail themselves of a good School without any necessity of their being admitted to a share in its Management'.[10]

The amended scheme was however approved, and to Mr. Codd's threat to oppose it in Parliament, Mr. Fitch replied on 3 May 1872 as follows:[10]

> you are entirely mistaken in supposing that the proposal to utilize the Board of Guardians was inserted by the Commissioners merely, as you phrase it, to 'satisfy a handful of Dissenters'. It is one very frequently made in cases such as Beaminster, in which the School is intended to serve an agricultural district as well as a particular parish.

The Congregationalists were well represented on the new governing body: not only was Alfred Hine a co-optative member, but John Hine was nominated as a representative of Beaminster Vestry.[38]

Between 1875 and 1882 the 'Middle Class School' was held in the old Tucker's Charity premises at Shortmoor; there were 38 scholars in 1876. In April 1882 Barton End (Fleet Street) was rented for 10 years from Samuel Symes Cox. All this time the governors were trying to find suitable permanent premises for the school; it was now thought that the number of scholars was likely to be nearer 75 than 50. Brook Lodge (now Hams Plot) was turned down by the Charity Commissioners in 1876 and again in 1892, and they also rejected a proposal to purchase part of Woodlands in 1881. Barton End was rented for a further year, and when the lease finally expired in April 1893 the school was closed for a time 'to enable the nursing of income', there being few pupils.[38]

It was eventually decided to purchase the site of the former potteries in Hogshill Street. The dwelling house was enlarged to provide a residence for the Master and a schoolroom was erected; the cost of the work was raised by public subscription, a tender from Messrs. Hann (£537) being accepted.[38] The school was reopened in January 1897 with 22 boys.[42] Later that year £150 was contributed by Beaminster residents towards the erection of a chemical laboratory and workshop in commemoration of Queen Victoria's Diamond Jubilee. In 1904 it was felt that the time had come for girls to be admitted, both as boarders and day pupils. New buildings for girls were erected in 1905, C. & A. Hann's tender for £968 being accepted; two adjoining cottages were purchased and demolished in order to enlarge the Master's house. Arrangements were made with Miss M. A. Warr, who was discontinuing her school at Brook House, for this to become the girls' hostel. Two women were to be included in future among the governors who were co-opted.[38] In 1909 a new scheme provided for 15 governors, 10 of whom were representative (two nominated by Dorset County Council, three by Beaminster Rural District Council, three by Beaminster Parish Council and two by Netherbury Parish Council) and five co-optative.[41] The lands constituting the endowment were sold for over £5,000 in 1919.[43]

As early as 1904 Dorset County Council established an agricultural centre at the school to provide special instruction under a qualified teacher, and land surveying came back into the curriculum; four agricultural scholarships were offered for the sons of Dorset farmers, and these were much sought after.[38] The 'Agricultural Field', which before 1933 was off Clay Lane, was divided into a number of plots, and experiments were carried out under the latest scientific conditions with different varieties of vegetables and using various artificial manures. The school magazine has regular reports on these over the years, mostly written by the boys themselves. The agricultural section was transferred to the large garden at the rear of Tucker House in the autumn of 1933.[44]

The school was enlarged in 1912 to provide more accommodation for boarding and the total number of pupils had increased to about 80 by 1915.[45] By this time the school had developed into an educational centre not only for the immediate neighbourhood but for much of West Dorset. In 1923, out of 112 pupils, 91 came from the area of Beaminster Rural District Council, 36 of them from Beaminster itself. Of the other 21 pupils, 14 were from Bridport and Dorchester and villages in the vicinity of these towns, but the remaining seven came from more distant parts of Dorset and Somerset and from as far away as Maidstone and Aldershot. Thirty-five day pupils who came to school on foot, by bicycle or in a trap had to travel a distance of between two and eight miles. In 1926 there were 22 boys boarding in the school house and three boarding in the town; the 10 girl boarders were then boarded around the town, Miss Warr's hostel having long since closed. In 1934 Tucker House opposite the school was opened as boarding accommodation for girls and, when they were transferred to Woodlands in 1953, Tucker House was used for junior boys.[46]

In the 1930s there were some 130 scholars.[44] Llewellyn Skyrm, who was headmaster for 17 years (1916–33), speaking at an Agriculture and Trade dinner in 1930, described his 'trade' humorously in the following terms: 'My shop is well stocked, it has never been fuller. I keep my stock four years, and I hope it gets better every year; I hope it is good stock — at any rate, it is Dorset stock'.[47]

Private schools

After 1870 the number of private schools in the town diminished; William Gardner's academy had already closed in 1868-9, but no doubt Mr. Gardner had reached retiring age. The girls at Brook House Ladies School, which was run by Miss Warr, were transferred to the grammar school in 1905.[48]

Charities

Strode almshouse. In 1899 the Charity Commissioners appointed three trustees to administer the charity. The Oglanders, who had paid a regular sum for the maintenance of the inmates and had kept the building in repair, were no longer at Parnham, and the income — now restricted to the legal entitlement — was not adequate to meet the outgoings. The two-thirds share of Bilshay Farm was sold in 1903, the proceeds being invested, and the number of inmates was reduced from six to four.[49] In 1980 Gertrude Forsey, then aged 94, recalled how as a young girl she had visited her godmother in the almshouse on Sunday after church and described the conditions at that time:[50]

> The building was divided by a central wall, with fireplaces at each end; each room was divided into two by a green curtain drawn across. The two ladies who lived at the steps end were gentry, and the other two were poor folk. Each person had a chest of drawers in which she kept her clothes and her food, and they each received a shilling a week and a loaf of bread.

Peter Meech Pension Charity. This was founded under the will of Peter Meech, proved in 1909: six poor people — five from Beaminster and one from Powerstock — were to receive not less than three shillings a week. The Vicars of Beaminster and Powerstock were *ex officio* trustees and four representatives were appointed by the parish councils; the first six pensioners were selected in January 1911. Peter Meech seems to have intended to build six cottage homes on the site of two houses in Church Street, one of which was his birth-place, but he made no financial provision for their erection in his will.[51]

All the nine parish charities then in existence were amalgamated in 1967.

Community Life and Leisure Activities

We cannot of course pretend that life in Beaminster was just the same at the end of the period under review as it was at the beginning, but many features did persist and in some ways there was less change over these 100 years than there has been in the last 30 or so. Our chief commentator in Victorian times is Percy Codd, son of the vicar, who gives a delightfully vivid picture of life in Beaminster in those days. Then there is J. R. Bridle (for 30 years, until his death in 1920, Beaminster correspondent of the *Bridport News*) who reported on events and personalities in the town, with lively notes, often humorous, written under the pen-name 'Beaminsterian'. Beaminster has been able to boast a number of long-lived residents whose recollections have also been drawn on as well as those of younger townsfolk.

Changes did occur in connection with two venerable Beaminster estates, Parnham and Beaminster manor house. The Oglanders, who had been at Parnham for 130 years, died out with Louisa, widow of Sir Henry Oglander, in 1894. Parnham went through the hands of several owners over the next 50 years. The farms in Beaminster at Coombe Down and Hewstock were sold off separately, and in 1896 Vincent Robinson bought the residential estate of about 70 acres for £6,500; he made a number of alterations to the interior and furnished it with antiques and works of art.[52] On the death of Mr. Robinson in 1910, an estate of 157½ acres was acquired for £22,000 by Dr. Hans Sauer, who among other things restored the western windows between the great hall and the dining room which had been blocked up by Nash. Dr. Sauer also made extensive alterations to the grounds: new iron gates were set up at the main eastern entrance, where a forecourt was made, and three extensive terraces were created on the south side (the upper terrace flanked by a Ham stone balustrade with gazebos) with lawns leading down to a lake.[53]

In 1913 Parnham became the property of Mr. and Mrs. Edward Moorhouse. The purchase was really prompted by their son Will, recently married, who wanted to put down roots. Will (Flight-Lieutenant W. B. Rhodes-Moorhouse, the first airman V.C.) was killed early in the First World War but his son William was brought up at Parnham. In 1927 William's grandmother, now a widow, wanted to make Parnham over to him, but his mother, realising that 'houses of its size belonged to a dying age', decided that the struggle to keep it up would eventually rob her son of all the activities which were most important to him.[54] W. H. Rhodes-Moorhouse was killed during the Battle of Britain early in the Second World War, and both he and his father are buried in a small private graveyard on a hillside in the park.

Parnham was sold in 1927 and was run for a short period by the Yeo Vale Country Club. In the 1930s it was the home of Eric Bullivant; it was requisitioned at the start of the Second World War, first as an army hospital and later as the headquarters of the 16th Infantry Division of the American Army. In 1955 Mr. Bullivant sold an estate of 338 acres, including land in Netherbury,[55] and Parnham was turned into a home for the National Association of Mental Health.

The Cox family, who had been at the Manor House for about 140 years, except for a short interruption in the earlier 1860s, ceased to live in Beaminster after the death of Colonel Cox's second wife Mary in 1909. The house and residential estate were sold in 1911,[56] and subsequently had a number of owners.

Before the First World War

The old landowners had been closely involved in the affairs of the town, chairing boards and committees and contributing to all the good causes and projects, and their disappearance from the Beaminster scene must have made quite a difference. The professional people however remained, and with the leading farmers and business folk — what Percy Codd called 'the upper middle class'[57] — there was never any lack of able and hardworking men to promote the varied interests of the town.

National events were celebrated with great enthusiasm locally in the days before Bank Holidays. On the occasion of Queen Victoria's Golden Jubilee (1887), the town was splendidly decorated and illuminated. A procession, consisting of the Ancient Order of Foresters, Independent Order of Oddfellows, Beaminster Brass Band and the few remaining members of the old Beaminster Friendly Society, perambulated the streets. Dinner was provided in a large marquee in the park of the Manor House, and was followed by sports in the afternoon with a substantial tea, and dancing, fireworks and illuminations in the grounds in the evening.[58] Similar celebrations at the Diamond Jubilee, when 500 of the younger children marched to the park with banners, made a red-letter day for Gertrude Forsey, who died in 1982 at the age of 95, having lived in Clay Lane all her life. Gertrude, who had to look after her invalid mother, recorded on tape how she expected to have to miss the procession:

> I remember Miss Eva Burnside my Sunday School teacher saying 'Now girls, you are going to have a very nice time I'm sure' and I said 'Well, I shan't be there because I've got to stay home with my mother for my sister to go'. That went back up Manor House and Gertrude was sent for and told she was going with the Sunday School and that is just what happened . . . They lifted my mother into the bath chair and we got her into the road and up to the Manor House. Lady Cox — they used to call her that but I don't think she was a titled lady — she said 'I will open my Drawing Room for her and she shall be inside' . . . But the people wouldn't consent — they said 'She's come up here — lets see her', so she sat in that chair for 24 hours.

At some stage Gertrude's mother, stationed in front of the *Knapp Inn*, saw the procession twice encircle the pound at the junction of Stoke and Broadwindsor Roads, for her especial benefit![59]

At the celebrations for the coronation of George V in 1911, the various societies paraded as usual, being followed on this occasion by a lengthy cavalcade consisting of individuals dressed up as historic and mythical personages, on foot and on horseback, and costumed groups mounted on waggons. Many people walked up to Storridge Hill, where the bonfire, one of a chain, was lit about 10 p.m.[60]

Victorian society had a great capacity for supplying its own entertainment and education, and a large number of societies were started, usually presided over by the gentry and clergy, who were keen on providing the means of self-improvement for the working classes. As Percy Codd says, Beaminster was scarcely 'the sort of dead alive country town it and others like it are now [after the First World War] supposed to have been'.[57] His father (Rev. Alfred Codd) mentions an 'Institute' meeting in his diary for 1857,[29] and this is probably a reference to the Beaminster 'Church Institute' which the Rev. William Barnes is understood to have visited in his capacity of adult educator. William Barnes lectured to clubs in rural communities over a wide area of the West Country, and from 1859 he was a frequent visitor to Bridport.[61]

A 'Mutual Improvement Society' was set up in Beaminster in 1854 and it may be that this and the Institute are one and the same. A small room attached to the 'town hall' (above the market house in the Fore Place) was initially rented as a reading room where national and local newspapers were provided for about 70 members; lectures, concerts and 'penny readings' were given during the winter. Some of the readings tended to be, as Percy Codd puts it, 'for the higher culture of the few rather than the general amusement and interest of the many', and included items like Pope's 'Essay on Man'; the Beaminster Mutual Improvement Society came to an end, owing to lack of support, in 1868. Penny readings of a more 'popular' kind had been started about 1867, first at Tucker's school at Shortmoor and from 1868 at the new girls' school in Hogshill Street. In December 1867, for instance, the programme included 'John Gilpin' and 'How I heard my own will read', interspersed with light music. The readings continued until about 1877.[62]

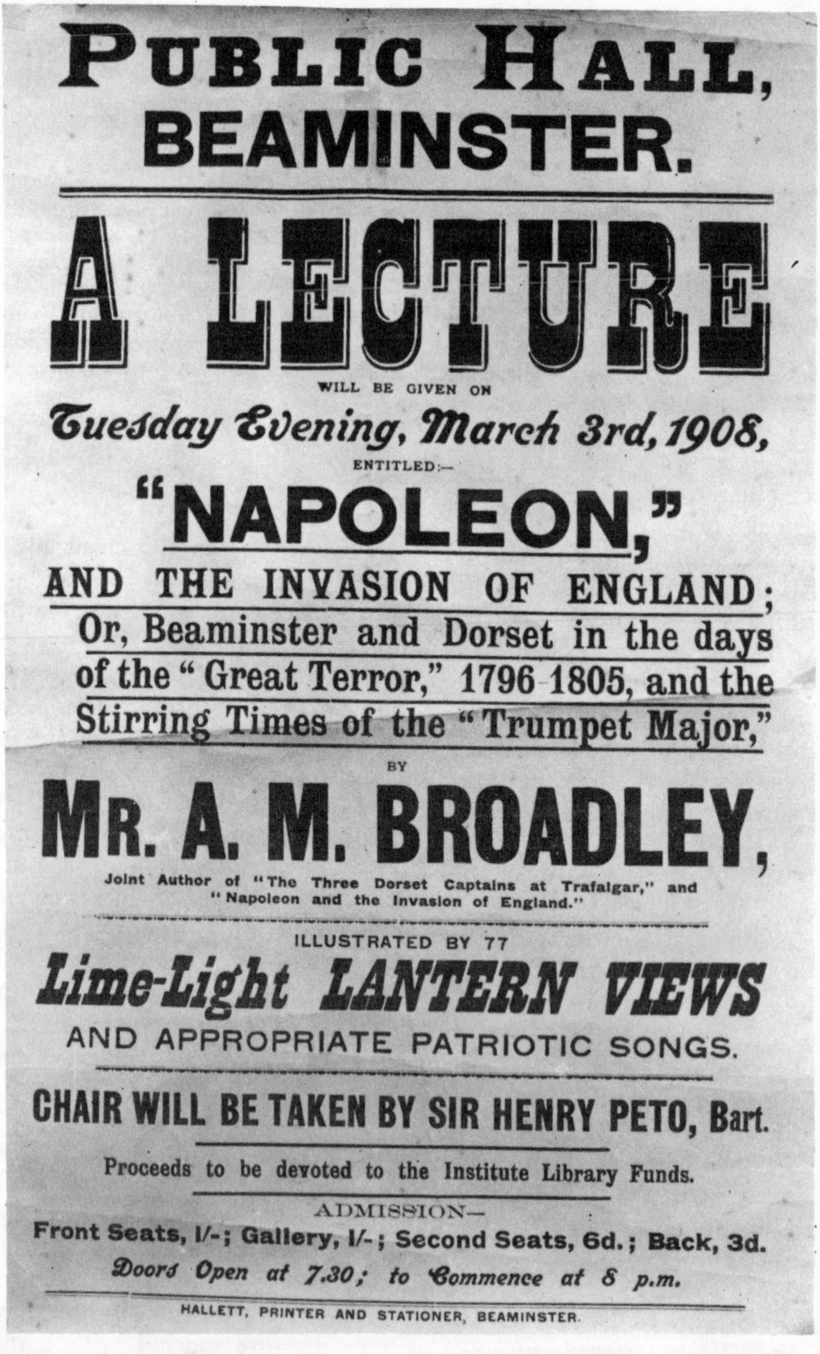

Fig. 12. Programme for a lecture on 'Napoleon and the invasion of England' at the Public Hall in 1908.

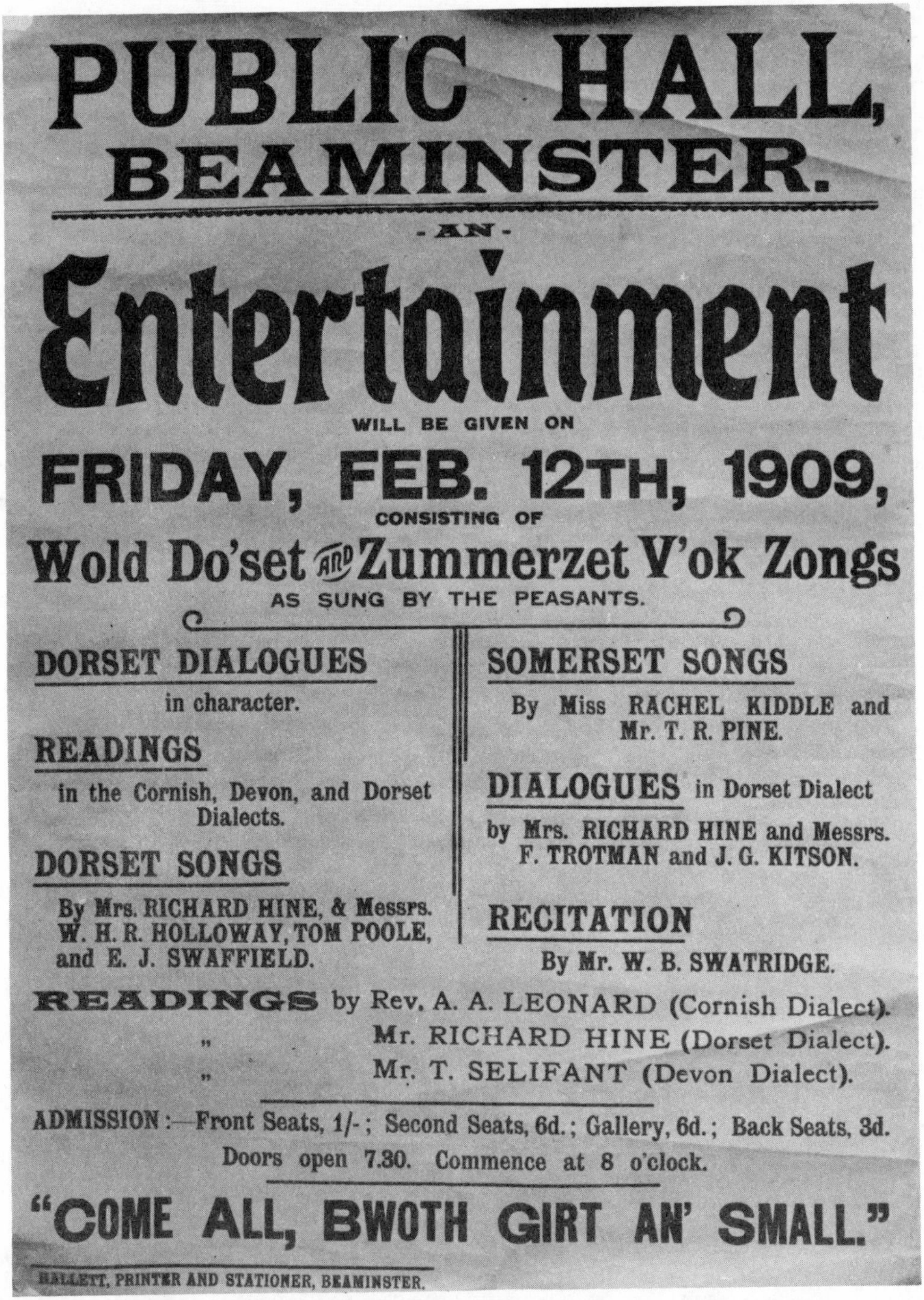

PUBLIC HALL,
BEAMINSTER.

- AN -

Entertainment

WILL BE GIVEN ON

FRIDAY, FEB. 12TH, 1909,

CONSISTING OF

Wold Do'set AND Zummerzet V'ok Zongs

AS SUNG BY THE PEASANTS.

DORSET DIALOGUES

in character.

READINGS

in the Cornish, Devon, and Dorset Dialects.

DORSET SONGS

By Mrs. RICHARD HINE, & Messrs. W. H. R. HOLLOWAY, TOM POOLE, and E. J. SWAFFIELD.

SOMERSET SONGS

By Miss RACHEL KIDDLE and Mr. T. R. PINE.

DIALOGUES in Dorset Dialect

by Mrs. RICHARD HINE and Messrs. F. TROTMAN and J. G. KITSON.

RECITATION

By Mr. W. B. SWATRIDGE.

READINGS by Rev. A. A. LEONARD (Cornish Dialect).
" Mr. RICHARD HINE (Dorset Dialect).
" Mr. T. SELIFANT (Devon Dialect).

ADMISSION:—Front Seats, 1/-; Second Seats, 6d.; Gallery, 6d.; Back Seats, 3d.
Doors open 7.30. Commence at 8 o'clock.

"COME ALL, BWOTH GIRT AN' SMALL."

HALLETT, PRINTER AND STATIONER, BEAMINSTER.

Fig. 13. Programme for an entertainment at the Public Hall in 1909.

In 1877 a Working Men's Institute was established at a public meeting, and a house in North Street was rented; a games room was provided downstairs, with a reading room upstairs. Colonel Cox took a great interest in the Institute, and for some years it flourished, with a membership of about 60. However, after it was transferred to smaller and less suitable premises in 1888, the membership declined, and it came to an end in the winter of 1893-4. Only three years later the Beaminster Institute was started in Hogshill Street with some 80 members, under the auspices of the vicar (Rev. A. A. Leonard) and the Congregational minister (Rev. F. Coram).[63]

These attempts to establish a permanent institute were hindered by the lack of suitable premises in which a substantial body of parishioners could get together in a large hall while other smaller rooms could be used for reading and games. In November 1901 Fiennes Trotman, chairman of the parish council, announced at a public meeting held at the girls' school that, in response to a memorial signed by 150 parishioners, promises had already been received of just over £500 towards the cost of building a public hall and institute. As soon as subscriptions reached £1,000, plans were prepared by B. Vaughan Johnson, and the lowest of three tenders, one of £1,170 from Benjamin B. Chambers of Beaminster, was accepted. On 17 June 1902 the foundation stone was laid by Peter Meech, the principal subscriber; the building, which was erected in commemoration of the coronation of Edward VII, was completed in April 1903. It is of local stone with Ham stone string course and dressings, and at that date it comprised, on the ground floor, the public hall with accommodation for 300 people, a reading room and a recreation room; above were the billiard room and the library. Richard Hine comments (1914) that 'it is universally acknowledged that the building is a very great boon to the town and neighbourhood'.[64]

A Penny Bank was started by Rev. Alfred Codd soon after he came to Beaminster in order to encourage thrift among the working classes.[65] In 1855 Richard Hine was manager of a branch of Bridport Savings Bank which in 1867 was open every Thursday between 1 p.m. and 2 p.m. at No. 12 The Square; this was continued by subsequent occupiers of the premises, T. P. Coombs (printer) and W. Oxley (stationer).[66] Friendly societies and other bodies provided mutual help and company for those of like interests. The original Beaminster Friendly Society revised its rules and restarted the club in 1862 and again in 1872, these changes leading to a certain loss of members. In 1892 there were only 76 members and it was decided to dissolve the club.[67] The Beaminster Working Men's Benefit Society was established in 1863 by some former members of the friendly society, but this too came to an end in 1883. Beaminster Manor Lodge (Freemasons) was founded in 1872.[68] The Beaminster Friendship Lodge of the Oddfellows Society, which was started in 1859, first met at the *New Inn*, later at the Congregational church, and finally at the Methodist church.

One of the great social gatherings was the Beaminster Fair which continued to be held every September. W. B. Swatridge, whose recollection of the fair went back to the 1850s, said that it was then looked upon as one of the principal events of the year: 'few people living within reasonable distance of the town cared to miss it . . . By two in the afternoon the crowd had become very dense, there was no open space at all, and the only way to get through the town was to work your way slowly and patiently, squeezing as best you could, step by step through the throng.' Though many tradesmen still displayed goods for sale, the fair had become more and more of a pleasure fair, with roundabouts and variety turns. By 1900 steam roundabouts had succeeded the primitive little wooden horses, propelled by boys, which Richard Hine remembered from his childhood.[69] As time went by, other amusements became available and tastes changed; many people complained of the cluttering up of the Square and the debris left behind.

All sorts of hobbies and sports were catered for by the various clubs in the town. Canon Codd's diary shows that he took an interest in some of these which he was probably instrumental in starting. A preliminary meeting to establish a Cottage Garden Society was held in August 1858, and there was an annual exhibition of fruit, vegetables and flowers up to 1877.[29, 65] Owing to lack of support the show then lapsed, but in 1896, on the suggestion of Rev. A. A. Leonard (a keen horticulturalist), it was revived as the Beaminster Vegetable and Flower Society, the first secretary being J. R. Bridle;[70] the society continued until the 1930s.

Another society started in 1858 was the Beaminster Musical Society. Percy Codd tells us that his mother, who was an excellent pianist and also had a fine voice, 'did a great deal to raise the musical level of Beaminster'. There was no lack of other talent, with soloists like J. L. Kitson, Frances Cox (daughter of Peter), Georgina (sister of Col. Cox) and others. Concerts were given with choir and orchestra all provided by Beaminster residents.[71] T. Beale, who was schoolmaster at the union workhouse from 1868 to 1872, formed a Fife and Drum Band from the children there, and this used to head processions in the town before the formation of the Beaminster Brass Band in 1878.[72] (The brass band gained the title 'Prize Band' in the 1930s, when it won the Wessex Band Association Festival.)

The bellringers of Beaminster church tower have a long history, but St Mary's Ringing Guild was constituted on its present basis in 1873, when T. P. Coombs became Captain of the Tower.[73] The bells used to be rung on the day of the annual fair but this was stopped by Canon Codd in 1858.[29] (When Cecil Poole completed 60 years of ringing in 1980, the Poole family had given 144 years of continuous service, beginning with Samuel Poole, Cecil's grandfather, in 1836.)

It is not known when a cricket club was first established in the town, but about 1845 cricket was played on a field called Long Ground at Hollymoor, and this continued on and off until 1866. In 1869 a proper pitch was laid down in a field off Tunnel Road and a regular club formed;[74] this was probably the scene of William Gardner's verses 'On a Cricket Match'. A football club had been started by 1896. The West Dorset and Beaminster Races (point-to-point horse racing) were held on Beaminster Down from September 1867 to 1870 inclusive. Horse races took place annually in the early 1900s — in 1907 these were held at Long Ground and a bicycle race was included.[75] Beaminster Bicycle Club had been started in 1880, with T. P. Coombs riding in front with a warning bugle to blow when necessary. The new riders were not too popular with the old ones, for when Richard Hine (secretary of the club) sent him a copy of the rules, Peter Meech replied as follows:

I cannot in any way patronize any such affair, in fact I am prejudiced against such obstacles on the public highway having had on various occasions narrow escapes (probably from serious injury) by having my horse run into by persons mounted on what in my opinion is an unsightly machine.

The machine in question was the original 'High Bicycle' or 'Ordinary'; when the chain-driven 'Safety' model first came in about 1885, the club treated such bicycles with derision until it was found that they were easy winners in a race.[76] In 1898 the Cyclists Touring Club applied to Beaminster Rural District Council for permission to put danger notices at the top of White Sheet Hill and Hackthorn Hill.[77]

In the early years of this century amateur dramatic performances, annual concerts given by the boys of the elementary school, and dances with the Beaminster String Band, all contributed to the gaiety of the town. One of the most popular societies was, however, the Beaminster Debating Society. This was formed in 1910, and one of its first debates was on 'Women's Suffrage': E. E. Wise, master at the boys' elementary school, spoke in favour and J. L. Kitson opposed. In 1912 the society had 123 members, but as many as 250 attended some of the debates, and a team went to Dorchester to debate with the debating society there.[78]

Beaminster men played their part in national emergencies. Volunteer forces again came into existence in Dorset when invasion from France was expected in 1859. The Beaminster Sub-Division of the First Dorset Rifle Volunteers was officially established in 1869; it consisted of about 30 recruits with John Hine, who took the leading part in its formation, as sergeant. In 1900, during the South African War, the total strength of the Beaminster Detachment was 66, and 12 members, with H. L. Kitson as captain, served in South Africa in the Volunteer Service Company of the Dorset Regiment. Together with Trooper Robert Leigh of the 26th Company Imperial Yeomanry, they were given a heroes' welcome in the town on their return in 1901.[79]

From the First World War to 1950

Thirty-six men from Beaminster lost their lives in the First World War. A memorial was erected to their memory in the church, and a captured German gun, which was presented to the town in recognition of the gallantry of Lieut. Rhodes-Moorhouse, was set up on a stone plinth in the Square; the names of all those who had served in the Forces were inscribed on the plinth.

It was generally commented soon after the war that class distinction had been diminished through all classes serving together in the ranks. Percy Codd, while affirming that such distinctions 'did not greatly trouble us at Beaminster', was of the opinion that they were more pronounced than in late Victorian times.[80] Perhaps there was more expressed consciousness of class, which had simply been taken for granted before the war when all automatically kept to their proper station. In the 1930s the three tennis clubs in Beaminster were widely referred to as 'the cream', 'the milk' and 'the skimmed milk'! The Second World War was to be the great leveller.

Many of the clubs and societies already mentioned continued or were restarted after the First World War. Early in 1921 the revived Beaminster Debating Society debated the proposition 'That Trade Unionism is played out'! Among those supporting the motion were A. A. Pim and Richard Hine; Mrs. Rhodes-Moorhouse and A. W. Graveson (master at Beaminster Grammar School) spoke against it.[81]

One of the important new societies was the Beaminster Women's Institute, which holds the distinction of being the second W.I. to be formed in Dorset; at the time it was the only organisation for women in the town. The first general meeting was held in January 1918 and three months later there were some 50 members, including representatives of all the well known Beaminster families; by the end of 1919 membership had grown to about 100. Women now had the vote, and the varied programme of talks given at the public hall included one in May 1921 on 'Women and Citizenship'. In July 1921 the W.I. held a garden fete in the grounds of Parnham, at which entertainments included a baby show, a variety show, pony rides, and music from the Beaminster String Band and the W.I.'s own 'Glee Party'. Groups of sightseers 'eagerly listened to Mr. Richard Hine's brief account of Parnham House and its ancient glories', and were then conducted over much of the house by Lady Monkswell or Canon Hutchings (the vicar). The following year a 'Fancy Fair' was held in the manor house grounds; as well as stalls and sideshows, there was boating on the lake and a concert in the house. Six hundred people came to the event, and we are told that, had the weather been kinder, there would have been at least 1,000.[82]

The cricket club and football club used the first Parnham field for a number of years from 1919, and there was also a Parnham Tennis Club. A hockey club was started in 1929. Several attempts were made to establish a proper recreation ground for the townsfolk. This had first been suggested in 1910, to commemorate the accession of George V, but there was not enough support. In 1919, as part of the war memorial schemes, Mrs. Edward Moorhouse offered a piece of ground at Mill Ground, on the west side of the Brit between the river and Clampits Coppice. She said in her letter: 'the people of Beaminster already seem to have a distinct partiality for it [this area]', which conjures up pleasant pictures of young couples strolling and children playing there. The proposition was carried with great acclamation at a parish meeting, and plans were made for bowling green, tennis courts and children's playground. However, in 1922 the offer had to be declined because there was not enough left in the fund to pay for the fencing which would be needed.[83] In April 1934, following on a resolution of the annual parish meeting, a committee was set up to find a field which would be suitable, particularly for children. Rack Close (behind Champions) was selected in October 1936, but in June 1938 a parish meeting decided not to proceed further when it was explained that the cost of acquisition and laying out would come to £1,585.[84] The Memorial Playing Fields were finally purchased and laid out in 1947 in memory of the men who fell in the 1939-45 War.

The Silver Jubilee of George V (1935) and the Coronation of George VI (1936) were celebrated in some of the traditional style with processions of schoolchildren and friendly societies, but with the popularity of radio, cinema and other new attractions, the nature of entertainment was changing.

During the Second World War the public hall was requisitioned for the Services and The Square was used for parking Services vehicles. After the war, men and women returned to a place which had on the face of it altered very little. The population of the parish, when last counted in 1931, had been only 1,612, the lowest since census records began, and probably not dissimilar to the population of the mid-18th century. In 1951 the population was 1,785, less than it had been in 1775. The people who lived in the still compact little town and the farmers coming in from the outlying farms, all as yet knew one another. But far-reaching changes were soon to be on the way, and Beaminster would never be the same again.

POSTSCRIPT

BETWEEN 1951 AND 1981 the population of Beaminster went up from 1,785 to 2,369, an increase of 33 per cent. The town has continued as a commercial and educational centre, and up to 1974 as an administrative centre, the headquarters of Beaminster Rural District Council. Further council houses and flats have been built at Gerrards Green, Hogshill Mead, Pattle and Willow Grove, and some elderly people's housing at St Mary's Gardens. The main feature has however been an influx of retired people and the development of private estates, mainly of bungalows, such as Champions Gardens, Culverhayes, Styles Close, Myrtle Close, Manor Gardens, Monmouth Gardens, Hollymoor, Riverside and Millfield. The visual impact of the new development has been reduced by the fact that most of the post-war housing is on the less exposed surrounding land, and is of a high standard. There has been little ribbon or sporadic development on the main approach roads.

A water-borne sewerage system was laid down in the late 1960s, with a new main outfall sewer to the sea. Beaminster Comprehensive School replaced the grammar school, with new buildings erected in Fleet Street in 1963, but like its predecessor it attracts pupils from a distance and has a boarding section. St Mary's Primary School, built in Clay Lane in 1973, replaced the two elementary schools. St John's Roman Catholic church was opened at Shortmoor in 1966, but Holy Trinity was declared redundant in 1978 and the Methodist church was closed in 1979. The Skyrm Room, named for the former headmaster of the grammar school, was built as an adjunct to the Public Hall in 1968, and the Strode Room was converted from the old almshouse in 1977.

There are several small but substantial industries, besides the usual servicing industries, in the town. Francis Bugler Ltd., still in Hogshill Street, are agents for agricultural machines, which they service; they also manufacture some items in metal. The former milk factory in North Street is now Aplin and Barrett, producers of food preservatives. The engraving and printing factory of Abbot Brown in Fleet Street is the largest employer, having expanded after its establishment in 1946. The most recent addition is the Numatic Factory in Broadwindsor Road, manufacturers of industrial cleaning equipment. It is hoped to establish other small industries nearby.

The town today provides a good centre with varied shops and facilities, and a great range of interests can be pursued through more than fifty clubs, societies and youth organisations. Beaminster has adapted many times to changing circumstances. It retains however its essential character as a lively and friendly small town where old Beaminsterians and newer residents work together for the best interests of the community.

APPENDIX I
Population of the Parish of Beaminster 1801–1981

1801	2,140	1901	1,702
1811	2,290	1911	1,860
1821	2,806	1921	1,651
1831	2,968	1931	1,612
1841	3,270	1941	no census
1851	2,832	1951	1,785
1861	2,614	1961	2,000
1871	2,585	1971	2,346
1881	2,130	1981	2,369
1891	1,915		

APPENDIX II
Chairmen of Beaminster Parish/Town Council* 1894–

1894–1900	Rev. A. A. Leonard
1900–1915	F. Trotman
1915–1929	R. Hine
1929–1931	L. Skyrm
1931–1946	R. Hine
1946–1952	L. Skyrm
1952–1961	W. A. Stiby
1961–1963	J. W. Sill
1963–1964	Miss V. Small
1964–1968	J. Hine
1968–1975	R. C. Bugler
1975–	N. C. Welsford

* Title 'Town Council' adopted 1979.

APPENDIX III
Chairmen of Beaminster Rural District Council 1895–1974

1895–1901	E. G. Legg
1901–1915	Rev. F. Williams
1915–1943	W. W. Sampson
1943–1947	Capt. N. H. Carter, R.N.
1947–1962	Col. G. A. Pinney
1962–1967	Adml. Sir V. A. C. Crutchley, V.C.
1967–1974	P. F. Tiarks

NOTES

Abbreviations

BN	*Bridport News*
DCM	Dorset County Museum
DRO	Dorset Record Office
Hine	R. Hine, *History of Beaminster* (1914)
Hutchins	J. Hutchins, *History and Antiquities of the County of Dorset*, 3rd edn. (1861–74)
PRO	Public Record Office
Proc. DNHAS	*Proceedings, Dorset Natural History and Archaeological Society*
RCHM	Royal Commission on Historical Monuments (England)
SD	*Notes and Queries Somerset and Dorset*
VCH	*Victoria County History, Dorset*

NOTES

Chapter 1. The Framework

1. A. Fagersten, *Place-Names of Dorset* (1933), pp. 275, 283.
2. *Proc. DNHAS*, vol. 84 (1962), p. 111.
3. Ibid., vol. 86 (1964), p. 114.
4. R. Good, *Old Roads of Dorset*, 2nd edn. (1966), pp. 13–16.
5. RCHM, *Dorset*, vol. 1 (1952), p. 27; Hine, p. 3.
6. *Proc. DNHAS*, vol. 77 (1955), pp. 136–7; J. B. Calkin, 'Population of Neolithic and Bronze Age Dorset', *Proc. DNHAS*, vol. 90 (1968), p. 228.
7. Ibid., vol. 84 (1962), p. 112.
8. Ibid., vol. 87 (1965), pp. 107–8.
9. G. Webster, 'Final report on the excavations of the Roman Fort at Waddon Hill, Stoke Abbott, 1963-69', *Proc. DNHAS*, vol. 101 (1979), pp. 51–90.
10. *Proc. DNHAS*, reports in vols. 89–104 (1967–82).
11. Ibid., vol. 81 (1959), p. 107.
12. *SD*, vol. 28 (1968), p. 320.
13. E. Ekwall, *Oxf. Dict. English Place-Names*, 4th edn. (1960), p. 32; M. Gelling, *Signposts to the Past* (1978), pp. 177–8.
14. Dean and Chapter Glouc. Cathedral, Reg. A., ff. 9rv, 10; G. R. C. Davis, ed., *Medieval Cartularies of Gt. Britain* (1958), p. 51; Hart, *Cart. Glos.*, vol. 1, pp. lxxi-lxxiv; Birch, *Cart. Sax.* 535; see also P. H. Sawyer, *Anglo-Saxon Charters* (1968), nos. 70, 209, 1782.
15. H. P. R. Finberg, *Early Charters of the West Midlands* (1961), pp. 153–63.
16. Ibid., p. 165.
17. Not 872 as in printed texts.
18. F. Barlow, *The English Church 1000-1066*, 2nd edn. (1979), p. 164 n.
19. *Register of St. Osmund*, ed. by W. H. Rich-Jones (Rolls Series, 1883-4), vol. 1, p. 198.
20. See A. M. Armstrong *et al.*, *Place-Names of Cumberland*, Part II (1950), pp. 430–31.
21. Fagersten, *op. cit.*, p. 262.
22. W. Stuart Best, 'The Early Church in Dorset', *Proc. DNHAS*, vol. 96 (1974), pp. 45–47.
23. K. Barker, 'Early Ecclesiastical Settlement in Dorset: A note on the Topography of Sherborne, Beaminster and Wimborne Minster', *Proc. DNHAS*, vol. 102 (1980), pp. 107–9.
24. V. I. Evison, 'The Anglo-Saxon Finds from Hardown Hill', *Proc. DNHAS*, vol. 90 (1968), pp. 232–40.
25. W. Page, 'Some remarks on the Churches of the Domesday Survey', *Archaeologia*, vol. 66 (1915), p. 71; R. Lennard, *Rural England 1086-1135* (1959), pp. 301, 396–402.
26. J. Fowler, *Medieval Sherborne* (1951), pp. 58, 60.
27. *VCH*, vol. 3 (1968), pp. 132–3.
28. Kemble 1309, 1322.
29. G. B. Grundy, 'Dorset Charters', *Proc. DNHAS*, vol. 57 (1935), pp. 130–39; for first charter, see also C. D. Drew, 'Earnley: a lost place-name recovered', *Proc. DNHAS*, vol. 71 (1949), pp. 84–87.
30. Hutchins, vol. 2, pp. 145-6.
31. DRO, P57/IN11.
32. *Bridport News*, 12 Feb. 1909.
33. Ordnance Survey, Southampton, Remark Books 13426, 13427, 13156.
34. Copy of survey in Beaminster Public Libr.; the author was co-ordinator.
35. Finberg, *op. cit.*, p. 161.
36. *VCH*, vol. 3 (1968), p. 72.
37. Hutchins, vol. 2, p. 120.
38. Fagersten, *op. cit.*, p. 262, n. 3.
39. *SD*, vol. 10 (1907), pp. 195–200.
40. DRO, Parl. Surveys, photo-copies 379 (Prima & Secunda), 385.
41. DRO, 7117, minute book 1813-57.
42. K. J. Penn, *Historic Towns in Dorset* (DNHAS Monograph 1, 1980), p. 15.
43. DRO, Inclosure 65.
44. PRO, PROB 11/6, will of John Curteys 1471.
45. DRO, 6291; Hutchins, vol. 2, pp. 120–23.
46. Hine, pp. 261-3, 257.

47. Hutchins, vol. 2, p. 127.
48. *Cal. Charter R.*, 1257–1300, p. 454.
49. *Registers of Roger Martival 1315–30*, ed. by K. Edwards (Cant. and York Soc.), vol. 1 (1959), p. 32.
50. Wilts. RO, Court of Dean of Sarum.
51. Wilts. RO, Bishoprick 443–3.
52. Wilts. RO, Bishoprick 444, 15 leases 1661–1826.
53. Wilts. RO, Bishoprick 468.
54. Hine, pp. 146–7.
55. DRO, MW/M4, Sir John Strode's notebook.
56. *SD*, vol. 10 (1907), p. 264.
57. *VCH*, vol. 3, p. 90; Hutchins, vol. 2, p. 158.
58. Lennard, *op. cit.*, p. 69.

Chapter 2. The Medieval Settlements

1. *VCH*, vol. 3 (1968), pp. 72, 90; *Domesday Book: Dorset*, ed. by C. and F. Thorn (1983), 3, 10; 3, 18; 32, 5.
2. Wilts. RO, Bishoprick 468.
3. H. C. Darby, ed., *Historical Geography of England before 1800* (1969), p. 209, fig. 25.
4. DRO, Inclosure 65; Hine, pp. 263–4.
5. DRO, 6296, Beaminster Secunda court book 1782–1806.
6. DRO, 6269, Beaminster Prima presentments 1651–79.
7. DRO, 6281, Prima court book 1616–30.
8. Hutchins, vol. 2, p. 133.
9. R. Hine's notebook with extracts copied from J. B. Russell's MS. (in possession of Mr. G. Crew), hereafter referred to as Hine (Russell), f. 16v.
10. DRO, 7120, Secunda presentments 1618–54; 6283, Prima court book 1654–88; 7117, Parsonatus minute book 1813–57.
11. *SD*, vol. 11 (1909), pp. 167–8.
12. *SD*, vol. 10 (1907), p. 197.
13. *Dorset Lay Subsidy Roll of 1332*, ed. by A. D. Mills (Dorset Rec. Soc., 1971), p. 39.
14. A. Fagersten, *Place-Names of Dorset* (1933), pp. 263, 264.
15. *Salisbury Charters and Documents*, ed. by W. D. Macray (1891), p. 365.
16. *Proc. DNHAS*, vol. 81 (1959), p. 107.
17. *Dorset Lay Subsidy Roll of 1327*, ed. by A. R. Rumble (Dorset Rec. Soc., 1980), p. 62.
18. *Lay Subsidy 1332*, p. 38.
19. *SD*, vol. 11, pp. 164–7.
20. Hutchins, vol. 2, p. 131, notes to Strode pedigree.
21. DRO, MW/M4; Hine, p. 338 n.
22. *Registrum Simonis de Gandavo*, ed. by C. T. Flower and M. C. B. Dawes (Cant. and York Soc., 1934), Intro. pp. xxviii, xxxiii, xlii; *Registers of Roger Martival*, ed. by K. Edwards, vol. 4 (1975), Intro. pp. xxxvi, xxxviii.
23. PRO, C 53/72.
24. J. H. Bettey, *Church and Community* (1979), p. 33.
25. *SD*, vol. 10, pp. 197, 198, 199.
26. Hine (Russell), f. 9v; Hutchins, vol. 2, p. 136; Hine. pp. 19–20.
27. PRO, PROB 11/14, will dated 10 Feb. 1503/4 but *not* a legacy (see Hutchins, vol. 2, p. 135).
28. Hutchins, vol. 2, p. 145.
29. G. D. Squibb, 'Dorset Incumbents 1542–1731', *Proc. DNHAS*, vol. 73 (1951), p. 145.
30. *Cal. Papal Letters*, 1.558; *Cal. Chanc. R.*, 35; *De Banco R.* 315.46d. and 329.252; *De Banco R.* 499.15d; *De Banco R.* 673.270d; *De Banco R.* 878.425; information from Rev. P. May, former Vicar of Netherbury.
31. *Cal. Pat.*, 1374–77, pp. 23–4; *Valor Ecclesiasticus*, ed. by J. Caley and J. Hunter (Rec. Com. 1810–34), vol. 1, p. 231.
32. *Register of St Osmund*, ed. by W. H. Rich-Jones (Rolls Series, 1883–4), vol. 1, p. 198.
33. *Reg. Gandavo*, pp. 16, 130–2, xxxiii.
34. *Leland's Itinerary in England and Wales 1535–43*, ed. by L. Toulmin Smith (1964), vol. 1, pp. 246–7.
35. For further historical and architectural details, see RCHM, *Dorset*, vol. 1, pp. 17–21, and Hine, Chapter 2.
36. PRO, PROB 11/11; Hutchins, 2nd edn., vol. 1 (1796), p. 452.
37. *Cal. Pat.*, 1405–8, p. 279.
38. Hutchins, vol. 2, pp. 136, 138.
39. J. Fowler, *Medieval Sherborne* (1951), pp. 208–10, 62, n. 3.
40. Hutchins, vol. 2, pp. 135, 138–9.
41. Hutchins, vol. 2, p. 564, pedigree of Grey.
42. *Registrum Henrici Chichele*, ed. by E. F. Jacob (Cant. and York Soc.), vol. 2 (1937), pp. 222–3.
43. Hist. MSS. Com., *55 Var. Coll. IV*, p. 127.
44. *Valor Eccles.*, vol. 1, p. 232.

45. *Proc. DNHAS*, vol. 27 (1906), pp. 225, 228; ibid., vol. 31 (1910), p. 87.
46. *Proc. DNHAS*, vol. 30 (1909), pp. 16-18.
47. DRO, KF 20.
48. Devon RO, 96M/Box 100/1.
49. Hine (Russell), f. 24 rv.
50. Wilts. RO, Court of Dean of Sarum.
51. Hine, pp. 37-39.
52. Wilts. RO, Dean of Sarum, churchwardens' presentments 1685.
53. Hine (Russell), ff. 5, 21 rv, 23.

Chapter 3. Town and Parish (1500-1700)

1. *Dorset Tudor Subsidies granted in 1523, 1543, 1593*, ed. & publ. by T. L Stoate (1982), pp. 39, 40.
2. J. Cornwall, 'English Towns in the 1520s', *Economic History Review*, 2nd series, vol. 15 (1962-3), pp. 54-69, suggests other formulas.
3. *Dorset Tudor Muster Rolls 1539, 1542, 1569*, ed. & publ. by T. L. Stoate (1978).
4. Wilts. RO, Dean of Sarum, churchwardens' presentments 1558-1603, no. 20; *Proc. DNHAS*, vol. 89 (1967), p. 231.
5. *Protestation Returns 1641-2* (Dorset Records, vol. 12, 1912), pp. 77-79.
6. *Dorset Hearth Tax Assessments 1662-4*, ed. by C. A. F. Meekings (1951), pp. 88, 89.
7. Ibid., p. 119.
8. Wilts. RO, Prebendary of Netherbury in Ecclesia, churchwardens' presentments 1632-40.
9. DRO, P57/CW5, churchwardens' accounts 1646-1719.
10. Hine, p. 33, quotes J. B. Russell.
11. C. M. Heighway, ed., *The Erosion of History* (CBA, 1972), p. 9.
12. See J. Patten, *English Towns 1500-1700* (1978), pp. 21-28.
13. Ibid., pp. 112-16.
14. Hutchins, vol. 2, p. 119; DRO, Q.S. Order Books 1625-38, 1663-74.
15. DRO, Q.S. Order Book 1625-38, f. 614 rv.
16. *Leland's Itinerary in Eng. & Wales 1535-43*, ed. by L. Toulmin Smith (1964), vol. 1, pp. 246-7.
17. DRO, P57/RE15, note at back of register of christenings,

18. DRO, 6281 and 6283, Beaminster Prima court books.
19. *Dorset Lay Subsidy Roll of 1332*, p. 38.
20. Hine, p. 185.
21. Hine, p. 142, quotes J. B. Russell.
22. DRO, Q.S. Order Book 1625-38, f. 229 v.
23. Hine, p. 154, quotes J. B. Russell.
24. *SD*, vol. 15 (1917), pp. 83-4.
25. Hine, pp. 360-1.
26. Wilts. RO, Court of Preb. of Netherbury in Eccl.
27. Hutchins, vol. 2, p. 119; Hine, pp. 118-22.
28. DRO, 8212.
29. Hine, pp. 125-7.
30. DRO, LN6, LN8, LN9.
31. DRO, LN8, LN10.
32. PRO, C 8/193/133, info. from Dr. J. Bettey.
33. DRO, LN8.
34. Info. from Mr. R. Machin.

Chapter 4. Agriculture and Industries (1500-1700)

1. *Leland's Itinerary in Eng. & Wales 1535-43*, ed. by L. Toulmin Smith (1964), vol. 1, pp. 246-7.
2. J. H. Bettey and D. S. Wilde, 'The Probate Inventories of Dorset Farmers 1573-1670', *Local Historian*, vol. 12, no. 5 (1977), pp. 228-31.
3. Wilts. RO, Court of Dean of Sarum.
4. Wilts. RO, Bishoprick 443-3.
5. Wilts. RO, Bishoprick 468.
6. Wilts. RO, Bishoprick 444.
7. Wilts. RO, Court of Prebendary of Netherbury in Ecclesia.
8. DRO, 6269, Beaminster Prima presentments 1651-79, ff. 8 rv, 91 rv, 242-3.
9. R. Machin, *The Houses of Yetminster* (1978), pp. 142-5.
10. RCHM, *Dorset*, vol. 1 (1952), p. 21.
11. DRO, MW/M4.
12. J. D. Wilson, 'Medieval Deer-Parks of Dorset XVII', *Proc. DNHAS*, vol. 100 (1978), p. 33.
13. Hutchins, vol. 2, p. 138.
14. Info. from Mr. Cleal and Mr. N. Welsford.
15. T. Fuller, *The Worthies of England* (1662), p. 309.

16. J. H. Bettey, 'The Dorset Wool and Cloth Industry', *SD*, vol. 29 (1974), pp. 240-2; W. B. Stephens, 'The Trade Fortunes of Poole, Weymouth and Lyme Regis 1600-40', *Proc. DNHAS*, vol. 95 (1973), pp. 71-73.

17. D. Defoe, *Tour through the Whole Island of Gt. Britain* (Penguin 1971), pp. 260-1.

18. J. H. Bettey, *The Landscape of Wessex* (1980), p. 116.

19. DRO, 6283, Prima court book 1654-88.

20. Hutchins, vol. 1, p. lxxvi, illustrated after p. lxxii, no. 6.

21. J. Pahl, 'The Rope and Net Industry of Bridport', *Proc. DNHAS*, vol. 82 (1960), pp. 143-5.

22. H. C. Darby, ed., *Historical Geography of England before 1800* (1969), p. 436n.

23. T. Fuller, *op. cit.*, p. 310.

24. Hutchins, vol. 2, p. 119n.

25. Hine, p. 93.

26. In possession of Mr. and Mrs. D. J. Barrett.

27. Hutchins, vol. 2, p. 146.

28. A. Everitt, 'The Marketing of Agricultural Produce' in J. Thirsk, ed., *Agrarian History of Eng. and Wales vol. 4 1500-1640* (1967), pp. 589-92.

29. J. H. Hamer, 'Trading at Saint White Down Fair 1637-49', *Proc. Somerset Arch. Soc.*, vol. 112 (1968), pp. 61-70.

30. *The Journeys of Celia Fiennes*, ed. by C. Morris (Cresset Press, 1947), p. 12.

31. DRO, P57/CW5, churchwardens' accounts 1646-1719.

Chapter 5. People and Society (1500-1700)

1. DRO, Q.S. Order Book 1625-38, ff. 213v, 229v.

2. Ibid, f. 272v.

3. Ibid., f. 529v.

4. Hine, p. 429 n.

5. DRO, P57/OV9.

6. Hutchins, vol. 2, p. 119 n.

7. DRO, Q.S. Order Book 1625-38, f. 509.

8. Ibid, f. 13v.

9. Wilts. RO, Court of Dean of Sarum.

10. Hine, pp. 184-6.

11. Hine, p. 215.

12. *Charity Commissioners' Reports for Dorset 1818-37*, pp. 158-9.

13. DRO, LN13; Hutchins, vol. 2, p. 125.

14. DRO, P57/CW5, churchwardens' accounts 1646-1719.

15. Hine, pp. 159-65.

16. Wilts. RO, Dean of Sarum, churchwardens' presentments 1634.

17. Hine, pp. 216-17.

18. Wilts. RO, Dean of Sarum, churchwardens' presentments 1606-8.

19. *Proc. DNHAS*, vol. 26 (1905), p. 114.

20. Wilts. RO, Dean of Sarum, churchwardens' presentments 1630/31.

21. Ibid, 1558-1603.

22. G. D. Squibb, 'Dorset Incumbents 1542-1731', *Proc. DNHAS*, vol. 73 (1951), p.145.

23. G. J. Davies, 'Early Dorset Nonconformity', *Proc. DNHAS*, vol. 97 (1975), p. 27; Hine, p. 90.

24. Davies, *Proc. DNHAS*, vol. 97, p. 29.

25. Hine, pp. 93, 92, 91.

26. *Dorset Tudor Muster Rolls* (1978), and *Dorset Tudor Lay Subsidies* (1982), ed. and publ. by T. L. Stoate.

27. *Protestation Returns 1641-2* (Dorset Records, vol. 12, 1912).

28. Hutchins, vol. 4, pp. 144-6; *Visitation of Dorset 1623* (Harl. Soc. XX, 1885), and *Visitation of Dorset 1677* (Harl. Soc. CXVII, 1977).

29. DRO, Q.S. Order Book 1625-38, f. 229v.

30. Wilts. RO, Bishoprick 443-3.

31. Wilts. RO, Dean of Sarum, CP/CR. 72 Misc. 3.

32. See Hutchins, vol. 4, p. 146.

33. *Dorset Hearth Tax Assessments 1662-4*, ed. by C. A. F. Meekings (1951), p. 88; DRO, P57/CW5.

34. Hutchins, vol. 2, p. 123.

35. Hutchins, vol. 2, pp. 126, 128, 88.

36. *SD*, vol. 11 (1909), pp. 165-6.

37. Wilts. RO, Prebendary of Netherbury in Ecclesia, churchwardens' presentments 1683-94.

38. Hutchins, vol. 1, p. lxxvi, illustrated after p. lxxii, no. 80.

39. Hutchins, vol. 2, pp. 135, 133.

40. Hutchins, vol. 1, p. lxxv, illustrated after p. lxxii, no 4.

41. Info. from Dr. R. Conway.

42. Hine, p. 157.

43. Hutchins, vol. 2, pp. 127, 128, 126, 132.

44. Hine, pp. 122-3.

45. DRO, Q.S. Order Book 1663-74.

46. Hine, pp. 244-6.

47. Hine, pp. 246-51; grave X, subsequent burials of Mary Ann Daniel (1929) and Emily Marion Parsons (1940).

Chapter 6. Town and Parish (1700–1850)

1. Bristol RO, EP/A/2/2.
2. DRO, P57/CW23.
3. DRO, P57/RE3.
4. Congregational Church, register of baptisms 1777–89; copy of original register 1796 (Nov.) – 1836 sent to London (PRO, R.G. 4/2403).
5. DRO, P57/RE3, RE11.
6. DCM, Hine Collection, scrapbook no. 2.
7. DRO, 6268, Bridport & Beaminster Turnpike Trust minute book 1754–1812.
8. *BN*, 11 Nov. 1910.
9. Hutchins, vol. 1, p. lxix.
10. Hine, p. 429.
11. Hutchins, vol. 1, p. lxviii.
12. A. P. Codd, *Life in Beaminster 1864–1910* (1969), p. 289, fig. 39.
13. 59 Geo. III c. 88; 11 Geo. IV & 1 Will. IV, c. 5.
14. Hine, pp. 127–8.
15. Hine, pp. 129–33.
16. Hine (Russell) notebook, f. 48.
17. Throughout the chapter, the following dates refer to commercial directories: 1793 *Universal British*; 1824, 1830, 1842 Pigot's; 1885 Kelly's.
18. Hine, p. 134.
19. M. Weinstock, *More Dorset Studies* (1960), p. 62.
20. DRO, P57/CW5, churchwardens' accounts 1646–1719.
21. DRO, P57/OV10, overseers' accounts 1729–69.
22. DRO, photocopy 498/17.
23. DRO, P57/VE3.
24. DRO, P57/OV11, overseers' accounts 1768–90.
25. DRO, P57/OV15, overseers' accounts 1824–34.
26. Hine, pp. 358–9.
27. DRO, P57/OV16.
28. Hine, p. 355.
29. Hine, p. 84.
30. Hine, pp. 356, 357n.
31. Hine (Russell), f. 6v.
32. Hine, pp. 142–3.
33. Hine, pp. 144–6.
34. Congregational Church, minute book 1796–1890, p. 93.
35. Hine, p. 146.
36. Hine, pp. 150–1, quotes J. B. Russell.
37. Hine, pp. 149–50.
38. Guildhall Libr., MS.11936, 49/75197.
39. Deeds in possession of Mr. & Mrs. D. J. Barrett.
40. Wilts. RO, Court of Prebendary of Netherbury in Ecclesia.
41. *Census report*.
42. DRO, P57/OV6, rate book 1850.
43. See Hine, pp. 385–7.
44. *Dorset County Chronicle*, advert. 5 July 1832.
45. DCM, Hine Collection, scrapbook no. 3.
46. *Chard in 1851* (Chard History Group no. 5, n.d.), p. 35.
47. DRO, alehouse keepers' recognisances.
48. Guildhall Libr., MS. 11936, 148/200408.
49. DRO, 6296, Beaminster Secunda court book 1782–1806.
50. DRO, P57/VE4.
51. Inclosure Award 1809.
52. DRO, D473/T1, T2, T3, T6, T9.
53. Architectural details from RCHM, *Dorset*, vol. 1 (1952), pp. 23–26, and Statutory List of Buildings of Special Architectural or Historic Interest (1984) with advice from Mr. S. Alford. The history of the houses is given in outline only, and to about mid-19th century: for some houses, considerable further information exists.
54. Deeds in possession of Mr. A. G. Tomkins.
55. Info. from Mr. N. Sjogren.
56. Hutchins, vol. 2, p. 124.
57. DRO, P57/OV3, rate book 1842.
58. Hine, pp. 351–3.
59. Deeds in possession of Mr. H. Russell.
60. Samways monument in north aisle of church; see Hine, p. 54.
61. DRO, D141/T1.
62. Info. from Mr. R. Machin.
63. DRO, land tax returns 1780–1832.
64. Hine, p. 109.
65. Hine, p. 48; M. Hadfield, 'The Bells of Beaminster', *Country Life*, November 1969.
66. Deeds in possession of Dr. & Mrs. M. K. G. Hudson.
67. DRO, 10841.
68. DRO, D473/T4, 5, 7, 8, 10, 11, 13.
69. DRO, D279/E1.
70. Codd, *op. cit.*, p. 258.
71. Info. from Miss K. Pim.
72. DRO, P57/CW6, churchwardens' accounts 1720–64.
73. DRO, 9663, plan of Charity lands.
74. DRO, D265/1.
75. See Hutchins, vol. 2, p.130, Strode pedigree.

76. Hutchins, p. 132, note to Strode pedigree.
77. DRO, D279/E4.
78. Hutchins, vol. 2, p. 134, Oglander pedigree.
79. DRO, MW/M8.
80. A. Penny, 'Icehouses in Dorset', *Proc. DNHAS*, vol. 86 (1964), p. 219; photos (1965) at DCM.
81. DRO, Highways Diversions, Q.S. Cert. no. 33, bundle 1.
82. W. Gardner, *Poems* (1872).

Chapter 7. Agriculture (1700-1850)

1. W. Marshall, *Rural Economy of the West of England* (1796), vol. 2, pp. 141-2, 148-9.
2. DRO, D279/E4.
3. D. Defoe, *Tour through the Whole Island of Gt. Britain* (Penguin 1971), p. 268.
4. Netherbury Church, parish docs. transcribed by E. Nevill c. 1905.
5. Marshall, *op. cit.*, vol. 2, pp. 129, 141-2, 144.
6. W. E. Minchinton, 'Agriculture in Dorset during the Nap. Wars', *Proc. DNHAS*, vol. 77 (1955), pp. 162-73.
7. J. H. Bettey, '1801 Crop Returns for some Dorset parishes', *SD*, vol. 29 (1968-73), p. 101.
8. W. Stevenson, *General view of the agriculture of the County of Dorset* (1812), p. 204.
9. Ibid, pp. 235, 236.
10. DRO, P57/CH1.
11. Stevenson, *op. cit.*, p. 197.
12. DRO, MW/M8.
13. H. S. L Dewar, 'Flax, hemp, and their growers in W. Dorset', *Proc. DNHAS*, vol. 91 (1969), pp. 216-19.
14. Stevenson, *op. cit.*, p. 287.
15. Ibid, p. 267.
16. Ibid., pp. 91, 340, 351.
17. Ibid., p. 348.
18. Ibid., p. 423.
19. Ibid., pp. 152-3, 149.
20. *Holden's directory.*
21. Marshall, *op. cit.*, vol. 2, p. 131.
22. Hine, pp. 266-72.
23. DRO, Inclosure 65; Hine, pp. 263-4, 273-5.
24. *Census report.*
25. Hine, p. 284; *Dorset County Chronicle*, 15 Sept. 1831.
26. Architectural details from RCHM, *Dorset*, vol. 1 (1952), pp. 26-27, and Statutory List of Buildings of Special Architectural or Historic Interest (1984) with advice from Mr. S. Alford.
27. DRO, P57/OV10, overseers' accounts 1729-69.
28. Hutchins, vol. 2, p. 133.
29. DRO, Inclosure 65.
30. DRO, 6296, Beaminster Secunda court book 1782-1806.
31. Deeds in possession of Dr. and Mrs. M. K. G. Hudson.
32. Hutchins, vol. 2, p. 127.
33. DRO, MW/M9.
34. DRO, 9827.
35. DRO, NY1.
36. DRO, P57/CW5, Churchwardens' accounts 1646-1719.
37. DRO, 9850, 9851.
38. DRO, 9853-9873 incl.
39. Hutchins, vol. 2, p. 135.
40. DRO, P57/OV21.
41. DRO, KE6, KE7, KE18, KE25, KE26.
42. DRO, 8203; Hutchins, vol. 2, p. 128.
43. Hutchins, vol. 2, p. 126.
44. Wilts. RO, Dean of Sarum, churchwardens' presentments 1634.
45. Hutchins, vol. 2, pp. 126-7; DRO, 8576B.
46. In possession of Mr. S. Oliver.
47. DRO, KF 20.
48. Hutchins, vol. 2, pp. 638-9, Larder pedigree.
49. DRO, 10776.
50. Hutchins, vol. 2, p. 499, Richards pedigree.
51. Wilts. RO, Court of Dean of Sarum.
52. DRO, P57/CW23, Cox survey.
53. DRO, 8218, 8217.
54. DRO, 8240; P57/OV1.
55. DRO, D418/T1, 8222, 8221, 8229, 8231 *et al.*
56. See Hutchins, vol. 2, pp. 201, 692, 128.
57. DRO, 9663, plan of Charity lands.
58. Wilts. RO, CP/CR. 72 Misc. 3.
59. Hine, p. 160.
60. DRO, 9658, 9695, 9698, 9699, 9701, 9702 *et al.*
61. DRO, 9698.
62. DRO, 9887, survey of lands of H. C. Compton.
63. Info. from Mr. R. Machin.

Chapter 8. Industries and Communications (1700–1850)

1. Throughout the chapter, the following dates refer to commercial directories: 1793 *Universal British*; 1811 Holden's; 1824, 1830, 1842 Pigot's; 1855, 1867 Kelly's.
2. Wilts. RO, Court of Prebendary of Netherbury in Ecclesia.
3. K. Ponting, 'Dorset Textile Mills 1727–71', *SD*, vol. 30 (1980), pp. 171, 174–9.
4. DRO, 9663, plan of Charity lands 1776.
5. DRO, 6298, Beaminster Secunda court book 1823–47.
6. Guildhall Libr., MS. 11936, 175/246049.
7. Guildhall Libr., MS. 11936, 168/234530.
8. Hine, p. 307; DRO, P57/OV33.
9. DRO, P57/CW23, Cox parish survey.
10. Hine, p. 306.
11. Tithe map and Award 1843.
12. DRO, 6296, Secunda court book 1782–1806.
13. J. Claridge, *General View of the Agriculture of the County of Dorset* (1793), pp. 37–38.
14. B. Kerr, *Bound to the Soil* (1968), pp. 74–76.
15. DRO, P57/OV21, apprenticeship indentures.
16. Guildhall Libr., MS. 11936, 49/75197.
17. DRO, P57/OV10, overseers' accounts 1729–69.
18. Congregational Church, minute book 1796–1890, p. 101.
19. *Return of mills and factories*, H.C. 41, pp. 178–81 (1839) xlii.
20. [Cd. 510] H.C., p. 84 (1843) xii.
21. Hine, p. 305.
22. Hine, p. 308.
23. *The Church of St Giles and the village of Hooke*, (n.d., priv. print., Hooke Church Council.)
24. F. C. Warren, 'Dorset Industries in the Past', *Proc. DNHAS*, vol. 59 (1937), p. 37.
25. Date and initial F on inside wall, top floor of mill building.
26. H.C. 97, p. 58 (1837) l.
27. Info. from Dr. R. Conway.
28. A. H. Shorter, 'Paper Mills in Dorset', *SD*, vol. 25 (1950), p. 300.
29. Hine, p. 133.
30. Hine, pp. 311–12.
31. DRO, lists of freeholders.

32. W. Stevenson, *General View of the Agriculture of the County of Dorset* (1812), p. 450.
33. Hine, p. 309.
34. DRO, P57/CW6, churchwardens' accounts 1720–64.
35. Hine, p. 84.
36. T. Tribe and P. Whatmoor, *Dorset Clocks and Clockmakers* (1981); P. N. Dawe, 'Beaminster clockmakers', *SD*, vol. 29 (1974), pp. 229–31.
37. DRO, MW/M8, loose sheet inside.
38. M. B. Weinstock, *Old Dorset* (1967), p. 172.
39. Wilts. RO, Court of Dean of Sarum (will).
40. DRO, 10841.
41. W. Marshall, *Rural Economy of the West of England* (1796), vol. 2, p. 131.
42. DRO, D279/E4.
43. Hine, p. 370.
44. *SD*, vol. 5 (1897), p. 185.
45. *The Story of the Roads of Chard* (Chard History Group no. 2, 1968), p. 8.
46. C. Hadfield, *The Canals of the South West of England* (1967), pp. 67–74; R. Russell, *Lost Canals of England & Wales* (1971), pp. 66–71.
47. *Pigot's directory of Somerset* (1842), under Chard.
48. 27 Geo. II c. 32; 29 Geo. II c. 54.
49. DRO, 6268.
50. 5 Geo. III c. 75.
51. See also R. Good, *Old Roads of Dorset*, 2nd edn. (1966), pp. 134–5.
52. 59 Geo. III c. 88.
53. Hine, p. 413.
54. 18 Geo. III c. 95.
55. DRO, 7112, J. B. Russell's ledger.
56. DRO, NY1.
57. DRO, turnpike plan no. 4, 1818.
58. *Dorset County Chronicle*, 5 July 1832.
59. 11 Geo. IV & 1 Will. IV, c. 5; DRO, turnpike plan & ref. book nos. 19 & 20, 1829.
60. Hine, opp. p. 404; DRO, photocopy 24, dated 1827 in cat.
61. DRO, TP1, Gen. Statements Acc., Bridport 2nd District.
62. Hine, p. 403.
63. A. J. Wallis, *Dorset Bridges* (1974), p. 85, and further info. from Mr. Wallis.
64. D. Young, 'Brickmaking in Dorset', *Proc. DNHAS*, vol. 93 (1971), p. 238.
65. Info. from Mr. Brian J. Murless.

66. J. Newman and N. Pevsner, *The Buildings of England: Dorset* (1972), p. 89.
67. Obituary notice, I.C.E., Mins. of Proceedings, vol. 30.
68. W. Gardner, *Poems* (1872).
69. Good, *op. cit.*, pp. 142, 144.
70. DRO, Maiden Newton Turnpike Trust minute book 1778–95.
71. DRO, LL89.
72. DRO, P57/CH1, trustees' account book.
73. Good, *op. cit.*, p. 145.

Chapter 9. The Poor (1700–1850)

1. DRO, P57/OV10, overseers' accounts 1729–69.
2. DRO, P57/OV11, overseers' accounts 1768–90.
3. DRO, P57/OV33, workhouse ledger etc. 1796–1833.
4. DRO, P57/CW23, Cox survey.
5. DRO, P57/OV12, overseers' accounts 1790–1804.
6. DRO, P57/OV43.
7. DRO, P57/OV13, overseers' accounts 1804–15.
8. DRO, P57/OV38, yearly lists of inmates 1810–23.
9. DRO, P57/OV14, overseers' accounts 1815–24.
10. DRO, P57/OV15, overseers' accounts 1824–34.
11. DRO, G1/A1, Board of Guardians' minutes 1836–40.
12. G. Body, 'Administration of Poor Law in Dorset 1760–1834', unpublished D. thesis, University of Southampton 1965 (copy DRO), p. 186.
13. DRO, P57/OV34, workhouse daily disbursements with earnings 1796–1804.
14. W. Stevenson, *General View of the Agriculture of Dorset* (1812), p. 452.
15. DRO, P57/OV35, workhouse daily disbursements with earnings 1833–36.
16. Body, *op. cit.*, pp. 205–8.
17. *Rep. R. Com. on Poor Law*, H.C. 44, App. A, Pt. I (1834) xxviii.
18. DRO, P57/OV26.
19. DRO, P57/OV27.
20. DRO, P57/OV21, apprenticeship indentures 1697–1821.
21. DRO, 7112, J. B. Russell's ledger.
22. Hine, pp. 229–31.
23. *Charity Commissioners' Reports for Dorset 1818–37*, p. 158.
24. DRO, D279/R2.
25. *Charity Commissioners' Reps.*, pp. 159–60.
26. DRO, 9663, plan of Charity lands 1776.
27. *Charity Commissioners' Reps.*, pp. 160–1.
28. Hine, pp. 208, 209.
29. *Charity Commissioners' Reps.*, p. 157; DRO, P57/CW6.
30. DRO, P57/CH1, Tucker's Charity accounts 1708–1873.
31. *Charity Commissioners' Reps.*, p. 156.
32. Hine, p. 178.

Chapter 10. People and Society (1700–1850)

1. William Salt Libr. (Stafford), Compton census SMS. 33.
2. A. Everitt, *The Pattern of Rural Dissent: the 19th Century* (1972), Table II, p. 69.
3. PRO, H.O. 129/277.
4. Congregational Church, R. Hine MS.
5. Hine, p. 94, quotes J. B. Russell.
6. B. Short, *A Respectable Society* (1976), p. 34.
7. Hine, pp. 92–3, quotes MS. in Dr. Williams' Libr. (London).
8. Cong. Church, R. Hine MS. book concerning chapel; Hine, pp. 93–94.
9. Cong. Church, minute book 1796–1890.
10. Cong. Church, account book 1762–1825.
11. W. Densham and J. Ogle, *Story of the Congregational Churches of Dorset* (1899), p. 11.
12. Cong. Church, register of baptisms.
13. Cong. Church, minutes of committees 1824–34, 1859–62.
14. Hine, pp. 102–3.
15. Hine, p. 104.
16. Capt. G. A. French R.N., *Stoke Abbott* (1974), p. 22.
17. Hine, p. 112 n., quotes J. B. Russell.
18. Devon RO, MS., 1857, John Stevens, 'History of Wesleyan Methodism in Bridport and its Vicinity', pp. 30, 33.
19. Ibid., pp. 518–19.
20. Ibid., p. 45.
21. Ibid., p. 521.
22. Hine, p. 114.
23. Stevens, *op. cit.*, p. 522.
24. Ibid., p. 63.

25. Ibid., pp. 522-3.
26. Hine, p. 115.
27. Stevens, *op. cit.*, p. 239.
28. Ibid., p. 491.
29. Ibid., p. 493.
30. Ibid., pp. 442-3.
31. J. H. Temple, *The Mighty Oak: the Story of the Devon and Dorset Mission* (1974).
32. Stevens, *op. cit.*, pp. 144-5.
33. Ibid, p. 523.
34. Hine, p. 31, and opp. p. 60 for drawing by J. Buckler of earlier porch.
35. DRO, P57/CW6, churchwardens' accounts 1720-64.
36. DRO, P57/IN11.
37. Hine, pp. 418-20.
38. Hine (Russell), f. 2v.
39. *Dorset County Chronicle*, 15 Sept. 1831.
40. Hine, p. 391.
41. Hine, pp. 281-5.
42. Hine, full list opp. p. 282.
43. Tomb n. side St Mary's churchyard. Except where otherwise stated, genealogical details are from parish registers and monumental inscriptions. (Few inscriptions in the churchyard are legible in their present state, but G. P. R. Pulman gives brief particulars — some inaccurate — in *Book of the Axe* (1875 edn.) pp. 133-7.)
44. Hutchins, vol. 2, p. 124; see Hine p. 351.
45. A. P. Codd, *Life in Beaminster 1864-1910* (1969), p. 264.
46. Hine, p. 351.
47. Hine, pp. 419n., 416.
48. The following dates refer to commercial directories: 1793 *Universal British*; 1824, 1830 Pigot's; 1867, 1880, 1899 Kelly's.
49. Info. from Mr. H. Russell; Hine, pp. 223-4.
50. DRO, P57/CW23, Cox Survey.
51. Info. from Kitson & Trotman.
52. Hine, p. 416.
53. Hine, p. 249.
54. Hine, p. 250.
55. Tithe map and Award.
56. DRO, photocopy 631, various docs. incl. wills Thomas (1780), Richard (1844).
57. Cong. Church, register of baptisms 1777-89.
58. Deeds in possession of Mr. A. G. Tomkins.
59. DCM, R. Hine collection, scrapbook no. 3.
60. DRO, land tax returns.
61. DRO, 5098.
62. Codd, *op. cit.*, p. 249.
63. DRO, LN39.
64. DRO, P57/OV6, 7, 8 (rate books).
65. Hine, pp. 286, 290.

Chapter 11. Town and Parish (1850-1950)

1. *Census reports.*
2. Vestry minutes 1842-86.
3. Hine, p. 33.
4. *BN*, 7 April 1911; Beaminster Rural District Council, MOH report for 1911. (Copy in possession of Mr. R. C. Travers).
5. J. H. Bettey, *Dorset* (1974), p. 88.
6. G. P. R. Pulman, *The Book of the Axe*, 4th edn. (1875), p. 104.
7. *BN*, 14 Feb. & 18 Dec. 1908.
8. DRO, P355/PC4, parish council minutes 1920-32.
9. T. Rowley, *Villages in the Landscape* (1978), p. 22.
10. PRO, M.H. 12/2705.
11. The following dates refer to commercial directories: 1830, 1842 Pigot's; 1855, 1867, 1880, 1885, 1899, 1915, 1923, 1935 Kelly's.
12. Hine, p. 183.
13. Sir F. Treves, *Highways and Byways in Dorset* (1906), p. 298.
14. Hine, p. 135.
15. DCM, R. Hine collection, scrapbook no. 2.
16. DRO, P57/OV6, 7, rate books.
17. DRO, P57/SC4.
18. Hine, pp. 147-9.
19. Hine, p. 150; A. P. Codd, *Life in Beaminster 1864-1910* (1969), p. 280.
20. Codd, *op. cit.*, p. 271.
21. Info. from Mr. and Mrs. J. Brooks; *BN*, obituary 26 April 1912.
22. Info. from Mr. T. G. Crew.
23. J. Hine, *Parish News*, May 1981.
24. Info. from Miss F. Reynolds.
25. B. Short and J. Sales, *The Book of Bridport* (1980), p. 49.
26. *BN*, 28 July 1961, and info. from Mr. P. G. Perry.
27. Info. from Mr. R. C. Bugler.
28. Info. from Mr. G. Frampton.
29. Hine, pp. 315, 320.
30. DRO, DC3, Beaminster Rural District Council Water Supply cttee. minutes 1907-31.
31. Info. from Mr. G. Runyard of J. W. R. Newman & Co.
32. Codd, *op. cit.*, pp. 282, 284.
33. Info. from Mr. J. Hine.
34. Info. from Miss K. Pim.
35. Grave in Holy Trinity churchyard.

36. Info. from Kitson & Trotman.
37. *BN*, 30 Nov. 1917; DRO, D279/B1, 2, 14.
38. *BN*, 3 Mar. 1911.
39. *BN*, 12 Aug. 1921.
40. Hine, pp, 360-2.

Chapter 12. Agriculture and Other Occupations (1850-1950)

1. *BN*, 15 Nov. 1918, 14 Jan. 1921.
2. For reasons of space, details of later owners and tenants of most of the farms have had to be omitted.
3. The following dates refer to commercial directories: 1855, 1867, 1880, 1885, 1899, 1915, 1923 Kelly's.
4. Info. from Mr. J. Dunell.
5. *BN*, 19 March 1920.
6. *BN*, 4 April & 29 Aug. 1919.
7. L. E. Taverner, 'Dorset Farming 1900-50', *Proc. DNHAS*, vol. 75 (1955), pp. 102-3.
8. A. P. Codd, *Life in Beaminster 1864-1910* (1969), p. 280.
9. Info. from Mr. F. J. Sprackling.
10. *BN*, 19 June 1908 (rep. MOH); Hine, p. 310.
11. Info. from Mr. J. Hine.
12. Taverner, *op. cit.*, p. 111.
13. Info. from Miss S. Stenhouse.
14. DRO, P57/VE2, vestry minutes 1842-86.
15. DRO, P57/VE4.
16. DRO, P57/CH6, note by unknown writer with earlier document.
17. Info. from Mr. S. A. Oliver.
18. Info. from Mrs. I. Elix of S. Australia.
19. L. Powys, *Dorset Essays* (1935), pp. 80-1.
20. Codd, *op. cit.*, p. 282.
21. G. P. R. Pulman, *The Book of the Axe*, 4th edn. (1875), p. 104.
22. Hine, p. 306.
23. *BN*, 18 May 1917.
24. Dorchester Ref. Libr., 262.2.
25. Hine, pp. 314-16.
26. Hine, pp. 317, 319.
27. Hine, pp. 318, 320.
28. *BN*, 4 Nov. 1927.
29. DRO, P355/PC5, parish council minutes 1932-46.
30. W. Gardner, 'Beaminster & Surrounding Scenery', *Poems* (1872).

31. J. H. Lucking, *Railways of Dorset* (1965), pp. 16, 18.
32. Ibid., pp. 32, 33; *Dorset County Chronicle*, 19 Nov. 1863, 29 Dec. 1864.
33. *Dorset County Chronicle*, 21 Nov. 1878.
34. Hine, p. 310.
35. Hine, p. 371.
36. R. C. Anderson & G. Frankis, *History of Western National* (1979), p. 36.
37. *BN*, 11 Nov. 1910.
38. DRO, P355/PC2, parish council minutes 1894-1907.
39. *BN*, 24 May 1912, 21 Mar. 1913.
40. *Parish News*, Aug. 1981.
41. DRO, P355/PC3, parish council minutes 1908-20.
42. *BN*, 21 Mar. 1919, 20 May 1921.
43. Anderson & Frankis, *op. cit.*, pp. 47-8.
44. Ibid., pp. 191 (App. B), 54.

Chapter 13. Public Services (1850-1950)

1. DRO, P57/VE2, vestry minutes 1842-86.
2. PRO, M.H. 12/2705.
3. DRO, G1/A1, Beaminster Board of Guardians' minutes 1836-40.
4. DRO, G1/A3, Guardians' minutes 1859-65.
5. DRO, P57/OV32.
6. *BN*, 1 Apr. & 15 July 1910.
7. *BN*, 16 Apr. & 7 May 1909.
8. DRO, · DC3, Bridport Highway Board minutes 1863-79.
9. DRO, DC3, Beaminster Rural Sanitary Authority minutes 1872-91.
10. DRO, DC3, Beaminster Rural District Council (abbreviated hereafter to RDC) minutes 1895-97 (with Sanitary Authority minutes 1892-94).
11. DRO, DC3, RDC minutes, Highways only, 1895-97.
12. *BN*, 26 Mar. & 2 Apr. 1920.
13. DRO, DC3, RDC minutes 1907-13.
14. DRO, DC3, RDC minutes 1924-27.
15. DRO, DC3, RDC minutes 1897-1906.
16. DRO, DC3, RDC minutes 1913-19.
17. DRO, DC3, RDC minutes 1931-37.
18. DRO, DC3, RDC minutes 1937-43.
19. DRO, DC3, RDC minutes 1919-24.
20. DRO, DC3, RDC minutes 1927-31.
21. DRO, DC3, RDC minutes 1944-49.
22. DRO, P355/PC1, annual parish meetings 1894-1927.

23. *BN*, 8 Mar. 1907.
24. *BN*, 29 Mar. 1907.
25. DRO, P355/PC5, parish council minutes 1932-46.
26. DRO, P355/PC4, parish council minutes 1920-32.
27. DRO, P355/PC2, parish council minutes 1894-1907.
28. DRO, P355/PC3, parish council minutes 1908-20.
29. Hine, p. 438.
30. DRO, P57/OV28, Beaminster Union returns 1849-53, 1857-58.
31. 6 Jan. 1911.
32. Hine, pp. 315-16.
33. Hine, p. 320.
34. DRO, P57/VE3.
35. Hine, pp. 318-19.
36. DRO, P355/LW1, ratepayers' meetings 1855-71.
37. DRO, P355/LW2, LW3, Lighting Inspectors' meetings 1866-79, 1894-1914.
38. Hine, pp. 138-9.
39. *BN*, 5 May 1911.
40. Hine, pp. 139-40.

Chapter 14. More about Public Services (1850-1950)

1. DRO, P57/VE2, vestry minutes 1842-86.
2. DRO, DC3, Bridport Highway Board minutes 1863-79.
3. DRO, DC3, Highway Board minutes 1879-92.
4. DRO, 10400.
5. DRO, DC3, Beaminster Rural District Council (abbreviated hereafter to RDC) minutes 1927-31.
6. DRO, DC3, RDC minutes 1907-13.
7. DRO, DC3, RDC minutes 1913-19.
8. DRO, P355/PC3, parish council minutes 1908-20.
9. DRO, P355/PC1, annual parish meetings 1894-1927.
10. DRO, P355/PC2, parish council minutes 1894-1907.
11. *BN*, 11 Dec. 1908.
12. DRO, DC3, RDC minutes 1919-24.
13. DRO, DC3, RDC minutes 1924-27.
14. DRO, DC3, RDC Clerk's file, Roads Administration scheme 1929-30.
15. DRO, P57/VE4.
16. DRO, DC3, Beaminster Rural Sanitary Authority minutes 1872-91.
17. DRO, DC3, Sanitary Authority minutes 1892-94.
18. DRO, DC3, RDC minutes 1897-1906.
19. *BN*, 31 May 1907.
20. *BN*, 6 Sept. 1907.
21. DRO, DC3, RDC Water Supply cttee. minutes 1907-31.
22. *BN*, 14 Oct. 1927.
23. *BN*, 26 Apr. 1929.
24. W. Gardner, *Poems* (1872).
25. Hine, p. 145.
26. *BN*, 21 Feb. 1908.
27. *BN*, 20 Mar. 1908.
28. DRO, DC3, RDC minutes 1931-37.
29. DRO, DC3, RDC minutes 1944-49.
30. DRO, DC3, RDC minutes 1937-43.
31. DRO, P355/PC4, parish council minutes 1920-32.
32. *BN*, 7 Oct. 1927.
33. *Census report.*
34. *BN*, 22 Feb. 1907.
35. *BN*, 24 Jan. 1919.
36. DRO, DC3, RDC Housing cttee. minutes 1919-21.
37. RDC MOH reports for 1919 & 1921 (copy in possession of Mr. R. C. Travers).
38. DRO, DC3, RDC register of houses 1926-44.
39. Info. from Mrs. A. Welsford.
40. RDC MOH report for 1926 (copy in possession of Mr. Travers).
41. DRO, P355/PC5, parish council minutes 1932-46.

Chapter 15. People and Society (1850-1950)

1. *BN*, 26 Jan. & 23 Feb. 1912.
2. Hine, p. 20.
3. Hine, pp. 55-6, 65.
4. A. P. Codd, *Life in Beaminster 1864-1910* (1969), p. 256.
5. J. Newman & N. Pevsner, *The Buildings of England: Dorset* (1972), p. 87.
6. W. Densham & J. Ogle, *Story of the Congregational Churches of Dorset* (1899), p. 14.
7. Congregational church, minute book 1796-1890.
8. Cong. church, minutes of committees 1859-62.

9. Cong. church, minutes of finance cttee. and church meetings 1869--83.
10. DRO, P57/CH3, Tucker's Charity schemes.
11. *BN*, 7 Mar. 1913, obituary of John Hine.
12. Hine, p. 108.
13. Info. from Mr. W. Riglar.
14. J. H. Temple, *The Mighty Oak: the story of the Devon and Dorset Mission* (1974).
15. Devon RO, MS. 1857, John Stevens, 'History of Wesleyan Methodism in Bridport and its Vicinity', pp. 445-50.
16. Stevens, *op. cit.*, p. 437.
17. Hine, p. 115; *BN*, obituary 12 Feb. 1909.
18. Temple, *op. cit.*; Hine, p. 116.
19. Devon RO, 2399D/68, 69.
20. Hine, p. 117.
21. *Methodist Recorder*, 18 Sept. 1902.
22. Devon RO, 2399D/158, trustees' minute book 1922-38, 1954-59.
23. W. F. E. Gibbs, 'Development of Elementary Education in Dorset from early 19th cent. to 1870', unpublished M.A. thesis, University of Southampton 1960 (copy DRO), App. II, list of schools reported to Parl. Enquiry 1818, p. 228; Hine, p. 79.
24. DRO, P57/SC2, account book 1830-52.
25. DRO, P57/SC3.
26. Hine, pp. 376, 79.
27. DRO, P57/SC4.
28. DRO, P57/SC5.
29. DRO, P57/IN18, 19, diaries 1857-66.
30. Hine, pp. 378-9.
31. Hine, p. 377.
32. DRO, D209/3, plans of National school 1866.
33. DRO, P57/SC6.
34. DRO, P57/SC7.
35. Hine, p. 384.
36. *Return of Non-Provided Public Elementary Schools 1906.*
37. Hine, pp. 382-3.
38. DRO, S94/1, Beaminster Grammar School governors' meetings, minutes 1872-1905.
39. DRO, P57/SC8.
40. Gibbs, *op. cit.*, pp. 121-2.
41. DRO, P57/CH4, Tucker's Charity schemes 1871-1909.
42. Names in school magazine, June 1924.
43. *Kelly's directory* 1923.
44. Info. from Mrs. J. Graveson; school mags. from 1920.
45. DRO, ED12, Beaminster & Netherbury Grammar School brochure *c.* 1915.

46. Grammar School mags., Dec. 1923, Dec. 1926, summer 1934, summer 1953.
47. *BN*, 14 Mar. 1930.
48. Hine, pp. 386-7.
49. Hine, pp. 203-4.
50. *Parish News*, Sept. 1980.
51. Hine, pp. 209-11.
52. DRO, D279/E3, sale cat. 1896; Hine, pp. 340-2.
53. Dorchester Ref. Libr., D1 Beaminster 728. 84.381.17, sale cat. 1910; Hine, pp. 343-7.
54. Linda Rhodes-Moorhouse, *Kaleidoscope* (1960), pp. 50, 57, 86-7.
55. DRO, D599a/3, sale cat. 1955.
56. Hine, pp. 352-3.
57. Codd, *op. cit.*, p. 270.
58. Hine, pp. 392-4.
59. *Parish News*, Dec. 1978, Mar. 1982.
60. *BN*, 23 June 1911.
61. P. Keane, 'Prophet in the wilderness — Rev. William Barnes as an adult educator', *Proc. DNHAS*, vol. 100 (1978), pp. 11, 19.
62. Hine, pp. 422-3; Codd, p. 276.
63. Hine, pp. 423-4.
64. Hine, pp. 424-7.
65. Codd, p. 280.
66. *Kelly's directories* 1855, 1867, 1880, 1885.
67. Hine, pp. 232-3.
68. Hine, pp. 237-40.
69. Hine, pp. 152-4.
70. *Western Gazette*, 7 Aug. 1896.
71. Codd, pp. 266, 276, 278.
72. Codd, p. 274; Hine, p. 439.
73. Hine, p. 29.
74. Hine, p. 392.
75. Hine, p. 352; *BN*, 26 July 1907.
76. Codd, p. 284; letter dated 3 Jan. 1880 in possession of Mr. W. A. Stiby.
77. DRO, DC3, Beaminster Rural District Council minutes 1897-1906.
78. *BN*, 18 Nov. 1910, 22 Nov. 1912.
79. Hine, pp. 286-301.
80. Codd, pp. 286-8.
81. *BN*, 18 Feb. 1921.
82. Beaminster W.I., minute book 1918-31; *BN* 20 May & 22 July 1921, 30 June 1922.
83. DRO, P355/PC3, parish council minutes 1908-20; PC1, parish meetings 1894-1927.
84. DRO, P355/PC5, parish council minutes 1932-46.

BIBLIOGRAPHY

(Principal Sources)

MANUSCRIPT SOURCES

Dorset Record Office

Manors of Beaminster Prima, Beaminster Secunda and Netherbury in Ecclesia:
  Court books and presentments 17th-20th cent.
Parish of Beaminster:
  Registers of christenings and burials, and copies of bishop's transcripts, from 1585 (some gaps).
  Churchwardens' rates and accounts 1646-1764 (2 vols.).
  Overseers' rates and accounts 1630-74, 1729-1834 (6 vols.).
  Overseers' bills and receipts 1747-1836.
  Apprenticeship indentures 1697-1821.
  Workhouse accounts and disbursements 1796-1836 (4 vols., various dates).
  Lists of workhouse inmates 1810-36 (2 vols.).
  Poor rate books 1842-76 (6 vols., certain years only).
  Tucker's Charity School, trustees' account book 1708-1873, grammar school management schemes 1870-1909 (2 bundles).
  National School, admissions 1830--36, accounts 1830-52, building and management cttees.' minutes 1866-80, misc. papers.
  Vestry minutes 1842-86 (2 vols.), misc. Vestry papers 1833-66.
  Lighting and Watching cttee., minutes of inspectors' and ratepayers' meetings 1855-1914 (3 vols.).
  Beaminster Parish Council, minutes 1894-1946 (4 vols.), annual parish meetings 1894-1927.
Beaminster Inclosure Award (and map) 1809.
Beaminster Tithe Award (and map) 1843.
Beaminster and Netherbury Grammar School, governors' minute book 1872-1905.
Beaminster Board of Guardians' minutes 1836-1930 (7 vols.).
Bridport Highway Board minutes 1863-94 (3 vols.).
Beaminster Rural Sanitary Authority minutes 1872-94. (2 vols.).
Beaminster Rural District Council:
  Minutes 1895-1949 (10 vols.).
  Beaminster Water Supply and Sewerage Cttee. Minutes 1907-31.
  Housing Cttee. minutes 1919-21.
Deeds, etc. 16th-20th cent.
Dorset Quarter Sessions Order Books 1625-38, 1663-74.
Licensed victuallers' returns 18th cent.
Land tax returns 1780-1832.
Turnpike Trusts:
  Acts and Plans 18th and 19th cent.
  Gen. Statements of Accounts 1822-82.
  Bridport 2nd District (Bridport and Beaminster) Turnpike Trust, minute book 1754-1812.
  Maiden Newton Turnpike Trust minutes etc. 1778-1873.

Wiltshire Record Office

Diocese of Salisbury:
  Bishop: manor of Langdon (Church Commissioners' records), survey *c.* 1663, leases etc. 17th–
    19th cent.
  Dean: visitation records (churchwardens' presentments) 17th and 18th cent.; Dean's court, wills
    and inventories 16th–19th cent.
  Prebendary of Netherbury in Ecclesia: visitation records (churchwardens' presentments) 17th and
    18th cent.; Prebendary's court, wills and inventories 17th–19th cent.

Devon Record Office

Devon and Dorset Mission of Methodist Churches, Bridport circuit:
  Circuit preaching plans 1854–90 (2 bundles).
  Beaminster trustees' minute book 1922–70.
  J. Stevens, 'History of Wesleyan Methodism in Bridport and its Vicinity', *c.* 1857.

Dorset County Museum

Richard Hine Collection (scrapbooks relating to Beaminster).

Congregational Church, Beaminster

Register of baptisms 1777–89.
Register of baptisms 1796–1837, 1868–74, incl. marriages 1837–55.
Account books 1762–1825, 1866–80.
Minute book 1796–1890.
Minute books of cttees. 1824–62, 1869–83.
Communion roll 1864–89.

TEXTS AND CALENDARS AND OTHER PUBLISHED PRIMARY SOURCES

Register of St Osmund, ed. by Rev. W. H. Rich-Jones, 2 vols. (Rolls Series, 1883, 1884).
Registrum Simonis de Gandavo 1297–1315, 2 vols. (Cant. & York Soc., 1934).
Registers of Roger Martival 1315–30, vols. 1 & 2 (Cant. & York Soc., 1959, 1962), vol. 4 (Devonshire
    Press, 1975).
Register of Robert Hallum 1407–17 (Cant. & York Soc., 1982).
Salisbury Charters and Documents, ed. by W. D. Macray (1891).
Historical MSS. Commission, *55 Var. Coll. I*, Dean and Chapter of Salisbury, pp. 338–88; *55 Var.
    Coll. IV*, Bishop of Salisbury, pp. 1–12.
Dorset Parish Registers: Marriages, ed. by W. P. W. Phillimore, vols, 1 & 3 (1906, 1908).
Cal. Dorset Wills 1568-1799, 2 vols. (Index Libr. vol. 53 for Courts of Dean of Sarum and Preben-
    dary of Netherbury in Ecclesia).
Cal. Dorset Wills proved in P.C.C. 1383–1700 (Dorset Records, vol. 11, 1911).
Dorset Protestation returns 1641-2 (Dorset Records, vol. 12, 1912; index 1960).
Dorset Hearth Tax Assessments 1662-4, ed. by C. A. F. Meekings (1951).
Dorset Lay Subsidy Roll of 1332 (Dorset Record Soc., vol. 4, 1971).
Dorset Lay Subsidy Roll of 1327 (Dorset Record Soc., vol. 6, 1980).
Dorset Tudor Muster Rolls 1539, 1542, 1569, ed. by T. L. Stoate (1978).

Dorset Tudor Subsidies granted in 1523, 1543, 1593, ed. by T. L. Stoate (1982).
Domesday Book: Dorset, ed. by C. and F. Thorn (Phillimore, 1983).
Leland's Itinerary in England and Wales 1535-43, ed. by L. Toulmin Smith (1964), vol. 1.
Universal British Directory of Trade and Commerce, vol. 2 (1793).
Holden's *Annual Directory* (1811-16).
Pigot's/Slater's *Directories of Dorsetshire* (1824-52).
Hunt's *Directory of Dorsetshire* (1851).
Kelly's *Post Office Directories* (1848-1935).
Census Reports (H.M.S.O., 1801-1951).

MAPS

Geological Survey, one inch to one mile: 327 Bridport, 312 Yeovil.
Isaac Taylor, Dorset, one inch to one mile, 1st edn. 1765, 2nd edn. 1795.
O.S. one inch to one mile, 1811.
O.S. six inches to one mile, 1890, 1903-4.

BOOKS, BOOKLETS AND ARTICLES

Anderson, R. C. and Frankis, G., *A History of Western National* (1979).
Barlow, F., *The English Church 1000-1066*, 2nd edn. (1979).
Best, G., *Mid-Victorian Britain 1851-1875* (1971).
Best, R., *Poorstock in Wessex* (1970).
Bettey, J. H., *Church & Community* (1979).
Bettey, J. H., *Dorset* (1974).
Bettey, J. H., *The Landscape of Wessex* (1980).
Bettey, J. H., *Rural Life in Wessex 1500-1900* (1977).
Bowley, M., *Housing and the State 1919-44* (1945).
Chambers, J. D. and Mingay, G. E., *The Agricultural Revolution 1750-1880* (1966).
Chisholm, M., *Rural Settlement and Land Use*, 3rd edn. (1979).
Claridge, J., *General View of the Agriculture of the County of Dorset* (1793).
Cornwall, J., 'English Country Towns in the 1520s', *Economic History Review*, 2nd series, vol. 15
    (1962-63), pp. 54-69.
Codd, A. P. (ed. by J. Stevens Cox), *Life in Beaminster 1864-1910* (Monographs on Life, Times
    and Works of Thomas Hardy, 1969).
Cox, Eric H., *Corscombe* (1970).
Dacombe, Marianne R., ed., *Dorset: Up Along and Down Along* (c. 1935).
Darby, H. C. and Finn, R. W., *The Domesday Geography of S.W. England* (1967).
Denshaw, W. and Ogle, J., *The Story of the Congregational Churches of Dorset* (1899).
Douch, R., *A Handbook of Local History: Dorset* (1962).
Dyos, H. J. and Aldcroft, D. H., *British Transport* (Penguin, 1974).
Dunning, R. W., 'Ilchester: A Study in Continuity', *Proc. Somerset Arch. Soc.*, vol. 119 (1975),
    pp. 44-51; 'The Minster at Crewkerne', *Proc. Som. Arch. Soc.*, vol. 120 (1976), pp. 63-67.
Everitt, A., *The Pattern of Rural Dissent: the 19th Century* (University of Leicester, Dept. Eng.
    Local History Occasional Papers, 1972).
Fagersten, A., *Place-Names of Dorset* (1933).
Finn, R. W., *Domesday Book: a Guide* (1973).
Fowler, J., *Medieval Sherborne* (1951).
French, Capt. G. A., R.N., *Stoke Abbott* (1974).
Gay, John D., *The Geography of Religion in England* (1971).
Gelling, M., *Signposts to the Past* (1978).
Good, R., *The Old Roads of Dorset*, 2nd edn. (1966).
Groube, L. M. and Bowden, M. C. B., *The Archaeology of Rural Dorset* (DNHAS Monograph 4, 1982).

Harrison, J. F. C., *The Early Victorians 1832-51* (Panther, 1973).

Haslam, J., ed., *Anglo-Saxon Towns in Southern England* (1983).

Hine, R., *History of Beaminster* (1914).

Hinton, David A., *Alfred's Kingdom* (1977).

Hutchins, J., *The History and Antiquities of the County of Dorset*, 1st edn., vol. 1 (1774); 2nd edn., augmented by R. Gough and J. B. Nichols, vol. 1 (1796); 3rd edn., ed. by W. Shipp and J. W. Hodson, vols. 1, 2 and 4 (1861-74).

Jackson, B. L. and Tattershall, M. J., *The Bridport Branch* (1976).

Kerr, B., *Bound to the Soil* (1968).

Large, E. H., *Broadwindsor* (n.d.).

Lennard, R., *Rural England 1086-1135* (1959).

Machin, R., *The Houses of Yetminster* (University of Bristol, 1978).

Machin, R., ed., *Probate Inventories and Manorial Excerpts of Chetnole, Leigh and Yetminster* (University of Bristol, 1976).

Mann, J. de L., *The Cloth Industry in the West of England from 1640 to 1880* (1971).

Marshall, W., *The Rural Economy of the West of England*, 2 vols. (1796, reprinted 1970).

Mingay, G. E., *Rural Life in Victorian England* (Futura, 1979).

Newman, J. and Pevsner, N., *Buildings of England: Dorset* (1972).

Orwin, C. S. and Whetham, E. H., *History of British Agriculture 1846-1914* (David and Charles, 1971).

Patten, J., *English Towns 1500-1700* (1978).

Penn, K. J., *Historic Towns in Dorset* (DNHAS Monograph 1, 1980).

Pitfield, F. P., *Dorset Parish Churches A-D* (1981).

Ponting, K. G., *A History of the West of England Cloth Industry* (1957).

Ponting, K. G., *The Woollen Industry of South-West England* (1971).

Poole, H. S., *Powerstock: A Short Social History* (1979).

Postan, M. M., *The Medieval Economy and Society* (Penguin, 1975).

Pulman, G. P. R., *The Book of the Axe*, 4th edn. (1875).

Rackham, O., *Trees and Woodland in the British Landscape* (1976).

RCHM, *Dorset: vol. 1 — West* (1952).

Ruegg, L. H., 'Farming in Dorsetshire', *Jour. Royal Agric. Soc. of England*, vol. 15 (1854).

Sanctuary, A., *Rope, Twine and Net Making* (Shire 51, 1980).

Saville, J., *Rural Depopulation in England and Wales 1851-1951* (1957).

Sawyer, P. H., ed., *Medieval Settlement — Continuity and Change* (1976).

Sellers, I., *Nineteenth Century Nonconformity* (1977).

Sellman, R. R., *Illustrations of Dorset History* (1960).

Smellie, K. B., *A History of Local Government*, 4th edn. (1968).

Stevenson, W., *General View of the Agriculture of the County of Dorset* (1812).

Taverner, L. E., 'Land Classification in Dorset', *Trans. Inst. British Geographers*, vol. 6 (1937), pp. 50-61.

Taylor, C. C., *The Making of the English Landscape: Dorset* (1970).

Taylor, C. C., 'The making of the English landscape — 25 years on', *Local Historian*, vol. 14, no. 4 (1980), pp. 195-201.

Taylor, C. C., *Roads and Tracks of Britain* (1979).

Thomas, David St John, *A Regional History of the Railways of Gt. Britain: vol. 1 — The West Country*, 4th edn. (1973).

Treves, Sir F., *Highways and Byways in Dorset* (1906, reprinted 1927).

Tribe, T. and Whatmoor, P., *Dorset Clocks and Clockmakers* (1981).

VCH, Dorset, vol. 2 (1908), vol. 3, (1968).

Webb, B. and S., *The Story of the King's Highway* (Frank Cass, 1963).

Weinstock, M. B., *Studies in Dorset History* (1953).

Weinstock, M. B., *More Dorset Studies* (1960).

Weinstock, M. B., *Old Dorset* (1967).

Whitaker, W. and Edwards, W., *Wells and Springs of Dorset* (Memoir Geological Survey, 1926).

Whitehead, T., *Fire Engines* (Shire 68, 1981).

Wilson, V. *et al., Geology of the Country around Bridport and Yeovil* (Memoir Geological Survey, 1958).

PERIODICALS AND NEWSPAPERS

Bridport News.
Proceedings Dorset Natural History and Antiquarian Field Club/Natural History and Archaeological Society, vols. 1–104 (1877–1982).
Notes and Queries for Somerset and Dorset, vols. 1–30 (1888–1980).

An old Beaminster gas lamp

INDEX OF PERSONS

GENERAL INDEX

LIST OF SUBSCRIBERS

L. E. Allen
Ann and Margaret
Mrs M. Appleton
L.L.D. & D.L. Baker
Florence & Mary Bamford
Mrs J.H. Banfield - née Nancy Mason
Joyce Banks
Mrs Charmian Barker
H. Howard Bax
D. Beach
Beaminster School
Douglas Beazer
Monica Bennett
Mrs Mollie Betchley
Kathleen and Kenneth Bland
Bernard Bonte
Doug. Boston
Mr & Mrs I. Boyer
J.V. Boys M.A.
S.L. Bridle
Miss B. Brierley
Anthony J. Bright
Harold Brook T.D.
Leslie & Marjorie Brooke
Edward Brooks, Canon
Nesta M. Brooks
Ray Brown
John & Jean Brushfield
Elsie Buck
Buck Buckhurst
Mark R. Budden
D.R. Bugler, P.R. Bugler
Warren Bugler
Lt. Col. D.J. ff. Campbell
Mr & Mrs A.H. Carter
Mr. K.H. Carter
F.W. & R. Chubb
B.P. Clark
Mr Robert Clarke
Janet P. & William C. Cogswell
Horace W. Colby
Ronald D. Colborne
Mr & Mrs A.P. Coleman
Dr. Robert G. Conway
Dr. Alcon Copisarow
Olive Crabbe
Robert Crabbe
Gordon Crew
G.L. & M. Cummins
Mr L.J. & Mrs J.E. Cummings
Mr G. Curtis & Mrs C.L. McDonnell
Murdoch Dahl
Desmond H.J. Danes
Daniels House Antiques
M.E.S. Dart
Terence Davis
Mr A.C. Dawe
Mr W.F. Dawe

William A. Day
Dr. Anne Dearlove
Chloë & Jonah Dearlove
Giles & Judy Dearlove
Dr. Oliver Dearlove
Mr G.C.J. Denning
J.H. Dennis
Edward Dicker
Gwendolen V. Dimmick
Mrs Caroline Dimmock,
    Mr Geoffrey John Dimmock
Mr John Gibbs, Mrs Frances Gibbs
Lydia A. Dixon
David Down
Yvonne Down
E.H. Draper
John Drayson
W.E. Duirs
Madeleine Dunell
Mrs D. Dupont
Marie & John Eedle
Mrs Cecillia Evans (née Perry)
Mr Glyn Evans
Sylvia M. Fletcher
Mr & Mrs H.P. Forsey
B.M. Fournier
Giles Frampton Snr.
Giles Frampton
Grace M. Frampton
Isobel G. Frampton
Linda Frampton
Mrs T.P. Frampton
Robert Fripp
Margaret & Geoffrey Fry
R.A.E. Fursey
Mr & Mrs G. Gale
Christine Galliott
J.D. & S.B. Gane
Jocelyn A. Gardner
Cdr. T.J.H. Gedge, A.F.C., R.N.
Mrs Joan Gent
Elisabeth Gibson
Mr & Mrs W.C. Giddings
Frank A. Gilson
Stanley & Rosemary Godsell
Good Hope Antiques
Nina Audrey Gould
Una M. Grain
Rene & James Gordon Grant
The Green Family
Tony Greenham
D.A. Greening
L. Greening
M. Greening
Elsa Guignard
Irwin J. Gunning
Edward L. Hallett
E. Hancock

Mr M.D. Hannam
Maurice Lionel Hannam
S.M. & E.V. Hansen
Miss M.M. Harborough M.B.E.
Mahala A. Hardinge
Pauline Hardwill
Mr & Mrs Harold Harris
Mrs Margaret Harvey B.A.
Ann Elizabeth Hawker
Mr F.A. Hayward
Guy E.S. Hereward
I. Hewitt
Audrey Jean Burtonwood-Hill
Miss Daphne A. Hills
Eva Hillyer
David J.B. Hindley
I.M. Hine
Mr & Mrs James Hine
Jean E. Hobson
L.A.F. & J. Holland
F.H.E. Holt
Brian Holtam
Dr. & Mrs A.S. Horner
N.G. House
Dr. & Mrs M.K.G. Hudson
Barbara Hughes
Mr Michael Hussey
Hugh Jaques Esq
Jude James, B.A., Dip. English
    Local History
Mr R.H. Jasper
C. & D. Jeans
R.S.A. & G.F. Johnson
H.F.V. Johnstone
Cynthia & Royston Jones
Mrs Irene Jones
Mr Richard M. Jones
Mrs Esmée K. Julyan
Mr & Mrs W.J. Campbell-Kease
Jacob Kemsley
Ivan C. Kent
P.A. Knight
John Knowles
Alma Lavery
Lawrence, Chartered Surveyors
Cora Lawrence
Mr & Mrs John F. Leggett
Edward & Lois Lewis
Derek M. Lipington
Peter Lockyer
Mr A.G. Luke
Miss Sally Lunn
The Lyme Regis (Philpot)
    Museum
Flora McKenzie
M.J. McKinlay
Kenneth Macksey
Mr & Mrs R.T. Maling
Janet Margrie
C. & A. Markley
Mr H.E. Marsden
Mr & Mrs Bertram Marsh
John & May Messer
J.S. Moon
Jacquie Morgan (née Down)
Gemma Murley
C. Nielsen
Jack Notley

Mr Sydney A. Oliver
Pamela Olsen
J.H. & D.M. Orr
Edna G. Pannell
Mr Ronald H.T. Parham
Philip M. De Paris
George A. Parkins
Vita & Roy Patmore
Mrs E.M. Paulley (née Hunt)
Mr Bill Payne
K.J. & M.C. Payne
Roger Peers
Alicia Penman
John & Josephine Pentney
W.T.G. Perrott
Mrs J.N. Perry
Philip G. Perry
Mrs Pauline E. Phillips
Kathleen Pim
A.M.J. Pomeroy
Cyril J. Poole
F.H. Port
N. & M. Pye
Chris Randall
T.J. & I.M. Rendell
Mr & Mrs W.R. Richards
Ken & Eileen Richman
Mr Peter Riglar
J. Rivett
Charles Rockett
George Roderick
J. A. Roe
Mrs Diana Rumsey
H.G. Russell
St Mary's Church of England
    Primary School
Margaret M. Saint
Susan E. Scott
Mrs Ivy Scott
P.J. Shakespeare
Mr & Mrs G.E. Shipton
J. Shipton
W.H. & I.M. Shord
R. Neville Sjögren
Edward J. Smith
Somerset & Dorset Family History
    Society
Mrs Betty Spencer (née Hooper)
N.M. Travers-Spencer
John Edward Spooner
Mr & Mrs P.G. Spooner
Ivy E. Sprackling
W.A. Stiby
Virginia Strange
F.W. Strevens
Eunice Sutherland
Louise Tattershall
Valerie Tattershall
Ken Taylor
Norah Meddows Taylor
Miss A.E. Thrift
Jo, Elli & Tom Thimbleby
Michael F. Tighe
Mr & Mrs K.F.E. Tilley
A.G. Tomkins
Miss Elizabeth Toogood
Cecilia Mason-Toohill
E. & H. Toovey

Mima Towers
Mr & Mrs B. W. Trask
Mr & Mrs R.C. Travers
Mr R.G. Travers
Mr R.J. Travers
Charles & Mary Treacher
Miss E.S. Trotman
H. Bernard Tucker
R.A.E. Turbefield
F.D. Veal
Mr & Mrs L.G. Wakely
M. Walbridge
Cynthia & Michael Walcot
Mrs Cecil Ward
Jesse & Lewis Warde
Neville & Joy Warnes
Peter & Joan Warren
J.P. & G.P. Watt
Edgar & Ruth Watts
Mr & Mrs R.J. Watts
Andrew McM. Webster
L.K. Webster
Mr & Mrs A. Welsford
N.C. Welsford
John Wetherden
John Whatmoor
Mr Jack M. Whitaker

Joan E. White
Mr & Mrs J. Whitehouse.
T.R. Wightman
J. Anthony Wigzell
Clifford J. Williams
Jill Williams (née Down)
John R. Wilson
Mrs M.T. Wilson
Robert J. Woodbury
Mrs B.M. Woodeson
Marjorie Woodward (Miss)
A.D. Wotton
D.S. Wragg
J.A. & G.M. Wright
Dr. C.J. Wrigley

PRESENTATION COPIES

Miss Kathleen Pim
Beaminster Town Council
West Dorset District Council
Dorset Natural History &
    Archaeological Society
Dorset Record Office
Wiltshire Record Office
Beaminster Library